Desi

Desire for Origins

New Language, Old English, and Teaching the Tradition

Allen J. Frantzen

RUTGERS UNIVERSITY PRESS
New Brunswick and London

Library of Congress Cataloging-in-Publication Data

Frantzen, Allen J., 1947–
Desire for origins : New Language, Old English, and Teaching the Tradition / Allen J. Frantzen
p. cm.
Includes bibliographical references.
ISBN 0-8135-1590-4 (cloth) — ISBN 0-8135-1591-2 (pbk.)
1. English literature—Old English, ca. 450–1100—History and criticism—Theory, etc. 2. English philology—Old English, ca. 450–1100—Study and teaching. 3. Civilization, Anglo-Saxon—Study and teaching. 4. Anglo-Saxons—Study and teaching. I. Title.
PR173.F73 1990
829′.09—dc20 90-31077
CIP

British Cataloging-in-Publication information available

Manufactured in the United States of America

For George R. Paterson

Contents

Preface

This book relates the study of two topics of general interest—language and history—to a topic that is considered quite specialized: the role of Anglo-Saxon studies in the postmodern age. I use the term "postmodern" to designate the variety of relatively recent critical movements, known collectively as "literary theory" or "critical theory," that preoccupy departments of English. This is an era in which complaints from the public sector about student reading and writing are commonplace, implying a significant disparity between the preoccupations of professors and the needs of their students. Teachers of the English language and its literature are viewed as working in a highly specialized system that is carefully divided into elaborate structures of literary periods and genres. "Theory," understood to be a special subject all its own, has made these structures even more complex. The need to specialize has narrowed the appeal of literary study, making it seem isolated from public understanding and unresponsive to the public's concern with the reading and writing skills of college students. In such an atmosphere, Anglo-Saxon studies (also known as "Old English") seem to be a luxury. Yet I consider the study of the early English language and its culture an opportunity for exactly the kind of work that higher education is supposed to undertake: making connections across disciplines and exploring the history and operations of language and texts.

Although this book addresses neither critical theory nor the verbal skills of students directly, it connects both subjects to the study of Old English. In the late nineteenth century, philology dominated English departments in high schools as well as colleges, and Anglo-Saxon language study was central to the business of higher education. Language study was the chief business of the department of English, and Old English, included in "Germanic philology" or simply "philology," was one of the department's staple subjects. Departments of English, in their early manifestations, did not teach literature. Instead, English professors studied language within the framework of the classical tradition, for traditional humanistic reasons: to encourage the development of responsible citizens, to promote good character, and so on. Old English literature as it has come to be understood—the heroic world of *Beowulf* and the gold and gore of epic poetry—was not then part of the discipline. Language, including public speaking, was studied as a valued part of the cultural tradition; it was not undertaken as a means to entering specialized realms of literary criticism.

But neither was the discipline thus constituted taken for granted. In 1885, in the very first issue of *PMLA,* the journal of the Modern Language Association of America, Francis B. Gummere reported a college president's claim that Anglo-Saxon, Icelandic, and Quaternions (a form of calculus) were "intellectual luxuries." Given the judgment of "so prominent and learned a man," Gummere wondered what "that robust personage, the 'average citizen,' impatient as he is of all that is recondite and out of touch with the practical," would think of a proposal for teaching philology in elementary schools. Nevertheless, Gummere assumed "that the fortunes of English Philology in college and university are no longer doubtful." Of course he was wrong. Philology did not become part of the elementary school curriculum, and a century after he wrote it was rare enough in doctoral programs.[1]

Although directly descended from the philological tradition that began with classical studies, Anglo-Saxon studies had, long before the postmodern era (let us say that the era began about 1970), lost nearly all of their prestige and, for general audiences, most of their value. The process by which this occurred is easy to trace. First, the study of literature became as important as that of language; then literary criticism was elevated to parity with language study and soon given precedence over it. In the meantime, Anglo-Saxon studies, tied to language study and long indifferent to literary criticism, dwindled into obscurity. Today many scholars consider Anglo-Saxon the academic heir to the classics, due for retirement as modern literature becomes the academic heir to Old English. I submit that a reassessment of Anglo-Saxon studies in the context of language study and cultural history can help recover the value of the subject, not only for teachers and their students, but for all those interested in the way language and language study shape culture and make history, as well as report the vicissitudes of both.

In the hope that this work will reach an audience beyond the specialized circles of medieval scholars, I would like to explain a few key terms whose meanings should not be taken for granted. I use "Anglo-Saxon" to designate the Old English language and its literature, between approximately A.D. 700 and 1100, and the term "Anglo-Saxon studies" to refer to scholarship concerned with the language, texts, ideas, and traditions—whether historical, literary, ecclesiastical, or secular—that document the early medieval period of English culture. I use a term borrowed from Reginald Horsman, "Anglo-Saxonism," to refer to the use of Anglo-Saxon culture and texts for ideologically motivated and political ends.[2]

A related term, philology, must be also be defined. It has acquired a very narrow and specialized meaning as the scientific study of changes in language (morphological, phonetic, syntactic, semantic), but in its earliest sense, "philology" meant much more. Theophilus Gale in *The Court of the Gentiles* (1669) defined philology as "a universal love, or respect, of human literature." In *The New World of English Words* (1706), Edward Phillips wrote that a "philologer" was a "man of letters, a humanist." George Campbell, in *The Philosophy of Rhetoric* (1776), declared that the "branches" of philology covered literature, jurisprudence, grammar, language, criticism, and all kinds of history.[3] In large part, the story of Anglo-Saxon studies in the modern era is that of the diminution of philology, which ceased to relate to a broad range of subjects and became an isolated, highly specialized form of language study.

Three additional, rather innocuous terms, "history," "textual criticism," and "origin," will be important throughout this work. By "history" I mean the reconstruction of the past by those who did not know it firsthand, a definition I have adapted from the opening words of Fritz Stern in *The Varieties of History*.[4] Another scholar who stresses the interaction of past and present in historical studies is R. G. Collingwood, who defines history as "a re-enactment of past experience."[5] Reconstruction and re-enactment are essential both to historical linguistics and to the closely related work of textual criticism, the study of where texts came from and how they took shape. A standard textbook defines textual criticism as "the analysis of existing forms or states of a text" to determine its earliest version, and as emendation that removes error and as far as possible restores the text to its earliest form.[6] I will use the term textual criticism to indicate not only the production of editions, but also the history of a text from its first appearance through various historical and literary accounts produced by editors and readers—in a word, the text's reception. The term "reception" must not be understood to denote a passive process, which is how so many people view the work of reading. Rather, reception, like reading, is part of the activity of interpreting, editing, and publishing texts. The notion of reception covers the response to textual information as it is reproduced and recycled, as well as the revision of that material. A formidable body of commentary and editorial information accrues to ancient texts as, century after century, they are repeatedly read and re-edited. Although less information of this kind has accumulated in the history of Anglo-Saxon studies than in the history of classical or biblical studies, the tradition is vast and nearly as difficult to circumscribe.

My attempt to define history and textual criticism within the context of reception and reproduction is designed to emphasize the subjectivity inherent in both scholarly practices. The technical nature of historiography and textual criticism has sometimes caused both to be understood as objective. Yet it is obvious that, just as history requires a writer to reconstruct the story being told, textual criticism requires the scholar to reconstruct the text to be read—not just to "edit" it, but do so within a specific, reconstructive, and hence *interpretive,* framework. To call either practice "objective" is to forget its hermeneutic function.

Literary and linguistic history and textual criticism are the most important practices in Anglo-Saxon studies. They have been, and continue to be, avenues to origins of many kinds, including national, spiritual, and psychological. "Origin" is itself a commonplace word that nevertheless requires definition. I use it to designate that from which a thing or person begins—a source or root, and also a cause. The search for origins is never disinterested; those wishing to trace an idea or tradition to its historical, linguistic, and textual beginnings have always done so with a thesis in mind, and the origin they have found has often been an origin they have produced. Their reasons for going to the source—their desire for origins—is my concern.

Beginning in the Reformation, the study of Anglo-Saxon texts and ideas played a formative role in political controversy. Not simply "antiquaries" (an epithet always used to suggest that their endeavors were gentlemanly dilettantism), early Anglo-Saxonists argued about authorship, gender, and the needs of the reading public. Nor were they only gentlemen; one of the most important of the early Anglo-Saxonists was Elizabeth Elstob; her influence reached beyond early eighteenth-century England to colonial America and Thomas Jefferson, who learned Anglo-Saxon from her *Grammar.*

My thesis—and thus my own reason for seeking the origin of Anglo-Saxon studies—is that engagement with political controversy has always been a distinctive and indeed an essential motive for studying language origins and therefore for studying Anglo-Saxon. The corollary to my thesis is that disengagement from politics and an attempt to justify the study of linguistic origins for their own sake are innovations in the modern Anglo-Saxon scholarly tradition; these developments, I believe, explain why Anglo-Saxon subjects have failed to retain a place in the mainstream of modern intellectual and political life. I pursue the argument in two parts.

Part I, Teaching the Tradition, contains three chapters that outline and elaborate the problem. Chapter 1 situates Anglo-Saxon studies in the current debate about academic culture and cultural literacy and their respective functions. Although my immediate concern is the state of Anglo-Saxon studies in the United States, the problems found in this country can also be found in Canada and England, where Old English requirements have been dropped. (In Germany, however, Old English still forms a required part of undergraduate programs in English.) Chapter 2 sets Anglo-Saxon studies in the context of nineteenth-century intellectual history and the phenomenon of Orientalism; surveys the development of Anglo-Saxon studies in the Renaissance; and reassesses the meaning of the "turning point," that moment when amateur scholarship is thought to have given way to professional and academic Anglo-Saxon studies. In contrast to the volatile backdrop of nineteenth-century Anglo-Saxonism, chapter 3 focuses on specifically American developments in Anglo-Saxon studies in order to demonstrate that, as Anglo-Saxon language and literature became established in American universities, professionalization was achieved at the expense of popular appeal and cultural relevance. The research projects dominating the field at present typify the isolation that such specialization promotes.

Part II, New Language and Old English, elaborates on the theoretical concepts introduced in the earlier chapters and puts them into practice. Chapter 4 explains what it means to call texts and contexts "eventful," and explores deconstruction and the archaeological analysis of Michel Foucault as a means of reconceptualizing the reconstructive and re-enacting functions of Anglo-Saxon studies. The two chapters that follow focus on two key Anglo-Saxon texts—the Old English version of Bede's *Ecclesiastical History* and *Beowulf*—not to "read" or interpret them, but to recover, in the history of their reception, their cultural significance for earlier ages, and to suggest their cultural implications for our own.

Chapter 5 examines the editorial tradition of Bede's *History* in the Renaissance, in the context of ecclesiastical upheaval and reform, focusing on one of the major canonical texts in Old English, "Cædmon's Hymn." Chapter 6 examines the treatment of *Beowulf* in the nineteenth century, the period when what we today tend to think of as disinterested scholarship replaced religious and nationalist polemic as a motive for undertaking the study of Anglo-Saxon texts. This chapter discusses the textual history of that most famous of Old English poems in order to illustrate how editorial methods and philology have conspired to rewrite the text. The final chapter describes the beginning phases of teaching Anglo-Saxon language in American schools in the nineteenth century, demonstrating that the textbooks still used in Anglo-Saxon courses retain ideas that took shape early on in the subject's development. I conclude with some hypotheses about the potential of Anglo-Saxon studies for renewing the place of language in the literary tradition that colleges and universities carry on.

Both parts of my argument follow chronological patterns, but neither seeks to be comprehensive. Part I contrasts Anglo-Saxon studies in the Renaissance and nineteenth and twentieth centuries; Part Two relates contemporary literary theory to Anglo-Saxon studies and uses the examples of *Beowulf* and Bede to demonstrate how contemporary theory can revive the cultural and linguistic significance of major Old English texts. I discuss Bede's *History* and *Beowulf* in their editorial and scholarly contexts because these texts are included in the first volume of the *Norton Anthology of English Literature* and are therefore easily available to readers outside as well as inside the academy. Both texts can, I think, be subject to rereadings that indicate how one might "reread" many other works of Old English poetry and prose. I avoid a continuous narrative that would organize the subject in a progressive sequence, and I make no claims to have achieved comprehensive coverage of the subject. I treat eighteenth-century developments in Anglo-Saxon studies quite briefly. Although this period stands midway between the two periods I focus on, I have not used it to connect them in an evolutionary process. My approach is selective rather than encyclopedic; it allows for the discussion of history as contradiction and discontinuity, or rupture, as well as smooth progression. The history of Anglo-Saxon studies has not been a simple process of discovery and disclosure of the Anglo-Saxon past through increasingly sophisticated, reliable, and objective scholarly means. That process is the paradigm of progress, and because the paradigm reduces the complex history of Anglo-Saxon studies to a simple formula, I resist it.

There are many ways to consider the history of one's scholarly discipline or profession. I have chosen to undertake this venture in terms of cultural contexts. I see Anglo-Saxon studies as a form of cultural studies. "Nothing is more indeterminate than this word," wrote the German historian Johann Gottfried von Herder (1744–1803) of the word "culture," "and nothing more deceptive than its application to all nations and periods." Marxist critic Raymond Williams has defined culture as both a process of development and the product of that process.[7] The processes and products of Anglo-Saxon studies are richly connected to other subjects, from the history of education to enforcement of the rules of language. The values and beliefs of Anglo-Saxon language, literature, and history were always—and only—asserted in the presence of an opposing set of values and beliefs; the study of Anglo-Saxon culture is thus unavoidably multi-cultural and full of conflict.

The history of all areas of English literature could, perhaps, be said to involve similar ideological endeavors. Nevertheless, I claim a special status for Anglo-Saxon studies as a form of linguistic and cultural history useful to twentieth-century readers. Anglo-Saxon studies treat the first writing in the English language, preserve the first forms of the English language, and were the first subject, after the classics, to achieve academic and professional status. They are a beginning that has been produced for us by our predecessors, rather than a mystical or mythical origin. But there is no phase of English history or literature, and there is little in American literature before the twentieth century, that was not powerfully and directly influenced by them. Readers who are interested in the origins of democratic government, religious freedom, and national self-consciousness are, whether they realize it nor not, studying traditions in which Anglo-Saxon texts and Anglo-Saxon studies have played a formative part.

A word about the theoretical orientation of this book is in order. My use of various historians of ideas—Michel Foucault, Hayden White, Jerome J. McGann, Edward W. Said, and a number of others—is an interpretation of their contributions to the problem of history rather than an application of the large conceptual systems within which they place their work. By borrowing their insights I leave myself open to charges of eclecticism. However, since critical texts are as susceptible to interpretation as any others, I make no apology for treating these authors as they treat others—that is, for acknowledging both general and particular debts, and adapting what I have understood from their writing and research to my own purposes. By extending their concepts to include the development of Anglo-Saxon as an academic discipline from the sixteenth century to the nineteenth, I wish to suggest how Anglo-Saxon studies might today benefit both from a fuller recognition of this history and from the sharper awareness provided by self-consciously theoretical methods. Recent work by John P. Hermann has urged Anglo-Saxonists to examine their concepts of theory; I urge them to examine the founding principles of their discipline.[8]

If few readers expect to find that the political connections of Anglo-Saxon studies continued beyond the nineteenth century, fewer still are prepared to believe that they extend to our own era, and that the state of the discipline can be improved by attention to the significance of Anglo-Saxon studies in ages whose prejudices we hope to have left behind. Anglo-Saxon studies are a way to recall what our cultural memory has begun to forget, and a way to recover connections that have been weakened. But nostalgia is not my interest. As Hayden White has maintained, "One of the ways that a scholarly field takes stock of itself is by considering its history."[9] This book considers the history of Anglo-Saxon studies in the various cultural contexts that mark their emergence as a scholarly discipline, and in the critical contexts that surround them today. I seek not so much to take stock of this discipline as to restock it with its history; not to muster an ideological critique—which would, in an age thoroughly familiar with feminist and even Marxist revisionism, be superfluous—but to draw attention to the ways in which pedagogy, history, and literary theory can join to enrich Anglo-Saxon scholarship, revitalize Anglo-Saxon studies, and return them to an active role in the study of culture.

Acknowledgments

It is a pleasure to thank Helen Bennett, Martin Irvine, Clare A. Lees, and Gillian R. Overing for their enthusiastic interest in this book. Parts of it were read by Peter Baker, Graham Caie, Kevin Kiernan, and Tim William Macham; Seth Lerer read the complete manuscript. These scholars offered cautions that I have often but not always been able to observe, and I have valued their advice and learned much from them. Colleagues at Loyola University Chicago, especially Thomas Kaminski, Karma Lochrie, and Barbara H. Rosenwein, were sources of good counsel, and to graduate students at Loyola I have many debts. Glory Dharmaraj and Deborah Frisby were especially generous with comments, and others who participated in a *Beowulf* seminar in 1987 and in a Newberry Library seminar in 1988 helped to test some of the ideas elaborated here. I owe special thanks to Sharon Brennan, who contributed much to my revisions of the manuscript, and to Jeffrey Nealon, Jon Grant, Alan Kozlowski, and Douglas Swartz. In early stages of this work I collaborated with Charles Venegoni, and I am grateful for his interest. Richard W. Clement's knowledge of Renaissance libraries was a great help, and I thank him, librarians at the Spenser Research Library at the University of Kansas, and librarians at the Newberry Library, Chicago, for assistance.

I am grateful to Paul E. Szarmach and Harold F. Mosher, Jr., for permission to incorporate material I first published in *Old English Newsletter* Subsidia, vol. 15 (1989), and *Style*, vol. 20 (1986). This book has been written with the support of a fellowship from the National Endowment for the Humanities. I hope that Jess B. Bessinger, Jr., Roberta Frank, and Fred C. Robinson will not be too startled at what I have done with the opportunity for which they most graciously recommended me. I happily acknowledge my debt to Loyola University Chicago for research support and to Leslie Mitchner at Rutgers, who helped to direct and inspire my work. Most of all, I thank George R. Paterson for his unmatched editorial acumen, unvarying moral support, and good will.

Part 1

Teaching the Tradition

1

Desire for Origins: Postmodern Contexts for Anglo-Saxon Studies

Teaching English ■

When people ask me what I do, I say that I teach English. Two reactions to this unassuming statement are nearly universal. The first is, "An English teacher? I'd better watch my grammar!" The second is, "English? That was my worst subject in school—I hated it." What are we to make of these statements? Two points among others that come to mind concern attitudes toward language, and I wish to relate them to the state of Anglo-Saxon studies. First, inferior teaching seems to be widespread within the discipline, although I would not be inclined to emphasize the point. English is surely not alone in this. The people who hated their English classes probably did not hate English any more than they hated philosophy or history. I do not know if philosophy or history teachers regularly hear how hateful others found courses in those subjects. But if English teachers hear such complaints often, that is because English courses are about language and about understanding how language, the attainment of which is the cause of much consternation for many people, works. One's language is unavoidably connected to daily acts of writing, speaking, and reading, to conversation, and thus to cultural status. This matter of status raises my second point, which is about correctness.

The association of English with grammar and English teachers with command of grammar suggests that many people think of English in terms of decorum and therefore think of English teachers as grammar police. (A friend says, "Not police—missionaries," but advocacy of an unpopular cause often entails enforcement.) This connection between speech and decorum is reasonable. Language is a set of rules, and people who are not sure they understand rules are self-conscious about following them. In a social situation, the English teacher may find that this insecurity, and its implication of a student-teacher paradigm, work to the professor's disadvantage. The former student may not have a command of grammar, but he or she may well command a salary much higher than the English teacher, who takes mastery of such rules for granted. Thus does society reward pedagogical tyranny.

For the medievalist and Anglo-Saxonist, one's reception inside the academy is rather like society's reaction to English professors in general. Once again, attitudes toward language are the key. Many specialists in modern literatures regard medievalists, and especially Anglo-Saxonists, as "antiquaries," a term used in the past—and often used derisively—to denote those who studied the past for its own sake while willfully neglecting the present.[1] Many modernists doubt that a subject so technical, philological, and remote as Anglo-Saxon still merits a place in the business of the undergraduate or graduate degree. Once again, bad pedagogy comes to mind. Many former doctoral candidates recall their graduate courses in Old English, and courses in *Beowulf* in particular, as a horror of monotonous grammar drills and tedious translation of words that were to be found only once or twice in a text but that still, for some reason, had to be looked up many times. To make matters worse, presiding over this philological busyness were proponents of a culture typified on the one hand by the machismo of carousing in beer halls, of treasure-giving, longing for exile, or complaining about being in exile, and, on the other hand, of piety and guilt, constant reminders of the need to repent in anticipation of the terrors of the Last Judgment. Thus, Anglo-Saxon language and literature recall both the oppression of philological discipline—translation and memorization—and the vague, violent primitivism that cliché has attached to Anglo-Saxon culture.

The response of non-medievalist scholars who encounter an Anglo-Saxonist differs in one obvious respect from the public's response to the English teacher: other scholars do not expect the Anglo-Saxonist to correct their speech. Specialized knowledge of the Anglo-Saxon language or its literature is not seen as having either academic or personal, immediate interest. Speaking is one thing, knowing where speech patterns come from is another; command of a language is one thing, knowledge of its history is another. Professionals in the academy are not today necessarily less conscious of language than they were in previous eras. But they have, by and large, stopped valuing linguistic history or regarding Old English as relevant to other periods of English literature. The isolation of Anglo-Saxon studies within the English department is particularly disturbing. Those who teach outside Anglo-Saxon studies far outnumber those who pursue them, and what the many do not value, their students will not learn about.

I wish to frame the split between Anglo-Saxon studies and the main business of the department of English in terms of scholarly practice—the tedium of translation; and the cultural subject of that study—the ethos of the beer hall. These reference points juxtapose preconceptions about language study with those about cultural study. In traditional Anglo-Saxon courses, connections between the history of the language and cultural history are, if not taken for granted, conceptualized in traditional, rigid, and limited terms. Most students in Old English courses never get beyond a rudimentary grasp of the language and a basic introduction to a few short prose texts and a small group of elegaic poems, including "The Wanderer," "The Seafarer," and "The Wife's Lament." These are texts more or less related to the heroic code, a social institution which could be—but rarely has been—seen in gender-conscious ways, or otherwise connected to pressing social concerns. The separation of instruction in grammar from socially significant issues, and from texts outside the preferred heroic and elegaic canon, is a fatal error. It suggests that translation skills are acquired either for their own sake or for the sake of appreciating antiquities. But few people see the merit of studying a "dead" language for its own sake or believe that the effort involved in learning such a language is worth the modest reward of appreciating the texts written in it.

Indeed, given a choice between language pursued in an outmoded philological fashion, and literature that responds—as the Old English elegies do—to comfortable formalist or "New Critical" criteria, students and their teachers act reasonably. They either prefer modern literature to the exclusion of Old English, or prefer to experience the literature of the Anglo-Saxons in translation. Translated, both linguistically and culturally, is exactly how the *Norton Anthology* represents Old English literature to its widest audience.[2] *Beowulf* is rendered in prose rather than verse, although a short section is given in Old English to convey something of the atmosphere of the original. Old English is not the only form of English that the *Norton Anthology* must translate. Chaucer continues to appear in Middle English, causing some students, for whom "Old English" is always the oldest form of English they have read, to think that Chaucer's English is older than the language of *Beowulf*. Chaucer's dialect is still considered readable, with the assistance of heavy glossing, but the Middle English of his contemporary, William Langland, is not. *Piers Plowman* appears in the *Norton Anthology* in translation, as does *Sir Gawain and the Green Knight*. As the anthology supplies Old English literature without the Old English language, it passes on texts second-hand, as it were, to teachers who do not read Old English and whose knowledge of Anglo-Saxon culture is likely to be derived from the anthology's own introduction.

That language matters less in the study of modern than of medieval texts is a doubtful proposition. The matter of translating English literature for speakers of the language will, in all probability, not always be limited to Old English. What is true for Anglo-Saxon culture and some Middle English texts is also true for other ancient subjects, in particular the classics, as scholars of Latin, Greek, and other medieval languages, literatures, and cultures already know. The fortunes of classical studies and Anglo-Saxon studies are closely connected. Philological study, once limited to the classics, was altered when Old English and the history of the English language emerged as the focus of the linguistic curriculum. Both have since given way to a curriculum dominated by literature, and specifically literary appreciation, with only minimal attention to the linguistic and philological basis of literary texts. Yet it is very likely that more students learn Latin and Greek than learn Old English. Classical studies will continue because major research universities and prestigious colleges realize that they must provide at least some place, however small, for Latin and Greek. But these very institutions have learned that they can dispense with Old English and still have an English department that includes "medieval studies," beginning with Chaucer rather than King Alfred.

The dependence on translations for earlier or pre-modern texts (that is, those written before 1800) will almost certainly increase, for many reasons, and scholars of Renaissance and eighteenth-century literature should realize what may be in store for them. Shakespeare is taught in translation in some high schools where Milton and Spenser cannot be taught at all (who would translate them?). Pope's "The Rape of the Lock" requires so much extratextual explication that we can say it too must, in effect, be translated, or reframed in more accessible terms. In the *Essay on Criticism,* Pope wrote, "And such as Chaucer is, shall Dryden be." Later in the eighteenth-century, Thomas Sheridan feared that Shakespeare and Milton would "become two or three centuries hence what Chaucer is at present, the study only of a few poring antiquarians, and in an age or two more the victims of bookworms."[3] Linguistic competence should not be taken for granted.

Anglo-Saxon studies are an important component of cultural study because linguistic competence is essential to the responsible reading of documents, whether old or new. This is a far more significant reason for studying Anglo-Saxon than that of admiring the formal properties of Old English texts or learning the operations of a dead language. The study of Old English is connected to the larger objectives of learning about linguistic and cultural history, and grammar is itself a system of teaching that is historically situated rather than "scientific" and natural. Indeed, the role of Anglo-Saxon studies in the English curriculum involves nothing less than the role of the past in the present, a role constituted not only by the antiquity of the Anglo-Saxon language and its texts, but also by the history of the study of language, documents, and objects that preserve it.

Academic Politics ■

Scholarly and pedagogical traditions together explain how and why Anglo-Saxon studies and the classics gave way to modern literature in the department of English. These traditions are not the dry stuff of academic history; rather, they can be seen only in the social circumstances in which departments of English took shape. They address the interaction of the professional and the political status of scholars, an interaction that links scholarship to individual and communal political interests. The scholarly and pedagogical traditions of medieval studies, ranging from Anglo-Saxon to the classics and medieval scholarship more generally, are invested with the ideological concerns of Germanic, English, and American nationalism. Inquiry into the formative circumstances of medieval, and specifically Anglo-Saxon, scholarship is still rare. There is, however, a healthy tradition of inquiry into the roots of modern scholarship. Because my work stands in a tradition of modern inquiry into academic politics, and seeks to extend that inquiry to Anglo-Saxon studies, I wish to identify certain institutional and theoretical issues raised in some of the studies that have influenced mine.

Richard Ohmann has twice critiqued the structures and social operations that relate the academy to American society and, specifically, that connect the teaching of writing and reading—which is the business of the department of English—to shaping and maintaining the individual's place in a capitalistic system. In *English in America: A Radical View of the Profession* (1976) Ohmann claims that "the function of English teachers cannot be understood except within the context of a given society and politics." He argues that English classes help create and maintain a contented and productive work force. This assertion is made even more pointedly in *Politics of Letters* (1987), in which Ohmann contends that English teachers help to sort out students according to class origins, "preserving and reproducing class structure" and, even more maliciously, concealing "the real workings of the society from those most hurt by it."[4] In a commentary on Ohmann's first book, William E. Cain concedes that Ohmann's main point is "indisputable," and notes that subsequent developments in the discipline, in particular the onset of critical theory as a specialization, have had almost no success in bringing about the changes Ohmann seeks.[5]

Ohmann's case is made, from the perspective of British academic institutions, in Terry Eagleton's *Literary Theory: An Introduction,* one of the most popular books outlining the tradition of modern literary scholarship. Eagleton offers a swift and frequently amusing account of "The Rise of English" that outlines the process by which literature came to be an academic subject that encoded and perpetuated the cultural values of a few influential critics.[6] Both Eagleton and Ohmann—but especially the latter—argue that the structure of liberal capitalism has dominated the institutions in which literature and language are studied; they believe that traditional ways of teaching and writing have isolated literature from social contexts and situated it instead in a homogenized "literary history" that registers only the values of dominant classes, and of male readers in particular. As a result, the tradition has become exclusive; it serves the interests of a conservative state at the expense of the divergent views and needs of its citizens.

Eagleton and Ohmann are both indebted to the eminent British Marxist, Raymond Williams, author of several studies—*Politics and Letters, Problems in Culture and Materialism,* and *The Country and the City* among them—that analyze the connections between scholarly criticism and the emergence of culture as an academic ideal.[7] With an attention to the historical development of such terms as "culture" and "civilization" that is still far too uncommon, Williams seeks to return criticism to political values encoded in key concepts that, once ensconced in academic tradition, acquired both the appearance of neutrality and the familiar and reassuring aspect of old friends.

Few writers assert political claims more insistently than Eagleton and Ohmann, but others have recently discussed the institutional aspects of linguistic and literary analysis in ways relevant to the history of Anglo-Saxon studies. The institution of English in America is the subject of recent work by Gerald Graff. In *Professing Literature: An Institutional History* (1987), Graff supplies a history of the English department that is notable not only for its historical breadth, but for its critique of the indulgences of contemporary theorists. With Reginald Gibbons, Graff edited an essay collection, *Criticism in the University* (1985), that analyzes the status of literary criticism as a scholarly subject and explores the political implications of the various "-isms" of contemporary critical theory. With Michael Warner he has collected a series of essays, *The Origins of Literary Studies in America* (1989), written by American scholars who influenced the first form of the department of English.[8]

Along the lines of Graff's work is a challenge to theorists by Robert Scholes, who analyzes the pedagogical possibilities and dangers of literary theory from a revisionist perspective in *Textual Power: Literary Theory and the Teaching of English* (1985), which critiques contemporary theory in a call for political awareness in classroom practice. Scholes warns the theory-conscious teacher that, at the outset, it is wise to "avoid works too remote in culture, that need too much annotation in order to be read at all."[9] The medievalist might counter that Scholes' emphasis on the ways in which texts encode culture is particularly well-suited to medieval texts, since they must be decoded in even more ways than modern texts. The history of the study of the medieval text is, in scholarly editions and even in translations presented in the *Norton Anthology*, often manifest in annotations and textual notes. It is there, in the modern apparatus, that the study of those texts should begin, for we decode the text and its history at the same time as we recode and reinterpret them.

The studies by Ohmann, Graff, and Scholes are responses, from a cultural tradition that is politically liberal, or what I would call "left-leaning," to a series of publications from culturally and politically conservative educators. Chief among them is William Bennett, who, as Chairman of the National Endowment for the Humanities, published *To Reclaim a Legacy*,[10] and who, as Secretary of Education, pursued policies that stressed traditional values in the classroom. Publications by E. D. Hirsch, Jr., including *Cultural Literacy: What Every American Needs to Know* (1987), and the *Dictionary of Cultural Literacy* (1988), take up the discussion much to the benefit of Bennett's argument, since Hirsch demonstrates how little Americans know about the traditions of their culture. Allan Bloom's *The Closing of the American Mind* (1987) has made similar points but a rather different case.[11] These works, to which I return at the end of this book, assert traditional values in a scholarly tradition that has become polarized, politicized, and pluralized.[12]

None of these works, whether from conservative or liberal sides, analyzes the place of English linguistic history, or Anglo-Saxon studies, in the controversy. Apart from a few pages in Graff's *Professing Literature*, the topic is untouched. These commentaries by themselves demonstrate my claim that Anglo-Saxon studies have lost the prominent place they once held. Indeed, since the role of classical culture is taken up in detail by Hirsch and Bloom,[13] the field of Anglo-Saxon seems to be alone in its neglect. Confronted by this failure, one turns from critiques of the modern tradition of literary studies to histories of

Anglo-Saxon scholarship only to be struck by the lack of political perspective in works recounting the development of Old English studies in the academy.

This is not to say that excellent histories have not been written. Eric Stanley's *The Search for Anglo-Saxon Paganism,* a series of short notes published as a book in 1975, demonstrates the many ways in which scholarship prior to our own time was misguided and amateurish.[14] Stanley maintains a perspective similar to that of Eleanor N. Adams, who in a 1917 review concluded that "our debt to these early scholars is not lessened by a frank recognition of the fact that their work is practically worthless to the modern student."[15] A somewhat more benign view of the profession emerges from essays included in *Anglo-Saxon Scholarship: The First Three Centuries,* a collection commemorating the work of several important early Anglo-Saxonists but containing not a single essay exploring the volatility of the Anglo-Saxon political tradition. Nor did any suggest that the political motives of the Renaissance antiquarians outlived them and indeed continue to manifest themselves in the form they helped to give Anglo-Saxon studies.[16] All these studies define the tradition of Anglo-Saxon scholarship around a unifying theme of progress. Their omission of politics, no doubt, reflects the widespread view that Anglo-Saxon studies can only be traced back to their "scientific" or properly academic beginnings in the nineteenth century. The theme of progress appears in virtually all histories of Anglo-Saxon studies written to date. The title of one very good essay by Michael Murphy on Anglo-Saxon studies in the sixteenth century speaks for all: "From Antiquary to Academic: The Progress of Anglo-Saxon Scholarship."[17] The paradigm of progress supports the image of modern Anglo-Saxon studies as a highly specialized, refined discipline. It is clear that Anglo-Saxonists have imposed this inhibiting paradigm on themselves. Each new generation of scholars is seen as correcting the errors of the previous generation; each age celebrates its own advancement of historical and textual methods.

There is, however, a recent book that critiques the tradition of progressive scholarship. Lee Patterson's *Negotiating the Past: The Historical Understanding of Medieval Literature* begins with an incisive review of Chaucer scholarship that examines what, in terms of English political history in the nineteenth-century, it meant to be a medievalist. Patterson claims that medieval scholars in this period held to one of two political persuasions, a conservative, authoritarian tradition that valued the social harmony and unity of the medieval world, and an opposed tradition that valorized the individualism of the Middle Ages, its primitivism, and its freedom of spirit.[18] Patterson juxtaposes the twin forces of Chaucer scholarship in the early twentieth century—historical or exegetical criticism, and formalism or New Criticism—with this bipartite nineteenth-century tradition, and outlines the development of various theoretical perspectives, including Marxist criticism and New Historicism in particular, as forces in medieval studies.

As astute and agile a survey of medieval critical traditions as one is likely to find, Patterson's book is a call to defend a heretofore undefined but often-invoked "humanism"; and in a critical climate in which the word "humanism" is frequently part of a chain that usually begins with either "bourgeois" or "liberal," this defense is appropriate. There is, Patterson writes, "something scandalous in the fact that the current, virulent attacks on humanism issue from two diametrical points on the political compass, the religious right and the theoretical left." And he pointedly asks, "How is it that the academic intellectual has come to conspire in his own demise?"[19] Yet Patterson's critique excludes almost entirely the place of Anglo-Saxon studies in the humanistic tradition, even though the humanism Patterson defends was, in England, shaped in the political climate in which the recovery of Anglo-Saxon records was first undertaken.[20] It is symbolic and symptomatic that these concerns, once closely connected, are now seldom linked; many debate the meaning of humanism in the Western tradition, but few acknowledge that Anglo-Saxonism and humanism entered the tradition together.

A timely reminder of how little Anglo-Saxon culture means to literate Americans appears in Hirsch's *Cultural Literacy,* and the *Dictionary of Cultural Literacy,* a compendium of information for those who wish to be culturally literate by Hirsch's definition. Hirsch's much-discussed (and, I believe, much-misunderstood) list of "what literate Americans *know*" contains not a single reference to Anglo-Saxon culture.[21] It omits the entire range of key figures and events: Alfred, the King of the West Saxons (871–899) and often called "the father of English literature" and "father of the English nation"; the terms "Anglo-Saxon" and "Old English"; Bede (d. 735), who is known as the "father of English scholarship"; and *Beowulf* (although *Beowulf* does appear in Hirsch's *Dictionary*). However, "Norse myth" is included, as is "King Arthur," and this suggests that myth plays a greater role in cultural literacy than history, literary or otherwise. Likewise, the brothers Grimm, founders of Germanic philology, are included, although "philology" is not; they earn their place, I feel sure, through their fairy tales, not their study of language origins. On the other hand, Hirsch's list does include 1066 among its dates (along with 1492, 1776, and the dates of the U.S. Civil War and the first two World Wars); it also includes "Norman Conquest," "Battle of Hastings," and William the Conqueror.

Although literate Americans do not know about Anglo-Saxon

literature, they do supposedly know (or at least know of) the achievements of Homer and Virgil—both of whom are included in the list—as well as other Latin and Greek authors. For the medieval period generally, Hirsch includes "Dark Ages" and "medieval," but not "Middle Ages." When we recall that the Anglo-Saxon age belongs to the infamous "Dark Ages," a gap between the included authors Augustine (d. 432) and Chaucer (d. 1400), the omission of Anglo-Saxon texts becomes understandable. It is left to the acronym WASP ("white Anglo-Saxon Protestant")—a term that is obviously derogatory these days—to convey the importance of Anglo-Saxon to American culture. That is the sole term on the list that includes "Anglo-Saxon."

Hirsch and his co-compilers are not setting values on the terms they include in the list. The subtitle of the book, "What Every American Needs to Know," is different from the title of the appendix, where the list appears. The appendix is entitled "What Literate Americans Know," and it is merely an attempt to describe what, near the end of the twentieth century, literate Americans know about—and care about—in their cultural heritage. It is instructive to compare this list with Hugh Blair's *Lectures on Rhetoric and Belles Lettres* (1798), a precedent to which Hirsch, in his discussion of national language, refers. Hirsch calls Blair the "first definer of cultural literacy for the English national language" and his book "one of the most influential textbooks ever issued in Great Britain or the United States." It was written for students in Scotland so that they could be introduced to the "study of the belles lettres, and of composition," learning that British students, Hirsch suggests (in a mismatched metaphor), "had absorbed through their pores."[22] Blair's book was also used in the United States. The 1850 "University, College and School Edition" came equipped with "Copius Questions; and an Analysis of Each Lecture," supplied by Abraham Mills. In his "Editor's Preface," Mills claimed that the questions and summaries had been "used by a number of classes of young ladies, educated by himself, . . . with entire success."[23]

Like Hirsch's list, the index to Blair's three volumes makes no mention of Anglo-Saxon culture. When Blair was writing, *Beowulf* had not yet been published in a modern edition, King Alfred was known only to a few scholars, and knowledge of the Anglo-Saxon language was very limited. Today, after a century of teaching Anglo-Saxon language and literature in American colleges and universities, the knowledge of literate Americans about Anglo-Saxon culture can be recognized, in Blair's list as well as Hirsch's, by its absence. *Beowulf* has now found a place in Hirsch's *Dictionary;* however, the average literate American still confuses King Alfred with King Arthur.

Beowulf and the Opera ■

The decline of Anglo-Saxon studies in the registers of general culture mirrors the decline of the subject in the academy, where that decline is recent and thus easily traced. Most scholars agree that it became obvious only in 1954, when Harvard University discontinued its traditional requirement that doctoral candidates in English had to study Anglo-Saxon. Abandoning the requirement should be seen as not as the onset of decline, but rather as the beginning of its final phase. Eventually other major English doctoral programs followed suit. A survey of forty-five universities conducted in 1979 showed that half of them had once required a course in Old English for the doctoral degree but had dropped the requirement since 1954.[24] A 1989 survey of twenty-one institutions with doctoral programs in English in the South Atlantic region of the Modern Language Association (MLA) indicated that only five required a course in Old English for the doctoral degree and that four had dropped the requirement recently.[25] Outside of doctoral programs, Old English and the history of the language tend to be required only for those undergraduates who wish to be certified to teach. Old English is now most frequently taught in classes that mix graduate and undergraduate students, but not in sufficient numbers to reverse the decline. Robert F. Yeager, who conducted the 1979 survey, suggested that the decline in the teaching of Old English at the graduate level resulted in part from the lack of undergraduate courses in the subject. Without exposure to Old English as undergraduate English majors, students entering graduate school tend to view the subject as "dour and alien and threatening."[26]

American undergraduates learn little or nothing about Anglo-Saxon culture. Those who go on to graduate school are not likely to pursue it, and if they do not learn about it at the graduate level, they will not, as teachers of survey or other courses, encourage their students to cultivate a subject they themselves know little or nothing about. It is necessary to consider these points in the context of reduced interest in the humanities in general. The number of bachelor's degrees in the United States increased by eighty-eight percent between 1966 and 1986, but bachelor's degrees in the humanities increased by only thirty-three percent. Approximately eighty percent of students who earn a bachelor's degree do so without ever taking a course in a foreign language, American history, or Western civilization, so it is likely that they never hear about Anglo-Saxon England at all.[27]

Anglo-Saxon scholars have been rightly concerned about the

consequences of the decline in the popularity of their specialty. One response was the publication of *Approaches to Teaching* Beowulf, a book which appeared in 1984 under the auspices of the MLA. The *Beowulf* volume contains numerous models for courses in which *Beowulf* and other Anglo-Saxon texts can be taught, many of them aimed at an undergraduate audience, and some of them arguing for novel ways to help students value Old English. For example, one teacher, in order to stimulate discussion, compared the armor in *Beowulf* to that in *Star Wars*.[28] The volume also describes a variety of attempts to emphasize the "cultural relevance" of *Beowulf*, including several "performances" of the poem, most memorably a sunrise reading in Central Park in the summer of 1982, sponsored by the *Village Voice;* this odd event had an even odder precedent, a rock opera based on *Beowulf* performed in New York in 1977.[29]

The editors of the MLA volume take an indulgent attitude towards such uses of *Beowulf*. But they remark rather dolefully that few graduate schools "can still afford to cater to a taste or a need for the Dark Ages in an educational market increasingly and restrictively competitive, egalitarian, technocratic, professional, popular, and geared to preparation in law, medicine, and business."[30] As this statement implies, the study of Anglo-Saxon culture is widely viewed, even within the academy, as elitist (as the words "egalitarian" and "popular" indicate). Limits to its practical applications limit its value. Outside the academy, *Beowulf* may be adapted to opera or to neo-primitivist rituals, but more generally it is ignored.

Let us contrast the gloomy picture of Anglo-Saxon in the United States with the annual International Congress on Medieval Studies, held every Spring since 1965 on the campus of Western Michigan University, Kalamazoo, where the serious business of medieval scholarship is done. In 1989 over two thousand scholars of medieval and early Renaissance culture participated in 336 sessions, during each of which usually three or four papers were read. Thirty-four sessions were in progress at any given hour of the program, and sometimes two-thirds of these sessions focused on linguistic or literary subjects. At one point, four simultaneous sessions were devoted to Anglo-Saxon, and another to Old Norse. An observer could well conclude that Anglo-Saxon studies, and the field of medieval studies more generally, had never been so prosperous.

Evidence from many other sources would seem to confirm this impression. In 1989, Bruce Mitchell, an eminent Anglo-Saxonist, listed a dozen projects that indicated the well-being of Anglo-Saxon studies world-wide;[31] his is only the most recent in a series of surveys of major current projects in the field, and it is a fair sign of how positively Anglo-

Saxonists regard the state of their profession.[32] At the head of Mitchell's list is the new *Dictionary of Old English* (*DOE*), the culmination of an enormous, computerized research program that was announced in 1973 in *A Plan for the Dictionary of Old English.* Before individual fascicles of the *DOE* began to appear—fascicles C and D have appeared, D alone covering 950 pages—a two-part microfiche concordance to the entire corpus of Anglo-Saxon literature was published.[33] Another vast project is the Old English Thesaurus, part of the Glasgow University Historical Thesaurus, which seeks to provide "a notionally classified" arrangement of vocabulary found in the *Oxford English Dictionary* and its supplements, with the Old English material produced by new work in other projects, including, of course, the *DOE*.[34] Two projects are cataloguing the sources of Anglo-Saxon texts. In the United States, *The Sources of Anglo-Saxon Literary Culture* (SASLC) collects information about manuscripts, texts, editions, and commentaries in a step preliminary to revision of yet another project, J.D.A. Ogilvy's *Books Known to the English, 597–1066.*[35] A simultaneous and similar undertaking, based in England, is the *Fontes Anglo-Saxonici,* "The Sources of Anglo-Saxon," which will identify exhaustively—that is, line by line—the sources of all Anglo-Saxon poetry and prose.[36]

In addition, Mitchell listed several fairly new journals and organizations. They include *Anglo-Saxon England,* published in Cambridge and affiliated with the International Society of Anglo-Saxonists; the *Old English Newsletter,* published in Binghamton, New York, in affiliation with the Old English Division of MLA; a new research center devoted to Anglo-Saxon studies at the University of Manchester; and other organizations and research projects designed to promote the exchange of ideas and research. This explosive growth is by no means confined to England, Canada, Germany, and the United States, although most of the research is carried on in these countries. A recent issue of the *Old English Newsletter* chronicles the growth of teaching and research in Old English in Japan,[37] and a new Japanese journal, the *Mediaeval English Studies Newsletter,* features a series of articles on the history of Old English studies in universities world-wide, showing that almost everywhere—except for France, where poststructuralism is singularly dominant—the subject seems to be booming.[38] This activity is, however, extremely specialized; its impact on undergraduate training appears to be slight. Little research in Anglo-Saxon studies concerns the needs of undergraduates, which are usually assessed in the context of "approaches" to Old English (i.e., how to teach grammar, how to use visual aids). This is useful work, but it is work that assumes an audience rather than helps to build one. Highly specialized, with a small undergraduate clientele, Anglo-Saxon studies demonstrate the gap between research and teaching that has been assailed by such critics as Charles J. Sykes. In *ProfScam: Professors and the Demise of Higher Education,* Sykes denounces the irrelevance of much university-level research and its isolation from undergraduate education. Sykes deplores a call for theoretical work even with *Beowulf* and identifies critical theory as an especially dangerous form of specialization.[39] He is not alone in alleging that research is too specialized and that the connection of conferences to larger cultural and social realities is virtually nonexistent. Reviewing the state of research in intellectual history, a discipline to which, as I see it, the study of Anglo-Saxon culture is closely related, Dominick LaCapra has written that "increased professional confidence" in the work of historians has resulted in "decreased public interest" in their research.[40] One could say the same of the specialized research of Anglo-Saxonists and public indifference to their efforts.

The audience attuned to Anglo-Saxon studies has shrunk for many reasons, some of them outside the power of Anglo-Saxonists. The chief reason is the failure of the university to persuade the educated public that language skills are important. Two decades ago, when universities began to abandon the requirement that undergraduates study foreign languages, they abandoned a principle fundamental to Anglo-Saxon studies. That principle, simply put, is that universities should lead students to new awareness by exposing them to information outside the domain of their prior experience and, therefore, difficult to gain access to. It is a principle that must be observed if the study of any remote culture—including the remote past of one's own culture—is to flourish. In the 1960s, when distribution requirements began to disappear in both graduate and undergraduate education, universities presumably thought that students could be persuaded to take courses in remote cultures and languages if those courses were appealing. But when languages were no longer required, the cultures they were part of lost importance rather than appeal. The result was not that Old English and other once-required subjects, including foreign languages, were taught more creatively or persuasively; they were simply taught less often, and to fewer students.

The blame for the decline of Anglo-Saxon studies does not lie entirely with university administrations or pragmatic students. Modern Anglo-Saxonists are the first in the history of their subject to neglect its history, but then they are also the first Anglo-Saxonists for whom the subject, long propped up by academic fiat, had acquired professional status without demonstrating cultural relevance. When universities deemphasized training in foreign languages, Anglo-Saxonists suffered quite unnecessarily; they had reduced Old English to the study of language, without attention to the cultural and political contexts in which

Anglo-Saxon studies had, in all previous periods, been carried out. Anglo-Saxonists contributed to the decline of their subject by ignoring its history, which, with all its conflict and power, they left for others to study. Philological practices used to study Anglo-Saxon, highly specialized in their appeal, were separated from the political controversies in which those practices developed—that is, from their history, whose appeal was much more general. Increasing professionalization and technical sophistication significantly expanded the ability to study early English language and culture, but failed to build an audience of readers curious about Anglo-Saxon England and interested in learning more about its language and culture and their influence on our world. Once a wedge of expertise divided Anglo-Saxonists from their wider audience, the enormous institutional structure of conferences, journals, and projects would grow in size but, outside the circle of Anglo-Saxon scholars, shrink in significance.

Because Anglo-Saxon has not usually been taught in terms of its cultural and historical connections, many educated Americans assume that Anglo-Saxon studies have nothing important to offer them, and, given their experience of Old English, they are, in the main, right. Anglo-Saxonists have sustained the impression that the subject is a horrendous complex of grammatical mysteries and an abstruse relic of a best-forgotten Germanic past. Society, usually willing to pay lip service to the humanities, but also usually conscious of the cost of irrelevance, has responded accordingly, manifesting an indifference to Anglo-Saxon studies that is more damning than contempt.

Thomas Jefferson and Bede's *History* ■

Let me offer an example of the failure of Anglo-Saxonists to address significant social and cultural concerns, a failure related to the resultant structure of the university curriculum. In discussing the history of Anglo-Saxon studies with students and colleagues in recent years, I have invariably found them startled to learn that Thomas Jefferson was an Anglo-Saxon scholar and that he was so concerned with the need to teach the Old English language that he planned to write his own grammar. As part of Jefferson's legacy, the Anglo-Saxon language was introduced into the curriculum of the University of Virginia; it was also to be taught in elementary schools.[41] Jefferson believed that Anglo-Saxon social organization was a model for American democracy. He was so impressed with two mythical Anglo-Saxon heroes—Hengst and Horsa—that he wished to see them pictured on the Great Seal.

Here we have a stunning illustration of the political power of

Anglo-Saxon studies. In the *Ecclesiastical History* Bede tells us that British chief Vortigern requested "the race of the Angles or Saxons," led by Hengst and Horsa, to help defend Britain from enemies to the north, probably in or around 449 A.D. They came ostensibly "to fight on behalf of Britain," Winston Churchill wrote, but their real intention was to conquer it.[42] Horsa was apparently killed early in the conflict; Hengst and his son Æsc betrayed the British and conquered them.

Jefferson thought that these warriors stood not only for bravery but also for democracy; according to John Adams, to whom he communicated his plan for the Great Seal, Jefferson saw Hengst and Horsa as representing "the form of government we have assumed."[43] The larger significance of Hengst and Horsa is suggested by Jefferson's plan for the reverse side of the seal, an image of the pillar of fire that led the Chosen People into the Promised Land (Exodus 13:21–22). The pillar served as a sign of God's favor and guidance, and hence marked the way for those who followed it into a new land. Opposite Hengst and Horsa, however, the pillar of fire acquires ominous significance: not a sign of guidance or protection for safe passage, but an emblem of conquest. Jefferson's idealization of Anglo-Saxon culture, and the scriptural allegory of the pillar of fire, vividly picture the ambitions of early settlers for westward expansion.

What does Jefferson's plan for the Great Seal, which encapsulates the makings of Manifest Destiny, tell us about Anglo-Saxon language, literature, and history? A teacher who wished to raise this obviously important, if disturbing, topic in an introductory Anglo-Saxon class could begin in as obvious a place as *Sweet's Anglo-Saxon Reader,* which includes the episode of Hengst and Horsa in its excerpts from the Old English translation of Bede, or another introductory text containing the episode. Many connections are possible. Students could begin to study Jefferson's knowledge of Bede in a recent, prominently placed article on Jefferson's Anglo-Saxon scholarship, which reveals that Jefferson owned the first edition of Bede's *History* in Old English, published in 1644. (I discuss it in detail in Chapter 5.)[44] As they explored the unfamiliar territory of Bede's text, students would uncover many familiar issues. Those who had read *Beowulf* in translation might wish to connect Bede's Hengst to the Hengst mentioned in the poem (understandable, but probably fruitless; they are different characters).[45] They would finish their first Old English course knowing something about both Bede's *History,* Bede's history, and the place of Old English in the history of American education. This is an obvious example of an exercise in "reception." It demonstrates that an important Old English text, which expresses an immensely important part of early English culture, can be intelligently and productively related to other Anglo-

Saxon texts, editorial history, and the scholarly habits and political concepts of a figure of great importance in American cultural history. It is an exercise that shows how the reception of an earlier culture—Jefferson's understanding of Hengst and Horsa, and the student's understanding of Jefferson—can lead to new ideas about one's own.

A related example is the nineteenth-century argument that Beowulf, hero of the only epic in early English culture, was a pirate.[46] Was this a sound suggestion or a misreading of the Old English text? It was the latter, surely. But seen as a misreading with a motive, it is a potentially arresting idea about expansion and settlement in Anglo-Saxon society, topics that also emerge in the background of Bede's *Ecclesiastical History. Beowulf* overflows with treasure and the significance of exchanging it; material riches are always seen as the reward for virtue and courage. Hengst and Horsa were mercenaries, not pirates, but the entrepreneurial character type existed in the culture, although its application to Beowulf (rather than to Hengst or Horsa) strikes us as outrageous. Expansionism was surely the reason early Britain was successively conquered twice by the Romans—once by Caesar, once by Christ—and by the Angles, Saxons, and Jutes. One cannot consider either Bede's *History* or *Beowulf* without thinking of expansionism, which was, of course, no less important to Jefferson than it was to nineteenth-century merchants and admirals.

These examples demonstrate, I believe, the kinds of connections that are possible when Old English is seen through its connection to other subjects in the curriculum, and to periods in English and American history subsequent to the Anglo-Saxon age. Students then perceive the cultural relevance of the subject, and Anglo-Saxon courses become as likely as any others in the humanities—and more likely than many—to play some part in the development of students' social views.

As they ponder modern critical response to Jefferson's Anglo-Saxonism by various Anglo-Saxon scholars, students may detect a certain narrowness, perhaps, and would find that linguistic matters were considered far more important than historical or cultural issues. Although Jefferson planned a grammar of Old English (it was never given final form) and engaged in numerous scholarly and scientific enterprises, his Anglo-Saxonism was not "disciplined," even by the academic or scholarly standards of his own time. Stanley Hauer, the first Anglo-Saxonist to explore in detail Jefferson's extensive work with language, grammar, and education, notes that the work of the Danish scholar Rasmus K. Rask, published in 1817, remained unknown to Jefferson throughout his life-long pursuit of Anglo-Saxon subjects, even as Jefferson continued with his grammar in 1825.[47] Rask's work, however, was not translated into English until 1830 and was largely unknown even in England until then, so Jefferson should hardly be blamed for being unaware of it. Hauer finds his ignorance "excusable," and applauds both Jefferson's "eloquent defense" of Anglo-Saxon and his efforts on behalf of the cause of Anglo-Saxon language studies. But Hauer avoids the much more significant, and politically volatile—that is, racist—beliefs that, at least in part, motivated Jefferson's fascination with Anglo-Saxon culture, even when quoting Jefferson's 1818 *Report* to the commission assigned to develop the University of Virginia. In this document, Jefferson explicitly connected expansionist views to language study. Anglo-Saxon, Jefferson wrote, "a language already fraught with all the eminent science of our parent country, the future vehicle of whatever we may ourselves achieve, and destined to occupy so much space on the globe, claims distinguished attention in American education."[48] Jefferson's potent mixture of ideology and Anglo-Saxon scholarship was by no means uncommon, as Reginald Horsman has shown. Jefferson and other early American revolutionaries were immersed in myths of Anglo-Saxon democracy, and among the patriots discussing them were George Washington, Patrick Henry, and Benjamin Franklin.[49]

It is remarkable that few Anglo-Saxonists teaching Old English language and literature today should be aware of the interest the framers of American government took in the cultural myths that had accumulated around Anglo-Saxon texts. Why have Jefferson's own Anglo-Saxonism, and the amateur efforts of many others, found no place in Anglo-Saxon studies? The answer is that those studies have been rigidly defined to include only primary materials and methods of language inquiry, and to exclude the history of reading and writing, the scholarship of Jefferson and other early Anglo-Saxonists.

Three Oppositions ■

Jefferson's Anglo-Saxon scholarship and his relation of global space to knowledge of the Anglo-Saxon language can be used to establish exactly the kinds of connections between Old English and other periods, and between language study and history, that make Anglo-Saxon studies important. His Anglo-Saxonism falls outside the specialized categories that now order the professional activity of Anglo-Saxonists and that capture their self-image. I see this specialization as a three-fold series of binary oppositions.

The first pair concerns the material Anglo-Saxonists study, and that which they do not. The former is comprised of a body of language and literature written between the seventh and twelfth centuries. That material is "Old English," and everything else—everything written before or after—is simply "not Old English." Few texts are earlier than this (apart from inscriptions and runes), and everything dated after approximately the year 1100 is considered "early Middle English" rather than "Old English." The processes through which these divisions were formed are the processes through which Old English was defined as a "field." "Fields are constructed by an initial attention to the borders which demarcate them," John Frow writes, "but the visibility of limits then tends to be replaced by the details of rules derived from the founding principles."[50] The boundaries between "Old English" and "not Old English" are produced and maintained by method, articulated by linguistic systems that graduate stages of the language and divide historical periods as precisely as possible.

Such systems are method—Frow's "details of rules"—and in my second pair, method is opposite to meaning. Jefferson's linguistic methodology was imprecise in regard to the differentiation of dialects and stages of the language. Unlike modern scholars, who distinguish sharply between method—which is technical, even "scientific"—and the meaning derived from that approach, Jefferson showed no awareness of the notion of neutral method or scholarship removed from culture and politics. It is true, certainly, that anyone wishing to learn Anglo-Saxon easily or well would not want to rely on the system Jefferson constructed, which was based on problematic but very popular assumptions about language and its origins. But the meaning of Jefferson's methods cannot be dismissed simply because those methods have been found defective; the semantic value of those methods can be seen, and appreciated, only in the context of the cultural value they expressed for him. Jefferson cared about method and meaning; he made plans for a dictionary of etymology and was even concerned about the readability of Old English in print.[51] But he made these efforts to refine method only because Anglo-Saxon history was, for him, vital to American democracy. Its value was its ideological currency. In Jefferson's Anglo-Saxon scholarship, method served meaning; in Anglo-Saxon scholarship today, "meaning," either as political significance or, more generally, literary interpretation, is secondary to method. From our perspective, the inadequacy of Jefferson's method is its only meaning. His linguistic contributions to American culture—his work with Anglo-Saxon grammar—are considered less valuable than his political contributions, or even his architecture. These latter contributions have transcended his own time, while subsequent research has rendered the former obsolete.

In my third pair of opposites, as in the second, the study of language is preferred to the study of contexts. I am calling this the division between documents—which can be dated by their language and scrutinized—and culture. If culture is, as Raymond Williams writes, both a process of development and the product of that process,[52] the processes and products of Old English culture are, in the first instance, political, and, in the second, documentary or textual. The study of Anglo-Saxon texts and history was always undertaken by those who were engaged in pursuit of self-definition. Early Anglo-Saxon studies trace the obsessive efforts of the learned to define their tradition in terms of the remote rather than the immediate past. This process was, of course, a means to procuring certain rights and privileges; as such, it was also a response to a threat—a challenge to one tradition from another, a demand for a share in those rights and the status they conferred. Although language is an inherent part of culture, languages—especially ancient languages—can and usually are taught as if they had nothing to do with either modern or ancient culture. Anglo-Saxon studies are, to a very great degree, taught as the history of the document, which is seen as a container for language and a vehicle of language change. The history of culture is much more difficult to teach, and I refer here not only to the content of the course, but the place of the teacher. One who wishes to teach the paradigms of grammar can remain outside the material, much as a police officer can direct traffic without moving in it. One who wishes to teach the cultural dimensions of Anglo-Saxon studies—connections to race, expansionism, and class status—is immediately inside a discussion of values and beliefs, a web of lived experience into which Anglo-Saxon texts and all their teachers, readers, editors, and hearers are woven.

Modern Anglo-Saxon scholarship favors one member in each of my three pairs of binary oppositions. First, it is concerned only with texts from the Old English period and does not consider texts that are "not Old English." Second, this scholarship is methodologically rigorous; it regards method (e.g., learning the language) as prior to meaning (interpreting the texts). Third, Anglo-Saxon scholarship analyzes documents in a narrowly textual way, leaving other aspects of Anglo-Saxon culture to other disciplines (art, history, philosophy, and so forth). In each case, Anglo-Saxonists in the twentieth century have traditionally preferred the philological to the historical option, and the result has been to limit the appeal of Anglo-Saxon studies by portraying them as rarified and unrelated to contemporary issues. In each case, I believe that the historical option should be exercised, not to the exclusion of the philological, but brought to parity with it.

In an era obsessed with overspecialization and cultural literacy, the history of the discipline of Anglo-Saxon studies is a timely topic. The boundaries now limiting Anglo-Saxon studies are merely theoretical ideas, and they are susceptible to challenge and to revision through theoretical debate. That debate does not pit "theorists," who are interested in change, against "traditionalists," who are dedicated to cultural continuity; it is not, as it is often said to be, a contest between "theory" and "tradition,"[53] but a dialogue between old theory and new theory. "Old theory" includes literary history, language study, and all the accustomed practices of the Department of English that have been in place for so long that many seem to think they are synonymous with the professional study of literature. Some "new theory" may be relatively new in its formulation, as is deconstruction, while other "new theory" is new only in its application, as is the case with Marxism and feminism; in either case it is seen as a pushy, postmodernist latecomer.

Yet the most powerful force working against Anglo-Saxon scholars today is not the postmodernism of others, but the modernist view of their own. Modernity, Wlad Godzich writes, is characterized by the idea that "thought progresses from enlightenment to enlightenment in history," and that this progress is achieved by "re-examining critically the very ground of its origin so that this ground becomes ever more secure." Thus "the new is immediately made valuable, becomes a value in itself, because it is constituted by means of a reappropriation of the original ground."[54] The history of Anglo-Saxon studies is conventionally understood as a march from amateurism to professionalism within the paradigm of primitivism and progress. The idea of progress not only reduces the disputatious process through which disciplines have developed into a list of the victors—there being from the failures, apparently, nothing to learn—but confers on those who chart progress the prestige of the originary ground. Hans Aarsleff has made the point rather bluntly. "It is not the forward march that misleads," he writes, "but rather the conviction that the top has been reached."[55]

The major defect of the paradigm is its impoverished view of human experience. To admit only the successes of scholarship into the discussion—the origins of those concepts that have been accepted as forerunners of modern methods—is analogous to the famous dictum that winners write the history of the war. Scholarship is not a war, and its "losers"—Thomas Jefferson as an authority on the structure of the Old English verb, for example—have had as much as the "winners" to contribute. It is no wonder that a view of the past so predictable, reductive, and dull has failed to build an audience for Anglo-Saxon. The subject—both its Old English texts and the history of their reception—is rife with conflict, but its presence in the academy is an ocean of calm.

I have rejected this paradigm and its forward-looking movement as organizing principles because I believe that the idea of progress itself is inadequate, both as a theme for history and thus as a principle according to which history can be constructed. I wish to set this paradigm against a model of conflict and its context. The "contexts" in which Anglo-Saxon studies took shape differ from "the history" of Anglo-Saxon studies as a comprehensive account that fits pieces together into a narrative celebration of the modern condition. Those contexts expressed desire for the establishment of origins, and were, as a result, fraught with conflict. This desire is both personal and relative to scholarly purposes; the search to which it leads invariably leads to conflict.

Desire for Origins ■

In the second half of the nineteenth century, when "Anglo-Saxon Studies" became an academic subject, Anglo-Saxonists were vigorously engaged in issues of social and cultural change; they did not pursue knowledge for disinterested reasons. They used Anglo-Saxon studies to identify, and then to recover, their cultural beginnings. Early Anglo-Saxonists identified closely with their subject. They recognized themselves in the texts they studied and were aware that they shared a horizon of interests with the horizons expressed in Anglo-Saxon texts. In their desire for origins, they studied Anglo-Saxon texts in a spirit of unabashed self-interest. Their work with the texts sometimes resulted in "misreading," as in the assumption that Beowulf was a pirate. But misreadings of Old English texts are not simply mistakes. They represent the intersection of an "Old English" and a "not Old English" point of view; they are points of connection between the Anglo-Saxon and the post-Anglo-Saxon world. Readers and writers in both worlds desired originary status—the status that, through its antiquity and its lofty position, a particular origin was believed to confer on those who claimed it. Anglo-Saxon texts, ancient representations of Germanic as well as English character, furnished historical accounts in which scholars recognized early versions of their own interests. They saw their own disputes anticipated and acted out in Anglo-Saxon texts, which thereby became extensions of their horizons, of their views. Anglican reformers saw their struggles against Rome mirrored in Anglo-Saxon homilies; Thomas Jefferson saw his ambitions for democracy foreshadowed in Anglo-Saxon laws and chronicles. Their Anglo-Saxon studies were narratives of their origins.

In the origin, early Anglo-Saxonists posited an ideal point, ancient and continuous with the present. We call belief in such a point "primitivism," and distinguish two kinds, cultural and chronological. Cultural primitivists have long portrayed the Anglo-Saxon era as a time of simple, "natural" social organization and political order. This myth interacts with (and is not entirely distinct from) chronological primitivism, which is less concerned with specific social or political organization than with a generalized view that life in the past was free of inhibition and restraint.[56] It was chiefly cultural primitivism that inspired early Anglo-Saxonists. Generations of English and American writers elaborated the myth of an ideal and innocent Anglo-Saxon culture, and, as if longing for an earthly paradise, looked back on it as an image of their own beginnings.

But primitivism can be seen as crude and uncivilized as well as ideal. Aspects of Anglo-Saxon culture that appeared ideal and innocent to some scholars seemed violent and barbaric to those for whom the Norman Conquest was the beginning of real civilization in England; for them the origin had been corrupted and needed to be revised. In the eighteenth century and after, the image of Anglo-Saxon culture veered between the idyllic and the barbaric. Early scholars were free either to revere the origins described in the texts or to despise them; in either case, what mattered was that they believed in those origins and connected them to contemporary circumstances. Their scholarship formed a link between origins and beginnings. Edward W. Said defines an origin as "divine, mythical and privileged," and a beginning as "secular, humanly produced, and ceaselessly re-examined," "designated in order to indicate, clarify, or define a *later* time, place, or action." Said pays particular attention to the role of education in this process of designation, since, he notes, the question "How should one begin to write?" contains four issues: one's training, subject, point of departure, and, for the literary critic, the status of criticism as an institutional practice isolated from historical, psychological, or cultural study. [57] The act of designating beginnings is an act that places one in a tradition and also shapes one's departure from it: it is an act that acknowledges and crosses boundaries.

In the Reformation, when Anglican scholars sought to prove that the Church of England was independent of the Church of Rome, and had been so for centuries (rather than for decades, which was actually the case), they asserted the integrity and the antiquity of documents referring to a specifically English Church. Several Anglo-Saxon texts, including homilies and letters to priests, seemed to give witness that such a Church had descended from the Apostolic era, but from Paul, not from Peter. The scholars' task was clear: They had to determine that certain documents were genuine, and others altered. The first step was to establish a beginning for ancient texts. The second was to claim that those texts attested to the origin of nothing less than the "true" religion, a religion older than and hence superior to Rome's. The designation of beginnings in Anglo-Saxon texts was a way to justify and enhance the status of the English Church in the sixteenth century. This is what Said means when he says that beginnings are designated in order "to indicate, clarify, or define a *later* time, place, or action."

The relationship of origins to beginnings is hermeneutic: a point of departure is a boundary crossing, a point at which history is rewritten. Once history is rewritten, the frame of reference or system (e.g., a theological system) within which the rewriting takes place is altered, and the point of departure for future beginnings is designated. Hermes, Frow reminds us, was not only the gods' message bearer: Hermes was also "the god both of boundaries and of the crossing of boundaries, and the patron of a special mercantile class of what Homer called 'professional boundary-crossers.'"[58] The means of rewriting historical boundaries in the Renaissance were the interpretive tools of textual criticism and historical narrative—both, of course, subsumed at the time under different and non-academic names. These procedures were interdependent and even mutually determining. A political crisis—the English Reformation—fostered scholarship, since, in order to justify the break with Rome, England needed a history that demonstrated the existence of an ancient, specifically English Church. Those who believed in the existence of such a Church traced enough evidence in religious Anglo-Saxon prose to substantiate the belief. Their historical and textual determination stemmed from religious conviction. We may say that desire for origins was their chief qualification for scholarship and their guarantee that textual criticism would inevitably bear out the historical view that inspired it. For them, textual criticism and history seem to have existed in a hermeneutic circle in which "individual features are intelligible in terms of the entire context, and the entire context becomes intelligible through the individual features."[59] Their history sought to explain its origin so that the origin could explain their history. Yet by designating a new mission of history and scholarship they both placed new limits on interpretation—scholarship had to confirm a newly official theology of origins—and made new kinds of interpretation possible: crossing one boundary, they designated another, which would in turn have to be crossed.

Traditional Anglo-Saxonists differ from early Anglo-Saxonists at virtually all points relating origins to beginnings. For us, an origin is merely a myth about the beginnings of a race or a nation, first an oral account that subsequently passed into written form and acquired a textual beginning. A textual account of an origin is a document, and although it is as close to the origin as a scholar can come, its fascination is that it is a document—an ancient artifact that we can pour over, analyze, and interpret. Its link to its mythical origins is not important, nor is it seen as a beginning to be used to designate one's *own* time and place. Designating one's own time and place in scholarly endeavors—that is, sharing horizons with the composers of Anglo-Saxon texts—is a form of subjectivity that is tantamount to misreading, a sign of partial, polemical scholarship to be avoided at all costs. We identify the subjectivity of earlier scholars as a weakness or fault from which improved scholarly methods save us. Without judging the profession, we can reconsider subjectivity as a response to a universally understood characteristic of Anglo-Saxon documents and culture, a collection of texts that are largely of anonymous authorship, sometimes incomplete, and usually undated and undatable. The ambiguity attendant on working with a corpus of such texts is considerable. One manuscript can supply the basis for many different—that is, conflicting—but plausible claims relating to its historical value and hence its originary status. This incompleteness in the origin has important consequences for those who decode and recode texts. Incompleteness is an aspect of textually, historically, and humanly produced beginnings. That data must be interpreted and those gaps filled: the origin, therefore, is incomplete. It is a question needing an answer; it is an origin needing a supplement.

The supplements proposed by one generation of scholars, or one race or nation of scholars, are relative to their immediate political and social contexts; another generation will wish in its turn to provide supplements to the work of their predecessors. Origins, to echo Said, have to be revised and ceaselessly re-examined. The history of the search for origins is, to this extent, a repetition of conflicts in different contexts rather than a progression from conflict to harmony. Since claims for originary status rest on evidence that is always in dispute, such struggle cannot be avoided. The history of Anglo-Saxon studies is the history of dispute about that evidence. Our own claims to methodological superiority will not be final; they will instead become part of this repetition, and they will be seen as such by future historians, whether they employ the paradigm of progress or not.

In this multiplicity of reading and writing, many desires—many visions of history, many understandings of a text—are possible. Perhaps the most disturbing aspect of the technical sophistication of Anglo-Saxon studies today is the implication that enough computers and databases will rid our work of subjectivity and will produce, to our satisfaction, a neutral, scientific, indeed ideal form of scholarship. Such objectivity is more than an illusion; it is also a means of cutting ourselves off from the past and denying that we have material interests in the study of culture.[60] The attempt to differentiate the scientific analysis of language—including philology and textual criticism—from the political or historical analysis of culture, has been detrimental to Anglo-Saxon studies. Originary status is instrumental, not ornamental. It is a powerful means, sometimes spiritual, always scholarly, to a material, worldly end.

The current concern with the tradition of Western culture and its place in our educational institutions should inspire us to rethink the cultural and social value of Anglo-Saxon language and history. Little well-informed or self-reflective discussion is available to readers curious about that heritage. There are numerous naive accounts of "our Anglo-Saxon heritage" in the form of popular books about King Alfred, or general histories describing the development of England's national greatness.[61] But these extremely simplified concepts of national heritage, designed to arouse patriotism, are admiring, even servile, and exclusive rather than inclusive intellectual models. I seek a perspective that engages historical change and conflict without seeking to direct response toward or away from national pride and prestige. It is not propagation of the tradition, but the critical *study* of that tradition, that is in question.

Early Anglo-Saxonists admired their image in the thing they studied; theirs was a self-conscious and idealized relationship to the culture they studied. We no longer idealize Anglo-Saxon culture, or, as a nation, know very much about it. The scholarly community that serves as the custodian of that culture does not idealize the culture, either, but idealizes the apparatus used to study it. Method, not the subject to which it is applied, sustains the self-image of modern scholarship of Anglo-Saxon England. We have effaced the myth of origin. In its place we worship the scholarly practices created to recover its textual beginnings.

Modern Anglo-Saxonists do not see themselves in the work of their predecessors; they do not believe in a shared horizon, either with Anglo-Saxon texts or with Anglo-Saxon scholars. Modern scholars may express devotion and even love for the subject, but they are careful to maintain a technical relationship to it, observing agreed-on professional rules in order to protect themselves from charges of self-interest. But just as early Anglo-Saxonists incorporated Anglo-Saxon textual perspectives into their own, we can relate their horizon to our own; we can recognize common and persistent problems of language, society, and government that confronted them and that confront us. In order to realize the importance of Anglo-Saxon studies, we need to see both the texts and their history differently—not to admire them as a chain of timeless classics, but, in the manner of early Anglo-Saxonists, to exercise their timeliness.

2

Origins, Orientalism, and Anglo-Saxonism in the Sixteenth and Nineteenth Centuries

Orientalism and Anglo-Saxonism ■

Anglo-Saxonists and those who teach other remote, and in that sense "foreign," cultures, have to struggle to demonstrate the importance of their subject. This is a burden not shared to the same degree by those who teach nineteenth-century fiction, for example, or those whose specialties are modern poetry and prose. The Anglo-Saxon language and its literature may be universally acknowledged as an important part of the English tradition, but a cursory glance at a text, in Old English or translation, reminds us of the distance between the language and art of that time and the language and aesthetics of our own. It is ironic that Anglo-Saxon culture should have come to bear this burden of otherness, since in earlier eras Anglo-Saxonists skillfully used their subject to define the characteristics unique to English civilization and thereby to designate the otherness of nations and languages outside the English tradition. In this chapter I shall juxtapose two important phases of the study of Anglo-Saxon language and texts, the nineteenth century and the Renaissance. I wish to use this juxtaposition first to demonstrate the similarity in nationalist outlook that links them, and then to suggest that the nineteenth century was not quite the watershed or turning point, to use a favorite phrase of Anglo-Saxonists, that it appears to be. The fundamental importance of the Anglo-Saxon heritage to nineteenth-century English thinkers is clear in the writings of Thomas

Babington Macaulay, one of many for whom Anglo-Saxon England supplied a context for national identity.

One of the most remarkable moments in nineteenth-century English intellectual history is preserved in Macaulay's "Minute of the 2nd of February 1835," written when he was member of the Supreme Council of India. Having just arrived in India, Macaulay found that the Committee on Public Instruction was divided between those who advocated education for Indians in the English language and those who wanted education in Sanskrit. Although he admitted to having "no knowledge of either Sanscrit or Arabic," Macaulay recommended to Lord Bentinck, the Governor General, that the dispute be resolved in favor of English. Macaulay was willing, as he said, to "take the Oriental learning at the valuation of the Orientalists themselves," not one of whom "could deny that a single shelf of a good European library was worth the whole native literature of India and Arabia." Macaulay wrote, "The intrinsic superiority of the Western literature is, indeed, fully admitted by those members of the Committee who support the Oriental plan of education." Macaulay allowed that poetry was the East's highest achievement, but maintained, "when we pass from works of imagination to works in which facts are recorded, and general principles investigated, the superiority of the Europeans becomes absolutely immeasurable." He continued:

> It is, I believe, no exaggeration to say, that all the historical information which has been collected from all the books written in the Sanscrit language is less valuable than what may be found in the most paltry abridgments used at preparatory schools in England. In every branch of physical or moral philosophy, the relative position of the two nations is nearly the same.[1]

Macaulay's comparison of the worth of Oriental and British literature reveals the Eurocentric, and indeed the specifically Anglocentric, point of view from which he saw the Orient. Given that the administrative objective of his "Minute" was not to select textbooks but to make English the official language of India, and to develop a school system to train bilingual bureaucrats for service in British administration, Macaulay's statement cannot be dismissed as a schoolmaster's quip. His writings about the East, which include a penal code as well as proposals for national education, are a rich index of British colonial and imperial attitudes.[2] Macaulay's "Minute" exemplifies a central characteristic of Orientalism: an acute consciousness of the superiority of Anglo-Saxon heritage without which the stereotypical British view of India would have been inconceivable.

Orientalism is a recognized cultural phenomenon, while Anglo-Saxonism, its ideological partner, is not. Because Orientalism belongs to the category of "not Old English," its close association with the formation of Anglo-Saxon studies has been ignored. Orientalism and Anglo-Saxonism intersect at many points. Scholarship in both areas developed when the history of the language began to be studied in the eighteenth century; Abraham Wheelock, one of the seventeenth century's most important Anglo-Saxonists and editor of Thomas Jefferson's copy of Bede's *History*, was a professor of both Old English and Arabic. From the late eighteenth-century (and in some regards earlier), the Orient served as a foil for the development of ideas about the maturity of the West; study of the history of the English language made the Orient, the site of the most ancient languages, particularly important.

According to Edward W. Said, "The constitution of a geographical entity called the Orient, and its study called Orientalism, realized a very important component of the European will to domination over the non-European world, and made it possible to create not only an orderly discipline of study but a set of institutions, a latent vocabulary (or a set of enunciative possibilities), a subject matter, and finally . . . subject races."[3] As Said shows, Orientalism comprised a wide range of scholarly topics—legal, literary, and linguistic; but its assumptions about the West went far beyond the scope of scholarly subjects. Orientalism deployed several disciplines of knowledge in a discourse of power. It enabled the European West to achieve academic mastery of the literature and culture of Arabia and India, and thereby to assure the irrelevance, inferior status, and ultimately the powerlessness of Oriental texts.

Orientalism did not, however, derive solely from enthusiasm for Oriental culture. Genuine curiosity about the East was always adumbrated by—always in the service of—political and religious ambitions, as several foundational studies have shown. *The Oriental Renaissance*, published by Raymond Schwab in 1950, was the first comprehensive survey attentive to the ideological implications of the subject.[4] Wilhelm Halbfass has written a magnificent study of the cultural relations of India and Europe from classical antiquity to the present, a study with detail and critical sophistication to rival Said's.[5] Donald S. Lach's analysis of Europe's need to learn Eastern languages for purposes of conversion as well as trade offers an extended view of Orientalism in its many-sided cultural role.[6] It was hardly coincidental that Orientalism and colonialism flourished together. Indeed, the literary and linguistic work of Orientalizing scholars can be seen as an academic form of colonization. Under scholarly watch, Said writes, "Oriental texts [came] to inhabit a realm without development or power," a realm "that exactly corresponds to the position of a colony for European texts and cultures."[7]

Like Orientalism, Anglo-Saxonism encompasses the study and the construction of history, language, and literature in an attempt to articulate the national values of English culture; in Macaulay's time, its "affirmative authority," to borrow a term Said applies to Orientalism,[8] was exercised not over the East, but over the English past. Orientalism suppressed and exploited the East, whereas Anglo-Saxonism glorified the West as English civilization constituted it. Unlike Anglo-Saxonism, Orientalism had a material motive—the East and its riches—always in view; the material concerns of Anglo-Saxonism existed but were not always tangible: They were forms of power that accrued to those who controlled the past and claimed originary status from it.

In Macaulay's writing on the past of his own nation, his Anglo-Saxonism is fully apparent and his Orientalism never far from view. His five-volume *History of England,* begun in 1839 but not published until 1848, is nationalist scholarship of a very popular kind. It was one of the most widely read and respected historical surveys of his day; some 13,000 copies of the first two volumes were sold in four months, and the next two volumes sold even faster—26,500 copies in ten weeks.[9] The *History* contains only brief pages on the Middle Ages, which Macaulay used merely to summarize the "plot of the preceding acts" leading to the Constitutional debates in the reign of James II (1685–1688).[10] The *History,* an extended argument justifying Whig rule by appeal to ancient precedent, shows how Macaulay's Whig (that is, essentially liberal) politics determined his view of the Anglo-Saxons in England's past.[11]

In the medieval pages of Macaulay's *History* the East is conceived not as a geographical entity but as an undifferentiated other, a "Mohametan power" (p. 6) threatening to overwhelm the Christian West. Macaulay commended the Church for rescuing Western Europe from the barbarians and thereby preserving classical culture. He saw the Church, like Noah's ark, as "bearing within her that feeble germ from which a second and more glorious civilisation was to spring" (pp. 6–7). As he defended medieval Christianity against those who expressed contempt for its institutions—pilgrimages, the Crusades, and monasticism—Macaulay stressed the role of Rome in shaping the political foundations that England shared with Europe. While he praised the "spiritual supremacy" of the Church, he was far less interested in doctrine than in the ability of doctrinal hegemony to unite Western European nations into "one great commonwealth," a federation of races and nations that "acknowledged a fraternal tie and a common code of public law" (p. 7), an alliance of "limited monarchies" and a "great coalition against Islam" (p. 21). Explaining the origins of this confederation, Macaulay noted that these nations shared institutions "derived partly from papal Rome, partly from the old Germany" (p. 21). This is a significant statement. With the coming of the Reformation, Macaulay's *History* reconfigures its oppositions. The old opposition between East and West disappears; in its place Macaulay divides England's history into Roman (pre-Reformation) and Germanic (post-Reformation) phases, and settles on a new opposition between England's Roman and Germanic heritage. Renaissance Anglo-Saxonists, we shall see, constructed the same opposition in only slightly different terms.

In the Middle Ages, when the nation's political institutions were forming, the presence of the Church was necessary to protect the social order. "Corrupt as the Church of Rome was," Macaulay said, "there is reason to believe that, if that church had been overthrown in the twelfth or even in the fourteenth century, the vacant space would have been occupied by some system more corrupt still." He added that, "In a darker age . . . , Christianity might have been distorted into a cruel and licentious superstition, more noxious, not only than Popery, but even than Islamism" (p. 34). Nonetheless, the Reformation was "an inestimable blessing" (p. 35). Once the king had become the head of the Church of England, it was possible not only to reject the Church of Rome but to deny the place of "papal Rome" in the institutional, religious, and cultural roots of the nation. After the Reformation, as Macaulay put it, the evil of Rome would be as "noxious" to England as the evil of the Orient.

The Reformation meant the rejection of Rome from England's past; it necessitated an urgent search for ecclesiastical origins and an English national culture with a distinctive linguistic, religious, and political history. With Germany leading the Reformation, English reformers' recourse to the Germanic past was not as unlikely as it may seem, for Rome was viewed as a long-standing enemy of Germanic civilization. According to Reginald Horsman, "German reformers drew an analogy between the earlier 'Germanic' or 'Gothic' destruction of the universal Roman Empire and the new destruction of the universal Roman Church."[12] This analogy between the old and the new Rome explains the importance of the "old Germany," as Macaulay called it (*History*, p. 21), as a precedent for the "new Germany" of the Reformation, to which English reformers searching for a "new England"—a new ecclesiastical order—turned.

Macaulay understood the importance of education and learning in disseminating England's new religion and newly claimed Germanic origins. When medieval England stood with the rest of Europe under the banner of Rome and tolerated the corruption of "Popery," the clergy controlled all access to learning; the people had no choice but to follow them. But during the Reformation, Macaulay claimed, lay literacy and printed books popularized a "new theology"—a singularly apt phrase—and divested the clergy of the monopoly that allowed their corruption to go unchecked. No longer "the sole or the chief depositories of knowledge," the clergy lost their hold on the popular imagination, and the Roman Church, under whose tutelage "the childhood of the European nations was passed" (p. 35), lost its intellectual pre-eminence.

Macaulay's conception of the Middle Ages as the "childhood of the European nations" invokes the paradigm of primitivism and progress in one of its most common forms, the paradigm of child and adult. This paradigm was used to explain transformation in all aspects of cultural life; it explained how a relatively primitive medieval legal system had, as Whig doctrine required, served as precedent for contemporary British political organization. According to Macaulay,

> In rude societies, the progress of government resembles the progress of language and of versification. Rude societies have language, and often copious and energetic language; but they have no scientific grammar, no definitions of nouns and verbs, no names for declensions, moods, tenses, and voices. Rude societies have versification, and often versification of great power and sweetness: but they have no metrical canons; and the minstrel whose numbers, regulated solely by his ear, are the delight of his audience, would himself be unable to say of how many dactyls and trochees each of his lines consists. As eloquence exists before syntax, and song before prosody, so government may exist in a high degree of excellence long before the limits of legislative, executive, and judicial power have been traced with precision. (pp. 22–23)

The link between the maturity of literature and maturity of government supported the conviction, expressed in the "Minute" quoted earlier, that a developed nation was entitled—and indeed, obliged—to replace the language and literature of a primitive society with those of a more advanced society. The conqueror's need for educational apparatus, and for tools of indoctrination, could be handsomely rationalized as intellectual progress for the conquered. Macaulay used scholarship merely as an analogy for the growth of England's great political institutions. His subject was political rather than literary history, but his view of primitivism has direct relevance to Anglo-Saxon scholarship. Primitive societies have language, Macaulay said, but enlightened societies also have grammar; primitive societies have versificaton, while later, better-developed societies also have the formal means of studying verse—meter, syntax, and prosody. The song of the minstrel, however beautiful, was primitive; later society abstracted, formulated, and "traced with precision" the rules that earlier peoples observed unconsciously. To characterize the movement from an unconscious grasp of a phenomonon to scientific study of it as progress is a venerable gesture; at the turn of the century, an American scholar connected eighteenth-century language study to later Germanic philology in just such a paradigm. The work of great Germanic philologists was "preceded by that of a long line of men whose primary aim was to purify, regulate, and in general improve the German language," wrote H.C.G. von Jagemann; likewise "the first astronomer was probably a sailor and the first botanist a gardener."[13]

Macaulay's *History* represents Victorian Anglo-Saxonism at its highest level of popularity and cultural power, but its world view was hardly unique. Anglo-Saxon scholars contemporary with Macaulay also linked literary sophistication to cultural maturity as they explained the superiority of the present over the past. Two of these scholars, very different from Macaulay and from each other, employed the paradigm of primitivism and progress that gives his *History* its shape. Sharon Turner and John Mitchell Kemble were among those who supplied the scholarly underpinnings, in history and in language study (i.e., textual criticism), to the tradition Macaulay popularized.

Sharon Turner (1768–1846) was the first modern historian of Anglo-Saxon England. His three-volume *History of the Anglo-Saxons* was published from 1799 to 1805 and was in its fourth edition in 1823. It deploys primitivism and progress in the fashion used later by Macaulay. "In no country can the progress of the poetical genius and taste be more satisfactorily traced than in our own," Turner wrote. The earliest stage of English literature could "have been scarcely more rude" (that is, primitive), but "it was preparing to assume the style, the measures, and the subjects, which in subsequent ages were so happily displayed as to deserve the notice of the latest posterity."[14] Concerning "the barren and peculiar state of the Anglo-Saxon poetry," Turner remarked, "If we call this style poetry, it is rather by complaisance than truth—rather with a knowledge of the excellences afterwards introduced into it, than of those which it then possessed." His developmental attitude towards English literature anticipates Macaulay's view of the level of literary sophistication in "rude societies": "When an infant first begins to talk,"

Turner wrote, "it uses only the nouns and pronouns of its language. By degrees it learns the use of a few verbs," and then acquires more complex and refined speech.[15]

More influential than Turner, if less popular, was the prolific Anglo-Saxonist, philologist, and historian, John Mitchell Kemble (1807–1857). Kemble, one of the reviewers of Macaulay's *History*, was a vigorous political partisan and one of the first editors of *Beowulf*.[16] A friend and, in a real sense, a student of Jakob Grimm, Kemble was, by his own account, "the first Englishman who has adopted and acted upon his [Grimm's] views."[17] Hence Kemble is associated with the introduction of newly scientific methods and new attitudes toward the past into Anglo-Saxon scholarship. His dedication to professional discipline appears in his criticism of both Turner and Macaulay. At the invitation of a French scholar, Kemble wrote an essay on the state of Anglo-Saxon studies that offers a tart but valuable digest of scholarship as he saw it in the early 1830s. He commented that Turner's *History* was "a learned and laborious work; yet in all that relates to the language and the poetry of our forefathers, often deficient, often mistaken."[18] For Kemble, philology, knowledge of the history of the language of the "forefathers," was the sole index to the quality of both history and language study.

Kemble's concern with method—proper procedures for identifying and analyzing evidence—also emerges in his measured response to Macaulay's *History* in a twenty-two page review of the last two volumes, which appeared in *Fraser's Magazine* in 1856. The first two volumes of the *History* had been criticized for faulty scholarship, in particular for Macaulay's failure to consult archival records. The second two volumes were, Kemble believed, "obviously written with much greater care." Nonetheless, he found Macaulay's scholarship deficient, especially in regard to his failure to consult German sources in his account of the Thirty Years' War. Kemble's review reveals his own familiarity with German sources—population figures and archaeological detail, for example—in abundant clarity; it might have been in response to his long critique that Macaulay later complained that "as to grubbing in Saxon or Hessian archives . . . I should have doubled my labour."[19] Kemble's specifically scholarly concern with documentation and research sets his work apart from the more popularly historical and less technically proficient writing of Macaulay.

Kemble's sober ruminations on *The Saxons in England*, first published in 1846, display an intellectual skepticism in keeping with the scientific methods of language study pioneered by Jakob and Wilhelm Grimm. We also catch the flavor of his scholarship in his edition and his translation of *Beowulf;* both contain prefaces attempting to trace the origins of the proper names in the poem and to relate them not only to the mythologies of Scandinavia and Germany but also to British place names. He was concerned, in other words, to use the poem to attest to the nation's ancient Germanic heritage. Yet, for all his superiority in scholarly discipline to Macaulay or Turner, Kemble shared their general idea of the service scholarship owed to nationalism. Victorian idealism suffuses the dedication to his *History:* "To the Queen's Most Excellent Majesty, this history of the principles which have given her Empire its preeminence among the nations of Europe." In the Preface, written during the revolutions of 1848, he notes, "On every side of us thrones totter, and the deep foundations of society are convulsed." But in England, "the exalted Lady who wields the sceptre of these realms, sits safe upon her throne, and fearless in the holy circle of her domestic happiness, secure in the affections of a people whose institutions have given to them all the blessings of an equal law." The introduction establishes his concept of England's Anglo-Saxon history: "it is the history of the childhood of our own age,—the explanation of its manhood," a remark repeated with evident approval by Walter de Gray Birch in the 1876 reprint.[20] Kemble may have been the first Anglo-Saxonist to introduce Germanic philology and its attendant scientific claims to England, but his scholarly idiom and nationalist outlook were fully traditional.

It is but a short step backward from the attitudes of these influential scholars, writing at the height of British colonialism, to those of the clergymen of the English Reformation, whose work with the Anglo-Saxon language and manuscripts supplied foundations on which the edifice of empire would rest. Likewise, it is but a short step forward from some of Macaulay's assumptions about literary and linguistic history to the views we call our own.

Renaissance Anglo-Saxonism ■

If nineteenth-century Anglo-Saxon scholarship can be divided into two traditions, one popular, the other learned, Anglo-Saxon scholarship in the sixteenth century can be said to mirror a comparable division into historical scholarship of a highly polemical nature and scholarship of a more technical and academic sort. In the Renaissance, writers in the former group were concerned with what Macaulay called the "new theology," their objective being to revise Roman Catholic dogma; John Bale and John Foxe were the major figures in this group.

Figures in the second group were also political, but their chief concern was the study of manuscripts and the production of editions; the leader of this group was Archbishop Matthew Parker. It is not necessary to suggest that this sixteenth-century division developed into the divisions apparent in the nineteenth century. It suffices, I believe, to recognize that Anglo-Saxon studies never constituted a monolithic project but rather a combination of activities, often complementary but divided into clearly polemical and ostensibly neutral camps, and that this division is maintained in the tradition down to the present era.

Our understanding of sixteenth-century Anglo-Saxonism depends on some familiarity with earlier attempts to read Old English and grasp its historical place. In the mid-fifteenth century Thomas Rudborne, a monk at Winchester, saw a manuscript of Bede's *Ecclesiastical History* at Southwick (south of Winchester). He thought that Bede himself had written it "in lingua Saxonica," and quoted the text in his *Historia maior.*[21] If Rudborne could read Old English—and N. R. Ker shows that he could—perhaps there were others, like him, working on Old English texts.[22] How this skill was developed and kept alive in the post-Conquest period is not well understood. After the Conquest, the language and the script of the Anglo-Saxons had gradually become unreadable. A Glastonbury library catalogue of 1247 describes several Anglo-Saxon manuscripts as "old and useless." Similar notes are used by N. R. Ker to support the view that little value was attached to Anglo-Saxon texts between the thirteenth century and the fifteenth.[23] Nearly forty manuscripts were altered in some way (glossed, or added to) before about 1200, while fewer than thirty received similar attention between 1200 and the Dissolution of monastic holdings under Henry VIII.[24] The number of manuscripts and texts had reached ninety by the end of the "early recovery period," which Ker takes to be the death of John Joscelyn (1529–1603; Joscelyn was secretary to Matthew Parker). The collection included most of the "principal" Anglo-Saxon manuscripts.[25] The role of sixteenth-century writers in this recovery is well-documented, but, Rudborne's excepted, earlier knowledge of Old English awaits attention.[26]

Between 1535 and 1540 monastic claims to property were dissolved by the Crown and the property redistributed. The fate of their libraries, which included charters and other important documents, was a matter of grave concern, and a new problem for the nation, since the Church was previously the unquestioned custodian of the written word. The destruction of books and sacred art that preserved Catholic practice and thus promoted sedition against the new Church reached alarming proportions under Henry VIII (1509–1547) and worsened in the reign of Edward (1547–1553). Under Edward VI, Parliament became involved in legislating doctrinal change and prescribing acceptable worship services in the Act for the Uniformity of Service of 1549, followed by the Act against Superstitious Books and Images of 1550.[27] These acts were part of a series of injunctions that not only forbade the use of images and ceremonies related to Catholicism, but required that children be taught to pray in the vernacular, and that the vernacular be used as a language for study and worship. The reform was temporarily reversed when Edward died and Mary (1553–1558) obtained the First Statute of Repeal in Parliament in 1553, following which many of the reformers, their work now endangered, fled to the Continent. But just as Mary's reign undid the work of Edward, her progress towards reconciliation with Rome was in turn undone by Elizabeth I and the Act of Supremacy of 1559; thereafter the course of the reform could not be turned back.[28]

Most of the Anglo-Saxon scholarship recognized as the beginnings of the tradition took place after 1560, as the count of known manuscripts clearly shows. Scholars working under Elizabeth enjoyed more security than their predecessors; their mission was to further and especially to justify—rather than to introduce and execute—the "settlement" of the Anglican Church as the new custodian of monastic property and the new authority for forms of worship and ecclesiastical conformity. The settlement was an immense and intricate material process of transforming religion and national culture; it required the appropriation of the physical and historical presence of the Roman Church into English history. C. E. Wright lists four predominant concerns: the establishment of royal supremacy (and thus the English monarch's independence from the Pope); the rejection of Transubstantiation or the Real Presence; the right to read the Bible in the vernacular; and the return to "the purity of the Primitive Church."[29] All of these objectives were assisted by the study of Anglo-Saxon manuscripts; the scholarly tradition too was "settled," and fragments of earlier work drawn together.

The two traditions I trace encompass historical and philological activity, and even the first, which was exceptionally polemical, was conscious of the dependence of historical vision on linguistic identity. Included in the first of these traditions is the work of early reformers and clergy: John Bale, John Foxe, Bishop John Jewel, and a number of English scholars in exile on the Continent. John Bale (1495–1563) was a prolific ex-Carmelite propagandist who made his acquaintance with early English history in part through local archives.[30] Bale collected manuscripts and wrote a great deal of history himself; his interest in the English past predated all official activity of the Reformation. Early scholars, Bale among them, worked during the long reign of Henry VIII and then under Edward VI, and their scholarship interacted with the political climate and was directly related to the fate of the great monastic libraries that were broken up, along with other Church holdings, during this period.

Although the development of Anglo-Saxon scholarship depended on the fortunes of the newly established Church of England, the impulses behind it reach into the fourteenth and fifteenth centuries. As Rudborne's work shows, there were efforts to inquire into local history and manuscript collections in the fifteenth century. More important is the tradition of denouncing clerical corruption, which was particularly venerable. At the end of the fourteenth century, John Wycliff had begun generating calls for reform and demanding that the authority of Scripture rule the clergy. He combined an attack on clerical corruption with a challenge to the doctrine of Transubstantiation, both issues of central importance in the Reformation, and a recent study characterizes this movement as "the Premature Reformation."[31]

Bale's passion for the past was not that of a bibliophile but that of an extraordinary malcontent, a sixteenth-century Wycliffite. Bale argued that the Church was corrupt and had ceased to serve its rightful mission; this argument was the formative principle for the history of his nation and its emerging national religion. He came to his reformist position through his first work, *Anglorum Heliades* (1536), a history of the Carmelite order in England (Bale later renounced his Catholic faith). The power of his argument derived partly from his passion, and partly from a shrewd sense of literary history. Bale's *Illustrium Maiorus Brittaniae Scriptorum* (1548) was perhaps his most important literary-historical text.[32] Dedicated to Edward VI, the book is a history of British authors organized into "centuries" or units of one hundred authors each, in five groups, each with a theme (a later version, in Bale's *Catalogus* of 1557, specified then nine groups). Within this sweeping chronology, Bale was able to organize English literary and church history into a single pattern of corruption that demanded radical reform.

In *The Image of Bothe Churches* (published in Antwerp in 1545 or 1546) Bale set forth a bipartite thesis, based on the Book of Revelations, about the development of the post-Apostolic Church. He argued that the Church had been corrupted during the reign of Constantine and had subsequently existed in two forms, a corrupt See of Saint Peter and an isolated community of those few who retained belief in the true Church.[33] Bale's image of two churches influenced a wide circle of like-minded reformers, the foremost of whom was John Foxe, and made

Bale the target of many Catholic (Marian, or Recusant) exiles writing on the Continent. One of these was Thomas Stapleton, who denounced Bale's highly contentious account of Church history. Stapleton was particularly upset by Bale's version of the famous episode in Bede's *History* that describes the origin of the mission from Rome to convert the English people, and how the English came to be called by that name. Bede reports that one day Gregory the Great saw several slaves being sold in the markets in Rome and, admiring their "fair complexions, handsome faces, and lovely hair," asked who these boys were. Told that they were heathens from Britain, he replied, "Alas that the author of darkness should have men so bright of face in his grip, and that minds devoid of inward grace should bear so graceful an outward form." They were called "Angli," he was told, of the kingdom of "Deiri," ruled by a king called "Ælle." Gregory then called them "angels," to be taken "de ira," or "snatched from the wrath of Christ" by conversion, and said "Alleluia" (the third pun, on Ælle).[34]

Bale's account of the episode in *The Actes of Englysh Votaryes* gave it a rather different flavor. Roman prelates were not allowed to have wives, Bale noted, and dared not have intercourse with women, for fear of impregnating them. Hence, he noted sarcastically, "other spirituall remedyes were sought out for them by their good prouvders and proctours," and that was how "Englysh boyes" came to be "solde at Rome."[35] "Baudy Bale" perverted the truth, Stapleton wrote, deliberately misread Bede's account, and charged Gregory "with a most outrageous vice and not to be named." Stapleton called Bale a "venimous spider being filthy and uncleane himself," an "olde ribauld" and "another Nero" who found "poisonned sence and meaning" where Bede, like a bee, had made honey.[36]

Foxe (1516–1587) helped bring Bale's theological and historical views to a wide as opposed to a scholarly reading audience. His much reprinted *Acts and Monuments* appeared first in Latin in 1563 and in English in 1570, an edition that included excerpts from Anglo-Saxon texts edited by Matthew Parker and his assistants. Publication in the vernacular was fundamental to Foxe's objective to enlighten the unlearned, "long led in ignorance, and wrapt in blindness for lacke especially of Gods Words, and partly also wanting the light of history."[37] Foxe devoted his book to the "true" history of the Church of Rome, the history of its English martyrs, "the story of those who were punished for dissenting from Rome" from the earliest phases of Christianity up to the sixteenth century. He was moved "to see the simple flocke of Christ, especially the unlearned sort, so miserably abused, and all of ignorance of history, not knowing the course of times, and true discent of the Church." The "Monkes or Clients to the sea of Rome" who wrote previous histories wrote only of "theyr owne sect of Religion," a Church that "flourished in this world in riches and iollity," causing the ignorant to think that there was no Church but that of Rome.

There was another Church, Foxe maintained, and that was the "true Church, always there, keeping sparkes of doctrine alive." The true religion, brought to England in the earliest age of the Church, had survived until the arrival of Augustine to Canterbury, who brought with him "Romish" influence. Ælfric used the texts of the true Church before they were destroyed by "papists" writing during the time of Lanfranc (the first post-Conquest Archbishop of Canterbury). Lanfranc and others destroyed the authentic Latin sources they transcribed; "studying by al measures how to preserve and further this their newcome doctrine," he wrote, these conspirators "did abolish and rase out of Libraries and Churches, all such bookes which made to the contrary" of their views. According to Foxe, all "heresies," including celibacy of the clergy, Transubstantiation, worship of the Blessed Sacrament, auricular confession, and Masses of satisfaction, among others, were "new nothynges lately coyned in the minte of Rome without any stampe of antiquitie." Foxe raised this matter of forgery, heresy, and "newcome doctrine" in his discussion of the "Statute of Six Articles" of 1539, also known as "An Act Abolishing Diversity in Opinions," which supplemented earlier definitions of heresy and considerably strengthened the hand of Henry VIII in enforcing ecclesiastical conformity. It was to this discussion that Foxe appended his own version of important Anglo-Saxon texts published earlier by Parker (I discuss Foxe's editing of these texts below).[38]

While Foxe cared deeply about ignorant readers, he showed few scruples in leading them astray. It is not easy to see an origin for modern Anglo-Saxon studies in the polemics of Bale or Foxe (or, from the Catholic side, Stapleton). Yet Foxe's theory of post-Conquest meddling, however unattractive, was very influential; the belief that pure sources had been corrupted seems to have been held by virtually all scholars of the first tradition, and many of the second. What separates the second from the first is that they worked directly with manuscripts, transcribing them, exchanging them, editing them, and at the same time developing an awareness of the need for tools, including dictionaries and glossaries, on which solid language study could be based. Not unexpectedly, this group of writers is composed of predecessors Anglo-Saxon scholars seem eager to claim. McKisack calls these writers "archivists and record-searchers," and that sounds promising already.[39] They were textual scholars whose research concerned constitutional and linguistic issues rather than theology. Although their interests lay outside theological controversy, they were not untouched by it, and the laws and grammars they worked with were known and listed, along with theological tracts, in the early collections by Leland and Bale. The methods of the two groups varied little, and the cultural and historical meanings they derived from Anglo-Saxon texts were fundamentally the same.

Writers in the second tradition of sixteenth-century Anglo-Saxonism concentrated on language and law, especially on the systematic study of language (i.e., study based on glossaries and dictionaries). We might characterize its interests as philological; scholars belonging to it are, not unexpectedly, those most frequently mentioned in surveys of early Anglo-Saxon studies. These writers busily traced routes to the past and focused not on early Christianity, the Rome of the pope, but on England's connection to the Roman empire. Among them were Leland, William Camden, William Lambarde, and William L'Isle. This movement also depended on earlier impulses, especially those from the universities and the arrival in England of continental humanism. Humanists were concerned with ecclesiastical reform. Erasmus had called for the use of the vernacular, in particular for translations based on Scripture, so that the plowman should have Scripture in his own tongue. The attempt to make forms of worship more intelligible to the laity was, of course, designed to limit dependence on the clergy, and evidence of prayers, forms of worship, and Scripture in Old English was cited throughout the Reformation as precedent. James McConica has suggested that the establishment of St. Paul's School by John Colet at Oxford in 1499 is a significant moment; Leland and Camden both studied there, and their inquiries into linguistic and legal subjects may well have been fostered by their days at Oxford.[40]

The two traditions I have discussed here interacted. Bale dedicated his *Anglorum Heliades* to Leland (1503?–1548), whom Joseph M. Levine calls "the first English antiquary of any consequence."[41] Leland was a scholar of moderate political views; he studied in Paris and brought a strain of continental humanism to his office as "antiquarius" to Henry VIII, a term designating one who studied the Roman past in the provinces of the Empire.[42] Leland obtained books for the library of Henry VIII but published little of his own scholarship during his lifetime. His catalogue of early historians and their works first appeared in an edition by Antony Hall in 1709; the rest of Leland's notes towards an unrealized massive history, which was to be called *De Antiquitate Britannica,* appeared in 1715. Leland contemplated an inventory of all Roman antiquities in Britain; he made notes on learning Celtic, Welsh, and what

Bale called "Saxonlike" languages; and he planned other massive projects that only decades of scholarship could bring to completion.[43]

By training and in range and nature of his interests, Leland stands in sharp contrast to Bale. Leland's interest was in Roman Britain rather than early Christian Britain, and he utterly lacked Bale's polemical fervor. But he was, after his death, commandeered by Bale. Leland went mad in 1548; he spoke to his century not in his own voice but through Bale, who in 1549 published *The Laboryouse Journey & Serche of Iohan Leylande,* a book urging the nobility and London merchants to subsidize the purchase of early English chronicles. The publication was important to the revision of English history in this period because it addressed a vital issue that had generated little response: the preservation of libraries and collections of texts. No significant response was forthcoming, and plans for national archives were many years in taking shape.

Directly linked to both Bale and Leland as a distributor of texts was Robert Talbot, who is considered to be the first serious gatherer of manuscripts after the Dissolution. Talbot had a copy of Bede's *History* (although the manuscript is unknown), and lent manuscripts of Ælfric's *Grammar* and his translation of the *Heptateuch* to Bale and manuscripts of the *World History* of Orosius and the *Anglo-Saxon Chronicle* to Leland.[44] Talbot is one of five figures named by Ker as major owners and users of manuscripts between 1540 and 1603, the others being Parker, Joscelyn, Laurence Nowell, and William Lambarde. Of this group, Joscelyn left his mark on more manuscripts than any of the others, but Nowell exercised greater influence on texts and textual traditions.[45]

Tutor to William Cecil, Elizabeth's Lord Treasurer (himself a collector of manuscripts), Nowell compiled the first dictionary in Old English, transcribed important and since-destroyed manuscripts, and acquired the *Beowulf* manuscript. In 1562, while in Cecil's service, he transcribed a manuscript containing Bede's *History*, the *Anglo-Saxon Chronicle,* and "The Seasons for Fasting" (which we know only through Nowell's transcript).[46] Nowell also copied a few lines of Anglo-Saxon, including the opening of King Alfred's will, from another manuscript.[47] Particularly important as a rewriter of Anglo-Saxon texts, Nowell was in the habit of completing texts he transcribed if he found gaps in them. When transcribing the laws, for example, he compared the Old English texts to Latin translations of them made in the twelfth century; where the Latin contained material missing in the Anglo-Saxon, he translated it into his own Old English, which was not very good, but which was good enough to fool Felix Liebermann, the formidable twentieth-century editor of the laws.[48]

What Nowell wrote, Lambarde (1536–1601), who worked from Nowell's transcripts, copied. Lambarde was the first to treat Nowell's "not Old English" as Old English. Lambarde initiated the use of Anglo-Saxon in legal studies.[49] He studied manuscripts of Anglo-Saxon laws and, in 1568, published a collection of them based in part on Nowell's transcriptions.[50] Lambarde carved an impressive path through Anglo-Saxon codices, consulting many manuscripts of the *Anglo-Saxon Chronicle* and the law codes in particular. Because his work, like Nowell's, was textual, it has won the respect of modern scholars, while Bale's achievement, like Foxe's, remains something of a controversialist joke, seemingly far outside Parker's powerful circle.

Matthew Parker (1504–1575) had been chaplain to Anne Boleyn; he retired during Mary's brief reign, while other more vocal reformers, including Bale and Foxe, took refuge in exile. In 1559, he was plucked from the scholarly life at Cambridge (he was Master of Bene't Hall, later Corpus Christi College, to which he donated his extraordinary manuscript collection) and consecrated by Elizabeth as the first Anglican Archbishop of Canterbury.[51] Parker took office at a crucial point in the history of the English Church. As Elizabeth reasserted the claims to reform, she required "constitutional and doctrinal principles" on which the Church would rest. Parker was equal to this scholarly, historical task of moving the reform forward without provoking excessive resistance. He recognized the importance of his position, since Canterbury was, at the time of Theodore of Tarsus, the gateway of Catholicism into England and one of its most important early centers of learning. Parker's mission, broadly seen, was "to justify the independence of the national church from the papacy and to claim antiquity for [its] departures from the consensus of late medieval theology in such matters as the nature of Christ's presence in the Eucharist."[52]

Parker supervised a small "school" of scholars working on Anglo-Saxon manuscripts gathered from all over England. The archbishop's correspondence is replete with requests for searches to be made for manuscripts in provincial churches.[53] Parker was not a scholar of Anglo-Saxon language or history, but he occupied a position of institutional significance. He was the first Anglican official whose mandate was to supply a textual basis for the settlement and liturgical reform already in effect.

Parker's most famous publication, *A Testimonie of Antiquitie,* appeared in 1566/1567. Perhaps the first edition of Anglo-Saxon texts set in type, it contained, in addition to the so-called Easter homily of Ælfric, Anglo-Saxon texts of the Lord's Prayer, the Creed, and the Ten Commandments, and rules found in two of Ælfric's pastoral letters, addressing questions of clerical celibacy and other matters of canonical concern.[54] These texts touched on several controversial points in Anglican theology, including the position of the early English church on the sacraments and clerical discipline, including marriage. The English Church denied Transubstantiation and insisted that the Eucharist was Christ's body only in a figurative or "spiritual" sense. The homily appeared to take a similar position, so Parker and his assistants used it to document objection to the Real Presence in the Anglo-Saxon period, and thus to demonstrate the antiquity of their own opposition. The homily subsequently became one of the most frequently reprinted Anglo-Saxon texts.[55] Contrary to what is nearly a universal claim on its behalf, *A Testimonie of Antiquitie* neither initiated contact between Protestant theology and the study of the Anglo-Saxon past or its language and literature nor was, with absolute clarity, even the first publication from the "arsenal" that was, according to Wright, Parker's library. Dorothy Whitelock has observed that another publication from Parker's group, *A Defence of Priestes Marriages,* may have appeared at the same time as, or even before, *A Testimonie*. Both publications make use of the *Peterborough Chronicle* and its account of Anglo-Saxon church life.[56]

Standing as he did at the confluence of these two related but distinct traditions, Parker was, from a receptionist point of view, in a remarkably good position both to intercept and to produce texts. Numerous Anglo-Saxon texts passed under Parker's eye and through his authority. Following *A Testimonie,* an edition of Anglo-Saxon laws by Lambarde, *Archaionomia,* appeared in 1568 (Wheelock's 1644 edition reprinted this text). Foxe's edition of the Anglo-Saxon translation of the Gospels appeared in 1571;[57] Parker's *De Antiquitate Britannicae Ecclesiae Cantuariensis,* including the life of King Alfred by Asser and the Preface to the Old English translation of Gregory the Great's *Cura Pastoralis,* appeared in 1572, and *Ælfredie Regis res gestae* in 1574. Both Bale and Foxe were directly linked to Parker and his establishment. Parker and Bale corresponded, the archbishop requesting information about manuscripts (and also about historical traditions) and Bale responding generously. It is clear that Parker's work would have been impossible without both the traditions, the historical and polemical, and the legal and linguistic, that he drew together.

The effect of these publications can only be measured if we remember that they appeared along with other works advancing the same historical arguments—not only Foxe's, but also those of Bishop John Jewel. Jewel's *A Defense of the Apologie of the Churche of Englande* was published in 1571. It had appeared in Latin in 1562 and was translated in that year and again in 1564 by Ann, Lady Bacon, this time with a preface by Parker. Jewel's was the first systematic (indeed, at 764 pages, encyclopedic) expression of the Church's doctrinal differences with Rome.[58]

Restoring and Rewriting ■

Within the large rewriting of English church history undertaken by Bale and Foxe were attempts to reconstruct the evidence in a physical sense. One of the most striking features of the recovery of Anglo-Saxon texts in this period is their rewriting of manuscripts. Many Anglo-Saxon manuscripts are physically defective, and the texts they contain are aesthetically (as well as sometimes physically) defective. These defects—whether physical (burns, tears) or aesthetic (faulty meter or grammar)—are invitations to editors reconstruct or "write," and thereby interpret, that which they claim only to restore. The hermeneutic moves of Parker and his assistants go well beyond anything scholars today would imagine. They wrote in many manuscripts in red chalk, leaving marks that usually, but not always, took the form of notes and comments. One of Parker's assistants, according to V. H. Galbraith, defaced a manuscript of the *St. Albans Chronicle* by "writing over the margins, crossing out words in ink, inserting headings, enclosing passages in brackets, interlining passages for insertion, keying up the manuscript to the pages of the printed version." "Deplorable methods no doubt," writes McKisack, "but they were the methods of an age which did not regard the Latin text as sacred and approved the restoration, physically as well as conjecturally, not only of what the author was believed to have written, but of what he might have written had he been in possession of other sources of information."[59] More extreme was Parker's habit—which we have also seen in Nowell—of "completing" manuscripts by supplying missing information and adding to texts in hands that imitated the hand of the original. He was pleased to have the services of his scribe Lyly, who "customarily used to make old books complete, that wanted pages." Yet Parker claimed not to want to remedy defects, lest "that what Cornelius Nepos writ to Sallust might be verified of him, 'that they [the texts] might not seem so much their histories as writ them, as his own'" (that is, lest the texts might seem to be the history not of those who wrote them, but of the editors). Parker's citation of classical scholarly standards for his own work indicates that he too was influenced by the humanist tradition.[60]

If they were careless of manuscripts, about printed texts themselves the scholars were very careful. Typography contributed to Parker's plan to create a new national consciousness. He believed that letter forms (the alphabet of Anglo-Saxon characters) were important to the authenticity of his publications, and wanted to use Anglo-Saxon letter forms to interest readers in Anglo-Saxon texts, so "[t]hat being arrived to the knowledge of the Characters, they might concert their Endeavours towards the Saxon writings." He believed that letter forms could "testify to the faithfulness" of his editions."[61] The role of printing in this effort was consciously emphasized by Foxe and others; the title page of Foxe's *Acts and Monuments* juxtaposed readers and reciters, Protestants with books in their laps, and Catholics with rosaries in theirs.[62]

The rewriting of manuscripts at the level of the letter had its counterpart at the level of the text. Parker's scholars assumed that manuscripts had been tampered with late in the Anglo-Saxon era, or during the Conquest, when Lanfranc reformed monasticism and so altered scribal (and textual) culture, and that, as a result, evidence of both the pure early Church and its degradation had been destroyed. The charge that earlier scholars had rewritten texts for political ends is richly ironic, for those activities describe precisely the scholarly endeavors of Bale and Parker and his assistants. One famous example of an "edited" text identified by Foxe as popish meddling survives in a Worcester manuscript, Cambridge, Corpus Christi College 265 (donated to the College by Parker). According to Foxe, words denying the Real Presence ("Non est tamen hoc sacrificium corpus eius," p. 177) were erased; they were restored to the manuscript by Joscelyn from an Exeter manuscript, Cambridge, Corpus Christ College 190.[63] When he complained about the rewriting of early sources by corrupt Roman clergy, Foxe demonstrated a canny sense of textual emendation. His reediting of the "Easter" homily deliberately distorted the text to sharpen its polemical edge.[64] His rewriting of shows that he too understood the need to "rase out" information contrary to his own views.

The assumption of Norman meddling had a direct bearing on the reception of Anglo-Saxon historical texts in the mid-sixteenth century, including Bede's *Ecclesiastical History* and texts attributed to King Alfred. Bede's authority was appropriated by both Protestants and Catholics, but the early date of Stapleton's reply to Bale—1565—suggests that the reformers had taken up Bede's evidence first. Stapleton's was the first translation of *History* in modern English, dedicated "To the Right excellent and most gratiouse princesse, Elizabeth by the grace of God Quene of England, Fraunce, and Ireland, Defendour of the Faith." Stapleton's translation takes Bede as an authentic witness and denounces Reformist doctrine. He sent his text to Elizabeth hoping that she would find in Bede a clear view of matters that the "pretended refourmers" had departed from (p. 3). He intended to juxtapose "a number of diuersities between the pretended religion of Protestants, and the primitive faith of the english Church," and contrasted the authority of Bede, who wrote without prejudice, with that of Bale, Foxe, and other "pretended doctors." Stapleton's translation of Bede was bound with another text, *A Fortresse of the Faith* (also 1565), written "to the deceived protestants of England." There is a subtext to his writing—as there is to Bale's and Foxe's—that bears scrutiny. Stapleton was aware of the Catholic missions in the East and claimed the conversion of India as a sign of the power of the Catholic faith. Only Christ, he wrote, could make so many converts in such an unhospitable land (74a–75b). Stapleton's indignant reaction to Bale's allegations about Gregory's homosexuality points to an intriguing subtext in the polemic; sexual difference, like Orientalism, served as a means of distinguishing the Anglo-Saxon center from the excluded "other." Bale linked the corruption of Roman religion to sexual perversity; Stapleton could not permit the Christ who conquered India, and who converted England, to be represented by a pope any less pure than the "angels" whose beauty he admired.

Intervention and Institutions ■

Renaissance antiquarians concerned either with ecclesiastical history and polemic, or with language, law, and classical culture, were in similar positions. When they beheld Anglo-Saxon texts and artifacts, they recognized cultural meaning long before they knew how to elucidate its documentary form. In a sense, they understood the material before they knew what it said; their mission was to explain how it yielded to their claims. They believed in broad similarities between their culture and Anglo-Saxon culture before they had evidence to make the comparisons convincing. The Anglo-Saxon church was almost as unknown to them as was the East, and was nearly as rich a storehouse of lore and expectation.

The antiquarians also shared a view of the past as a ruin. The dissolution of monastic libraries prompted unsuccessful requests for the foundation of a Royal library to house national treasures. Wright quotes powerful statements by John Bale about the export of manuscripts for sale and their desecration; they found use, for example, as toilet paper.[65] Obviously no apparatus was at hand to provide for national archives, and even records of immediate rather than historical or "antiquarian" interest were poorly kept.[66] However, collections of manuscripts were growing so fast that already in 1600 Thomas James, the first keeper of the library of Sir Thomas Bodley at Oxford, compiled a catalogue of manuscripts in the college libraries of Cambridge and Oxford.[67]

In seeing the past as a ruin, these English scholars were not unique. Levine begins his important discussion of antiquarianism in this period with a reference to the Italian humanist Poggio Bracciolini as Edward Gibbon recalled him, "sitting on the Capitoline amid the ruins of ancient Rome, reflecting on the vicissitudes of fortune." Poggio's horror at Rome's decay prompted him to "take an immediate inventory of the visible remains, as though he could somehow reverse that terrible decline of fortune and restore some part of the original grandeur to the awful scene."[68] It was a similar desire for restoration that sent William Camden in search of antiquities; it was a similar desire for origins that sent earlier scholars to inventory the "visible remains" of their "Saxon" ancestry. For early Anglo-Saxonists, the "awful scene" was the devastation of texts at the end of the Anglo-Saxon period; their goal was to reconstruct them.

One of the ongoing concerns of scholarship in this period was the development of a national linguistic history and of a distinct sense of a national language. There was nothing new in this, of course; concern with a national language (along with a repertory of genres equal to that of French and Italian) was important to Chaucer.[69] In the next chapter I demonstrate how nineteenth-century Anglo-Saxonists assumed an attitude toward texts similar in important ways to those of the first Renaissance writers to work with early English manuscripts. Although in the later period intervention into manuscript evidence was rationalized by means of a formidable philological apparatus, the results were not unlike the extraordinary rewriting of texts that Parker and his assistants undertook. There is another similarity between Anglo-Saxon scholarship in these two periods, and that is its movement towards institutionalization in league with larger, nationalist impulses.

Of the two traditions I have traced in Renaissance Anglo-Saxonism, the second, dominated by the legal and linguistic inquiry, was already seeking the authority of official, institutional status in 1586, when the Society of Antiquaries was founded. The Society, the first official, and hence "institutional," group of Anglo-Saxonists, was short-lived, but it gave credibility to the of work the antiquaries and opened the way for scholarship outside the demands of theological reform.[70] The major Anglo-Saxonist of this era was Camden (1553–1623). In the spirit of Leland, Camden toured Britain to catalog its ancient glories and in

1605 published them in his fabulously successful *Remaines of a Greater Worke, Concerning Britaine, the Inhabitants Thereof, Their Languages, Names,* a compendium of information about the language and geography of England, reprinted numerous times, and arguably the most influential of all early discussions of Anglo-Saxon history.[71]

Camden's *Remaines* celebrated the martial excellence of the Saxon forebears of the English nation, ardently tracing language as well as national character to the "warlike" and "stowt" Saxons, whose complete conquest of England was confirmed by their three-fold domination of language, law, and dress.[72] What had even after Camden's time remained a rather vague if enthusiastic connection between English and other Germanic languages was already the subject of intense learned labors and, by the middle of the seventeenth century, would result in the first printed Anglo-Saxon dictionary.

In the same year that Camden's *Remaines* appeared, Richard Verstegan, a Dutch Catholic, published *A Restitution of Decayed Intelligence.*[73] Verstegan printed a list of "our most ancient Saxon words" in his linguistic history, which accepted the legend of the Tower of Babel as the moment at which human languages were differentiated. In this he resembles the other historians of his age; but his list of Anglo-Saxon words has won him high praise as a linguistic historian, for of its nearly seven hundred items some 615 are correctly identified as "Old English" rather than later forms of the language, and in almost all cases he correctly differentiated words of Germanic origin from words borrowed from French and Latin. Verstegan's work "tends to correct our notions of the linguistic naivete of this pre-scientific era."[74]

William Somner's *Dictionarium Saxonico-Latino-Anglicum* appeared in 1659, the first dictionary of Anglo-Saxon to be produced since Nowell's manuscript dictionary of a century earlier.[75] Then in 1689 George Hickes published *Institutiones grammaticae Anglo-Saxonicae, et Moeso-Gothicae,* [76] a set of massive tomes reprinted in 1705 with the monumental addition of Humphrey Wanley's catalogue of Anglo-Saxon manuscripts. It was the first comprehensive list of these manuscripts ever compiled, although Thomas Smith, in 1696, published a catalogue of manuscripts in the library of Sir Robert Cotton.[77] Wanley's catalogue, Kenneth Sisam wrote, "was and still remains the key to the Anglo-Saxon manuscripts."[78] Hickes' work was edited and reprinted by Sir Henry Wotton (1708) and by George Thwaites (1711).[79] Another dictionary was produced by Edward Lye in 1772.[80] The linguistic projects listed here are significant indications of the extent and ambition of inquiries into the Anglo-Saxon language, its origins and its structure.

Yet much Anglo-Saxon scholarship produced during this period sounds an ominous note: inquiry into "Saxon" texts and history proceeded in the face of strong opposition. Commendatory verses attached to Somner's dictionary, for example, look back to the turmoil of the Civil War, a period of great destruction of church property amidst the greatest political crisis in seventeenth-century English history. The poet asks what it matters, "What *Hengist* utter'd, and *Horsa* writ?" Somner should not expect his "Treasury of *Saxon* words" to be valued "amidd'st unlettered swords." The poet continues:

Last, think'st that we, who have destroy'd what e're
Our Grandsires did, will with their language bear?
That we (who have all famous Monuments
Raz'd, and defeated thus all good intents
Of former Piety:) will honour give
To antique Characters? Shall Paper live,
And Inke, when Brasse and Marble can't withstand
This iron ages violating hand?[81]

The political ties of Anglo-Saxonists writing during this period seem to have had a direct bearing on the status of Anglo-Saxon studies. Hickes was a non-juror who remained loyal to the exiled king, James II, who was forced to abdicate in the "Glorious Revolution" of 1688.[82] The Revolution had brought to the surface the question of limits to the monarchy and the authority of Parliament.[83] The unpopular political stance of some these Anglo-Saxon scholars no doubt slowed the spread of work in the field.

The Eighteenth-Century Establishment ■

In the eighteenth century, England's Roman heritage was more highly prized than the nation's Anglo-Saxon origins. Research into local antiquity eventually shrank to only provincial importance. Lambarde led the way when, seeing the manuscript of Camden's vast *Brittania,* he "immediately deferred to the younger man" and confined himself to the county of Kent, "thereby inventing a new antiquarian genre, the county or local history."[84] For neoclassical scholars in the age of Pope and Johnson, the polemic and passion of the early scholars was bad form based on a misguided notion of the nation's past, and the rustic concerns of local history, compared to Rome, were, of course, merely a trifle.

A popular history of the English language tells us that, in the eighteenth century, "the ancient languages had been reduced to rule; one knew what was right and what was wrong. But in English everything was uncertain," and an age desirous of order, organization, and authority, dominated by the linguistic structures and historical study of Latin and Greek, turned nervously to the state of its own tongue.[85] The most striking aspect of eighteenth-century authors concerned with linguistic standards was their hostility towards the scholarly tradition linking the origins of the English language to Germanic worlds. Yet eighteenth-century scholars were fascinated with Anglo-Saxon primitivism as a source of democratic cultural roots. Passionate insistence on the purity of the northern peoples and their system of government was an obsession that took firm hold early in the century, and, by the century's end, had become linked to the philological and comparative bases for studying European languages. Renaissance recovery had meant inquiry into Roman as well as Saxon origins. Roman antiquity reflected what was held to be by far the more pleasing aspect of British history, and everybody, it seems, knew it. Anglo-Saxon origins manifested the dual nature of the primitive—purity and barbarism—to their disadvantage. The classical heritage of England was pure, but it had been sullied and sacrificed to Saxon culture, its ancient monuments destroyed. By the middle of the eighteenth century, there were as many voices despising Anglo-Saxon culture as praising it. But inquiry into the origins of the language continued the Anglo-Saxon tradition, and the reputation of the Anglo-Saxons and their language cannot be said to have increased or decreased in the eighteenth century. For every author condemning Anglo-Saxon barbarity we can find one interested in the origins of the English language and admiring of its "Saxon" heritage. Very little was written in this period to repudiate the historical vision of Bale, Foxe, and others—the vision that was the chief contribution of the polemical tradition—while much, obviously, was done to continue the research into language and manuscripts begun by Nowell, Lambarde, and others, and to acquire the necessary tools for that research.

As Anglo-Saxon scholarship moved into a more competitive arena and came face to face with classical studies, there was less emphasis on historical texts and greater emphasis on the place of early English in the family of human languages. Application of considerable intellectual resources to language study continued throughout the eighteenth century, and in fact the "new" philology of the nineteenth century could not have risen without the platform of previous work. So many scholars think Anglo-Saxon studies "died" in the eighteenth-century (a notorious metaphor for sexual intercourse in literature of the time) that the view has become standard. Sisam calls Wanley's 1705 *Catalogue* a "high-water mark" that "was not passed again for more than a century."[86] David C. Douglas concludes his study of the eighteenth-century tradition with a chapter entitled "The End of an Age."[87]

Although the eighteenth century is usually seen as a point of near-extinction in Anglo-Saxon scholarship, one may reasonably assert another view: as the focus of work shifted from the recovery of historical and theological texts, the face of the subject changed, and language study that situated Anglo-Saxon in the context of wide-ranging historical and linguistic inquiry became its predominant feature. As Janice Lee demonstrated, Anglo-Saxon texts and history were not marginal concerns in the period.[88] Major topics of reform debated in Parliament included suffrage and representation, both institutions which were examined anew in England in the wake of the French and American Revolutions. Scholars on both sides followed the example of the seventeenth century and turned to Anglo-Saxon legal and historical documents to support their views.

The works of Wanley and Hickes in particular can be cited as the most important sources for a view of the Anglo-Saxon past that had become a fundamental tenet of English linguistic scholarship in the early eighteenth century. In 1714, John Fortescue-Aland cited many authorities, including the important jurist Henry Spelman, for the opinion that Germany was mother of "most" of the laws of Western Europe (which was not to deny that England's laws had been made on the example of the Romans). Saxon, Fortescue wrote, is "Mother of our English Tongue," and Old English was a better—since "fuller"—tongue than Latin or Greek. Greek had been understood by the learned, Old English by the common people, Fortescue claimed, and English was the language of "the true religion" and the language of the progenitors of Queen Caroline.[89]

Fortescue-Aland's line of argument appears in the first grammar of Old English written in English, although along the model of that of Hickes, published in 1715 by Elizabeth Elstob, *The Rudiments of Grammar for the English-Saxon Tongue, First Given in English, with An Apology for the Study of Northern Antiquities.*[90] Elstob's title, like the poem attached to Somner's dictionary, indicates a countercurrent to the Anglo-Saxon scholarly tradition that she, as a disciple of Hickes, represented. Her preface begins with the apprehension that two charges will be made against her work: first, that as a woman she takes up a learned subject; second, that the subject taken up is the "Saxon" tongue. Elstob dedicated her grammar to Caroline, whom she sets in a tradition of great leaders, including Charlemagne and Julius Caesar, who were also scholars. Fully conscious of gender, Elstob writes that she was rewarded by her study of Anglo-Saxon, "this original of our Mother-tongue," and hoping "that others of my own sex, might be capable of this same satisfaction," she decided to supply "the rudiments of that language in an English dress."

Elstob's advocacy of Anglo-Saxon studies, especially as pursued by a woman, confronted an extremely hostile current of thought in which, among others, Joseph Addison, John Dryden and Jonathan Swift championed the idea of an academy of the English language to "fix" its forms and hence preserve it against decay. Swift published *A Proposal for Correcting, Improving, and Ascertaining the English Tongue* in 1712. The impulse towards an academy reflected the influence of French and Italian models for standardizing national language.[91] Elstob's view of these ideas is apparent:

> I cannot but think it is a great pity that in our considerations for refinement of the English tongue, so little regard is had to antiquity, and the original of our present language, which is the Saxon. This indeed is allowed by an ingenious person, who hath lately made some Proposals for the Refinement of the English tongue. . . . The author of the Proposal, may think this but an ill return, for the soft things he has said of the ladies. (pp. ix–xi)

Swift characterized those who studied Anglo-Saxon as "men of low genius" who labored with "that vulgar tongue, so barren and so barbarous." Many others shared the view that the earliest forms of English were unworthy of study and that England's scholars would do better to stick to Latin and Greek as subjects for study and objects for linguistic and literary imitation. A chorus was raised against the "nest of Saxonists," a term used specifically to deride those at Oxford, including Wanley and Hickes. Alexander Pope must also be included among the formidable foes of scholars of Saxon antiquity. Pope penned infamous ridicule of the antiquary Thomas Hearne (1678–1735?), a historian now much admired who published some forty volumes of medieval texts. "Esurient of antiquity, he became a whetstone of cheap wit," writes Douglas of Hearne. "He lacked urbanity." Less than six months after his death, Pope wrote, "To future Ages will his Dullness last / who hath preserved the Dullness of the past." And the bookseller who disposed of Hearne's library advertised the sale with a quip: "'Pox on't', quoth Time to Thomas Hearne, / 'Whatever I forget you learn.'"[92]

Yet it is easy to pay too much attention to the views of Swift and others who ridiculed early Anglo-Saxon scholars, and in the process to neglect the enormous output of other writers speculating on language origins at the time. These included Jeremiah Wharton, who published *The English Grammar* in 1654, in which he explained why Charles II wished for a grammar of the "Teutonick tongue" from which English had come (its purpose was to make Latin easier to learn). In 1699 Guy Miège, in *The English Grammar,* claimed that English and Dutch were both "germanic" dialects, a claim made all the more important when, in 1714, the English declared their preference for German Protestants over Stuart Catholics and the Guelph family of Hanover inherited the British throne.[93] In 1731, Thomas Stackhouse, in *Reflections on the Nature and Property of Languages in General,* firmly linked native languages and native tongues, asserted that "all tongues are equal," and said that they were born, and died, like men, an obvious refutation of arguments in favor of "fixing" the language and trying to halt changes in it. Opposition to such attempts was shared by Samuel Johnson, who wrote that "every man would have been willing, and many would have been proud to disobey" the decrees of Swift's academy.[94]

Indeed, the eighteenth century is replete with texts and ideas about language origin and language change, and all of them have some bearing on the place of Anglo-Saxon language and culture. L. D. Nelme, writing in 1772, claimed that Anglo-Saxon was a primordial language with the capacity to lead scholars to the languages of the Tower of Babel; he also wrote an Anglo-Saxon dictionary designed to bear out his etymological views.[95] Many writers believed in a universal and original language that was composed of primordial elements; Nelme at one time thought that Anglo-Saxon contained the symbols and sounds of this first language. Eventually he accepted the view Rowland Jones expressed in *Origin of Languages and Nations* that the original language was Celtic. This research self-consciously continued inquiries into the origins of languages in the Renaissance; among Jones' sources is Camden.[96] Many views were possible. In 1783, John Williams, registering a fuller perspective on Oriental languages, traced Celtic and Indian to common roots and proposed that the mother tongue was Hebrew.[97] The work of these and many other early language scholars has been set into context by Hans Aarsleff, who is one of the few historians to see the point and the purpose of the often misguided conclusions about language origins reached in the eighteenth century. "Error may be as influential as truth," he writes, adding, "To the historical understanding, the pseudo-science of an age may be as important as its science."[98]

In 1786 Sir William Jones delivered a famous paper to the Asiatic Society on Greek, Latin, and Sanskrit, showing that they belonged to a single family of languages. G.W.F. Hegel hailed the paper as the "discovery of a new world." Others were even more enthusiastic, believing that the "cradle of civilization" had been found in India whence the chosen people descended, like rays of light, westward. Thereafter Indian language and culture were used to develop theories of racial difference. Racialism—the scientific theory of "inherent, unchangeable differences between races"—acquired both form and respectability from the scholarly community's passion for scientific classification.[99] German and British scholars mined the "Indo-Germanic" languages, as the "Indo-European" languages were once known, for origins older than the classics and beyond Scripture.

Language study in England benefited only slowly from the new learning of the Orientalists. Aarsleff's splendid survey of the state of affairs at the time chronicles the overpowering mechanical influence of "universal grammar," which was based on the assumption that the sounds of letters were dictated by the natures of the things they signified. The most important English language scholar of the period was John Horne Tooke, a notorious partisan of the American side of the American Revolution (he was jailed for his views). Horne Tooke wrote *The Diversions of Purley* in reply to John Locke's essay, "On the Nature, Use, and Signification of Language." For him language was either the immediate sign of a thing, or a sign in abbreviated form; nouns and verbs belong to the first category, prepositions and other parts of speech to the second.[100] Tooke's theory can be illustrated by his work with the preposition, an "abbreviated" kind of word that had lost parts of the directly signifying elements in which it originated. Prepositions were forms of verbs or nouns and indicated the relation of words to each other, Tooke thought. Thus "by" was the imperative of the Old English "beon," to be ("byð), written either "be" or "by." "With" was the imperative of "wyrðan," to become. "Beyond" meant "be passed," since it came from "be" and "geond," which came from "goneð" and "gan," to go. To be "beyond" a place was, then, to "be passed that place." "Through" came directly from the Teutonic noun "dauro," meaning door.[101] Concrete nouns revealed etymologies instantly: since "bar" was a defense, "barn" was a place of cover or protection, "baron" an armed man, "bark" a strong ship, and so forth. Tooke made no distinction between Germanic and Romance languages (e.g., "baron" comes from Old French, "bark" from Old English), but he was not always dead wrong. "Truth" came from "to trow," to consider, he said, and modern scholarship indicates that "treow," meaning "to have faith in," is correct.[102] One must admit that it takes a great deal of learning and ingenuity not only to devise such explanations, but to compile nearly one thousand pages of them. Likewise, it takes a fair knowledge of the language to explain what is wrong with them.

Among the Anglo-Saxonists who followed Tooke's system was Samuel Henshall, who was, in 1800, an unsuccessful candidate for the Rawlinson chair in Anglo-Saxon at Oxford.[103] His small book, *The Saxon and English Languages Reciprocally Illustrative of Each Other,* shows him to have been as tendentious and nearly as inventive as Tooke. Henshall's thesis was that previous Anglo-Saxonists had badly misunderstood the corpus of Old English because they had attempted to translate it into Latin, which could not convey the "accurate ideas of the 'British-saxon,' 'Anglo-saxon,' or 'Norman-saxon' documents."[104] His book contains parts of several texts, including penitentials, law codes, and "Cædmon's Hymn," as well as some poetry composed by Abraham Wheelock and others in Old English.[105] Henshall espouses Tooke's ideas of language on nearly every page. The infinitive "to love" comes from "do love," meaning "to be in the act of loving." "D" was given soft pronunciation in the present tense (as in "th") and hard pronunciation in the past. Therefore, Henshall wrote, "*Present* Singular, I love, or love do, thou love-in-is, or lovenest, by abbreviation lovest, and loves,—he love-do or loveth." "Loveth" became "he love did" or "lovedd" in the past (pp. 53–54).

Tooke's theories of universal grammar were popular for many reasons. The simplest was that they offered a way to explain the world, its history, and the speaker's place in it. The history of the language mattered chiefly because the history of nations was contained in it. It was for no other reason that Hegel would have considered a paper on the families of Oriental languages the "discovery of a new world." Many quarreled with parts of Tooke's method, but virtually everyone who commented on it conceded its brilliance and usefulness. "For thirty years," Hans Aarsleff writes, "it kept England immune to the new philology until the results and methods finally had to be imported from the Continent in the 1830s."[106]

Nineteenth-century Anglo-Saxonists demonstrated the nationalism that motivated their scholarship; nationalism recalls in many ways the theological and political conditions in which Anglo-Saxon scholarship began in the Renaissance. Kemble, Turner, and Macaulay represented different historical methods, but they shared important assumptions about English history. They viewed England's medieval past as the nation's childhood, grasped the importance of the Anglo-Saxon—that is, Germanic—past as a foundation for contemporary claims to supremacy, saw scholarly discipline as essential to proper understanding of the past, and accepted as the historian's chief duty the commemoration of the nation's greatness. They saw the past as primitive, little more than a rudimentary version of the present, without values of its own; if they idealized childhood, they left no doubt that primitivism, whether cultural or chronological, was ideal only after progress transcended it. Macaulay and Kemble also shared antagonism towards the Catholic Church of the Middle Ages, Kemble reserving particular scorn for corruption of its judicial system, including penance and confession. His indignation almost equals that of the sixteenth-century Reformers themselves. The "canonical prohibitions" of the corrupt clergy betrayed "the innocent and ignorant into a condition of endless wretchedness," he wrote. "Engines of extortion, and instruments of malice" had led "to the intervention of the priest with the family, in the most intolerable form." He concluded that "thrice blessed was the day which left us free and unshackled to pursue the noblest and purest impulses of our human nature."[107]

The Point of the Turning Point ■

That Kemble, the pioneer of Germanic philology in English scholarship, subscribed to views shared by Macaulay and Turner and railed against papists with the vehemence of a Renaissance reformer is significant, for historians of Anglo-Saxon studies point to him and his period as a turning point, a moment in which ideas and methods of the past—antiquarian, polemical, partisan, and amateur—began to give way to the scientific methods of Germanic philology. Eleanor N. Adams concluded that the contribution of antiquarian or amateur Anglo-Saxonists did not play a part in the modern practice of the discipline.[108] Although uncertain "when the apologetic-polemical motivations of Anglo-Saxon scholarship were broken by a scholarship of more disinterested motives," Berkhout and Gatch locate the "great change" in the rise of Germanic philology in the nineteenth century. Michael Murphy accepts the 1830s, when Kemble began to publish his Anglo-Saxon studies, and when Thorpe published a translation of the Danish scholar Rasmus Rask's grammar of Old English, as the point of transition "from the enthusiastic to the 'scientific' in Anglo-Saxon studies in England." Richard C. Payne takes a more complex view. He notes that a new wave of scholars, trained in philology and Teutonic mythology on the Continent, brought back to England "the intellectual interests and prejudices that they had developed abroad." Nevertheless, he too claims that in this period "literary interest became the driving force behind Anglo-Saxon scholarship in England, replacing nationalism, the study of law, and ecclesiastical controversy, which had motivated students of the discipline since its beginnings."[109]

This widely recognized turning point—the "great change" in which "the 'scientific'" and "literary interest" "[replaced] English nationalism"—was supposedly effected by philology, the application of systematic linguistic principles that vanquished amateur polemic and produced scholarship as we know it: professional and, we like to think, disinterested. When Anglo-Saxon studies moved to the university, they became a profession. Confidence in the objectivity of scientific methods figures prominently in the conclusion of Daniel G. Calder's recent study of surveys and histories of Old English literature. Commenting on "the break with the past that the Anglo-Saxon literary historian can now make," he observes:

> We are in a better position than our predecessors have ever been to analyze the literature, both poetry and prose, without preconceptions. To our inherited philological base we have added a much improved technical understanding, encompassing advances in palaeography and in the study of sources and cultural backgrounds.[110]

Many Anglo-Saxonists would no doubt agree.

This passage, which I see as an epitome of its perspective, juxtaposes method, seen as technical understanding, with meaning, or preconceptions. This juxtaposition does much to explain why modern Anglo-Saxonists are content to ignore the political and ideological history of the discipline. The ideological content of philology can persist untouched by analysis because we have separated it, as a method, from its historical meaning, and have given it a historical meaning of our own—that is, we used the advent of philology as a turning point. We have seen that Macaulay, Turner, and Kemble did not share an attitude toward scholarship; however, they shared something more important: an attitude toward the past, which they saw in a vital relationship to the present. When they surveyed Anglo-Saxon history, they saw there the beginnings of traditions which they themselves wished to claim. In exactly the same way, although at first without comparable scholarly self-consciousness, Renaissance scholars set about recovering Anglo-Saxon texts where necessary, and rewriting them. The idea of a "turning point" is based on an attitude toward the "pastness" of the past; this attitude is, I think, fundamental to the change in Anglo-Saxon scholarship that we see in the nineteenth century.

In *Toward an Aesthetic of Reception,* Hans Robert Jauss suggests that the engagement of early scholars with the past, and their desire for access to the past, reflected their belief that the past spoke to the present and that important events in the past had, in the present, reached their culmination. For these historians, Jauss says, "To write the history of a national literature" was "the crowning life's work of the philologist. The patriarchs of the discipline saw their highest goal therein, to represent in the history of literary works (*Dichtwerke*) the idea of national individuality on its way to itself." The past was thought to "peak politically in the fulfilled moment of national unification or literarily in the high point of a national classic."[111] Like Macaulay, Johann Gottfried von Herder (1744–1803) organized the story of history around organic motifs. Hayden White describes them as "the motifs of change and duration and the themes of generation, growth, and fulfillment, motifs and themes which depend for their plausibility on the acceptance of the analogy between human life and plant life, the root metaphorical identification at the heart at the heart of the work."[112] For Herder, language had a life of its own, and developed in the same way a nation or a people did; Herder believed that speech began in song and collected "a truly international compilation of folk songs," as Aarsleff calls it, *Stimmen der Völker in Liedern,* which Aarsleff sees as a "forerunner" of the Grimms' fairy-tale collections."[113] The division of the past into "closed periods" allowed the historian to attribute a "completeness" to earlier periods, and, Jauss says, to describe them "in their own completeness without regard for that which followed from them." He continues: "Thereafter, when the unfolding of national individuality was no longer satisfactory as a guiding thread, literary history chiefly strung closed periods one after another."[114] This gesture of closure attributes "completeness" to the historical past, making it obsolete.

In Jauss's paradigm of closed and open historical periods, Macaulay and Kemble saw the past as open to the present. We see this sense of connection to the past in Macaulay's view of the change in national consciousness in the Reformation; he saw it as a turning point, as the end of ignorance forced on the nation by the corrupt clergy. Today Anglo-Saxonists use the trope of the "turning point" to illustrate the commonsensical idea that the past is superseded by the present, and to explain how progress seals off one epoch from the next. The most recent essay on the decline of Anglo-Saxon studies, in fact, uses the phrase in its title: "Some Turning Points in the History of Teaching Old English in America."[115] In the case of the history of a scholarly discipline, progress can be measured by improved methods; philology is (mistakenly) seen as effecting closure on romantic Anglo-Saxonism and as opening a new era of scientific study. This trope accounts for disciplinary change and development of the "field" of Anglo-Saxon studies as a concentrated core of methodology separate from social views.

Modern philologists have sustained the divorce of present from past: they have separated method from meaning. They set aside earlier centuries for two reasons: first, they recognize scientific, reliable scholarship only after nineteenth-century philology was emergent; second, they accept the claims that philology provides direct access to the Anglo-Saxon past. Aarsleff's maxim, that error may be as significant as truth, applies to much of the Anglo-Saxon scholarship produced in the Renaissance and eighteenth century: to Bale's vision of the two churches, which was an utterly false reconstruction of English history; to the numerous false etymologies produced by everyone from Elizabeth Elstob at the beginning of the century to Horne Took at its end. Elstob's edition and translation of one of Ælfric's homilies on the birth of Gregory the Great sums up many of the constant features of Anglo-Saxon scholarship from the Renaissance to the time of Macaulay, Kemble, and Turner. Elstob picks up the wordplay that Bede used to describe Gregory's discovery of the English (Angles and angels) in Rome. The "Angli" came from the kingdom of "Deiri," ruled by a king called "Ælle." Gregory's response, "Alleluia," a pun on Ælle, became the occasion for some puns of Elstob's own. She connected "ælle" to "ellen," the Old English for "virtue," and to her own name, which she says came from a place name, "Ellstow." Allowing for some phonological changes, she suggested that "Ellstowe" could also have been written "Ellstouue," and that the "uu" here "might easily pass in process of time" into "bb," thus rendering her own name.[116] She concluded:

> And that which may yet further excuse the tediousness of the Allusion, may be this; that as the Holy *Gregory's* Affection to the Subjects of King *Ella* was the Occasion of bringing Christianity to all the *Saxons*, so it hath fallen out by Providence, to one not only born within the Circuit of those Dominions, but nearly approaching to his Name, to show some sort of Gratitude, in restoring to the *English* this Memorial of their Apostle and Benefactor at so great a distance of time. (pp. 16–17)

Here is a scholar writing in her own language and rewriting as she does so the language of her "mother tongue." Her etymologies cannot pass muster, but of them, and of all the Anglo-Saxon scholarship left behind at the "turning point" and the advent of "new philology," one wants to remark as Halbfass did of early Christian missionaries to the Orient. The missionaries, he wrote, performed "detailed work in several areas."

> But primarily, in spite of or perhaps precisely because of their "prejudice" and dogmatic limitations, they have also helped to de-

> fine and clarify the central problems involved in approaching and understanding that which is alien: They, or at least their outstanding exponents, embody a desire to understand whose singular power and problematic nature arise from their deep and uncompromising *desire to be understood.*[117]

This desire to be understood, as "deep and uncompromising" in Elstob and other eighteenth-century "missionaries" in the cause of Anglo-Saxon studies, is a point larger than the turning point: It is a point of similarity between early Anglo-Saxonists and ourselves, and that similarity is the point of reconsidering our own work in the tradition of theirs.

3

Sources and the Search for Origins in the Academy

Philology and Romanticism: Lachmann and Grimm ■

Just as Renaissance theologians and scholars of early British constitutional law "sought the origins of Parliament beyond the earliest of its written records,"[1] philologists and textual critics in the nineteenth century sought the origins of speech. Describing the state of Anglo-Saxon scholarship in the early nineteenth century, T. A. Birrell writes, rather implausibly, that it was undertaken "for its own sake, not under the influence of the aprioristic religious and political theories of the 17th century, nor, indeed, under the influence of the aprioristic linguistic and racial theories of the later 18th century."[2] Birrell's phrase "for its own sake" masks the fact that the nineteenth-century study of Anglo-Saxon drew on the resources of "scientific" inquiries into language in order to bolster institutional positions that religion and politics had been unable to maintain. What was new in the later period was not scientific neutrality, but rather the academic, systematic context within which the desire for origins was realized. Investigations of universal languages in the eighteenth century and research into the origins of the English language both rested on romantic views about language. A tenet central to both was the principle that language had a life of its own and changed because of internal, natural causes rather than as a result of history.

Nineteenth-century philology, however "scientific," made no pretense to political neutrality. Historians of the language, including Hans Aarsleff and James H. Stam, have emphatically denied that philology represents the rejection of politically and ideologically motivated scholarship.[3] Aarsleff notes that the chief exponent of "linguistic finalism" was Max Müller, who wrote that "language is independent of political history," and later thinkers, including G.W.F. Hegel (1770–1831), maintained Müller's view that grammar was "the alphabet of the Spirit itself."[4] The newer "scientific" methods of philology were suffused with the ideological goals of German romanticism, which were created by, and which helped to foster, national culture. In German universities in the late eighteenth century, modes of linguistic and historical analysis were based on assumptions about the "spirit of the age" ("Zeitgeist") and the belief in the "biography" of a people.

In the nineteenth century, as Germanic philology was institutionalized as a university discipline, the meaning of "philology" narrowed from the study of all culture to the study of historical linguistics. Eugene Vance's definition of philology makes this professional focus, and its importance for origins, clear: it is "a historical discipline grounded upon the systematic and diachronic analysis of language, documents, legends, and myths whose purpose is to lead backward through the dim corridors of time to some specific source, intention, or moment of origin, of plenitude, or of truth."[5] The development of a specialized and narrowed definition of philology charts the most significant development in the history of Anglo-Saxon studies: not progress towards specialization and increasingly scientific methods of analysis, but a growing awareness of the distance between the subject and the scholar studying it, an awareness that eventually hardened into the belief that such distance could guarantee scholarly or "scientific" objectivity. Such specialization inspired confidence. Writing of *Beowulf,* J. M. Kemble claimed that "a modern edition, made by a person really conversant with the language which he illustrates, will in all probability be much more like the original than the MS [manuscript] copy, which, even in the earliest times, was made by an ignorant or indolent transcriber."[6] The scholarly reconstruction, therefore, produced a textual beginning closer to the origin than the Anglo-Saxon manuscript itself.

In characterizing these ideological perspectives on language, Aarsleff says that the "chief aspiration" of nineteenth century scholarship was "the confident ascertainment of ultimate origins in a distant past beyond the earliest written records," a "gap between documentation and essential beginnings" that was "breached by faith in a few powerful romantic doctrines."[7] We should correlate this gap with two others: the distance between what Edward W. Said calls "beginnings" (documents) and "origins" (myths, belief in the divine); and the gaps of the Anglo-Saxon literary corpus, with its anonymous texts, fragmented manuscripts, and other incomplete features.

Aarsleff attributes the success of philological criticism—its method—to its cooperation with and reinforcement of a larger romantic world view—that is, its cultural meaning—rather than its correction of that perspective. In other words, method and meaning served a single purpose. "The prestigious methods and procedures of positivism gave faith that the results had the quality of certain knowledge and established truth," Arsleff writes. "In humanistic scholarship romanticism and positivism joined forces in the enterprise of system building."[8] This "system building" itself took many forms. For the future of Anglo-Saxon studies, the important system was not the intellectual framework of philology, but the place of philology and literary history—indeed, philology *as* literary history—in the institutional framework of the Department of English. Romantic historicism cooperated with language study because they were, at a basic level, one kind of activity; the scholarly methods helped to institutionalize romantic ways of seeing the past without radically transforming them.

The fundamental similarity between romantic historians (to use that label for both Macaulay and Turner) on the one hand, and newer "scientific" analysts like Kemble, on the other, can be seen in their favorite image, the family; the historians linked past and present in the paradigm of parent–child relationships, in which the present was the fulfillment—the adult form—of the past. We might expect the paradigm to be inverted if we think of biological descent from parent to child, but descent was not in question: the focus was ascent, or progress. Philologists, as Martin Bernal has vividly called to our attention, were enamored of the image of ascension: the metaphor of the tree, roots deep in the earth, branches aloft in the sunlight, served the notion particularly well.

Bernal considers the tree to be the "ideal Romantic image." Trees "are rooted in their own soils and nourished by their particular climates; at the same time, they are alive and grow;" they "progress and never turn back," for they are laden with a "simple past and a complicated and ramified present and future."[9] Many institutions, human and otherwise, were classified in the pattern suggested by the tree. Just as manuscript traditions could be organized into trees or "stemmata," one branch of a tradition splitting into two, three, or four, so too languages could be organized into trees, branching off in various directions. Ultimately, even races and nations would be seen as possessing the same pattern. Powerful claims were made for the capacity of scholarship to recover the original language of the human race; language was seen as organic and even as having a life of its own, "with its own life and laws independent of speakers."[10] These ideas did not go unchallenged even at the midpoint of the nineteenth century; near the end of the century they were vigorously refuted, as Aarsleff has shown. But they aptly illustrate the atmosphere of romantic historical thinking in which the scientific principles of philology were developed.

In terms of linguistic and cultural origins, the tree is a map of textual and linguistic beginnings and a map of power. It traces origins from the visible present to their roots in the hidden past. It neatly emblematizes the cooperation of historical meaning—the continuous, organic development of national consciousness—and method, the techniques used to discover in the multiplicity of the present the unity of the past. The tree provided a model for the reconstruction of textual origins, enabling Kemble to assert that a modern scholar could produce a version of an Anglo-Saxon text closer to the original than the manuscripts, and it likewise gave historians of language the means to determine the origins of language and the sequence in which languages had been transmitted to the present.

These efforts to reach textual and linguistic beginnings, once formulated into scholarly procedures, became known as "source criticism," a term as clearly related to the desire for origins as "philology." Although source criticism was formulated in conjunction with the editing of classical and biblical texts, it was also widely applied to vernacular medieval texts. The prestige attached to this methodology derived in part from the antiquity of the cultural monuments to which it was applied. If scholars could trace the development of texts such as the epic *Gilgamesh* over some fifteen hundred years, or analyze the individual narratives conflated to compose Pentateuchal narratives, surely they could, using the same methods, recover the textual origins of younger (although no less important) cultural artifacts of the Germanic world. The relevance of the project to a search for origins was obvious.

Source criticism was not exclusively a product of nineteenth-century thought. Jeffrey H. Tigay claims that the objectives of source criticism were anticipated by the British scholar of Hebrew Richard Simon in *A Critical History of the Old Testament,* published in 1678 (1682 in London). Simon believed that the Torah "was composed of historical records kept by official scribes of Moses' time."[11] Simon's attempt to trace the *Torah* to its textual origins is an early example of a critical practice institutionalized by nineteenth-century source critics.

In the nineteenth century, Germany universities—the University of

Göttingen in particular—institutionalized source criticism and philology and ensured the prestige of both. Bernal calls the University of Göttingen the "embryo of all later, modern, diversified and professional universities." He continues: "It is true to say that while exclusive professionalism was the distinctive form of Göttingen scholarship, the chief unifying principle of its content was ethnicity and racism."[12] It was at Göttingen that Greece first was proposed as the alternative to Egypt as the source of European civilization; it was here F. A. Wolf had worked, beginning in 1777, and here, starting in the early 1830s, that Jakob and Wilhelm Grimm, Georg Gottfried Gervinus, and other German scholars refined and taught the methodologies that we recognize as source criticism, textual criticism, and philology. At Göttingen the brothers Grimm also, in 1833, met Kemble, creating the most important link between German and British scholarship of the period.

Anglo-Saxonism in the last century acquired its reputation for scientific neutrality largely through the success of the brothers Grimm—Jakob (1785–1863) and Wilhelm (1786–1859)—and Karl Lachmann (d. 1851). Two scholarly concerns define their common ground: a romantic reconstruction of the German peoples and their language and literature; and an elaboration of rules and systems of formal and textual classification that enabled the reconstruction to be carried out with "scientific" exactitude.[13]

The moving force in the development of textual scholarship, and the most important influence on later scholars, Lachmann developed the genealogical method of editing texts, sorting manuscripts into families and using "genetic" relationships to reconstruct lost archetypes.[14] So pervasive was Lachmann's influence that Aarsleff includes his approach to textual editing among "the fundamental doctrines of romantic scholarship":

> the oral tradition and long reliable transmission of early poetry; the historicity of early epic poems such as *The Song of Roland* and the *Nibelungen;* the distant oriental origins of the European folktale such as the fabliau; and the acceptance of Lachmann's principles for the editing of early texts.[15]

Such scholarship, which attempted to recover the text in its uncorrupted state, its purest form, was heavily organic in its underlying assumptions and techniques. Lachmann edited a wide range of texts, from Scripture to Greek and Latin classical texts, laws, and mythical (or folk) narrative.[16] When editing classical and biblical materials, Lachmann sought to capture the text as the earliest extant manuscript presented it, not the text as it might have existed in its earliest version. In

Said's terms, Lachmann concentrated on the "humanly produced" form of the text, its "beginnings" in manuscript form, not its origin. The form of the first manuscript was a very different thing from the first form of the text; in the unstable environment of a manuscript culture, many manuscripts could contain a single text in very different forms, since the manuscripts differed in size, were written in different hands, and so forth.

Lachmann's method of reconstructing textual history, known as "stemmatics," used error in the manuscript transmission—as evident in grammar, meter, orthography, and narrative coherence—to reconstruct a textual tradition. James Thorpe wrote in 1972 that it was "still generally accepted by classicists and by New Testament scholars."[17] But some of Lachmann's editions, and especially his work as a Germanist, were conceived of differently. For the literary history of Anglo-Saxon, the claim that special assumptions governed vernacular texts was, of course, of utmost importance, as was the assertion that genuine originality could be recovered through textual scholarship. Lachmann supported his search for textual origins with a set of "scientific," or at least highly regulated procedures, including the examination of meter and lexicography, that allowed him to differentiate genuine from corrupt versions of a text. Lachmann edited the *Nibelungenlied* not to recreate the original manuscript but to lead to the materials from which the original text had been compiled; his hope, as Lee Patterson writes, was to demonstrate that "the author of the *Nibelungenlied* was not a thirteenth-century poet . . . but *das Volk*.[18] These separate texts comprised what was known as the "inner history" of the text, the approach that influenced Wolf's edition of the *Iliad* and thereafter Lachmann's own.[19] Lachmann's edition of the *Nibelungenlied,* which appeared in 1840, went under the title of *Zwanzig alte Lieder von der Nibelungen* (*Twenty Ancient Tales of the Niebelungs*).[20]

Lachmann used textual criticism to explain away the gap between the date of manuscripts and the stories they told, or what Aarsleff calls "the gap between the texts and the postulated origins" of those texts in a time contemporary with the events they described.[21] This gap was closed by oral tradition, through which short poems, historical ballads, or *Lieder,* composed at the time of the events by witnesses, were transmitted and eventually combined to form epics. The origins of the epic, itself a culmination of national culture, were thus posited in primitive, "folk" literature. The *Liedertheorie,* an attempt to discover "origins that were by definition incapable of documentation,"[22] served immensely ambitious cultural purposes. It posited ancient origins for texts of national and historical importance, thereby validating the historicity of the events recounted in the texts, and explained the transformation of folk art into the high art of mature cultures. Lachmann furnished textual criticism with tools that claimed to recover non-textual or pre-textual origins. His theory had implications for *Beowulf* scholarship as well as for the study of epics in French and German.

Lachmann's theories were not successfully challenged until Joseph Bedier exposed the ideological, romantic prejudices behind German textual scholarship, especially regarding the epic. Just as he sought to dispense with mythological assumptions about ancient narratives, he dispensed with the bipartite Lachmannian approach to manuscript traditions. His own approach has become known as the "best-text" method and is still admired for its pragmatism. Bedier recommended that one chose a manuscript because it was "the manuscript 'one is the least inclined to correct.'" He did not chose a manuscript because "it was closest to the original, for he did not presume to know or be able to divine what the original would have been like," Aarsleff writes; he relied on "intuition and personal judgment" instead of "the old scholarly, objective rigmarole."[23]

Lachmann's influence on Anglo-Saxon studies was greatly enhanced by the work of Jakob and Wilhelm Grimm, Lachmann's contemporaries and regular correspondents.[24] What Lachmann did for the recovery of origins for vernacular texts, Jakob Grimm did for language itself in *Deutsche Grammatik,* published in 1819. The scholarly problem that Grimm, like Lachmann, set out to solve was the problem of concealed origins, the problem of detecting pure, native culture hidden beneath layers of Christian teaching. Grimm showed that the relationships of language families could not, as earlier philologists had claimed, depend on vocabulary alone. Other elements, including grammar and patterns in sound changes, were needed to document the fundamental similarities of related languages.

The arguments in Grimm's first grammar, which appeared in 1819, were not entirely new. The Danish scholar Rasmus K. Rask published *A Grammar of the Anglo-Saxon Tongue* in 1817. His work was translated into English by Kemble's friend and colleague, Benjamin Thorpe, in 1830.[25] It was Grimm's second, and much revised grammar, published in 1822, that articulated "Grimm's Law" of sound shifts (as it has become known), which demonstrated the relationship of sound changes in Greek, Gothic, and Old High German, and made Grimm famous. Grimm's revised *Grammar* was specifically in debt to Rask, but even the first edition (published too early to have benefitted directly from Rask's grammar) contained a tribute to Rask's learning.[26]

Grimm's contributions were not limited to systems of grammar and word study. He was a literary historian whose textual and linguistic research uncovered conflict between Germanic and Christian roots at the origins of Germanic civilizations. A dedication to the mysterious origins of the Fatherland occupied both the Grimms to the point of obsession; their function in the world of early German romanticism, as Louis L. Synder has written, was to supply it with critical scholarship. But it was their fairy tales, the *Hausmärchen,* that enjoyed wide-spread popularity. The same cultural ideals informing their linguistic scholarship were put forward for a general audience—specifically, an audience of children—in folktales supposedly gathered from peasants close to the German soil. The authenticity of many of the tales has been disproved. Snyder believes that the Germanic origin of the tales mattered less than the use the Grimms made of them to promote German nationalism, but he lets them off too easily.[27] Long before Synder wrote, there was substantial, devastating evidence that the Grimms either manufactured their tales or rewrote them so extensively as to obliterate their "folk" character. They "deliberately deceived their public by concealing or actually misstating the facts, in order to give an impression of ancient German folk origin for their material which they knew was utterly false," writes John M. Ellis. Ellis indicts a long list of Grimm scholars for either failing or refusing to see the fraud that the Brothers Grimm have perpetrated with astonishing success.[28] The tales advocated cruelty, violence, anti-Semitism, and, above all, submission to the authority of the state. Sometimes purged of sadistic elements and thus known in a relatively benign form, the tales were later restored to their complete versions as "Nazi literature designed for children."[29] But the authenticity of the tales was spurious, a fabricated point of origin.

Grimm also expressed the relationship between Christian ideology and native texts, not surprisingly, in terms of the tree. Christian teaching, he claimed in the preface to his 1840 edition of the Anglo-Saxon poem *Elene,* sought to "graft its mildness, its more profoundly, more fervently affecting feeling on the rough bark of the strong healthy wood of pagan conceptions." Georg Gottfried Gervinus, of like mind in the matter of the conflict between pagan and Christian origins, described the *Hildebrandslied* as "almost the only remain which allows us to glimpse the rich national poetry" that existed before the clergy erased "the ruins of paganism" from Germany.[30]

Although far more precise than any explanation yet offered—with the exception of that of Rask—Grimm's work was based on romantic myth, as Stam demonstrates. Grimm explained that his three-part system of patterns was a terminal and non-renewable process because "the spirit of language has completed its course" at the final, third stage, and "does not seem to want to begin anew."[31] Grimm's indebtedness to Romantic concepts of language was effectively demonstrated by E. Prokosch's *A Comparative German Grammar.* Prokosch identified Grimm's "purely psychological explanations" for certain linguistic features, including precise details of the "sound shift" (*Lautverschiebung*), which Grimm saw as "an expression of the impetuous character of the Germanic tribes during their early history."[32] Such views attempted to relate language change to climate (e.g., mountain air), national character, and other data that, although difficult to document to the satisfaction of modern linguists, were fully in accord with governing concepts of racial evolution. The difficulty was explaining what had happened to this pure origin. For both Germanic scholars of the nineteenth century and Reformation Anglo-Saxonists three hundred years earlier, the answer—as for Macaulay—was Christian Rome.

In *Deutsche Mythologie* (1844), Grimm showed how the peoples of Europe had developed as families branching out from ancient, shared roots; in his *Deutsche Grammatik,* Grimm solved the problem of racial origins by restructuring the Germanic languages into families and groups. According to Grimm, the history of native poetry, *Dichtkunst,* was drastically altered by "the blighting touch of Christianity," which caused "the freedom of the poetry and its roots in the people" to perish. Followers of Grimm and Lachmann sought to isolate genuine, early, and pagan Germanic culture from later layers of Christian meddling, a mission analogous to the task confronting Renaissance scholars who wished to remove traces of corrupt Roman Catholicism from the "true" stock of the Church of England. E. G. Stanley did not exaggerate when he wrote that "Grimm's method and attitude must be clearly understood [in order] to understand the methods and attitudes of Anglo-Saxon scholars for the rest of the nineteenth century and after." Stanley remarks that "scholars from the first half of the nineteenth century to the present day have followed, in varying degrees of ferocity, Grimm's relatively mild disparagement of the Christian element in the extant Germanic poetry."[33] But this trend, as is discussed in the next chapter, has been decisively reversed.

The systematic study of grammar and meter was valued not in itself, but for its power to penetrate accumulated history and take scholars directly to the pristine beginnings of their national culture. Philology lent a powerful aura of certitude to language study and textual criticism, and therefore to intellectual history (at this time inseparable from national history); philology demonstrated how these activities could be elevated to the level of the sciences. In her work on the linguistic means of dating Anglo-Saxon texts, Ashley Crandall Amos cited Rask as perhaps the earliest scholar to recognize that "linguistic forms can localize and date the works employing them." Scholars set out to study the "chronological implications of isolated linguistic forms" and, Amos writes, "aspired to create a system of objective linguistic tests that could unambiguously date all Old English poetry." Metricists in particular "attempted to identify specific linguistic changes that might serve, like chemical reagents, to put a text in chronological perspective." Amos quotes Gregor Sarrazin's 1913 statement that "effaced linguistic forms are conjured up again by the meter as if by means of chemical reagents"; the goal of such scholarship, Amos adds, was to penetrate "intervening deposits of scribal alterations" to reach the "objective and indisputable fossilized remains of the text itself, as it was first composed."[34]

The methods of Lachmann, Grimm, and Rask were not simply vehicles for originary myths prized by nationalist cultural historians: The philologists' methods themselves were produced by those same myths. The methods, however, could be formulated, presented as regulated systems, and set in an institutional situation; as subjects for teaching, methods would eventually be presented with all the prestige and certitude attached to science. Thus philology, although it was enlisted in specifically social and nationalist causes, was eventually able insulate itself from early ideological applications.

Against Philology ■

Anglo-Saxonists in England did not immediately recognize that philology was a better way of studying Anglo-Saxon language and literature than the approaches that preceded it. Kemble's early work, introducing the topic, is strident and defensive. For Kemble, Grimm's most important advance over previous philologists—John Horne Tooke and Joseph Ritson, for example, whose work Kemble ridiculed—was "*system,*" for it "enabled him to sweep away errors," correcting faulty editions on the basis of grammar alone and identifying correct forms without having to look at the manuscripts, which, Kemble said, always confirmed Grimm's hypothesis when compared to it.[35]

We can see the complex state of attitudes toward Anglo-Saxon scholarship two decades later in the work of Henry Sweet, one of the most important Anglo-Saxon scholars of the last century (who had the dubious honor of being the figure on whom George Bernard Shaw based *Pygmalion's* Professor Henry Higgins).[36] Sweet's views summarize the nineteenth-century developments, showing how thoroughly Anglo-Saxon studies had become institutionalized and confirming that the three oppositions of modern Anglo-Saxon studies—those between

"Old English" and "not Old English," "method" and "meaning," and "documents" and "culture"—had already emerged.

Sweet's views reflect both the nationalist meaning—the cultural meaning—of earlier scholarship and an intense concern with methodology that contributed to the specialization of the field as an academic subject. In 1872 Sweet edited *King Alfred's West-Saxon Version of Gregory's Pastoral Care,* declaring the text to be "of exclusively philological interest." Sweet drew the attention of "Aryan philologists in general, as well as specially Teutonic scholars" to linguistic details, but attacked those who accepted "blindly the theories of Rask and Grimm." Sweet's criticism was aimed not at philology but at English philologists who ignored manuscript evidence or failed to interpret manuscript evidence within a system of phonological change, who were "slavish and undeviating" in their adherence to manuscript readings and ignorant of "scientific" processes as Sweet understood them. In his introduction to the *Pastoral Care,* Sweet used "Old English" to refer to the "unmixed, inflectional state of the English language, commonly known by the barbarous and unmeaning title of 'Anglo-Saxon.'"[37] For Sweet, language study was the sole activity proper to Anglo-Saxonists.

Having explicitly discussed the opposition between "philological" and literary interest, Sweet then explained why one studied language, which was to acquire a sense of national history. Noting "cheering signs" of a revival of the study of English, he observed that, "even if Old English were totally destitute of intrinsic merit, it would still form a necessary link in the history of our language" (p. xi). He saw language study as a matter of national pride. In his introduction to *The Oldest English Texts,* Sweet lamented that he and other English scholars were reduced "to the humble role of purveyors to the swarms of young program-mongers turned out every year by the German universities," and that an English scholar could not compete with them "except by Germanizing himself and losing all his nationality."[38] These comments tell us that for Sweet method *had* meaning: if one had to adopt Germanic methods, one might as well be German ("Germanize himself"). Sweet's reaction was not exactly paranoid. By the end of the nineteenth century, there were 35 Anglo-Saxonists in Germany at work in 21 universities; Aarsleff produces the names of only five English scholars working in Old English at this time, a number easily exceeded by a rough count of Anglo-Saxon philologists in the United States.[39]

The guiding light shining forth from Germany universities was also resisted by others. In 1891, John Churton Collins, Oxford-educated but teaching (perhaps significantly) at Birmingham, declared that if literature were to have a future in British universities, it "must be rescued from its degrading vassalage to Philology." At Cambridge, he said, where there was already a "Chair of Celtic, a Chair of Anglo-Saxon, a Chair of Comparative Philology," a plan had been formed to endow a Chair of English Literature. But the plan was subverted and led to a chair "for the interpretation of Middle English." And there was a plan to found a "School of Literature," with Teutonic, Romanic, and Celtic branches, the Teutonic "to be subdivided into an English, German and Scandinavian section," and other divisions likewise divided.[40] Collins foresaw a "School of Literature" to be organized according to Grimm's divisions of Germanic languages. He saw the German system not as a marvel but as an abstract scheme for organizing languages that threatened to become codified as an institution. This was, however, precisely the effect of philology. It was an ideologically charged system rife with German nationalism that managed, through the mediating function of academic institutions, to lose its ideology, retain its scientific shape, and, for a time, rule intellectual life.

Many English writers became hostile towards Anglo-Saxon literary culture in this period.[41] Influential critics such as W. P. Ker, who wrote three literary histories touching upon Anglo-Saxon (published between 1897 and 1922), and George Saintsbury, who published *A Short History of English Literature* in 1898, regarded the literature as primitive—that is, as barbaric, undeveloped, and unsophisticated, or, to put it another way, "Germanic." That was the first charge against Anglo-Saxon literary culture. The second charge extended to Anglo-Saxon language and literature and was more serious; it was a charge against philology itself as method without meaning.

The nature of the objection to the primitivism of Anglo-Saxon culture is clear in the most famous reply to it, R. W. Chambers' essay, "On the Continuity of Old English Prose." Claiming that "few dogmas seem so firmly rooted as this of the decay of Anglo-Saxon civilization," Chambers challenged the views of Ker, Arthur Quiller-Couch, and G. P. Krapp, all of whom maintained that Anglo-Saxon England's was a "decadent" civilization. Quiller-Couch maintained that both Old English prose and poetry were decadent and (therefore) could have had only linguistic links to "our living Poetry and Prose." Quiller-Couch could accept philological but not cultural connections to a corrupt past; G. M. Trevelyan wrote that England before the Conquest was merely "a geographical expression," "an aggregation of races, regions, and private jurisdiction"—in other words, that it was not a civilization at all.[42] He too stressed the distance between his own age and that of the Anglo-Saxons.

Chambers' purpose was to reclaim origins by asserting the continuity of Old English literature with that of the Renaissance and insisting that the prose was historically as well as linguistically important.[43] It was because pure origins were essential not only for Old English literature, but for the Anglo-Saxonists who studied it, that the decadence of Anglo-Saxon culture had become an issue of dispute. It is significant that Chambers stressed the *continuity* of the English tradition as opposed to its isolation or periodization, its distance from the present. He defended Anglo-Saxon against the charge that it was not, as a literature, *good enough* to serve as the cultural origins of the England of the the twentieth century.

Admirers were to be found, such as Stopford Brooke, whose two histories of Old English literature appeared in 1892 and 1898, and W. J. Courthope, whose *History of English Poetry* appeared in 1895. Daniel G. Calder describes them as immersed in romantic illusions and "irritating cultural narcissism." Brooke asserted that, "Questions of race are often questions of literature," a view that suggests his acceptance of a Germanic heritage and racial outlook.[44] They valued Anglo-Saxon for reasons exactly opposite those feeding the dislike expressed by Ker, Saintsbury, and others. The difference between the idolizers and detractors was the importance of the past to the present. Admirers believed that the past was connected to present and that this link redeemed the past. Detractors considered the origin of Anglo-Saxon as language to be one thing, not to be despised since it contained data available for scientific, philological analysis, but thought Anglo-Saxon culture to be deplorable. The first charge, therefore, can be dismissed as a bias against the primitivism of Anglo-Saxon culture, a bias strong enough to devalue the literature even as it sustained interest in linguistic analysis. The second charge, which relegated philology to methodological pedantry, was important in American universities, for it helped to shape the department of English.

Philology in Nineteenth-century America ■

German nationalist perspectives were put forward at both a broadly popular level—the Grimms' fairy tales—and at the highest levels of university training; German culture was, as a result, suffused with racial and ideological arguments. Transplanted to the United States, philology nourished nationalism of a new but related kind; institutionalized in colleges and universities, it promoted patriotic goals and supplied the first methods for teaching and studying literature and language.[45]

The power of the university to instill national virtues was recognized very early in America. The first philologists in American colleges and universities were trained in Germany (the only place where graduate-level education was available) and returned to the United States well-versed in language study.[46] They promptly made philology the foundation of their own teaching and claimed that education should inspire patriotism. From the very beginning of college and university education in America, philology, including Anglo-Saxon studies and covering the earliest of the phases of English literature, was inextricable from the civic goals of the English department. The business of the department was to teach the history of the English language and a certain number of important—we would now say "canonical"—texts in a historical sequence that began, of course, with the earliest texts in English. At the MLA meeting of 1902, James Wilson Bright, author of an Old English grammar and reader, a version of which is still in wide use, declared that the philologist should take part in "the work of guiding the destinies of the country," since "the philological strength and sanity of a nation is the measure of its intellectual and spiritual vitality."[47]

As it was in England, the link of early philologists to Germany was very important. Among these philologists were James Morgan Hart (an American who studied at Göttingen), Theodore W. Hunt (an American who studied in Berlin), H.C.G. Brandt (a German educated in the United States), and Francis A. March, who did not study in Germany but who was the nineteenth century's most important Anglo-Saxon scholar. All wrote about the teaching of Anglo-Saxon and philology, but though their training seems to have been uniform, their attitudes towards Anglo-Saxon were not. Hunt asserted the need for college students to know Anglo-Saxon—to be, as he put it, "substantially conversant with First English Philology in Cædmon, Beowulf and Alfred"—but took a broad view of the place of literary knowledge in national culture and specifically commended the benefit of the study of English "to the general American public and to American letters."[48]

Hart had different ideas. He recognized literature as thought, and language only as speech. In a paper for the first MLA meeting (1883), he distinguished the disciplinary value of philology as a method—the grounds on which Anglo-Saxon could always be safely defended—and the cultural content of texts, their value as literary thought. Hart deplored what he considered the barbarianism of Anglo-Saxon culture. While he insisted that every teacher of language should study Anglo-Saxon language—that is, should be a philologist, in order to explain the history of the language—thought and culture were other matters.[49] "Were, now, the connection of thought between our King Alfred and Queen Victoria an unbroken continuity," Hart wrote, "I could spare my time." But he maintained that everything before the Conquest was as "foreign to our way of thinking as if it had been expressed in a foreign tongue." Hart was American, not British, and his reference to "our King Alfred and Queen Victoria" is especially illuminating. Moreover, the very "connection of thought" between King Alfred and Queen Victoria that Hart doubted was, shortly after he spoke, propounded in numerous essays published at her death in 1901, which was thought to have been exactly a millennium after King Alfred's.[50] His identification with British nationalism notwithstanding, Hart considered Anglo-Saxon culture adequate material for the study of language, but not for the study of "thought."

Hart's attitude towards Anglo-Saxon culture was shared by many who viewed the subject from the English perspective. The same animosity towards philology was afoot in America, where some scholars rebelled against the scientific claims of philology as apparatus unconnected to values appropriate to American education. Woodrow Wilson, then teaching at Princeton, decried the "scientific and positivist spirit of the age." Pillorying and parodying the methods of philologists (without naming them), Wilson wrote,

> You divert attention from thought, which is not always easy to get at, and fix attention upon language, as upon a curious mechanism, which can be perceived with the bodily eye, and which is worthy to be studied for its own sake, quite apart from anything it may mean. You encourage the examination of forms, grammatical and metrical, which can be quite accurately determined and quite exhaustively catalogued. You bring all the visible phenomena of writing to light and into ordered system. You go further, and show how to make careful literal identification of stories somewhere told ill and without art with the same stories told over again by the masters, well and with the transfiguring effect of genius.

Equating works of genius with stories "told ill," Wilson attacked the use of method for its own sake and mocked the application of method in the absence of suitable aesthetic criteria.[51]

Wilson was one of part of a generation of generalists who denounced overly specialized training (not, we see, a new objection to higher education). In 1895, Hiram Corson, author of *The Aims of Literary Study,* denounced the use of Germanic methods for their own sake as "piddling analysis which has no end but itself." Although philology was "a great science," he said, it was not "literature." "Students are taught methods," he wrote, "but comparatively few attain unto the proposed *objects* of the methods, which objects are often lost sight of, altogether, in the *grind* to which they are subjected."[52] If Corson, Wilson, and others rejected method—they seem to have opposed any systematic approach to studying literature except impressionism, or some equally vague assertion of mutually understood value—they left no doubt that meaning, or "objects" of method, was important.[53]

Both charges against philology—and therefore against Anglo-Saxon studies—were effective. The view that the culture it represented was, if not barbaric, too remote or foreign to care about, was easily paired with the view that philology was method without a purpose. The resulting dichotomy between literature and language is already foreshadowed in Wilson's oppositions of thought to language, and language and "anything it may mean." R. C. Alston, commenting on the decline of historical linguistics—"more frequently referred to as 'philology,'" he notes—remarks that in the modern university "the entire corpus of vernacular literature up to the fifteenth century" is regarded as "language," and everything thereafter as "literature."[54] When it became clearer that the real business of "literature" departments was "literature," and specifically literary criticism, the importance of language study decreased, and the value of Anglo-Saxon courses decreased with it. The paradigm opposing language and literature was used to distinguish factual research from interpretation, or mere speculation; to contrast objective knowledge with subjective reactions; and to rank the establishment of a text—source criticism—as the primary activity, and further work with that text—literary criticism—as secondary. This opposition came to encompass, in a sense, all three of the oppositions I outlined in my introduction in a single set.

Philology and Modern Anglo-Saxon Studies ■

In order to measure the significance of nineteenth-century thinking for the study of Anglo-Saxon culture today, it is important to review the purposes of philological instruction. In the last century in American colleges, philology was taught for two reasons. First, texts in Greek, Latin, and Anglo-Saxon were used as means to discipline young minds and build the spirit through "repetitive exercise on disagreeably difficult tasks."[55] Second, these texts incorporated a great tradition that educated citizens were expected to understand, although, as Gerald Graff repeatedly notes, culture was not actually "taught," since it was assumed that "the meanings of literature were self-explanatory and thus in need of no elaborate explication."[56] When Anglo-Saxon courses were widely required, Anglo-Saxonists could afford to present their difficult subject as a form of discipline. Nineteenth-century Anglo-Saxonists, in fact, thought that the difficulty of the subject matter was part of its benefit to students and they used it, as Robert F. Yeager put it, as a "disciplining rod."[57]

In the debate between philologists and scholars with wider, interpretive interests in literature, Anglo-Saxon studies had become connected to "research" and the "scientific" model, while educational theorists stressed the importance of teaching and writing about modern as opposed to ancient texts, in the "generalist" model (as Hunt, for example, was arguing).[58] By the second decade of the twentieth century, the movement towards generalism in the department of English decisively stressed aesthetics over history and produced a critical attitude very different from but complementary to historical analysis, New Criticism. New Criticism, focused on examination of the text without reference to outside materials, resembled and imitated, up to a point, the stress on method that distinguished philological criticism. That is, just as it was important to counter the force of historical criticism, it was important to reproduce creditable critical procedures.[59]

Thus, as Rene Wellek noted, once the "old philology with its definite methods and body of knowledge" was abandoned, critics had to put in its place "a new systematic theory, a technique and a methodology teachable, transmissible, and applicable to any and all works of literature."[60] The "old philology" was more than the study of language; it was also literary history—that is, literature with organized, historical dimensions. It was teachable because it was systematic: It consisted of rules and laws, it divided history into periods identified by major authors and key genres. What replaced it was, in the hands of Ivor Winters and others, equally "scientific." The difference between philological criticism and the New Criticism that replaced it was thus not belief in "scientific" method; early proponents of New Criticism, I. A. Richards, with his belief in "scientific psychology," chief among them, sought to establish the value of their approach along very specific, and indeed empirical lines.

Although New Criticism is often thought to mean only insistence on the autonomous status of literary texts, independent of contextual and historical information, it had a political agenda of its own. Early New Critics, as Graff and Terry Eagleton both stress, had clear social ambitions for literary criticism, since literature was seen as "a conscious ideology for reconstructing social order" in the years after the first World War.[61] But critics whose influence gave New Criticism its later—and most distinctive—voice were not political, and some of them even denied the political capacity of poetry. "[Cleanth] Brooks," Graff notes, "chose to deny that poems could assert ideas at all."[62]

In the main, Anglo-Saxon language and literature continued under the "old philology," using and refining all the apparatus of the nineteenth century. However, New Criticism did influence Anglo-Saxon studies, which—as Tolkein's essay demonstrated in *Beowulf*—had long been focused in a narrowly historical way expressive of national literary history ("old historicism," perhaps). Finally it was possible to write about the "literary merits" of texts whose literary merits had been considered minimal; such critics as Stanley B. Greenfield and Edward B. Irving, Jr., demonstrated the persuasive power of close reading to disclose the harmonies, balances, and patterns of texts.[63]

As New Criticism became established, traditional philological criticism, once fixated on the Germanic past, acquired a new, distinctly historical aspect that became known as "patristic" criticism. What was new about this kind of criticism was its attention to prose texts and ideas from Latin literature as they influenced the genesis of texts. The emphasis on Latin sources and backgrounds for Anglo-Saxon literature developed not in response to—or in opposition to—New Criticism, but in tandem with it. The mission of patristic criticism was to assert that Latin learning was a context for all medieval literature and that vernacular texts could not be correctly understood outside the framework of sacred literature. Patristic criticism not only asserted that historical background was essential, but defined that background narrowly in terms of the writings of the "Fathers of the Church"—an ample collection of texts, of course, but hardly a comprehensive index to medieval culture.

That patristic exegesis (i.e., explanations of Scriptural allegories by the Church Fathers) was a body of knowledge fundamental to medieval literature had already been asserted in 1931 by J. M. Campbell.[64] But the case was made most memorably by D. W. Robertson, Jr., and as a result the approach sometimes is referred to as "Robertsonianism." Robertson's 1951 essay, "Historical Criticism," claimed that all medieval literature, whether religious or secular in nature, was an allegory of Christian charity—a notion originating, appropriately enough, with Saint Augustine.[65]

Of particular consequence for Anglo-Saxonists was the work of R. E. Kaske, whose sympathetic review of Robertson's book accused Robertson's critics of being unfamiliar with Scripture and patristic exegesis, and whose defense of exegetical criticism extended to *Beowulf*. In *Critical Approaches to Medieval Literature*, Kaske and E. Talbot Donaldson debated the merits and failings of patristic exegesis.[66] Donaldson argued that historical critics put the requirements of their thesis before the artistic nuances of their texts, even as he demonstrated their misreadings of texts and contexts. "At certain periods source study, philology, historical orientation, and even some of the techniques of the new criticism have tended to obliterate the meaning of the poems with which they have associated themselves," Donaldson wrote (p. 25). He noted (with a wit notably absent from most discussion of the topic) that "such activities as source study, investigation of historical context, philology, editing, and patristic exegesis are salubrious vacations from the awful business of facing a poem directly," and then cautioned that for "a good many people the interest implicit in such studies and the fun of them will become more important than the poems themselves." In turn, Kaske asserted that the writings of the Fathers were "a sort of massive index to the traditional meanings and associations of most medieval Christian imagery," thus confirming the disquieting impression that "Robertsonianism" did intend the Church Fathers to speak for all medieval people.[67]

It is unfortunate that the assumptions of exegetical criticism were, apart from the work of Robertson, never presented in book-length form. The most influential practitioners of exegetical criticism in Anglo-Saxon—Kaske, Thomas D. Hill, and J. E. Cross—never developed the assumptions of patristic criticism in the context of a debate about, as opposed to an assertion of, the method; closer scrutiny (in the form of book reviews to extend and critique the method) would have been productive. Nonetheless, Kaske's exegetical analysis of *Beowulf* inspired numerous studies tracing the origin of Anglo-Saxon poetry and prose to Latin exegesis, and his influence is not to be doubted. Robertson's arguments about medieval texts were refuted more vigorously by R. S. Crane, who was not a medievalist, than by scholars working in either Old or Middle English. Crane observed that Robertson's method was bound to find confirmation in the texts, since Robertson began by assuming that his thesis about medieval literature was true. Robertson, said Crane, assumed that all medieval literature was about a single theme: the texts were "always allegorical," even when "the message of charity or some corollary of it is not evident on the surface."[68] Crane denounced the ahistoricism of New Criticism and that of Robertsonianism for the same reason. His point was not that the former seemed to dismiss historical circumstances and concentrate on the text "in itself," while the latter seemed to make the intellectual and historical context all-important, but that both began with unexamined assumptions, what Crane called the "high priori road."

There can be no doubt that Robertson intended his claims to be sweeping. The first page of *A Preface to Chaucer* quotes—in order to contest—David Hume's statement: "Mankind are so much the same, in all times and places, that history informs us of nothing new or strange in this particular. Its chief use is only to discover the constant and universal principles of human nature." Robertson argued instead that the people of the Middle Ages and their literature were interesting to us precisely because they were not like us; his perspective, I hasten to add, differs greatly from that taken by Hans Robert Jauss in his well-known work on the "alterity" (or "otherness") of medieval literature.[69] To account for the differences between their world and aesthetics and ours required Robertson to compose an exposition of their worldview. Robertson chose "the tendency to think in terms of symmetrical patterns" as the chief characteristic of the medieval mind (pp. 6–8) and allegory, clothing truth with a veil of fiction (pp. 15–16), as the predominant literary strategy or technique. He devoted most of the book to elaborating the medieval doctrine of love and order and, with some apology for his method, used Chaucer's texts to illustrate the general principles of the "background materials" (p. ix). This concept of "background materials" served as a new origin—an origin in Latin culture—for Anglo-Saxon literature.[70]

Robertson established the dominance of Latin in the study of medieval literature. He assisted in directing Anglo-Saxon studies away from Germanic or native culture to Latin, learned culture. Some reference to standard literary histories will demonstrate the influence of patristic criticism in helping refocus Anglo-Saxon studies on the Christian, Latin tradition. The 1949 edition of George K. Anderson's *The Literature of the Anglo-Saxons* (revised in 1966) analyzes both poetry and prose, but does not discuss Latin "sources" except in the case of King Alfred and the homilists, who translated Latin texts. In 1967, C. L. Wrenn wrote that Latin writings in Anglo-Saxon England were of "only indirect and secondary interest," and should be considered for the "light these may throw on Anglo-Saxon thought."[71] In 1965, Stanley B. Greenfield, in *A Critical History of Old English Literature,* only touched on the allegorical or patristic tradition and treated Latin and Anglo-Saxon prose together in a section of the book designed to convey "social and cultural history," since the prose tradition was clearer—although later—than the poetic tradition and could be used to clarify the poetry. But the revised version of Greenfield's history, with Calder, titled *A New Critical History of Old English Literature,* and published in 1986, contained an entire section on Anglo-Latin, written by Michael Lapidge. It begins with the assertion, "If we are properly to understand

Old English literature, we must know something of the circumstances and context in which it was composed; in short, we must study the Anglo-Saxon church."[72]

This assertion was fully in accord with Wellek's "old philology," what we would call traditional literary history, but not with the really *old* philology of one hundred, or even fifty years ago. By the 1970s, Anglo-Saxon studies had a completely new face. Volumes of sources and analogues appeared (not only Latin sources, however); volumes of essays about the sources of Anglo-Saxon literary culture, and projects related to them, multiplied. In just twenty years—from the mid 1960s to the mid 1980s—Latin, once a "background," had become a major component of Anglo-Saxon literary culture. The pagan North of Germanic philology, and the attendant (implied) barbarism of Anglo-Saxon literature, receded rapidly before the new wave of ecclesiastical learning, a *fons et origo* worthy of the name. The most striking change in Anglo-Saxon studies demarcating this period from the earlier part of the century is the replacement of the Germanic, nationalist ideal as an object of the scholarly search for origins with an entirely new point of origin—or, in modern parlance, "source"—for Anglo-Saxon in Latin literary culture. The origins desired in the last century were supposed to exist in the woodlands of Northern Europe; the origins desired by Anglo-Saxon scholars in this century seem to be in Rome, or failing that source, a monastic library in Anglo-Saxon England. When New Criticism asserted itself, Anglo-Saxonists were slow to grasp that their fortunes were falling with those of philology and historical criticism. And when this realization dawned, Anglo-Saxonists did not chose to fight on enemy territory. They did, it is true, begin arguing the literary merits of Anglo-Saxon literature, but this was a battle they were destined to lose, not because Anglo-Saxon lacks literary merit, but because its literary merits could not, apart from translations, be reached except through mastery of the language. There was no escape from philology, or so it seemed. Indeed, many scholars seem not to have considered New Criticism as anything more than another modernist fad, permissible in the study of modern literature but having little usefulness in the study of Old English texts. Those who had learned their philology well might be indulged if they chose to dabble in New Critical ideas, but they were not to be encouraged.

New Criticism sought to remove literature from the control of philologists and textual critics—and therefore from Anglo-Saxonists. These latter scholars were left with texts to edit and language to study, nothing more, and both activities were seen by non-Anglo-Saxonists as preliminary to literary criticism—a distinction between "lower" or textual criticism and "higher" or interpretive criticism. The orderly and ordering procedures of philology had little to do with the tasks of the rest of departments of English, which by the 1970s had moved through three phases in the United States: the philological, the historical, and the New Critical. Anglo-Saxon studies fared very well in the first two phases, finding in the first and second ample opportunity to develop textual-critical tools. Historical criticism brought the study of Latin sources and made them a predominant influence; New Critical work balanced these two phases by concentrating on the formal analysis of poetry. In other areas of the English department, including Renaissance studies and eventually studies in Chaucer and Middle English, further development followed as various kinds postmodern criticism were established. Separated from these periods, Anglo-Saxon scholars shunned more recent critical practices and regarded them as worse than new ways of applying critical approaches to texts in order to produce "readings" of them. Some of these approaches, they recognized, sought not only to overturn traditional interpretations of texts but to undo interpretive traditions themselves. Postmodern critical strategies invited wide-ranging inquiries into the structure of language, the relation of writing to speaking, and the role of origins in culture—a range of topics of obvious and fundamental importance to Anglo-Saxon studies. But in a reaction wonderful for the simplicity of its assessment, Anglo-Saxonists considered postmodern criticism appropriate for modern texts, but stuck to traditional philological analysis for their own.

The Search for Sources ■

The consequences of this decision are obvious in the two directions taken in Anglo-Saxon studies today: first, traditional literary criticism that identifies itself as "interpretation," and, second, traditional philology, work with language, manuscripts, and sources that does not directly concern itself with literary interpretation or critical readings (in the sense of New Critical interpretation). One can see this split in criticism published up to 1985. Anglo-Saxonists sympathetic to New Criticism, and aware of the need to discuss literary meaning, tended to write about poetic texts rather than prose. Alongside this work, Anglo-Saxonists interested in sources emphasized prose texts, and early in the 1980s launched the large-scale projects to study sources and lexicography that today dominate Anglo-Saxon studies. Having seen them in the larger historical context of Anglo-Saxon studies, we may now take a closer look particularly at how these projects influence Anglo-Saxon studies and how conscious they are of their hermeneutic function.

Although they are not, of course, limited to prose, these projects collectively reinforce the view that the study of Old English prose and its sources could be seen, early in the decade, as the direction in which Anglo-Saxon studies in the 1980s needed to move.[73] The emphasis on prose is significant, since many prose texts in Anglo-Saxon are translations or paraphrases of Latin sources. The scholarship of Germanic Anglo-Saxonists was, by contrast, chiefly devoted to poetry. Antagonism to "Germanic" myth in the sources projects is clear, since the role of German or native culture competes with the emphasis on Latin sources that the source projects favor.

I described these projects in Chapter One as frequently cited indications of the vitality of the discipline. The most ambitious and impressive of them, and certainly necessary, is the new *Dictionary of Old English.* Large-scale editing and lexicographical projects have long been linked to Anglo-Saxon studies, a tradition begun by Laurence Nowell's Elizabethan manuscript dictionary, an important step in Renaissance attempts to establish and systematize Anglo-Saxon scholarship. As we see in the case of the Early English Text Society (EETS) in the nineteenth century, dictionaries do not simply analyze existing texts. Rather, they influence methods of editing, the study of language, and the institutionalization of scholarly practices.[74]

The first priorities of the *DOE,* as set forth in 1973, are all related to producing new editions and analyzing the defects of available editions. The editors have declared that their first steps will be to fill in gaps left by previous editors—that is, to complete the corpus—and to supply newly detailed and reliable manuscript and linguistic evidence. Thus the project involves enlarging and altering the edited corpus of Old English texts, bringing into print texts as yet unedited, and re-editing those for which significant new manuscript evidence has been discovered since the previous edition. The editors intend to make "full use of the lexicographical work of the past," to "begin with a new and exhaustive collection of materials," and to "take a fresh look at Old English vocabulary."[75]

Given that the new dictionary has inspired many editorial projects, an assessment of its potential influence requires that we review the philosophy its editors advocate. The direction of editorial philosophy urged by the *DOE* is not Lachmann's but Bedier's. In his outline of recommended editorial procedures for texts produced for the *DOE,* Helmut Gneuss observed that the editors of Old English texts "have hardly ever made an attempt to reconstruct a critical text from the variant readings of several [manuscripts] or by means of conjectural emendation as is feasible and usual in classical texts." Gneuss recommends that editors choose as base texts "the oldest MS or the one believed to be closest to the original."[76] It should be noted, however, that although the search for a manuscript least likely to need correction is different from Lachmann's search for the Ur-text, it is a procedure as potentially ahistorical as Lachmann's own; it requires decisions about the "best" manuscript to be made in linguistic or philological terms, rather than in terms that measure significance in more culturally specific ways (e.g., number of copies made). Aarsleff's brilliant assessment of Bedier's "deconstruction of the origins doctrine"—that is, of Lachmannian editorial principles and the historical myth-making on which they were founded—should not only remind us of the ideological basis of philology, but also prompt us to inquire into the ideological assumptions behind the textual practices that have replaced Lachmann's.[77] Bedier's own ideological preferences—especially after Aarsleff expresses approval for their good common sense—are all the more difficult to spot.

The source-study projects seeking to catalogue the sources of Anglo-Saxon "literary culture" underscore and amplify the traditionalizing influence of the dictionary without the benefit of extended discussion of theory. The British organ, *Fontes Anglo-Saxonici,* is "a register of written sources used by authors in Anglo-Saxon England," a "large collaborative project aimed at identifying all written sources which were incorporated, quoted, translated or adopted anywhere in English or Latin texts which were written, probably or certainly, in Anglo-Saxon England." The *Fontes* intends to produce nothing less than a *sentence-by-sentence* register of sources for Anglo-Saxon texts rather than a general reference to Latin sources. This project will catalogue the results of a century-long hunt for sources, identify "what gaps still remain in our knowledge," and close them—more gaps like those of damaged manuscripts to be filled by editors confident of their abilities to make whole. The project is to be organized in two ways: first by listing sources for individual works, and then by listing all authors and works used as written sources. The *Fontes* hopes to enlist the energy of "young scholars, who may perhaps have little new information on sources to contribute themselves," and whose chief duty appears to be "putting the whole range of existing source studies into the *Fontes* fixed format." In other words, their role is to be for the most part clerical. There is an implication that the "major" work has been done, and that new scholars (i.e., graduate students) can make careers of moving around the pieces, although the *Fontes* literature, with a defensive candor rare in the "sources" explanatory literature, insists that contributing to the project "is not a simple mechanical exercise" but is instead "an advance in scholarship."[78]

The *Sources of Anglo-Saxon Literary Culture* (SASLC) is also described as a "collaborative project that aims to produce a reference work providing a convenient summary of current scholarship on the knowledge and use of literary sources in Anglo-Saxon England." It is intended to "complement other research tools," including the *Dictionary*, major bibliographies, and the *Fontes*. *SASLC* is intended to serve "as a preliminary publication to the larger, more comprehensive" *Fontes* project, but in fact the two projects are simultaneous.[79] *SASLC* defines its subject somewhat more broadly than the *Fontes*, however, including "less clear-cut evidence such as allusions to unnamed sources." It is not going to "present new research on source problems and related questions," as the *Fontes* seeks to do, but will be a summary of currently available information.

Although apparently distinct in scope and purpose, these projects function together in a complex network under the supervision of a few stalwart hands. To outsiders witnessing all this productivity, it seems that various groups of scholars are calling on colleagues to join a range of complementary projects designed for some larger audience. But in fact those who respond are also those calling for response. The boards of directors of these groups overlap and indeed are sometimes difficult to tell apart.[80] The appearance of widespread cooperation among many Anglo-Saxonists translates into cooperative ventures organized by a few.[81] Just as these projects share objectives, they share limitations. I will outline five. First, they have not defined key terms, including "fontes" and "books known," or "sources" or "literary culture." Obviously knowledge of sources increases our knowledge about literary culture, but "sources" can be variously defined according to the degree of dependence on the text that is the source. Is the *fons* of the Latin text a "beginning," a "source," an "origin," or a "cause" for the Anglo-Saxon? "Source" can mean these things, and more. No effort has been made to differentiate the various literary operations implied in this critical vocabulary. The discussion of "books known to the English" raises a basic theoretical problem in almost every word, since "books," "known," and indeed "the English" are all terms that require specific definition if we are to avoid characterizing Anglo-Saxon literary culture entirely in modern concepts. Many important works known to the Anglo-Saxons were hardly "books." Ogilvy's usage was anachronistic in 1967; surely a less misleading term, one distinguishing a text from its "title," perhaps, or at least a "text" from a "book," is needed. To "know" a book could mean to read, recite, listen to, copy, interpret, or remember a book; and there are other possibilities as well—for example, books "known of."

Second, these projects concentrate on the written aspect of the term "literary," thus further limiting the already oppressively textual reconstruction we have of Anglo-Saxon literary culture—a culture of the book, indeed, but also less exclusively a culture molded as well by oral tradition. Since the oral tradition was not recorded, it cannot of course be catalogued. But this tradition is not even accounted for in the source projects, although a theoretical model for the oral transmission of written texts—and the written transmission of texts once known only orally—is crucially important.[82] Failure to conceptualize culture as more than writing, and failure to see that texts are events as well as documents that can be spoken or written, are a key shortcomings of the picture of Anglo-Saxon literature and culture created by the source projects. Textually interactive processes—memory, for example—have no place in the sources models, although we are confident that memory was an important way to modify as well as retain texts in the Anglo-Saxon period.

Third, the projects emphasize Latin sources in a paradigm of translation that only partially represents evidence from the period. Latin texts are assumed to be the sources of those in the vernacular, as if Anglo-Saxon literary culture "progressed" from Latin to Old English as learning became more generalized. King Alfred would seem to be the chief inspiration, but this is a misleading reconstruction of Anglo-Saxon literary history. We know that the textual relations of Anglo-Saxon literary culture were more complex than the simple translation model ("from" Latin "to" Anglo-Saxon) allows. Once translated, Latin texts did not disappear; they "lived," as it were, in two languages. Moreover, new Latin texts were written as often as extant texts were translated. Vernacular texts were sources for Latin texts as late as the twelfth century, when Anglo-Saxon laws were translated into Latin, as were some other codes. Moreover, vernacular sources sometimes served as sources for other vernacular texts; and some texts may have had no source apart from inspiration. Some Anglo-Saxon authors such as Ælfric worked regularly in both languages; and King Alfred likewise worked in a world that was officially bilingual.

Fourth, source scholars have not fully considered the ends to which their research will be put. The identification of a Latin text as the source for a text in Old English seems to be self-explanatory, but it is not. The literary life of the information contained in that explanatory gesture is not accounted for. No attention is given to either the reader of the Latin or its writer, or to the readerly/writerly character of the Anglo-Saxon handling the source. What is the point of constructing a hypothetical model of the materials used by Anglo-Saxons authors? What will be the effect of such a model once it is made available, in updateable form, to every Anglo-Saxonist with a computer terminal? The power of such a system to influence scholarship—to control its direction—is alarming, for once *SASLC* and the *Fontes* are available, the corpus of criticism will include an entirely new, and potentially confining, layer. While the corpus of Anglo-Saxon primary texts is being modestly enlarged to meet the needs of the *DOE,* the corpus of textual commentary (sources, analogues) is growing much faster. As these projects increase the philological data to be gathered, they are not necessarily increasing the *knowledge* available, although they are multiplying tools and tasks.

Fifth, rich theoretical issues, themselves the subject of Anglo-Saxon texts, are ignored by the sources projects, which regard them as "thematic" (if they regard them at all). Until very recently, Anglo-Saxonists have taken little interest in theoretical issues outside the confines of historical criticism (patristics) or source criticism. This failure is, I believe, related to a failure to appreciate the importance of theoretical issues in the texts and culture we study. Anglo-Saxon texts present problems of language, interpretation, and translation—not merely as themes, but as large-scale cultural conflicts. Although the sources projects do not pretend to have solved these problems, they do present paradigmatic contexts that invite solutions along predetermined lines (e.g., from Latin to vernacular, concern only with written textual processes, etc.). Questions of reading and writing in Anglo-Saxon texts are devalued in the context of source study; such complex cultural issues as conversion, expansion, and the relationship of literacy to social position and authority are smoothly processed, and participants in related disputes (e.g., King Alfred) are understood to be advocates for those causes the scholars themselves champion (e.g., democratic government, literacy, social harmony, etc.), speaking for the causes, as it were, on the critics' behalf.

The sources projects posit a world of literary relations in which Latin governs vernacular as an older, superior culture determines the lower, newer culture. The intellectual universe of possibilities is Latinate; the sophistication of the vernacular culture is measured by its ability to recapture and understand Latin. Sources even promise to bring order to the chaos of the entire world of undated, anonymous Old English texts, although why, and for whom, we do not know. Although few Anglo-Saxonists writing about sources have attempted to rationalize their project, two examples displaying "the self-consciousness over methods and approaches that has characterized contemporary analysis" appear in a collection of essays, *Sources of Anglo-Saxon Culture,* presented at an early conference on the topic.[83] Let me summarize these discussions with reference to sources, and in particular with reference to their regard for previous scholarship—that is, to their identification of origins.

The first essay is I wish to discuss is, in a way, typical of current attitudes about source study. Addressing Anglo-Saxon literary history with a focus on the Old English poem *Christ III,* Thomas D. Hill de-emphasizes both historical and theoretical issues. Hill notes the lack of dates and known authors that bedevils this history: "the study of Old English poetry in relation to its sources will not necessarily permit us to date or to localize any given poem, but it could permit the literary historian of this period to analyze the relationship of one text to another with much more assurance and objectivity."[84] He also observes that once a source is known, the critic can speculate from the poet's choice to his "educational background and his attitude towards vernacular poetry." In other words, what we cannot know about Anglo-Saxon poetry because we have no evidence we can infer once we have additional evidence from Latin texts. Latin sources become the basis for an entire construction of Anglo-Saxon literary culture. In order to rationalize this model, Hill first organizes Christian Latin literature in a "descending order of sophistication." The objectivity of the construct for the vernacular texts can thus be ensured, since it would be "an ordering of Old English poetry on the basis of source study," an ordering "at least reasonably objective."[85]

A second essay in this *Sources* collection, written by Colin Chase, offers a view of sources inclusive of both historical perspective and critical theory.[86] This essay expresses a rare appreciation of the complexity of the seemingly routine subject of sources. Chase notes that source study invokes ideas of original genius, cultural origins, and the origins of scholarly methods; to study sources is, as he points out, to study origins. Chase's essay sets source study firmly in the context of nineteenth-century source criticism and portrays it as a kind of historical writing. He observes that, according to the *Oxford English Dictionary,* the first use of the word "source" to indicate "a work . . . supplying information or evidence (especially of an original or primary character), as to some fact, event, or series of these," appeared in William Robertson's *History of America,* written in 1778. One might add that John Lingard's history of the Anglo-Saxon church (1806) demonstrates comparable use of the term; in his preface he notes that he makes "frequent reference to the sources, from which I have derived my information," and comments that he has drunk "at the fountain head," or the pure sources of the Anglo-Saxon church.[87] Chase also notes the irony of using a concept perhaps "foreign or even incomprehensible" to the Anglo-Saxons to illuminate their culture, and draws attention to important issues about source studies—their indebtedness to Germanic scholarship of the last century, the appropriateness of using the post-Gutenberg concept to describe literary relations in an early medieval culture—that deserve renewed attention. Chase explains that the study of sources is related to the concept of "original genius" as well as to "the origin and spread of scientific textual criticism." Commenting on the relevance of contemporary criticism to source study, he writes, "We need not become deconstructionists to accept that the questions they have asked bear important implications for our study."[88]

Philological or textual criticism has been ascendent in Anglo-Saxon studies for precisely the reason that it is not seen as "meaning producing" or hermeneutic. In discussing the relationship of textual criticism to the classics, Jerome J. McGann has stressed that the editing of modern texts—what he terms "national scriptures"—calls for different procedures from those applied to biblical and classical texts.[89] Data about modern texts are much more abundant than data about classical texts, obviously, a point that forms the heart of McGann's call for critical procedures that not only produce a text but also take into account the text's reception in periods subsequent to its appearance. McGann has helped to restore an understanding of textual criticism as a practice that attempts to define various stages of a text's existence, rather than focusing on one moment only and thus culminating in the production of a "definitive" edition.[90]

Anglo-Saxonists who maintain the distinction between interpretive criticism and bibliography or textual criticism can heed the words of the traditional scholars Richard Altick and James Thorpe. Both argue that textual and literary criticism are interdependent and that both practices are hermeneutic. "All literary students are dedicated to the same task, the discovery of truth," says Altick at the beginning of *The Art of Literary Research.* He goes on, "Some prefer to regard themselves primarily as critics, some as scholars; but the dichotomy between the two is far more apparent than real, and every good student of literature is constantly combining the two roles, *often without knowing it*" (p. 3; emphasis added). Altick articulates the traditional division acknowledged in Anglo-Saxon studies: the "critic's business is primarily with the literary work itself," while the scholar "is more concerned with the facts attending its genesis and subsequent history" (p. 3). In much the same vein, Thorpe writes that "the role of textual criticism is to provide essential mediation between the author and his audience, between the creator and the responder." Thorpe allows for the hermeneutic function of textual criticism—"the textual critic is a go-between," he writes—and thereby puts textual criticism on the same phenomenological plane as literary criticism. Although he does not explore the implications of this link, Thorpe relates textual scholarship to history, and as he does so he illuminates one of the reasons why scholars are so concerned with gaps in texts, traditions, and critical apparatus (e.g., editions). Textual criticism, he writes, has a place in "the preservation of our literary heritage." It is, he says, "often a small place." He continues:

> Its practical importance hinges on one simple fact: the texts of the works which constitute our literary heritage become progressively corrupt. The process of the transmission of a text is full of chance for error at every step of the way. . . . A text is never self-correcting or self-rejuvenating, and the ordinary history of the transmission of a text, without the intervention of author or editor, is one of progressive degeneration.[91]

Thorpe's reference to "progressive degeneration" connects the paradigm of progress, the traditional view of textual scholarship in Anglo-Saxon studies, to attitudes towards historical writing. It combines the popular, traditional idea—that progress is a legitimate paradigm for improvements in scholarly methods—with another popular attitude, that history is decay that textual scholarship halts. In other words, textual scholarship preserves the tradition by preserving the texts on which the tradition depends. It is because textual criticism is charged with this conservative role that it is, as method, so conservatively approached. The belief that textual critics, like philologists, deal directly with texts rather than work through mediating, interpretive functions, is fundamental to the pairs of oppositions I have been discussing. Anglo-Saxonists thus are conceived of as handling in some unmediated fashion Old English and the methods needed to analyze its language and documents objectively. Because the corpus degenerates, scholarship must preserve it by maintaining the documents and completing the tasks of editing and analyzing them. Philological analysis, including analysis of manuscripts as well as the study of Latin sources, has already been identified as the best way to perform these tasks. The rest of the work with the corpus—interpreting it, for example, through literary criticism—is secondary. "Progressive degeneration" is fundamentally what the search for origins attempts to undo: The decay of time must be reversed and the pure beginning recovered.

Anglo-Saxonists do believe that history is decay and that the most effective means of resisting that corruption have been discovered. When, in a retrospective look at the profession in 1981, in which his share was to look into the future—a difficult and daring task, of whose pitfalls he was well aware—Carl T. Berkhout wrote that he did not "foresee any dramatic, sustained shift in major critical approaches to Old English literature and language." He added:

> The structuralists are still about, the deconstructionists will decompose for a while, and other theorists will bless Old English now and then, but what really lies ahead is a more refined pursuit of those approaches which by consensus have been the most successful, most illuminating, during the past generation or so, whether their emphasis be belletristic, philological, linguistic, historical, or a triumphant harmony of all such approaches.[92]

Berkhout is right to identify an intransigence toward theory and a complementary confidence that theory is different from the "approaches" of traditional scholarship. But the consensus about those approaches has already begun to change, in part because the community of Anglo-Saxonists has changed and because the theoretical climate has also changed. Both the community and its methods are more diverse, more openly aligned with historical and political positions, and, therefore, at least potentially more open to connection with scholars in other periods and disciplines.

The "beginning" for Anglo-Saxon scholars is the text in its original form or "best" form (to use Bedier's term). This is rather different from the origins sought by Lachmann and others. When Lachmann set out to prove that the "author" of the *Niebelungenlied* was not a medieval poet but *das Volk,* he was not searching for the origins of a poem, but for the origins of his culture. When Jakob Grimm attributed certain stages of development in Germanic languages to the "spirit," he was not thinking only of linguistic facts or the logic of their development; he too was thinking the origins of his culture. For Lachmann, Grimm, and for numerous early Anglo-Saxon scholars, origins were invested with significance of almost every kind; their desire for origins was not simply a wish to document textual or linguistic beginnings but to approach, clarify, and capture the wellsprings of their culture, its sources.

This desire for an origin rich with specific cultural meaning is ideological in that it reflects the material interests of a given class.[93] It has been replaced with a desire for origins of method. We look on Lachmann, Grimm, and others not, of course, as the founders of our social attitudes (heaven forbid), but as founders of scholarly methods, the developers of procedures for editing texts and laws for explaining language change. This desire for a method free of ideological meaning is itself part of the ideology of modern Anglo-Saxon scholarship, as particular to our age as Romanticism was to Grimm's.

The sources projects dominating Anglo-Saxon studies today, for all their learning and expertise, unfortunately perpetuate the illusion that traditional methods are neutral. That illusion is, in Marxist terms, indeed "ideological" not only in the specific sense of false consciousness, "occupation with thoughts as with independent entities, developing independently and subject only to their own laws," but also in the more general sense of an organized system of beliefs.[94] This illusion offers a self-serving concept of professional discipline in which method is always seen as prior to and productive of meaning, isolated from interested social circumstances and linked to technological improvement (more method) and therefore neutral. The problem is not with the traditional aspect of these methods—in Anglo-Saxon studies, obviously, methods of manuscript and linguistic analysis are indispensable—but rather with their exclusivity. In Anglo-Saxon studies, traditional methodologies are employed *exclusively* and unquestioningly, as if, as Berkhout maintains, the main tasks of the discipline had already been decided and now the mission was refinement rather than innovation. Thus, to the extent that modern Anglo-Saxon scholarship is concerned with origins, it is concerned with lexical origins—the earliest forms of words, for example, or the earliest use of a source or a meaning for a word—and methodological origins. Modern histories of Anglo-Saxon scholarship, dominated by the search for methodological origins, dismiss early scholars' concern for cultural and national origins as "polemic" and, with rich and unconscious irony, locate the "turning point," the point of departure from contaminated scholarship, in the early nineteenth century, a time when only the methodological elaborateness of procedures used to locate cultural origins was new, whereas the uses to which those procedures were put were already very old.

Rather than acknowledge and explore the separation of nineteenth-century method from the climate in which it took shape, Anglo-Saxonists are content to adapt those methods and neglect their context. We prefer the methods that bring us into immediate contact with the Anglo-Saxon sources; we trust as neutral methods for identifying sources and, presumably, for structuring them into "reasonably objective" hierarchies, and we assume that the structures thus made available are, if not wholly objective, at least significantly more so than earlier ways of organizing the corpus. This belief in a methodological originary point is as naive as the fascination of the Grimms with the literature of the Germanic folk. Although most of us would discount a system based on a belief in the primitive origins of culture, or such constructs as authorship by the *Volk,* we enshrine nineteenth-century developments in method as a pure origin. We see them as the beginnings of technically sophisticated and politically neutral scholarship and thus as the beginnings of Anglo-Saxon studies as we like to think we practice them.

The success of Germanic philology in surviving the ideological conditions of its early development can be seen in the extent to which philological vocabulary structures our study of early languages. One of the lasting influences of the nineteenth-century habit of dividing and subdividing cultural material into areas for academic study was the construction of language families along national boundaries. The structures established by Grimm, no less important than Lachmann's, find their echo in the introductions to virtually all grammars of Old English, where East, North, and West Germanic languages are set out and described as if those categories had always existed.[95] This was a distinction first made by Rask, who separated West from North Germanic and showed that Scandinavian and Anglo-Saxon were not as closely related as others believed.[96] As H. Munro Chadwick pointed out in 1945, these divisions and subdivisions of "German languages" shifted the vocabulary of historical-linguistic study.[97] What had been known as "Teutonic," a term for a whole group of languages, was divided into two parts, "Scandinavian" and "Germanic." This change in usage took time, and many ambiguities in "Teutonic" compared to "Germanic" remained, as Chadwick notes. Grimm's *Deutsche Mythologie,* for example, appears in English translation as *Teutonic Mythology.*[98]

This was, not incidentally, the period during which the Scandinavian element shrank in importance, at least for a time, and study of "Germanic" languages became specifically German. Rask, in a review of Grimm's *Deutsche Grammatik,* took note of the long tradition of Danish scholarship in Germanic languages, accurately pointing out that the advances of German and English scholars would not have been made "but for the emulation excited by the learned men of Denmark."[99] It is striking to see how quickly the Danes in particular lost their early reputation for philological work; Aarsleff observes that J. N. Madvig consistently reasserted Danish influence and denounced the entire range of organicist ideas about language that romantic scholars cherished. Madvig's resistance is particularly important for Aarsleff, who uses it to argue that the romantic phase of Germanic philology was not a norm—as it certainly became in Anglo-Saxon scholarship—but a "special phase" in which language was isolated from social contexts. Madvig and others, says Aarsleff, believed that "comparative historical grammar and philology do not encompass all of the study of language"; Aarsleff shares their view.[100]

Commenting on this division of Germanic languages, Chadwick wrote, at the end of World War II, apparently without irony, "In Germany the introduction of the new terminology had a most stimulating effect." He added, "It served to bring out the antiquity of the German nation and to impress upon the Germans of the present day that they were the descendants and heirs of the Germani who fought successfully against the Romans more than eighteen centuries before." The end result, wrote Chadwick—sounding very much like Macaulay at this point—was that Germany became regarded "as the head and source of all the Teutonic peoples," since Germany "had had an ancient culture more purely native and—to many people—more attractive than that of the Holy Roman Empire."[101]

"German claims to domination" are richly attested in the joint projects of philology and national history. Chadwick traced "the formation of modern German ideology" to "the first six centuries of our era," and—inevitably—to Tacitus, the Roman historian whose accounts of the Germani continue to influence our understanding of the early Germanic peoples. In his effort to explain the ascendancy of Germany in modern Europe, Chadwick did not deny the importance of "the apparent invincibility of their army," but laid great stress on their "intellectual achievements." "In particular through their discovery of the value of a University," Chadwick said, "they have actually succeeded in establishing a world domination." Chadwick found that German universities promoted "humanistic" studies (an echo of the popular refrain, "the pursuit of knowledge for its own sake") that were in England limited to Latin and Greek; that Germans contributed far more state support to education; and that in England, unlike Germany, a university education seemed to serve professional preparation, "most frequently for the Church." He added, "Among Germans of to-day it is a commonplace that all that they value most in their national characteristics and ideology is inherited from their heathen ancestors of long ago. Many are said to desire the restoration of the old forest cults in place of Christianity."[102] The return to forest cults is, of course, easy to dismiss; but Chadwick's comments attest not only to the success of German state education in instilling patriotic fervor through scholarship as well as fairy tales, but to the enduring appeal of that model to English scholars even after two world wars.

Part 2

New Language and Old English

4

Deconstruction and Reconstruction of the Origin

Progress and Politics ■

If the study of Anglo-Saxon texts in earlier periods, or "the history of the discipline," is to be incorporated into the teaching of Anglo-Saxon language and literature, those who teach medieval literatures, Old English in particular, will have to reach out to the new language—really many languages—of contemporary criticism. As a first step, the oppositions I have been discussing—between "Old English" and "not Old English," method and meaning, and texts and culture—will have to be reconciled. This task becomes more manageable, and more obviously necessary, when the oppositions are consolidated into a single opposition between history and philology, two "languages" medievalists already speak. In this pairing, history includes "not Old English," "meaning," and "culture"; philology is restricted to "Old English," "method," and "texts." So long as philology is understood, in Wilhelm Dilthey's words, as "a *personal skill and virtuosity in the scrutiny of written memorials,* " other interpretive procedures "can prosper only in association with philology," which must precede them. The "originary priorities" of philology, according to Eugene Vance, created traditional medieval disciplines. They are based on the "romantic belief" that "written language, though it is external to consciousness (whether individual or collective), nevertheless bears the stamp of that consciousness." As they analyze textual traces, philologists—and medievalists more generally—undertake "the exegesis or *interpretation of those residues of human reality preserved in written form.*"[1] They study "textual traces" in order to approach the consciousness of those who wrote the texts.

That texts give direct access to consciousness is not a proposition one finds in Anglo-Saxon studies, where it is considered too philosophical. The consciousness contained in Anglo-Saxon texts is seen as consisting of a pure and stable set of ideas and values; whether these ideas and values have been molded by textual systems, such as rhetoric or grammar, or by other forces in the culture that Vance calls "determinants"—for example, ideological pressures—is likewise not considered, since it is seen as a political matter rather than a literary or philological one.[2] The possibility that authorial consciousness is not itself a pure origin, but that it is instead determined by cultural and textual constraints, such as patronage or systems of education, is one of many theoretical questions about reading and writing that Anglo-Saxon studies have managed to avoid.

J.G.A. Pocock's contrast between the "history of consciousness" and "the history of discourse" frames this limited idea of "consciousness" in terms that incorporate the reader into the interactive process of textual reception. If consciousness is seen as static, a record of what the author *did*, a text remains only "a cultural artifact inscribed with a certain finality and published." In contrast we can speak of "discourse." By considering what the author "was doing," not only in writing, but in dealing with the world, we can examine more than the artifact: we also examine both the author's "acts of discourse" and "acts of discourse performed by others in response." The history of discourse is "concerned with speech acts that become known and evoke response"; it includes the response of all readers, whether they are contemporary with the text or come after it.[3]

Traditional Anglo-Saxon studies, engaged in what I have called "the history of the document," defer discussion of these and other equally important matters, assuming instead that the "meaning" of the text is arrested at the stage of consciousness we assign to its author or original audience. In pursuit of the history of the document, traditional medieval studies have compounded the romantic illusion of unmediated access to consciousness, as if philological method could approach consciousness without the mediating presence of those who studied the Middle Ages before them. Thus Anglo-Saxonists study texts as if they contained the traces of Anglo-Saxons only, and had no part of the consciousness of those people who followed them.

But the "textual residue" on which philological analysis is performed holds the remnants of more than one culture, for, at every point, our awareness of the Anglo-Saxons is mediated. It is mediated in manuscripts, which have histories of ownership and which often contain commentary, whether medieval or early modern; in editions, which represent texts within the confines of textual-critical reconstructions; and in critical commentary, the layers of analysis and argument about the text and its various meanings. Those layers, literally present on manuscript pages and in the apparatus of editions of Anglo-Saxon texts, are as directly involved in "Anglo-Saxon studies" as the Old English texts themselves. To isolate only one layer—that of language, for example—and to organize its data in a linear fashion around a conceptual program (for example, recovery of the earliest version of the text), is good philological procedure, but it disregards the complex history of events that surrounds the page and its linguistic data.

Isolation from sections of the Department of English in which theoretical debate has been taking place is one reason Anglo-Saxonists have not taken up these important questions. They operate instead within the reassuring confines of the paradigm of progress, a conceptual framework for knowledge that demonstrates the ultimate harmonious resolution of historical conflicts. Teaching progress requires that conflicts be presented in terms of their final resolution; teaching the history of Anglo-Saxon studies from the viewpoint of modern philology reduces that history to a series of largely mistaken ideas about language change out of which our methods slowly and painfully emerged. Teaching the history of Anglo-Saxon studies as conflict requires that we consider philology as but one part of a discussion, rather than its main part. This is a viewpoint in which the heart of the matter is not the resolution of the conflict but its constitution: what made the issue an issue, who cared about it, and why, and how Anglo-Saxon language and culture figured into the debate.

To see the past in this way is to reconceptualize "progress" as "change." As the British historian P. Carpenter has written,

> [W]henever a sequence of events is followed straight through from beginning to end and the final outcome is known, there is a strong tendency to attach more weight to endeavours which were crowned with success than those which resulted in failure. From there it is but a short step to adopt a modernistic view of the past, by applying to it the standards of the present and judging it by those standards.

Carpenter adds that much of this confusion "could be avoided if a clear distinction were maintained between progress and change."[4]

The effect of substituting "change" for "progress" is not recourse to relativism of a simplistic kind; such a substitution does not reflect a viewpoint that considers, for example, one way of teaching the Anglo-Saxon language to be as good as another. It is instead the rediscovery of what relativism means for important subjects: points of view that vary according to the persons who take them. This rediscovery is nothing more than taking the past seriously. Anglo-Saxonists of previous eras were proud of their relativism. They had no standard of professional objectivity or scholarly neutrality to adhere to; their pursuit of Anglo-Saxon language and literature was part of a larger moral purpose. Jefferson thought that the Anglo-Saxon language expressed the democratic ideals inherent in early English civilization; German philologists found Anglo-Saxon scholarship a way to identify their national origins; and American Anglo-Saxonists of a century ago thought that Anglo-Saxon studies were essential to understanding the place of one's language in one's political tradition.

Since contributions to progress now include the increasing sophistication and refinement of existing methods, such as the application of computers to "fixed formats," method *is,* in some cases, recognized as having meaning of its own. The "meaning" is progress in research in the humanities. This construct of the discipline is ideologically situated. Like other cultural and institutional constructs, it serves, and preserves, the interests of a specific professional class, not "all Anglo-Saxonists," but those of a certain training and academic position who define the cutting edge in the field and hence shape expectations and set standards for newer scholars.

Escaping the confines of the paradigm of progress requires that we identify it as a knowledge *system* held in place by tradition and authority. With the help of Michael Ryan's discussion in *Marxism and Deconstruction,* we can identify four normative beliefs that measure progress: positivism, idealism, naturalism, and objectivism. Following Ryan, I approach these characteristics from a deconstructive perspective. My purpose in characterizing Anglo-Saxon in terms of these four ways of regarding knowledge is to show how they limit our scholarship and to propose that, by confronting these assumptions, Anglo-Saxon studies can actively engage contemporary questions of cultural relevance by recognizing and analyzing the relativism that governed the study of Anglo-Saxon culture in the past.

Ryan seeks to establish the political and philosophical similarities between Marxism and deconstruction. To do so he outlines four "brands of knowledge" in a construction that I am using to schematize some prevailing attitudes in Anglo-Saxon studies. I have borrowed this rather formidable list as a way to present, in philosophical terms, some assumptions included within the broadly humanistic claim that knowledge constitutes growth, and therefore that history, when understood as the acquisition of knowledge, is marked by progress as opposed to change.[5] Ryan identifies these four as assumptions against which both Marxism and deconstruction "either explicitly or implicitly, write." He notes that he is thereby extending Derridian deconstruction in a political direction; Derrida, Ryan writes, "points toward, but does not develop, the conclusion that all knowledge (of the social world in particular) is a terrain of political struggle."[6] Ryan suggests that the "workshop of scientific and philosophic conceptuality" might, "like the "capitalist workplace," be a "contested terrain where such a simple thing as analytic method can become a tool of class power, as a way of deciding who can know and what can be known" (p. 50).

Let me relate each of these assumptions to predominant attitudes informing Anglo-Saxon studies. The most important of them, positivism, bears directly on the idea of the origin and informs the others. Ryan discusses positivism in terms of linguistic phenomena, specifically in terms of the relationship between words and objects (p. 54), or the "myth of the immediate 'natural' presence of meaning" (p. 55). Positivism assumes the ability of a hypothesis to confirm real conditions; it is based on the "perfect adequation between the instruments of knowledge—concepts and words—and the world," Ryan writes. Derrida complicates the neat equation of words and the world, a foundational assumption of early language theory, through the concept of "mediacy," which asserts that nothing is ever simply "present" in a unique or original sense, but that instead it "always refers beyond itself to something other, and it is always an effect, a re-presentation" (p. 50).[7] Ryan adds, "Nothing, in other words, 'is' without presuppositions and effects, without itself being a presupposition and an effect of other things, and conditions and effects circulate and interrelate in ways that deny the stability of presence required by positivist knowledge" (p. 50). The Derridian critique of idealism claims that Western metaphysics posits unity where difference is present, harmony where contradiction exists, or, as Ryan says, "cover[s] over rupture, difference, antagonism, and undecidability" with models in which conflict is resolved (p. 53). The illusion of the ideal gives rise to viewing the history of our discipline as a metaphysical abstraction that submerges many relationships into one forward movement.

Since idealized views of knowledge are also naturalist and therefore objectivist, Ryan treats them together. The relations of production, seen as "natural," neutralize class conflict; all power relations, in fact, seen as "natural," disguise the wishes of those who rule by portraying them as the wishes of those who are ruled. Social harmony is achieved at the expense of the governed, to the benefit of those who govern. Ryan observes that naturalism has a mystifying force. "By naturalism," Ryan writes, "Marx means the effacement of history and of social genealogy; something is made to seem outside the movement of time and the productive process of society" (p. 56). Thus naturalism seeks to conceal the constructedness of meaning and the apparatus that produces meaning, while enshrining meaning itself as natural and uncorrupted. A critique of naturalism seeks to demonstrate that processes are social, contested events, and in history, not above it.

Derrida's discussion of "naturalism" explores Rousseau's claim that speech was closer to the "natural voice" of consciousness than writing. This claim supplies the basis for Derrida's analysis of logocentrism, "the universal law pronounced by a consciousness that transcends the empirical world" (p. 55). It is therefore objective, or "nonsignifying" ground "from which language as a process of reference derives," or a "purely objective" presence "which language designates and in which the process of reference ends" (p. 56). "The myth of the immediate 'natural' presence of meaning and sound in the mind permits history, production (technological artifice), and institutionality to be declared external, fallen, and secondary," Ryan writes (p. 55). Objectivism and naturalism disguise power relations and constructed relations and present them as not derived, but as having always existed.

Ryan's double construction of the territory shared by Marxist and deconstructionist thought has the advantage of supplying an institutional critique for concepts that, in most discussions of Derridian deconstruction, have reference only to the pure abstractions of metaphysics. His "four brands of knowledge" describe some of the favorite assumptions of Anglo-Saxon studies. The humanities are seen in idealist perspective, as furthering knowledge and in the process improving life; power relations within institutions are rationalized as natural or objectively ordered; history and language are viewed with rigorous positivism, with "fact" and "language" taken as evidence of social conditions. Historical and linguistic revolutions are described as "natural" and orderly transitions, even though our sources sometimes maintain, to the contrary, that they took place in conflict, and that the English language and its literature did not grow from the ground like trees. Although we allow that the development of both language and literature is consistently marked by confrontation and dissention, we do not employ models that describe the political aspects of that development.

Anglo-Saxon studies are idealist in that they entertain the image of progress that idealizes and celebrates change as improvement. Objectivism allows Anglo-Saxonists to believe that their methods of analysis are conducted independent of arbitrary judgment because they appear to be highly disciplined, scientifically proven, and reliable, if not entirely error-free. These methods are not seen to be socially produced visions that articulate the attitudes and values of their historical periods. Rather, the historical circumstances that condition them are ignored and hence, in Ryan's (and Derrida's) terms, effaced.

Applied to Anglo-Saxon studies, Ryan's analysis of knowledge systems reveals one intellectual pattern rather than four: positivist, objectivist, idealist, and naturalist assumptions are ways to impose order on potentially chaotic subject matter and to confirm the wisdom and to rationalize the methodologies those forms express and embody. Since the history of the discipline is a steady march from darkness (i.e., philological ignorance) into light (dictionaries, glossaries, etc.), progress can be taken for granted; its endpoint—our own success—is already known. Thanks to these ever-improving methods, our work is objective, codified, and at least potentially complete; it is a field of inquiry with fixed methodological procedures and assumptions; and it occupies a limited area, distinct from other disciplines but equal or superior to them in scientific rigor, and accessible to all who master the technical aspects of the subject. Progress of this kind is continuous and harmonious, achieved without apparent cost. It is a dream of humanism without history.

As Anglo-Saxon studies construct meaning along procedural and methodological lines, they effectively conceal ideological bias and present the "terrain of conceptuality," to adapt Ryan's language, as uncontested and regulated by "scientific" rather than "political" principles. This effacement of the history of Anglo-Saxon studies is, ironically, accomplished by "history," philology, and other scholarly disciplines that are used to construct a continuous, chronologically-determined series of advances. This series, in turn, offers a systematic explanation for what has happened in the past and how the present is triumphantly related to it. The series must have an accessible beginning and, behind the beginning, a mythical origin. The beginning may be a naively imagined "turning point" or sign of maturation in scholarly discourse; the origin, much more remote, a romantic image of racial or national emergence, hardly needs to be thought of, for it is only a myth suffused with ideology that has no place in modern studies of the humanities. This concept of an origin can be dismissed, of course, only because it is seen as a matter of faith rather than as a matter of fact. It is merely a metaphysical assumption.

The Plot of History ■

The metaphysical abstraction that underlies the philological project is a static model, a plot. Viewed through four centuries of development, the literary history of Anglo-Saxon England and the history of Anglo-Saxon scholarship present a plot of social progress. We see that plot manifest in the "spread of literacy" and the adjacent development of literary sophistication, both in the means of producing and distributing texts, and in aesthetic or artistic achievement. This is the most predictable plot of all, "'optimism' and the doctrine of progress which usually accompanied it," Hayden White calls it, a version of Herder's organic romanticism.[8] The plot of progress assumes orderly transitions and hence de-emphasizes conflict; it assumes shared world views rather than world views that reflect and express individual personalities and circumstances. It has but one ending: satisfaction in the present. Those historical events that lead to progress lead to us: Anglo-Saxon England is a culture on its way to being our culture. This is an assumption with powerful consequences for the aspects of Anglo-Saxon culture that are selected for study: power, military might, aristocratic status, and so forth. There are other sides to the culture, of course—indeed, many sides, as the Marxist Margaret Schlauch claimed nearly fifty years ago, and earlier Vida Scudder made similar observations in her efforts to teach medieval and specifically Anglo-Saxon culture.[9] Why those sides of the culture are rarely examined has much to do with who has been doing the examining. The example of women's literature in Anglo-Saxon England is not only the most obvious, but also the most important. "Women's issues" mattered less to Anglo-Saxon studies fifty years ago than they do today simply because, fifty years ago, there were even fewer women teaching and researching the topic than there are today. The "feminist" side of Anglo-Saxon culture has always been present, but it has only lately been recognized.

Dissatisfied with the plot of progress, I offer another model for Anglo-Saxon studies that allows for many different and simultaneous plots enacted, as it were, on the same stage at the same time. This model, which I present as a prelude to my discussion of deconstruction and Foucauldian archaeology, emphasizes discontinuity and therefore disrupts the smooth continuities of the myth of progress in writing about Anglo-Saxon texts and Anglo-Saxon studies themselves. The myth of progress visualizes the past as a straight line, a chain of cause and effect in strict chronological sequence. Before I describe in theoretical terms what it means to approach Anglo-Saxon studies not as a continuous unfolding fabric but as a web, with interconnected, interdependent strands and, depending on where one stands, several centers, I would like to offer a vivid and specific illustration of the problem intellectual history confronts.

In *The Country and the City*, a powerful study of pastoral literature and its devastating cultural consequences, Raymond Williams describes paths, lanes, and roads around his boyhood home:

> At the end of the lane by the cottage where I was a child, there is now a straight wide motor road where the lorries race. But the lane also has been set, stoned, driven over; it is a mark on the land of no more than two generations. . . . In the field with the elms and the white horse, behind my own present home, there are faint marks of a ninth-century building, and a foot below the grass there is a cobbled road, that resists the posts being driven, today, for a new wire fence.[10]

In this complex, dense image of the past, a ninth-century building is still faintly outlined; nearby a now-buried roadway is crossed by newer paths, themselves to be crossed by more paths still. The tensions preserved in this passage are both vertical (seen in the contradictory patterns imposed on one landscape in successive centuries), and horizontal (seen in the boundaries, roads, ways around and through the landscape in any one era). With depth, division, intersection, and impenetrability (in the buried obstacle that resists the fence-makers), this image of the past is not a set, or single layer, of boundaries or margins around a center, but a collection of many margins, some buried, and many connections, some suppressed. These traces, not entirely obliterated by newer paths and links, record the role of the past in the present, which takes shape around them, not in spite of them.

The earth between the foundations and the writer functions as an image for the passage of time that lies between the historian and the subject of history; it relates the historian to history in a model more complex than the direct line of progress relating past to present through a succession of turning points or technical breakthroughs. Like the layering of patterns of generations past, the passage of time separates us from Anglo-Saxon culture and mediates our experience of it: thick, partially hidden, contradictory, and uneven, the layers of the past cannot readily be reduced to a single plot without loss; it tells many stories at once, not one story (the plot of progress) in many ways. Between the Anglo-Saxon past and the primary materials we use to study it—manuscripts, new editions and histories—is a many-layered network, comprised of more than texts. It also binds together objects and ideas—things, words, and the concepts linking and dividing them. This territory has been inhabited by both amateur and professional editors and readers of Anglo-Saxon texts. Their routes over and through this material record their reception of Anglo-Saxon language and literature; that reception is attested in early editions, treatises on the language and its culture, and grammars. Their traces remain; they mediate our experience of the past.

Williams's description of his home may seem unlikely as a point of departure for a discussion of deconstruction, though less so for a discussion of Michel Foucault's "archaeology of knowledge," with its emphasis on analyzing historical documents from within the site, as it were, like an archaeologist surrounded by the layered remains and semiobliterations of past ages. William's description is rich in metaphors for modern scholarship. Intellectual history structured according to such a model can never be complete; it can never adopt the paradigm of progress; it can never claim to be objective. Nor can this model of history ever claim to approach its origin, wherever the origin is to be found, without mediation; nor can it claim that the past on which it rests—of which it consists—was merely a prologue. Deconstruction, Foucauldian archaeology, and a focus on the eventfulness of texts are three interconnected ways of making such history possible. They are three ways of demonstrating the limits of modern scholarly practices, and three ways of exploring the conceptual limits of the origin.

Deconstruction and Undoing ■

"To undo" one model of intellectual history that has strongly influenced Anglo-Saxon studies does not mean "to do without" such models altogether, any more than to deconstruct is to destroy. Nor is to deconstruct to identify oppositions, as I have been doing throughout this discussion, only in order to collapse them into each other and subvert them (that is, deny that they are opposite or even that they exist); or invert them, replacing one model of "false consciousness" with another in order to divert attention from the historical matter at hand. As a way of exposing hidden assumptions, deconstruction is sometimes said to make knowledge or learning impossible. For example, Robert Scholes has recently defined deconstruction as "the aestheticizing of all discourse, the denial that any really persuasive, or informational, or speculative discourse can exist."[11] This remark is typical of the reputation that deconstruction has acquired among scholars urgently concerned, as Scholes is, with the political and institutional consequences of literary theory. But whatever the excesses of deconstruction, humorously lampooned by Graff and others, it is a way to expose the protective covering with which modern scholarship surrounds the origin—a center it cannot do without, and yet a center with which it can do nothing.

Deconstruction exposes limits. It proceeds by identifying oppositional pairs—culture and nature comprise a classic set—showing that while they are assumed to be "natural" or given, they are instead created or produced; the "deconstructive" gesture, in the words of Frank Lentricchia, is "a dismantling that enables a more intimate kind of knowing."[12] The effect of deconstruction on Anglo-Saxon studies is the exposure of some contradictions in the account of origins offered by Anglo-Saxon intellectual history and supported by the history of the discipline. A deconstructive approach discloses the rhetorical strategies—value-laden premises set forth as "proofs"—employed to organize the language and culture of Anglo-Saxon England into a rigid definition of primary and secondary patterns that conform to the paradigm of progress.

Under the guise of organizing and presenting information (knowledge) in disinterested fashion, disciplines actually control both the knowledge and access to it. A deconstructive analysis identifies the originary status of the data on which a discipline claims to be based as the creation of those who claim to follow the discipline. Using such an analysis, we can reveal and trace the rhetorical maneuvers by which Anglo-Saxonists have given Anglo-Saxon England both originary status and the form its objectivity requires it to have—the great periods of Anglo-Saxon literary history (the age of Bede, the age of Alfred, the age of Ælfric); families of languages and dialects; distinct literary genres; and other stereotypical forms into which data is poured. These and other assumptions have become premises long ago accepted as scientific, objective, and hence independent from us.

Looking back to Ryan, I take two essential ideas common to positivist and idealist thinking: the pure, simple origin, the place from which one begins; and the logic of cause and effect that explains the development of an orderly history leading from the origin to the present. Derrida's critique of the origin as a unified, simple and pure presence forms part of his discussion of Rousseau in *Of Grammatology.* Derrida's "effort to formulate an organized multiplicity of origins" has been analyzed by Rodolphe Gasché: Gasché describes

> the classical concept of origin as a point of presence and simplicity to which reflection tries to return as to an ultimate ground from

> which everything else can be deduced. The pluralization of the origin is a first step toward a deconstruction of the value of origin. This deconstruction begins with the recognition that the source or origin is characterized by a certain heterogeneity: "at first, there are sources, the source is other and plural."[13]

The lost origin is conceived of as a totality; deconstruction attacks this notion of totality, of a self-contained complete unity from which all else derives. No Anglo-Saxon scholar believes that such an origin could be recovered, of course. To do so would be to return to a prelapsarian world, or something equally unimaginable. Rather, one finds that Anglo-Saxonists—Renaissance, romantic, and modern—believe in the fragment, or part, as that from which the system of the whole can be reconstructed. That is, we find Anglo-Saxonists seizing a text—a homily by Ælfric, Bede's *Ecclesiastical History*—as a fragment from which the entire civilization of early England can be deduced. The fragment thus serves as the center or origin of the structure exterior to the origin and built around it. Derrida illustrates that this opposition between center and structure is contradictory. He denies the possibility of identifying that which is exterior to the origin, since the origin itself is exterior and is found only in the structure given to it by those who are in search of it. Without a fixed origin, the structure supposedly centered on and governed by the origin cannot be said to be grounded on an absolute and unchanging point; interpretation cannot cease in the identification or reclamation of the origin. As a result, interpretation cannot reach a final ground. The center or origin cannot be separated from the structure built around it, even though, in order to be identified as "the center" or "origin," it was initially assumed to be independent of structural identification. Derrida calls this contradiction—"the center that is not the center"—"coherence in contradiction." He adds, "And, as always, coherence in contradiction expresses the force of a desire."[14]

In Gasché's analysis of Derrida, the contradiction between center and structure is described by means of an analysis of Derrida's use of the terms "origin" and "supplement." Gasché summarizes the path leading to Derrida's concept of "supplementarity" as follows: (1) origins (nature, primitivism) are pure; (2) everything that comes after the origin (society, speech) is exterior, added on to the origin but leaving it whole; (3) there is no rational need for these additions, but they function as "secondary origins"; (4) these "secondary origins" threaten the primary origin (they can take its place). Rather than a pure origin, we have traces of or additions to the origin. Texts about Anglo-Saxon England, structured around the absent "origin" of Anglo-Saxon England, have *become* the origin of Anglo-Saxon England. The origin, in short, is the structure thought to be built around it.

The "supplement" or trace or fragment (by which I mean here merely the text or artifact from the Anglo-Saxon period) becomes *more important than* the origin it represents. The pure origin does not exist; the supplement could have been imagined only in the absence of the origin (as theology could take shape only in the absence of a god). Thus the origin is now oddly dependent on the supplement; it has taken second place and the supplement becomes primary, and cause (the origin) has become effect (the supplement).[15]

Cause and effect are a means of proceeding from the pure origin in an orderly way that can be narrated as the progress of history. Jonathan Culler uses Friedrich Nietzche's analysis of causality to explain what it means to deconstruct a discourse: "to show how it undermines the philosophy it asserts" by identifying those rhetorical operations in the argument that produce its premises, the supposed ground of the argument. The famous example from Nietzche is a pin and a pain. We think of a pin, at least one sticking into us, as causing pain. But this is the external, logical, interpretation of the event. Seen internally, the event may be reversed: We feel the pain first and it causes us to look for the pin; "the cause," Nietzsche writes—in this case the pin—"gets imagined after the effect has occurred."[16]

By analogy, I propose a reversal of the causal relationship of Anglo-Saxon studies to Anglo-Saxon England. Traditionally, we think of Anglo-Saxon England as causing Anglo-Saxon studies—as the pin, so to speak, that causes the pain. That is, the history and language of Anglo-Saxon England, as the manuscripts preserve it, are the stimulus; Anglo-Saxon studies, our work, is the response. We traditionally regard Anglo-Saxon England as the subject and hence the cause of our work; after all, it was there first and has chronological priority. It seems to constitute the origin of our language and history and is also the cause of our work in the profession. My deconstructive act invites us to reconsider that causal relationship and to think instead of "Anglo-Saxon studies" as the cause of "Anglo-Saxon England." The methods we use to conceptualize the manuscripts, data, images, and objects of early English civilization are responsible for giving that evidence significance, fitting it into patterns that demonstrate the social and political "realities" we select for them. This does not *invalidate* the methods or make them unusable, but it does qualify and reconceptualize what they accomplish for us. It does mean that method will not lead us to the origin or certify progress or objectivity.

Deconstruction, therefore, can be used to show that our scholarship, far from being eternal and lasting, must be treated as the one thing we do not want it to be: incomplete—that is, subjective, transitory, and historically interested. Rather than tools that lay bare basic rules governing the universe—revealing, for example, the structure of plants, the families of man, or the families of man's languages—our disciplinary procedures are limited because they are self-limiting. They study only that which they make it possible to talk about, to hold up for scrutiny. The systems of truth that define and enforce the rules used to determine what can and cannot be said control both the production and the application of knowledge.

The knowledge produced is thus different from but not independent of the system that uncovered it. The principles that admit evidence into the discussion, and that dictate how the evidence can be handled, allow that evidence to assume only certain patterns and not others. In a sense, those principles constitute a mold that receives the subject of the discipline, giving it a shape that it will retain once freed from the mold and allowed to stand on its own. These principles are, of course, exclusive as well as inclusive, but once the subject has taken shape, no obvious way remains for the identification and analysis of that which has been excluded. "Deconstruction," Culler writes, "couples a philosophical critique of history and historical understanding with the specification that discourse is historical and meaning historically determined, both in principle and practice."[17]

What this suggests is that although Anglo-Saxon studies assert transhistorical, idealizing theories about their evidence, their theories are actually "historical narratives" produced by "interpreting the supposedly less complex and ambiguous texts of a period." Of course, historians want to think that they write the truth about the past and that their expression does not "affect or infect the meaning that it is supposed to represent."[18] But no more than we can contemplate thought directly can we contemplate the past directly. In the mediation—in the writing about thought, in the writing about the past—there is the feared element of corruption or infection. I identify this "infection" as ideology or interest, by which I mean the unavoidable fact that scholarly discourse is ideologically situated. The scholar's interests and aims combine with other historical factors to work against the possibility of objectivity, or what Culler calls "transparency." If this idea of "infection" is one we particularly wish to resist, it is in part due, as Culler argues, to post-Romantic notions of historical progress that always put "us" at the end point, at the point of greatest "awareness and self-awareness."[19]

Deconstruction, as Ryan shows, can be used to demonstrate how conceptual apparatus is linked to political institutions; deconstruction can also demonstrate that discourses and disciplines repress information and observations that trouble or complicate their founding claims—the origin or center around which they claim to be structured. Normative procedures and ideas become so, and retain the status of normal or normative, only by excluding other values which then acquire the status of secondary, derived, and inferior.[20] In order to reconstruct our discipline, we must look at what we have excluded: the history of our discipline. Deconstruction offers us a chance to examine the primary and secondary definitions of the texts we study; it requires us to adopt methodologies that examine what stands between us and our manuscripts, and thereby to count the ways in which our discipline makes the meaning we claim to find in our sources. Deconstruction does not destroy anything, so far as I am concerned, but the illusion that certain humanistic perspectives are either natural or neutral; on the contrary, deconstruction makes productive use of self-consciousness and can also be used to insist on the "reinsertion" of its abstracted binary pairs, identified and examined, into history.

In setting deconstructive critiques against the traditional ideas of Anglo-Saxon studies, in particular attitudes towards language, I am not suggesting that the new perspective renders the familiar obsolete—only strange, or "other," the position Anglo-Saxon studies have so often reserved for their opposition but that Anglo-Saxonists have only recently learned about firsthand. Rather, I see many reasons to show that old and new not only can but must work together, not in a new synthesis in which the differences are neutralized, but in a new acknowledgment of difference and divergence. Historical criticism, Rene Wellek's "old philology," has been synthesized with the interpretive maneuvers of New Criticism in a two-step process in which one first determines philological or aesthetic problems, and then applies either aesthetic (to philological) or philological (to aesthetic) procedures in order to produce solutions that pave the way to literary interpretations. This is what Anglo-Saxonists mean by "traditional approaches," a mixture of philological procedures and critical interpretations of texts. But such interpretations are, in the history of the subject, a very recent innovation. As evidence, I point to J.R.R. Tolkien's much-discussed essay, "*Beowulf*, the Monsters, and the Critics," as a moment (1936) in which, at last, an eminent Anglo-Saxonist claimed that historical analysis had swamped the poetic merits of the text, and set about to assert the balance between history and criticism.[21]

Deconstruction should not find a place beside New Criticism in the interpretive techniques available to Anglo-Saxonists once they have mastered their philology. It should be employed instead as an ongoing challenge to the hermeneutic mission of philology and to all the procedures Anglo-Saxonists and others routinely apply to their texts and language, precisely to take them out of the routine, and the routine out of them.

Foucault and Archaeology ■

For Derrida, contradiction between center and structure expresses desire; Foucault sees desire differently, both in relation to power and in relation to sexuality. Like Derrida, Foucault has a reputation for avoiding politics; but his commentary is usually seen as more politically engaged than Derrida's. Indeed, the three critical strategies I am using in this chapter—deconstruction, archaeological analysis, and textual eventfulness—have been chosen because they are neither explicitly political nor programmatic. Revisionist criticism should, I believe, not substitute one kind of politically oriented and theoretically programmatic and exclusive set of scholarly procedures (which is how I see Anglo-Saxon studies at present) with another (e.g., with Marxism, which is both political and theoretically programmatic).

The archaeological metaphors used by Foucault to challenge traditional intellectual history are a good point of departure for the definition of contexts in Anglo-Saxon studies. Foucault's concept of history and his program for historical study (to the extent he offered a "program" as opposed to a series of statements) are discussed in a series of studies which began in 1965. He surveyed the development of the natural sciences, social institutions, including the clinic and the prison, and sexuality.[22] His statements on intellectual history do not form a coherent "system"; the extent to which his work has been codified is the extent to which others have extended his statements in analyses of his work.[23] Nearly everyone who uses Foucault's concepts is not only interpreting them (for in application they are interpreted) but is often doing so against Foucault's wishes; he seems to have regarded the wish to write about specific conditions of economic or social history as a futile and reductive effort to posit "facts" where only elaborate "conditions of emergence" are to be seen. Politically oriented commentators on culture such as Edward W. Said, Frank Lentricchia, and Hayden White are impatient with this distinctly apolitical aspect of Foucault's work.[24]

Foucault's "archaeology of knowledge" directly challenges the continuities of conventional historical analysis, especially the history of ideas. His model for history is not a search for continuity or plot, but a disclosure of discontinuity and contradiction. He writes a new kind of history (which has been called "antihistory," but this term seems to me misleading in a semantic field already very problematic).[25] The problem of history, Foucault writes, "is no longer one of tradition, of tracing a line, but one of division, of limits; it is no longer one of lasting foundations, but one of transformations that serve as new foundations, the rebuilding of foundations" (p. 5).

Foucault's most important statements about literary history treat "the questioning of the *document*." Historians, Foucault says, have become accustomed to using documents as a memory bank from which to reconstitute the past, "an age-old collective consciousness that made use of material documents to refresh its memory." Like the "Annales" historians, to whom he is often likened, Foucault focuses on discontinuity rather than a smooth evolution of ideas (the plot of progress).[26] He writes, "The document, then, is no longer for history an inert material through which it tries to reconstitute what men have done or said, the events of which only the trace remains; history is now trying to define within the documentary material itself unities, totalities, series, relations" (pp. 6–7). He juxtaposes the document to "the monument," a metaphor as important to his intellectual construct as the idea of archaeology. Let me examine briefly the relationship of documents to monuments, their appearance to the archaeologist-historian, and the meaning of these elaborate ideas for Anglo-Saxon studies.

Traditional historians, Foucault writes, "memorized" the monuments of the past and "transform(ed) them into *documents*," giving them human form, as it were, by letting them speak for the past. When he says that "history is that which transforms *documents* into *monuments*," he means that documents are treated as silent and inert things seen as constituted by forces and relations to other things:

> There was a time when archaeology, as a discipline devoted to silent monuments, inert traces, objects without context, and things left by the past, aspired to the condition of history, and attained meaning only through the restitution of a historical discourse; it might be said, to play on words a little, that in our time history aspires to the condition of archaeology, to the intrinsic description of the monument. (p. 7)[27]

All unities of thought—all the significant developments or "turning points" that give the shape of progress to the history of ideas—should not, Foucault believes, be seen from the outside, where the historian, at the end of the story, stands.

Documents should not be humanized or be said to "speak" for the past. Foucault sees them internally instead; archaeology, a metaphor for seeing from within and looking inside, is the basis for "intrinsic description." The historian, Foucault writes, can see the discontinuities: "for history in its classical form, the discontinuous was both the given and the unthinkable: the raw material of history, which presented itself in the form of dispersed events" had "to be rearranged, reduced, effaced in order to reveal the continuity of events" (p. 8). The reductions that made possible the writing of history in the past are themselves made possible by the forms that language gives to consciousness in any era, which simultaneously enable speaking certain things and prohibit speaking other things. "Speaking is a repressive act," White comments, "identifiable as a specific form of repression by the area of experience that it consigns to silence."[28] In order to enter the written monument, the documentary record, from the inside, one must become aware of the epistemological assumptions used by historians in various epochs to constitute truth, harmony, and the intellectual and social progress that shaped "the continuity of events," what I have been calling the plot. Foucault sees the document as an impersonal monument in what Mark Poster calls a "strategy of dehumanization" that makes the familiar (that is, the accepted pattern) appear strange.

Foucault argues that disciplines of knowledge—strategies for truth-telling—are discourses of power; they do not merely explore a subject but recreate or invent that which they "gaze upon" or study. He calls discourses "practices that systematically form the objects of which they speak" (p. 49). In his early work, Foucault wrote about discourses of power in terms of two social institutions, the prison and the clinic; his later work explored the concept in intellectual history. Common to these topics is the use of power by officially designated figures (doctors, law-makers) to supervise the behavior and control the lives of others, and to do so within an institutional context. Foucault is concerned with who speaks, the site from which the discourse is spoken, and the various ways in which the speaker relates to those over whom power is exercised. These relations include everything from medical textbooks to surgical techniques, systems of classification, and so forth (pp. 50–55). A discourse thus exercises power at several levels simultaneously; it imposes conditions on analysis that allow only certain kinds of data to be recognized while keeping other kinds from being seen.

Discourse is more than social control; this is a distinction easily forgotten because Foucault's work on prisons and clinics appeared in English translation, and came into prominence, at about the same time as his later (and more refined) development of the concept of discourse was articulated.[29] To study the operations of discourse is to study the rules through which power is exercised by the subject, a set of analytical procedures derived from observation of many practices (Foucault gives the examples of law and religious casuistry), through which the subject speaks to and directs the object, the other (pp. 32–34).

Since discourses are formed through the exercise of power, it is obvious that conflict or tension must arise in the act of expression. Hence the belief that every statement, or, as Foucault says, all "speaking," represses as it expresses insofar as it makes possible further statements about what has been accepted for expression, inhibiting inquiry into that which has been repressed. The silence is created, writes White in an explication of Foucault, because "in any given effort to capture the order of things in language, we condemn a certain aspect of that order to obscurity."[30] My aim in describing the "discursive function" of an academic discourse, and explaining how Anglo-Saxon studies constitute a particular discourse, is in no sense an attempt to engage Foucault's concept in all its complexity. Rather, I wish to use it to describe how Anglo-Saxon studies has been historically engaged with political forces—first explicitly, then implicitly, first openly and obviously, then indirectly and obscurely. To disclose these operations, and to see them in complex relation to other discursive conditions, will require a contextualization of Anglo-Saxon studies that is not only "eventful" on the level of "social control," by which I mean the overt operations of the power structure of the Church of England, for example, but also eventful in a covert way, on a rhetorical level, the level at which language meets ideology.[31] The discontinuities to be examined will be obvious clashes over public issues in written, or textual, forms—for example, contradictions, misunderstandings, and misreadings. At both public and private levels, we should remember Foucault's comment that discontinuity is not an obstacle to scholarship, but rather is its object (p. 9).

Foucault's "archaeology" is a conceptualization of how knowledge is ordered, represented, and created. It is a way of taking apart contexts to reveal conflicts hidden within them—in this it resembles deconstruction at least superficially—and a way of trying to make visible the invisible systems that order an intellectual system, and through that system, a social universe. Archaeological analysis can be applied to political systems used to acquire social power and thereby transformed into dominant social and intellectual codes. What it means to study a culture on the "archaeological level" of knowledge is to study it "on the level of what made it [knowledge] possible."[32] Re-examined in the context of

Foucauldian archaeology, Anglo-Saxon studies can be seen to be cooperating with specific political and cultural movements—for example, the recovery of texts during the establishment of the Church of England—and subsequently serving the interests of those cultural forces. Thus Anglo-Saxon studies can be said to have functioned primarily as academic or scholarly discourse, directed by political power but mediating it, and so appearing to be unrelated to the material interests that have presided over its formation.

Foucault's work is immensely valuable to intellectual history because, unlike Marxist historians, he does not insist that one totality (traditional history) be replaced with another. Instead, he has created an incomplete model that emphasizes the rhetorical nature of historical writing and the relation of that writing to many forms of power. For some of his critics, Foucault remained too distant from social issues and political engagement. While he showed that discursive analysis could be used to reveal the ideological basis of seemingly disinterested academic disciplines, he never refined the ideas or offered a complete practical model for it.

Foucault's archaeology assists deconstruction in destabilizing the idea of historical progress, a smooth chain of continuities leading from past to present; both can be used to create productive instability on the level of textual analysis. But Foucault himself remained wary of political engagement, and it has been left to his explicators, in particular to Said and Poster, to set Foucault in the context of Derridian deconstruction. Said's formulations, as I adapt them here, show how Anglo-Saxon studies, as a discipline of knowledge, include a discursive function.

Said—re-emphasizing Foucault's implicity political stance—reminds us that disciplines of knowledge, methods of inquiry, and systems of organizing data into intelligible, revealing structures, are not neutral. Instead, they assert a formative influence on the material they study. This claim allows us to say that the discipline of Anglo-Saxon studies created the Anglo-Saxon culture that it subjects to analysis and illumination. How can a discipline create what it studies? In one way: Anglo-Saxon culture exists predominantly in writing about Anglo-Saxon England. Scholarly books and articles, as well as exhibits and other cultural apparatus, vastly outnumber the artifacts and manuscripts that survive from the period. The paradox—the reversal of cause and effect—is a move essential to textual, or disciplinary, deconstruction.

Disciplines and institutions operate discursively and function as ordering agencies that express a desire for power—that power being the control of knowledge. Discursive formations, whether they are institutions or disciplines, disguise material interests, with the dominating will wrapped in disinterested language, such as scholarly claims to objectivity; but the discourse is used to justify material pursuits. Once its disinterested claims are established, especially as academic, professional objectives, the material concerns that govern and motivate the formation of the discourse seem to vanish. Said explains the discursive relationship between "what is written and spoken" as follows: "Foucault's contention is that the fact of writing itself is a systematic conversion of the power relationship between controller and controlled into 'mere' written words—but writing is a way of disguising the awesome materiality of so tightly controlled and managed a production."[33] Said's quotation marks alert us to the irony in his reference to "mere" written words. The "mere" written words in the case of Anglo-Saxon studies take form in histories and critical studies of Old English literature and language, the writing that mediates Anglo-Saxon texts as they are preserved in manuscripts and the scholarly public. It is especially important to note that we cannot avoid discursive intermediation in Anglo-Saxon studies since we cannot simply teach Anglo-Saxon texts from manuscripts, without grammars, readers, and editions, but must first write about them, translating them as we do so into our own academic discourse.

While warning against those who simply apply Foucauldian concepts as if they described social reality, Said translates "discourse" as social control and discusses "how the will to exercise dominant control in society and history has also discovered a way to clothe, disguise, rarefy, and wrap itself systematically in the language of truth, discipline, rationality, utilitarian value, and knowledge." The language of power seems to be characterized by "naturalness, authority, professionalism, assertiveness, and antitheoretical directness," and therefore maintains itself unobtrusively while controlling "the production of culture."[34] In the case I discuss, the culture being produced is the mythical culture of Anglo-Saxon England and the academic culture—and mystique—needed to preserve it.

Foucault, borrowing a concept from Nietzsche, proposes "genealogy" as a narrative that exposes rather than conceals truth claims. A genealogy is an analysis of history that does not take truth claims at face value, but instead juxtaposes the data highlighted by those claims with other data available to the historian. The declared power of history to recover Platonic, metahistorical origin depends on the demonstration of an originary point from which history continuously developed. Genealogy exposes that claim by portraying the history of a text or a movement in terms of discontinuities, gaps, and inconsistencies, identifying these as points of suppression, oppression, and conflict instead of harmonious transitions and transformations.

A genealogy is not a search for origins; indeed it makes the recovery of origins impossible. The genealogist, "if he listens to history," will find "that there is 'something altogether different' behind things: not a timeless and essential secret, but the secret that they have no essence or that their essence was fabricated in a piecemeal fashion from alien forms." The kind of history that emerges from a genealogy is not a continuum—not, for example, the plot of intellectual and cultural progress written in the conventional histories of Anglo-Saxon language and literature—but fragmentation and discontinuity. He writes,

> Genealogy does not pretend to go back in time to restore an unbroken continuity that operates beyond the dispersion of forgotten things; its duty is not to demonstrate that the past actively exists in the present, that it continues secretly to animate the present, having imposed a predetermined form to all its vicissitudes. Genealogy does not resemble the evolution of a species and does not map the destiny of a people. On the contrary, to follow the complex course of descent is to maintain passing events in their proper dispersion; it is to identify the accidents, the minute deviations—or conversely, the complete reversals—the errors, the false appraisals, and the faulty calculations that gave birth to those things that continue to exist and have value for us; it is to discover that truth or being do not lie at the root of what we know and what we are, but the exteriority of accidents.[35]

Many readers object to Foucault's relentless and ultimately reductive insistence that all discourse relates to power and that virtually all human endeavor can be reduced to a desire for control. They misunderstand this "will" as invariably evil, when for Foucault it is both necessary and sometimes good. The history of Anglo-Saxon scholarship cannot be reduced to terms of a relationship to politics and the desire for power. Without recourse to a conventional piety—that Anglo-Saxonists and scholars more generally work with the past because they love knowledge "for its own sake"—one can understand that not every project in Anglo-Saxon studies, either in its past or its present, reflects a malevolent urge to control the lives of others.

But the struggles uncovered in a genealogical or archaeological analysis do not have to be bloody; they can be as apparently benign as the inability of the ninth-century translator of Bede's *Ecclesiastical History* to grasp the syntax, and sometimes the logic, of his source. Or the struggle can involve the failure of a good scholar—Elisabeth Elstob—to find a patron for her Anglo-Saxon research and publication after her brother's death. If political motives of the first Anglo-Saxonists, and the use of the discipline to pursue power by later scholars, are striking and even characteristic of the history of our discipline, those motives are not the only points of confrontation and struggle to be studied. Genealogical analysis of Anglo-Saxon studies is timely, and even necessary to the history of the subject, because the conflict in that history, overpowered by dogma and tradition, has been tamed by the paradigm of progress.

Archaeology and genealogy create a new kind of intellectual history whose main contribution is that it prevents unified conclusions about complex events. It frustrates the ordering impulse of the historian, first by asserting the incompleteness of traditional narrative history and the false security that kind of history creates, and then by challenging the historian to rethink the treatment of documents. Rather than fit them into coherent patterns building towards great events and shaped around great figures, Foucault asks the writer to treat documents as belonging to networks of assumptions and assertions leading in directions that traditional history has chosen to neglect. Both deconstruction and archaeological analysis force a productive rethinking of continuous, progressive narratives which subsume both Anglo-Saxon texts and the early modern scholars who first studied them. I have sought to use Derridian and Foucauldian ideas to demonstrate the philosophical and the political liabilities—the conceptual limits—of continuously narrated history. These ideas foster a great deal of skepticism; one wonders if it is possible to observe their cautions and still analyze a topic in a useful way. My solution has been to use deconstruction and an archaeological description of history to demonstrate the limits of traditional methods—their exclusivity, their uniformity, their oversimplification of the past. Seen through deconstructive and archaeological perspectives, Anglo-Saxon studies appear to be structured around a naively imagined origin. This structure merely replicates another, that of Anglo-Saxon literary culture itself, which is also seen as centered on a naively imagined origin—an origin that is unified rather than multiple, an unsupplemented origin. The effect of deconstruction on the origin so seen is devastating; the structures built around the origin are built around nothing more than the idea of origin that they have themselves created. The origin is not the center that anchors the structure but the structure that anchors itself.

Such observations are nothing if not frustrating, since they undercut traditional methods without substituting other methods for them. This is why deconstruction, to take the most obvious example, cannot be posed as an alternative to New Criticism and seen as a means of arriving at new interpretations of texts. Deconstruction does not "take away" the meanings of conventional analysis but instead points to their circular nature and their exclusivity. Foucauldian archaeology makes a similar point: history contains more than progress. To place Anglo-Saxon studies in relation to the thought of Foucault, Derrida, and their numerous commentators emphasizes not only the language of criticism but also the extremely narrow limits of the scholarly tradition in the last century: philological analysis on one hand (much the stronger), literary criticism and interpretation on the other. There is more to the subject than either allows. But to describe that subject in archaeological language, or in the language of a metaphysical critique, is for me less beneficial than to describe it in the model of reception. Reception is open-ended without being formless, and structured without being programmatic. It is an integrative concept open to many strategies of reading.

Reception and Production ■

"Reception" theory, as articulated by Hans Robert Jauss, accommodates the ruptures, discontinuities, and contradictions exposed by deconstructed views of history. It does this without synthesizing "difference" into a homogenized construct in which oppositions are cancelled out and neutralized (i.e., rendered powerless) at a new level of thematized disjunction or pluralism. The reception model is particularly useful to Anglo-Saxon studies since Jauss concentrates on medieval literature and its "rediscovery" in the nineteenth century by "romantic philology." Romantic philology (the early manifestations of philology), Jauss writes, "produced only the ideology of new continuities in the form of the essential unity of each national literature, but did not enable one to draw the medieval canon of genres back into a new literary productivity."[36] The "new continuities" we have seen in the numerous shapes given to progress as a paradigm for the history of the English people and their language, and therefore to Anglo-Saxon studies. Jauss does not examine the essential unities of national literatures; instead he examines literary "productivity," which he conceptualizes as "reception."

Jauss's model of reception initially seems traditional and straightforward; in comparison to Derridian or Foucauldian concepts, it is in fact relatively straightforward, although no more traditional than the latter. Indeed, when first encountered, the "reception" model strikes some readers as almost self-evident: a constant, unchanging or "fixed" text—Bede's *History*, for example—is read or "received" in a chronologically distinct sequence of literary environments, which, although different from each other, are themselves fixed (that is, generalized, stereotyped): Bede as read in the eighteenth century, Bede as the Victorians saw him, and so forth. This is, quite simply, what is meant by traditional literary history, and it is not Jauss's concept at all.

After the manner of Hans-Georg Gadamer, Jauss uses the concept of "horizon" to link the cultural environment of a text to the cultural environments of its readers. The "horizon" expands as the text finds new readers and is realized in new environments. The text and its readers are seen as actively engaged. He asks, "If a text is an answer, what is (was) the question?" In other words, what evidence is available to document the expectations of the audience *contemporary* with the text? Jauss links this attention to the response of the early audiences with the response of the present audience. He asserts that "whoever believes that the 'timelessly true' meaning of a text is automatically available to him or to her has simply raised his or her own expectations to an unconscious normative position, and claims thereby to stand outside history." His discussion sets him apart from Gadamer, in regard to attitudes toward classicizing (pp. 30–31). By giving "back to the historical fact its basic character as an event," he says, we can define history and works of art not as classicized objects of the past but as "open field[s]" for interpretation, what Jauss elsewhere calls "the process of continuous mediation of past and present art" (p. 62).

Like Foucault and Derrida, Jauss exposes the myth of the pure origin, but in historical terms related to the position of medieval literature in the discipline of literary study. Arguing for the usefulness of "the theory and history of the literary genres of the Middle Ages," he writes, "What they may achieve, and wherein they may once again arrive at an actuality, can rather first emerge when our relationship to the Middle Ages is liberated from the illusion of beginnings, that is, from the perspective that in this period one might find the first stage of our literature, the beginning that conditions all further development" (p. 109).

The Middle Ages are not important because they led up to our own time, "not as a beginning that receives its significance only through an end that is distant from it." Rather, the Middle Ages show us literature newly forming in the vernacular, both the testimony of its historically unique conditions and "elementary structures in which the socially formative and communicative power of literature has manifested itself" (p. 109). Let us not mistake Jauss's language for that of a newly mystified origin, however; it is language that points to texts always in transition between writer and reader, and between one reader and the next.

The text is active on at least two levels, the horizon of its own time, reflected in the text and relating the text to others similar to or different from it; and the horizon of the text's later reader—a horizon that is extended with each new reader. These horizons merge; they exist in a "dialogue" between past and present in which the "pastness" of the text (i.e., its historically unique character) is preserved and set against its "presentness" (its reception by new readers). The "pastness" of Anglo-Saxon studies is a process of divergence and conflict, not the past "on its own terms," as conventional literary history prescribes them—as conflict resolved—but a past constituted by conflict on its way to resolution.

I will adapt Jauss's concepts in order to study Anglo-Saxon texts in two interactive perspectives, the textual level (semantic conflict, lexical inconsistency) and the contextual level (ideological applications and interpretations in reception). Conflict is an essential motivating force in both. Borrowing from the Russian Formalist concept of literary "evolution" (not to be understood as organic or continuous) Jauss emphasizes that "struggle" is part of the text's development, which may include a break with tradition in the text, a preference for something older that is inserted into a contemporary form. I suggest that a conversion such as is presented in Bede's story of Cædmon is one such account of struggle in a text that is paralleled in the contexts of its own and many later periods in which it was received.

The reception of the Anglo-Saxon past records the invention of Anglo-Saxon studies to serve the ideological ends of leaders in English culture and education. But in order to study the uses of the Anglo-Saxon past—the uses of Anglo-Saxon language, literature, and history—we need to do more than identify the ideological demands of Anglican theology or British imperialism. To identify such ideologies is comforting; they illuminate the past but also isolate the institutional pressures and ideological formations of the present from it. But ideological demands do not explain the deep attraction of the past for generations of Anglo-Saxonists. The reception of an early culture by a late one is not only a study of scholarly discovery but also a study of self-discovery and the invention of self-image.

How the past is received, how aesthetic response shapes the reception of the past, is a process of filtering, of admitting into discussion some aspects of the past and prohibiting others. Presiding over this process of selection is a figure of cultural significance—a scholar or politician—for whom the past has its uses. This figure functions as a gatekeeper, first as the author, and later as the readers who rewrite the text sometimes literally, sometimes figuratively by means of interpretion. In Brian Stock's terms, this figure stands at the center of a "textual community." Describing the medieval version of such a community, he writes, "What was essential to a textual community was not a written version of a text, although that was sometimes present, but an individual who, having mastered it, then utilized it for reforming a group's thought and action." The description of such a community requires both a textual and a historical basis; and it involves both audiences aware of authors and authors aware of their audiences.[37] In the language of Levine L. Schücking, an Anglo-Saxonist whose interest in aesthetics figures prominently in his Old English scholarship, this figure is a "guard" who stands "at the entrance to the temple of literary fame," a "selecting authority" who determines how a work is received by presiding over its production. Schücking was speaking of theater directors and publishers in German culture after World War I, but his analysis of how material considerations influence the course of texts in the world and thus how dramatic culture is shaped is applicable to Anglo-Saxon textual production in the Anglo-Saxon period.[38]

The Anglo-Saxonists who first forged a link between ideology and aesthetics in the sixteenth century were gatekeepers. Early scholars, drawn to Anglo-Saxon texts by their political usefulness but also by the capacity of these strange and little-known documents to reflect the scholars' self-images and to supply the illusion of origins, filtered the records they transcribed and edited. Anglo-Saxonists traditionally describe this filtering as a process of making and correcting errors, of finding or failing to follow the rules and procedures that govern our concept of the discipline today. But that is a simplistic, and indeed an ideologically motivated, interpretation of our past, transforming the struggles and contradictions of earlier scholarship into a matter of right and wrong. Indeed, such an interpretation of our past shows how we too function as gatekeepers, admitting certain features into our concept of the history of our discipline—the technical in particular—while holding back or refusing to recognize, except by historicizing in a naive way, the deeply interested and ideological motives that inspired the foundation of Anglo-Saxon studies.

The concepts described here can be used to study Anglo-Saxon texts themselves as well as the work of early scholars who used those texts for historical and ideological projects. By examining the interplay between events, actions, and ideas *in* texts and the corresponding events, actions, and ideas *outside* the texts, we can see that the history of Anglo-Saxon studies is not extraneous to the subjects of Anglo-Saxon language, literature, and history. The ideas and attitudes of readers accumulate around texts; the scholarship of each generation adheres to the subject and becomes *part* of the subject that the next generation then studies.

Hence, I wish to combine Williams's image of the "field" of his boyhood home, a model for both synchronic (or horizontal) and diachronic (or vertical) conflict, and Ryan's concept of a scholarly "field" as a contested terrain. Ryan challenges the complacency and security of traditional knowledge systems and argues that their security disguises conflict. Williams shows that his home was built over other homes and that the patterns of his life are superimposed on the patterns and the traces of other lives. I suggest that Anglo-Saxon studies can be seen as a field in both senses—as a contested terrain, and as a place built over other places, differently designed, differently experienced. Seen in these ways, Anglo-Saxon studies are interactive rather than static and fixed. The texts and contexts they involve can be seen and analyzed as events rather than as fixed statements and completed circumstances, cut off from us by history and accessible only through the complex analytical modes traditional in professional discipline.

In order to reconceptualize Anglo-Saxon studies *as a field,* we must discuss its constructions of both contexts and texts. Three hypotheses summarize the goals of this reconceptualizaton.

First, texts and events are "sites" of multiple and simultaneous conflicts. They are about conflict on many levels, from the most general level of cultural or social conflict (e.g., war), to a level of very specific conflict of competing rhetorical strategies, images, and linguistic structure in individual texts.

Second, the "eventfulness" of texts emerges only when self-consciously revisionist, and specifically oppositional, theoretical approaches confront (but do not replace) traditional modes of analysis. Although we will continue to apply traditional disciplinary methods, we must do so within the theoretical perspectives that challenge conventional expectations about textual coherence and cultural progress.

Third, the "eventfulness" of Anglo-Saxon texts requires a widened definition of both "text," to include initial and subsequent phases of a text's life, and "context," to include phases of textual production both contemporary with the text and subsequent to its own period—not just the Anglo-Saxon context, that is, but the contexts of later periods in which the texts were reproduced. The contexts that surrounded the document in subsequent ages—non-medieval and indeed modern—illuminate both the text and its cultural importance. A definition of textual criticism that is concerned with both the history of the text and with its linguistic dimension, which is always the focus of "definitive" editions, allows us to approach texts in this extended sense.

Many intellectual and literary historians have described texts as eventful. Said, for example, argues that "texts are worldly" and that "to some degree they are events, and, even when they appear to deny it, they are nevertheless a part of the social world, human life, and of course the historical moments in which they are located and interpreted."[39] Dominick LaCapra, addressing the assumptions of source criticism, believes that "all forms of historiography might benefit from modes of critical reading premised on the conviction that documents are texts that supplement or rework 'reality' and not mere sources that divulge facts about 'reality'." Documents process reality, therefore, rather than simply reflect it.[40] Along similar lines, J.G.A. Pocock proposes that we see texts as "utterances" that "compel" responses, a performative concept of historical sources that, like LaCapra's, admits "context to parity with the action." Pocock believes that as we read a text, we do not resolve a conceptual problem but rather reconstitute a performance: We view the past as a series of interconnected events and reconstitute the text as an event.[41] Jerome J. McGann asserts eventfulness in his claim that texts both mirror and model their societies.[42] And what LaCapra, Pocock, and McGann claim for history, and Said for texts, Paulo Valesio sees in rhetoric, "the dimension of language where all cultural contrasts are revealed as conflicts that, however grave and serious, never hinge on absolute distinctions; they always, at a certain level, interchange and merge some of their elements."[43] None of these approaches is simplistic in its conceptualization of documentary evidence, as the sources projects seem to be, and neither do they simply assert the political aspects of history. Pocock specifically notes that not every text (here, every source) can "be considered, exclusively or primarily, as contributory to political action."[44]

These statements address eventfulness at textual and contextual levels simultaneously: they see documents functioning in culture, and culture functioning through documents. When Jauss states, "The question of the reality of literary genres in the historical everyday world, or that of their social function, has been ignored in medieval scholarship, and not because of a lack of documents," he describes what I see as the dominant character of modern Anglo-Saxon studies as the history of the document. He laments "the humanist overemphasis on the written and printed tradition, a Platonic aesthetics according to which past literature can really be 'present' for us in a book at any moment" and stresses instead that literary genres are "primarily social phenomena, which means that they depend on functions in the lived world." When he cautions against "the naively objectivist equation of philological interpretation with the experience of the original reader or hearer," he addresses the dichotomy between method (philological interpretation) and meaning (subjective, not rigorous) in which the modern scholar's concern with lexical detail, for example, becomes the primary focus, the prerequisite, for more elaborate interrogations of the reader's response (pp. 99–100).

I began this chapter by discussing the limitations of philology without history, "Old English" without "not Old English," "method" without "meaning," and "documents" without "culture." The concept of origins, conceived within philology, is limited to the first member of each pair; it is only through a *combination* of the first with the second member—the traditional and the untraditional frames—that origins can be reconceptualized as events. For the literary historian, eventfulness begins with the document, the Anglo-Saxon text, its manuscripts, and their production. In addition to the chief text—for example, *Beowulf* or Bede's *Ecclesiastical History*—manuscripts hold other texts, such as glosses and marginalia, not always contempory with the manuscript; editions of the manuscript, and quotations or excerpts from it, extend the text and its "eventfulness." Texts seen as events relate writing to rewriting, which includes both editing and reading. Thus the relation of author to text has a parallel in the relation of reader or editor to text, for both are "rewriters": Just as the author produces the text in writing it, later readers and writers reproduce the text and produce new texts from it. Such rewriting is made possible by shared horizons that register the differences between past and present but prevent us from closing off texts as "written memorials," as Dilthey called them in the quote at the opening of this chapter, as static, fixed, and available for impartial exegesis. "Eventfulness" does not emphasize the isolation of authorial consciousness preserved in textual traces; rather it emphasizes the commonality of a text's readers and writers: Anglo-Saxons, early Anglo-Saxonists, and, of course, Anglo-Saxonists today.

Eventfulness is created by constraints, what Vance calls "determinants": eventfulness results from conflict. Texts are constrained when they are written—by the literary genres available, against which authorial desire may struggle in the urge to say something in a new way; by the statements of the author's predecessors; by the author's world view, which may be unorthodox; by the views of its readers, who may challenge the text. Texts are also the source of constraints, urging interpretations on the reader and encouraging the reader to take certain actions and avoid others. Textual eventfulness is not confined to the period in which the text was read and re-enacted by its contemporary audience, as in Pocock's distinction between what the author "did" and what the author "was doing." Instead, the text's "eventfulness" continues to engage all its readers and to respond to their desires.

Readers who approach a text as a "problem in the reconstruction of performance" are more likely to discover horizons within the text than readers who search the text for the resolution to a conceptual problem.[45] The question of origins has traditionally been seen as a conceptual problem only, a matter of searching for the points at which our scholarly practices were formed. I hope to view origins not as a solution to this conceptual problem but as a challenge to reconstuct "performance." The past I turn to now is not a romantic past or a "classic" past, "timeless," outside and above history. It is rather a social past, and it is not self-evident or fully recoverable from either text or context. The social past cannot look the same to us as it did to an earlier audience. It is a past, for all its historicity, relative to us. In *Speaking of the Middle Ages,* Paul Zumthor urges the "concretization" of texts made possible when we recall that they presuppose personal relations and that those relations involve history. "The order of desire," Zumthor writes, defines "the personal factor in our studies."[46] Williams's image resists our traditional wish to see the past "as it really was." Instead of the past "as it really was," there were many "pasts," all of them "real," all of them relative. It is to the past of Bede's *History* and its relation to the postmodern present that I now turn.

5

Polemic, Philology, and Anglo-Saxon Studies in the Renaissance

History and Philology ■

Bede's *Ecclesiastical History* is an eventful text. It has occupied numerous social and literary contexts, each a "moment" of reception for a community surrounding Bede's text. In each community, the text functions as a node within a Foucauldian network, both holding the community together and connecting it to other nodes, other texts, and other readers. These groups share horizons and are versions of Brian Stock's "textual communities." Stock focuses on an individual in each community who, having "mastered" a text, "utilizes it for reforming a group's thought and action."[1] Such individuals are gatekeepers who admit or prohibit texts and interpretations for others in the group. The concept of a textual community as I use it also owes something to Stanley Fish's "interpretive community," a social construct that influences the way an individual reads and receives texts. Readers who belong to one community read a text in a certain way; membership in such a community is sufficiently stable for "interpretive battles to go on" and sufficiently unstable "to assure that they will never be settled." Fish proposes this concept in a discussion of the Milton *Variorum;* it is a model especially appropriate to the history of reading Bede's *History,* which might well be called the "Variorum Bede." Abraham Wheelock's edition of the *History* in 1644, in fact, deserves precisely that title.[2]

Bede's text serves as a focus of communal interpretation and eventfulness at various levels, ranging from manuscript study, early and modern editions, and introductory Old English textbooks, to the *Norton Anthology*. These levels are opportunities to align the horizons of a contemporary reading audience with those of an Anglo-Saxon audience and an audience of Renaissance readers. Our awareness of Anglo-Saxon history and textuality is mediated through the consciousness of those who have contemplated Anglo-Saxon culture before us. This claim is not new, and the following versions of it will prepare us for a discussion of how editions and textbooks impose philology as a medium between us and the manuscripts and thus condition our awareness of the historicity of Bede's text in the name of seeing the past "as it really was."

One of the most significant protests against the developing distance between Anglo-Saxon records (history) and modern scholarly methods (philology) was made over 55 years ago by Kenneth Sisam in a lecture describing the achievements of Humphrey Wanley (1672–1726), the eighteenth-century Anglo-Saxonist whose catalogue Sisam calls "the key to the Anglo-Saxon manuscripts."[3] Sisam saw Wanley's work as a mixed blessing, for he was "so good an intermediary that the study of Anglo-Saxon tended to be cut off from the manuscript sources which should vitalize it." After Wanley, scholars saw no need for "all that slow rummaging in manuscripts and commerce of manuscripts so characteristic of the early English tradition." Sisam lamented that with Wanley "another stage was reached in the divorce of philology from history." "For," he concluded, "palaeography touches history at every point."[4]

Another Anglo-Saxonist who asserts the importance of manuscript contexts, broadly defined, is Fred C. Robinson, author of several studies arguing that medieval texts should be edited with their manuscript contexts—what he has called their "most immediate contexts"—in mind. Robinson's views are particularly important because he addresses editorial procedures. In an account of his examination of a manuscript of the *Anglo-Saxon Chronicle* (London, British Library, Cotton Tiberius B.iv), Robinson describes his initial impression that the manuscript was of "plain, unpretentious, utilitarian appearance," and that its binding was late, "probably nineteenth-century," and could therefore be "excluded" from his "range of responses." Then he came upon two pages larger than the others but folded to conform to their size. These folded pages proved to contain annotations by John Joscelyn, secretary to Matthew Parker and one of the most important Renaissance scholars of Anglo-Saxon. Robinson realized that in the nineteenth century a binder had trimmed the volume, cutting away the margins of all pages except those containing Joscelyn's notes. The codex, he realized, was not at all "modest," but rather "stately," and its history was more likely to have been distinguished than not.[5] The binder trimmed the pages of an ancient book, as if, after a millennium, the space on the page needed to be presented as economically as a modern printer would have wanted it. Luckily, in the case of Joscelyn's notes, the binder at least had respect for Anglo-Saxon literature "in context." Anglo-Saxonists of all stripes will agree that this type of "not Old English" work by other readers and writers is an important link between Old English and us.

This manuscript of the *Chronicle* offers a graphic image of my subject. In the nineteenth century, a curator's *idea* of an Anglo-Saxon book intervened drastically into the manuscript's history. Because the margins were worn, torn, or otherwise damaged, most of whatever evidence they contained was removed. Thus it happened that, except for two pages, what the sixteenth century added, the nineteenth century took away. And just as manuscripts were shorn of commentary attesting to their post-medieval meanings, the subject of Anglo-Saxon studies itself was stripped of its historical accretions, so that the philologist in the language laboratory could confront the Anglo-Saxon artifact unimpeded. "Accretion" is a messy model for historical narrative, but it is an archaeological metaphor that captures the density and complex interrelatedness of early Anglo-Saxon studies. I shall explore the metaphor in my discussion of Bede's *History* in the hands of early readers and editors.

Robinson demonstrated the practical consequences of treating a part of Bede's *Ecclesiastical History* in its manuscript contexts. Many medieval writers (or their scribes) concluded texts with requests for prayers from readers for the author's (or copyist's) salvation. In four of the vernacular manuscripts and in several Latin manuscripts, Bede's petition is given the form of two prose paragraphs, which I give below as Parts One and Two (the second of which at one time belonged to Bede's preface). But in a fifth vernacular manuscript, Cambridge, Corpus Christi College, 41 (from the eleventh century), the petition is in three parts; the third section, written in alliterative meter, asks not for prayers but for support from a "ruler of the realm" or secular authority.[6] Robinson suggested that this three-part text, clearly composed by different authors, could be considered an "envoi," a form of closure that is directed to the attention of a specific person. The text is as follows:

> (*Part 1.*) And I beseech you, Good Savior, now that you have mercifully allowed me to drink sweetly the words of your wisdom,

> that you also allow that I may at last come to you, the fountain of all wisdom, to appear eternally in your presence;
> (*Part 2.*) Also, I humbly beseech further that among those to whom this story of our nation may come, to be read or to be heard, that on behalf of my weaknesses, of both mind and body, they will often and eagerly intercede with the celestial mercy of God almighty; and that in each of their territories they will bestow on me this measure of their reward, so that I, who sought eagerly to record whatever I considered memorable and worthy of the inhabitants' thought concerning various provinces, or more important regions, might in all things obtain the fruits of their virtuous intercession.
> (*Part 3.*) I also beseech every man who is ruler of a realm (or) lord of men, who might read this book and hold its covers, that he kindly support the writer who wrote this book with his two hands so that he (the writer) may finish with his hands yet many more (works) according to the Lord's wish. And may the Lord of the heavens, he who has power over all, grant that (request) to him (the writer), so that he may properly acclaim his Lord until the end of his days. Amen. So be it.[7]

This "envoi" had "never been allowed by editors to stand as the composit unit which it was intended to be." Editors did not print it at the end of text, where it occurs in the manuscripts; they also printed the prose and verse parts separately. Robinson sought to "present a text of complex authorship and prose-verse form in the composite, integral state that its last shaper intended it to have."[8] He rejoined the sections of the text and thereby introduced this part of the text of one of the most famous of all Anglo-Saxon compositions to a modern reading audience.

But Robinson's edition does not account for all the "eventfulness" of this text, which is formatted on the manuscript page differently from the rest of the *History*. The script of the "envoi" is much larger than that used for main text; the lines are written in alternating brown and red ink ornamented with gold.[9] Both features would be difficult to transmit in print; but both are important to the appearance of the text on the page. The manuscript context of the "envoi" is also more complex than an edition could reasonably be expected to show. Robinson printed photographs of the three manuscript pages containing the three-part envoi (these are pp. 482–484 of the Cambridge text), a particularly good idea, given the inaccessibility of the manuscript. One who examines these pages will be astonished to see that each is covered with writing that has nothing to do either with Bede's text or with the "envoi."

The margins around each section of the "envoi" are filled with text of Masses and liturgical forms, written in crowded, small script. On page 482 is a liturgical text concerning John the Baptist, and Peter and Paul; on page 483 is the beginning of a Mass for the sick;[10] page 484 holds an illustration of Christ and a homily for Palm Sunday based on Matthew 26:27.[11] These additions are all subsequent to the "envoi" and were clearly transcribed onto these pages precisely because, as part of the design of the manuscript's creators, space used to emphasize the conclusion of Bede's text was available when a later copyist ran out of room. Already in the eleventh century, the Corpus Christi manuscript was caught up in a dense web of historical and textual events. The glorious aesthetics of one era gave way to the perhaps pedestrian need for space in another. Those conditions have much to tell us about copyists' attitudes towards texts; they form a material part of the reception of Bede's *Ecclesiastical History*.

One could hardly find scholars more admired than Robinson and Sisam for what Wilhelm Dilthey called "personal skill and virtuosity in the scrutiny of written memorials."[12] But their emphasis on manuscripts and on the work of early Anglo-Saxonists with those manuscripts contains the kernel of an unorthodox but very important point: If we dismiss the early modern history of a manuscript as "not Old English," we render the historical meaning of the manuscript purely in terms of philology. If we focus on manuscript contexts, we come into contact with other readers and can recognize the relationship of their interpretive strategies—the hermeneutic nature of their work—to interpretive strategies of our own.

Bede's text presents a challenging opportunity to teach Old English in a postmodern way—in a way that uses critical theory to confront conventional ideas about the remoteness of the past. If we teach the text in the context of its manuscript and later editorial reception, we pursue the study of language *in* history rather than *outside* it: we study Old English in the context of "not Old English." As we do so, we experience the self-reflexivity of teaching about reading and writing, or textual production, in the past as one reads and writes in the present. And other, less limiting preconceptions are challenged, in particular the tradition separating poetry from prose and the consequences of this practice for the expectations of a reading audience.

Robinson's observation that editors of the "envoi" printed its prose and poetic sections separately, each part without regard for the other, is a good place to begin discussing the reception of Bede's text, which is entirely in Latin prose, but which, in the Old English version, includes one very famous poem, "Cædmon's Hymn." The distinction between poetry and prose is an editorial convention reflected at both the level of a student's introduction to literary analysis and the level of an introductory Anglo-Saxon course. Such a course usually begins with examples of Old English prose translated from Latin, including Old English translations of the Bible, in particular the Book of Genesis, and Ælfric's *Colloquy*, especially interesting because it takes the form of a dialogue (a device imitated in a popular introductory textbook)[13]—and was used to teach Latin through Old English.[14] The function of the text is difficult to guess from a modern edition, in which the Old English, a gloss on the Latin in the manuscript, is printed in large type, and the Latin, the main text in the manuscript, is printed as a gloss.[15]

The use of prose early in the course is strategic. For many reasons, including elaborate diction, parataxis (lack of coordinating conjunctions or subordinate clauses), and alliterative meter, Anglo-Saxon poetry is much more difficult to read than prose, especially the prose found in relatively straightforward Old English translations of Latin texts. We can see this difference in the contrast between an Anglo-Saxon version of the Gospel and "Cædmon's Hymn." When the serpent asks Eve why she and Adam may not eat fruit from all the trees in Paradise, she replies, "Of þara treowa wæstme þe sind on Paradisum we etað": "We may eat the fruit of the trees that are in Paradise."[16] A transliteration—"Of the fruit of the trees that are in Paradise we eat"—can be quickly produced. The syntax of "Cædmon's Hymn" is not so simple:

Nu sculon herigean heofonrices Weard
Now let us praise of heavenly kingdom the keeper,
Meotodes meahte and his modgeþanc
the might of the creator, and his mind-thought,
weorc Wuldor-Fæder swa he wundra gehwæs
the work of the gloryfather, when he of wonders every one,
ece Drihten or onstealde
eternal lord, established (in) the beginning.
He ærest sceop ielda bearnum
He first shaped for the children of men,
heofon to hrofe halig Scyppend
heaven as a roof, holy shaper,
ða middangeard moncynnes Weard
then middle earth, the keeper of mankind,
ece Drihten æfter teode
the eternal lord, afterwards made,
firum foldan Frea ælmihtig
as a place for mankind, the eternal Lord.[17]

Much in the syntax of this short poem needs to be untangled. It is not obvious that "heofonrices Weard," "Meotodes meahte," "his modgeþanc," and "weorc Wuldor-Faeder," are in apposition (that is, all variations of the direct object); or how "swa" relates "wundra gehwæs" (each of wonders) to "ece Drihten"; or how one parses the last two lines (literally, then middle earth the keeper, the lord, afterwards made). The complexities of this short text are, of course, as nothing compared to those of vast poems, *Beowulf* being the longest, that have come to us in damaged manuscripts. Yet even the first two lines of the "Hymn" have merited notes unto themselves by eminent scholars.[18]

The use of prose to introduce Old English, a useful but unfortunate tradition, implies that prose is chiefly a form for teaching language and that, once students have acquired reasonable facility, they can move on to poetry. This sequence reinforces a prejudice many undergraduates have already, which is that poetry is literary, while prose is functional, and that literature majors should care more about deciphering poetry than prose. If the aim of a literary education is to help students admire and appreciate texts, poetry will be preferred, and, moreover, isolated from ideological analysis (i.e., politics). But if that education is to approach cultural context and engage the history of ideas, prose must be examined both for its affective merits or style and for its pragmatic function.

The appearance of "Cædmon's Hymn" in the *Norton Anthology* and in introductory Anglo-Saxon textbooks offers students and teachers the opportunity to discuss the relationship of prose to poetry at the outset. As we shall see, this is but one of several pedagogical issues that are thematized in the hymn by Bede. The *Norton* contains a translation of part of the Latin version of Bede's text, but prints the text of the hymn in Old English, with a translation (and a discussion of Old English meter). The linguistic juxtaposition is fortunate; some manuscripts of the Latin *History* include the hymn in both Latin (the form Bede gave it in) and the vernacular. A teacher with some familiarity with Old English thus has an opportunity to emphasize the eventfulness of the episode in its linguistic as well as more general textual aspects.[19]

Written in 734, Bede's *Historia Ecclesiastica Gentis Anglorum*[20] is a sweeping account of English history from the time of Gaius Julius Caesar (55 B.C.) to 731. It is also, thanks to its early and extensive manuscript tradition, a record of eighth- and ninth-century intellectual history.[21] Numerous manuscripts survive from the Anglo-Saxon period, the earliest having been written "in or soon after 737," shortly after Bede's death in 735.[22] The text was translated into Old English sometime near the end of the ninth century, but not by King Alfred, although it was long assigned to him. Bede's text appears in the list of books William of Malmesbury reported as King Alfred's translations; that attribution contributed greatly to the reputation of Bede's text in the Renaissance, when the service of ecclesiastical history to the state set scholars in the same relationship to Queen Elizabeth that Bede was thought to have had to King Alfred. It was not until Henry Sweet's *Reader* appeared in 1871 that the attribution was seriously questioned.[23]

The first modern translation of the Latin text was published in 1565 by Thomas Stapleton, a Catholic living on the Continent in exile made necessary after Mary, Queen of Scots, failed in her attempt to reverse the Reformation and Elizabeth I succeeded to the throne.[24] The first English edition of either the Latin or the Anglo-Saxon text in modern times was published by Abraham Wheelock in 1643; the edition was reprinted, with the addition of several other important Anglo-Saxon texts, in 1644.[25] In 1722, George Smith (1693–1756) re-edited both the Latin and Anglo-Saxon texts, completing the project begun by his father, John Smith (1659–1715); John Stevens translated Smith's Latin text into English in 1723.[26] J. A. Giles edited the Latin texts in an edition of Bede's works in 1843 (in 12 volumes),[27] but Smith's edition was considered standard until Charles Plummer's edition appeared in a collection of all Bede's historical works in 1896.[28] Thomas Miller re-edited the vernacular version at the end of the nineteenth century,[29] and his edition was almost immediately followed by another very different edition by Jakob M. Schipper.[30]

The *Norton Anthology* Cædmon ■

The *Norton Anthology* registers Bede's cultural presence for the widest possible reading audience. The *Norton* is a measure of fame scorned by Anglo-Saxonists, perhaps, but a wonderful opportunity for them to present their subject to undergraduate audiences and readers curious about the earliest phases of English literature. This audience of readers and teachers, as a textual and interpretive community, shares a horizon in the context of which the horizon of many previous communities can be seen. As modern readers of Bede look at Bede's text together, interpret it, and assess its values and its value, they join their concerns with Bede's. To recall the language of J.G.A. Pocock, we examine what he "was doing," not what he "did."[31] Since we have no choice but to read Bede through twentieth-century eyes, my objective is to complicate that vision and widen our horizons by aligning them with other communities held together in some sense by the shared experience of Bede's text.

The story of Cædmon presents reading and writing in an ideologically situated way. The episode is about the "textual power," as Robert Scholes calls it, of textual production, since it is about the use of writing to alter social status and redirect tradition.[32] This story, in which one author comments on the creativity and influence of another, has achieved mythical status in English literary history; it is a story whose author uses a character as a counterpart, and, I believe, a story whose character has managed to turn the tables on his creator. Cædmon is, in departments of English—if not in departments of History—arguably more important than Bede himself, for Bede wrote only in Latin, and he gave us "Cædmon's Hymn"—seen as a breakthrough for vernacular poetry—in Latin only.

The juxtaposition of Bede's authorship with Cædmon's status as author is, in any case, not frivolous, for the reader's relationship to Bede is a trope for Bede's relationship to Cædmon. Just as Bede argued a cultural thesis through Cædmon, so early Anglo-Saxonists argued their views on the English Church through Bede, and this is an interest that modern historians and Anglo-Saxonists share with them. Were it not for this "certain brother," as Bede fondly calls him, simple, unlettered, and very shy, his use of the vernacular, and the translation of Bede into Old English in the ninth century, the venerable Bede would probably not merit a place in the *Norton Anthology.* Indeed, in the nineteenth century, Cædmon was considered at least as important as Bede. The first volume of Anglo-Saxon poetry published in the post-Anglo-Saxon world appeared in 1655 as *Cædmonis Monarchi Paraphrasis Poetica Genesios;* it was translated by Benjamin Thorpe in 1832 as *Cædmon's Metrical Paraphrase of Parts of the Holy Scriptures, in Anglo-Saxon.*[33] What was then named for its supposed author is, appropriately, today known for its owner and first editor, the Dutch scholar Francis Junius, as *The Junius Manuscript.*[34] The collection begins with a poem about Genesis, so its attribution to Cædmon, whose poetical productivity Bede clearly outlines, was almost inevitable. If Cædmon had had the career Bede sketched, it would have included the writing of such poems as these—about the creation, the Exodus, the prophet Daniel, and a poem known as *Christ and Satan.* He is no longer considered to have been the author of any of these poems.

Cædmon was a simple man who lived near the monastery at Whitby and who was, one evening, given the gift of song. In the fourth book of the *History,* Bede describes how Cædmon, who had "lived in the secular habit until he was well advanced in years and had never learned any songs," used to withdraw from feasts when the harp was passed and each guest was expected to sing for the group. On one such evening,

Cædmon retired to the cattle shed, where it was "his turn to take charge" of the animals. Having removed himself from his immediate and accustomed textual community—the beer hall, where Cædmon was a would-be performer with an audience—he fell asleep and dreamed that "someone stood by him" and commanded him to sing. Cædmon replied that he could not sing and had for that reason left the feast. The figure insisted, "Nevertheless, you must sing to me." But Cædmon refused, was again commanded to sing, and this time "began to sing verses which he had never heard before in praise of God and the Creator." Bede supplies the text in Latin rather than Old English, and in a curious comment that bears further scrutiny, Bede then notes, "This is the sense but not the order of the words which he sang as he slept. For it is not possible to translate verse, however well composed, literally from one language to another without some loss of beauty and dignity." Once Cædmon's gift was discovered, his song became the center of an ever-widening interpretive community. Cædmon reported his gift to his supervisor, who in turn took him to see Hild, the abbess of the nearby monastery. There, as a test, learned men read stories from Scripture to Cædmon, who returned the next day and recited them in verse. Soon thereafter Hild "instructed him to renounce his secular habit and to take monastic vows." Cædmon joined the monastery and spent the rest of his life composing poems for the edification of the faithful.[35] His gift of song became the center of an enormous textual community whose literary traditions Cædmon, as a gatekeeper, revolutionized by adapting their content to a new form. In exactly the opposite way, he revolutionized the traditions of the community of the beer hall by adapting their form to new content.

The text, and its context in Bede's *History*, is explicitly about origins, and Bede's description of this episode has been accepted as an origin on both the literary-institutional and the linguistic level. In the modern era much commentary has been brought to bear on a conceptual problem—the question of the origins of Christian vernacular poetry in the Anglo-Saxon language—rather than on the eventfulness of the episode. The *Norton Anthology* informs us that Cædmon was "the founder of a school of Christian poetry." Stanley B. Greenfield and Daniel G. Calder (who cite several even more effusive comments), call the "Hymn" "the only authentic extant work of the first English Christian poet." They assert that the episode "lies at the heart of the fusion between native Anglo-Saxon and Latin-Christian traditions in the Old English period" and that it is "a case study of the difficulties involved in establishing definitive interpretations of Old English poems."[36] The conflict between Latin and vernacular literatures is easily forgotten in the version of that conflict supplied by Bede; the "fusion" of traditions and the foundation of "schools" of poetry are commonplace explanations that answer too easily some of the most important questions of cultural and social change in Anglo-Saxon England. Teachers discussing "Cædmon's Hymn" would do better to challenge the commonplaces rather than to repeat them.

Scholars are slightly apologetic in discussing the hymn's aesthetic merits. Sir Frank Stenton claimed that its nine lines "bear all the signs of unpracticed expression in an art which itself was as yet undeveloped."[37] But the importance of the hymn in the concept of origins and Anglo-Saxon literary history seems rarely to have been doubted. J. M. Wallace-Hadrill downplayed Bede's miracles, including this episode, saying that it was "part of the function of history to record what ordinary people believed," and that Cædmon's achievement was "sanctity working upon memorization."[38] Others have preferred to see the miracle as literary; C. L. Wrenn thought it was miraculous that an untrained singer could master a disciplined art; André Crépin suggested that the miracle was the adaptation of "ancient traditional themes and formulas to new revolutionary ideas."[39] Plummer suggested that Cædmon's gift rests on two truths, that poetry was a gift from above, and that, "in moments of heightened feeling, when 'We feel that we are greater than we know,'" we become conscious of new powers "previously dormant or non-existent."[40]

Few scholars either criticize the artfulness of the text or doubt that it demarcates a new beginning for English literature in the Christian idiom. Indeed, the "Hymn" has been a central text in the debate about oral formulaic literature in England and the preservation of Germanic elements in Christian verse. Cædmon's originality has prompted scholars to ask whether he actually *adapted* native techniques to Christian teaching, or merely *used* them as a "vehicle" for expressing common Christian vocabulary. The hymn has been compared to an episode in *Beowulf* called a "creation song" and thus connected to the "Teutonic creation myth" first discussed by Jakob Grimm and to the tradition of "catechetical *narratio*" (basic instruction in sacred history).[41] Robinson categorizes Old English poetic diction as "pre-" and "post-Cædmonian," arguing that an essentially unified, Germanic vocabulary became ambiguously Christian after the traditional verse formulas were adapted to Christian poetry.[42]

These paradigms—the power of poetry to lead to Christian conversion, transition from Latin to the vernacular, and so forth—are dangerous pedagogical devices. They assert and assume the historical value of Bede's account of Cædmon and proceed to construct literary history on it. Once freed from these comforting, pre-packaged contexts, certain features of Bede's account of Cædmon's gift require reexamination. Two of these features are among the most frequently referenced elements of all Anglo-Saxon literary culture. The native hall, with the harp at the feast, is set against the learned monastic songfest of holy worship; pagan verse from the hall is remodeled, through the dream, into Christian form. Hence the tradition of the pagan textual community is radically revised, and, simultaneously, the monastic textual community undergoes an immense transformation as the prose of Scripture, transmitted by the learned scholars to the unlearned layman, is popularized and transformed into song. The artist, having rejected pagan song, is as a result elevated in the Christian community, becoming a revered brother whose reputation rests entirely on this sudden gift. At the same time the learned teachers are humbled and become mere listeners when the student becomes the master, shades of Christ's performance before the doctors in the Temple (Luke 2:46). As the once-despised becomes privileged, the wayward individual becomes the object of communal admiration. When the voice mute in secular song suddenly, miraculously, speaks the new tongue of the new religion, the "out" becomes "in."

Bede leaves little doubt about which of these binary terms ought to be dominant; traditional literary history has accepted the episode of the hymn as a point of origin from which all moves smoothly forward. But once the traditional hierarchical relationships in the text are challenged, the text is dislodged from its conventional place in traditional literary history, where it has been frozen into paradigms of conversion without coercion and change without conflict, and conceptualized as wholeness striving for coherence beyond an artistic desire for congruence with reality. We are alerted to textual acts of suppression. The elaborately structured tale dichotomizes institutionalized discourse in an extensive arrangement of binary pairs, with one term in each pair set over the other in a gesture of appropriation, of declaring value without appearing to do so. The capacity of this text to communicate more than a traditional view of Anglo-Saxon literary history—that is, the text's eventfulness—is disclosed through deconstruction. Cædmon can be seen as countering the thesis of the text—that conversion is painless and without conflict or coercion—even as he demonstrates it. Jonathan Culler points out that deconstruction "involves an interest in anything in the text that counters an authoritative interpretation" and that deconstruction challenges the interpretation that the "work appears most emphatically to encourage." Texts "thematize" what Culler calls both "interpretive" operations and their consequences.[43] Bede thematized by deploying his oppositions in a way that silenced Cædmon and his resistance; and Bede's version becomes a conventional account of an origin, a "birth" of Christian Anglo-Saxon poetry.

Cædmon's deconstruction of Bede breaks the text into acts of speech, writing, and publication, acts that de-compose the text into what Pocock calls "the performance of many mutations in many idioms and contexts, for which the text at times appears as little more than the matrix or a holding pattern."[44] If Cædmon must be granted the historicity that Anglo-Saxon literary history allows him—that he really existed, and that something resembling Bede's narrative took place—let us go the whole distance and imagine him as an author with alternatives Bede does not mention. Cædmon himself disturbs the paradigms of Bede's narrative when he resists institutional and traditional pressures. He refuses to sing, leaves the celebration so he need not perform, and twice tells the figure who appears to him that he cannot sing. Yet, in spite of this protesting, he is made to do that very thing—he is coerced and converted by force, if only by a forceful command. Cædmon demonstrates his capacity to versify *in his sleep:* The figure comes to him "per somnium," in a dream; the Old English specifies that he reported his gift "þa aras he from ðaem slæpe."[45] Cædmon merely demonstrates the power of an outside force to move the individual to act against his will, and perhaps without his understanding. Ever dutiful and submissive to authority, Cædmon reports his new possession to the reeve, who takes him to Abbess Hild. When Cædmon has passed the tests of the learned, he is whisked into the monastery by the abbess, "who cherished the grace of God in this man." Thus appropriated, the artist is rewarded as he rises through the ranks. Formerly in self-imposed exile, skulking in the cattle shed, he is now installed as official versifier and, in a handsome irony, is compared to a "clean beast that chews the cud,"[46] when it was from the beasts he was to guard that poetry rescued him. Such are the benefits for those who direct their powers of speech to the service of God and the gospel.

Through his resistance and his acquiescence, Cædmon's deconstruction exposes the shifting and unstable grounds on which meaning rests. It leads us to the suppressed term in each pair: to "unlearned," rather than to "learned"; to "reluctant" rather than to "willing"; to "resistance" rather than to "cooperation"; to "silence" rather than to "speech." The effect of deconstruction is to de-center Cædmon's cooperation and focus on his resistance, and to show that there are, in this tale, two possibilities rather than one. It is the reader, and the reader's desire, that leads to preference for one term (cooperation, compliance) over the other. This is, in the first place, Bede's desire; he leads, we follow. Cædmon sings in Bede's voice.

Desire, says Derrida in a comment on Freud, is a contradictory unity; Freud's dream analysis showed that the satisfaction of desire required the simultaneous admission of incompatibilities. Desire for origins, as the literary history of Cædmon's hymn shows, does not recover unity but instead uncovers disunity and unites incompatibilities. The story of Cædmon describes a single moment supplied with all the ingredients necessary to furnish the beginning of a new tradition. It stands as a classical origin, which Rodolphe Gasché defines "as a point of presence and simplicity to which reflection tries to return as to an ultimate ground from which everything can be deduced."[47] But this claim to a pure, complete, single moment, narrated in a compact, unified form, conceals eventfulness—plural and contradictory wishes—and hence makes the text vulnerable to de-composition and deconstruction. The origin cannot stand without the supplement: Bede's story of the conversion of vernacular verse to religious themes cannot be told (indeed, cannot be imagined) without the addition of Old English to his Latin. The account itself is never—not even in the oldest manuscript—the whole and satisfying complete moment of origin that Anglo-Saxonists desire. It is only through supplementarity, through the marginal incorporation of the Anglo-Saxon text into the Latin, that the origin of a "Christian school" of vernacular poetry becomes possible.

Like Freud's dream, Cædmon's dream—which one more daring than I might say is also Bede's dream—admits incompatibility into the desire for unified and pure origins. Bede desired a narrative that collapsed (and reduced) native tradition and Christian doctrine into a new language and a new style; the traditional presentation of Cædmon and his hymn in English literary history, and in the classroom, not only grants Bede his wish, but may be said to fulfill a fantasy that was not only Bede's, in which the hostile proposition (pre-Christian verse) is not simply reconciled to the new proposition (Christian doctrine in verse form), but is obliterated in the process. Bede describes a narrative totality of system—the "whole course of sacred history" encompassed by Cædmon's song—and lauds its power to "turn his hearers away from delight in sin" and toward good works. But this totality of suppressed dissent is made to "tremble," is made "*insecure* in its most assured evidences" by Cædmon himself.[48]

Before Cædmon, Latin discourse in Anglo-Saxon England was a supplement to the "vain and idle songs" of the native tradition. After "Cædmon's Hymn," that relationship was reversed, and the native tradition—an origin—was replaced by the supplement. Because Bede's account of Cædmon describes a permanent change in literary tradition, Cædmon is seen as "prophetic."[49] But Bede's use of Cædmon is not prophetic as much as it is proleptic. It does not merely predict response, but also determines it. The story of Cædmon answers or replies to an objection before it has been made and responds to an event before its significance, which has shaped that response, could have been made known.[50] Bede directs Anglo-Saxon literary history to tell the story of the conversion of native poetry to holy use as Bede told it—as a story that explained the origins of Christian literature in the vernacular. His text tells us how to think about its theme for the simple reason that Bede's historical vision was an attempt to explain and justify events, not to foretell them. The originary interpretation of Cædmon reflects the originary significance long assigned to Bede himself as father of English history and father of modern scholarship. Bede's *History* is not only universally recognized as an important source for early English history but is also regarded with remarkable reverence by its modern readers as a keeper of the flame—not only of historical truth, but also of historical method. "Real history died with Bede," a recent admirer has written (Bede died in 735), "not to be reborn in England until the twelfth-century historians."[51] Donald Fry has compiled a long list of testimony to Bede's credibility among modern historians and those Fry calls "the most sophisticated professional readers."[52] Bede's originary significance is entirely the creation of those who came after him and who saw in him, through Cædmon, the beginnings of Christian poetry in Old English and the beginnings of modern historiography.

The point in countering testimony to Bede's credibility with a deconstruction of "Cædmon's Hymn" is not to parade Derridian claims about language through the *Ecclesiastical History*, but to demonstrate that the text advances what Edward W. Said calls a cultural "thesis." Texts place themselves in the world, and *are* themselves, Said writes, by "soliciting the world's attention," and by limiting "what can be done with them interpretively."[53] Historical change is one of Bede's themes and the triumph of Christianity is one of his theses. Deconstructing this text is a way to see what Bede "was doing," as opposed to what he "did," to prepare us to see Bede operating in a world of textual and social power, and to see that power circulating in Bede's *History* and in the reception of the *History* in later periods.

Cædmon in Introductory Old English Courses ■

My goal in using the episode of Cædmon to expand the horizon of textual communities in Bede's *History* is not only to produce new readings of the text reflective of postmodern preoccupations, but to construct a framework within which to view previous work with the text and to use the episode to examine aspects of the history of Anglo-Saxon studies. Excerpts from Bede's text in the *Norton Anthology* can raise these issues at the level of the survey class; anthologies of Anglo-Saxon literature and introductory grammars and readers raise them at the next level, the study of Anglo-Saxon language. The introductory textbooks have shown little variation in deciding which episodes from among the five books of the *History* are most deserving of the student's attention. *Bright's Old English Grammar and Reader* selects the conversion of King Eadwine (*EH* 2:9–11) and the story of Cædmon (*EH* 4:34), as does *A Guide to Old English* by Bruce Mitchell and Fred C. Robinson.[54] *Sweet's Anglo-Saxon Reader in Prose and Verse* includes the story of Cædmon and the arrival of the Angles, Saxons, and Jutes (*EH* 1:12).[55] *An Old English Reader,* edited by Otto Funke and Karl Jost, includes only the episode of Cædmon's hymn (with parallel Latin text from Plummer's edition of the *History*).[56] Alone among the texts I have sampled, *Sweet's Anglo-Saxon Primer* excludes Cædmon, selecting instead the description of Britain (*EH* 1:1) and the conversion of Eadwine.[57] There are many other introductory texts, of course, and I discuss only a sample of those that are currently available.

In the introductory course in Old English, the teacher can begin by suggesting that Cædmon's hymn has received much more attention than Bede's *History.* As a parallel, one may cite the frequency with which the preface to King Alfred's translation of the *Cura Pastoralis* is studied and the infrequency with which critics have commented on Gregory's text, one of the most important of all the books read in King Alfred's England. To emphasize the place of Bede's text, the *History* should be read with the Latin (and its modern English translation) at hand.[58] Bede's refusal to give the text of the *Hymn* in Old English was deleted by the translator and is apparent only when the Latin text is compared to it. Why Bede did not provide the vernacular text of Cædmon's hymn has always puzzled Anglo-Saxonists. Greenfield and Calder suggest that Bede gave the hymn in Latin "to avoid calling attention to the *Hymn*'s roots in the secular tradition." It is all the more interesting when we recall that Bede urged use of the vernacular in preaching and praying when he wrote to Archbishop Egbert, his pupil.[59] The refusal itself calls attention to some doubt on Bede's part about the institution whose beginnings he was narrating, as if Bede were of two minds about Cædmon's gift, and worried that Cædmon's artistry was combining "the new order of Christian poetry" with a degraded and dangerous native tradition.[60] Less restrained is George Hardin Brown, who comments that Bede's statement is "but a very early version of Robert Frost's remark that what is lost in translation is the poetry."[61] That the poetry should be "lost" in a story about the conversion of English poetry to Christianity seems not to matter if the episode offers yet another example of the ways in which Bede anticipated the good judgment of our own age.

In fact, quite early in the critical tradition, John Lingard suggested that the Old English text of the hymn was not as ancient as Bede. Lingard believed that Alfred had translated the hymn from Latin rather than transcribing an ancient copy already in the vernacular. It was, Lingard thought, written to be sung "to some favourite national tune." John Josias Conybeare, in 1826, thought that Lingard's thesis was not plausible, but allowed that "its direct refutation would be no easy task, and most readers would, in all probability, wish to be spared the discussion."[62] Unfortunately, Conybeare was right at least on the last point; there has been too little serious discussion of the possibility that the Old English text is significantly later than Bede's report of the event. A comparison between the language of the vernacular and Old English glosses on comparable Latin texts raises the possibility that the vernacular was created as a paraphrase of the Latin. Should this prove to be the case, or even a strong possibility, Old English literary history will be in for a refreshing period of revision of some of its most cherished commonplaces about translation and Cædmon's contribution to the tradition.[63]

Cædmon's gift allowed him to put into verse Scriptural text already translated into the vernacular. That Bede not only fails to give the poem in Old English, but also fails to give the text as a poem at all, is matter ripe for discussion. The Old English version gives the "endebyrdnes" or "word order" of the hymn, while the Latin offers only the sense, and *not* the order of the words "sensus, non autem ordo ipse verborum."[64] In other words, by turning poetry into prose, Bede reverses the process that made Cædmon famous and seems to turn against his (Bede's) own creation. As we would expect, the Old English text omits the statement about the aesthetics of translation and gives the hymn in the form of vernacular verse. David N. Dumville has pointed out that the Old English says no more than the Latin supposedly translated from it, causing him to wonder—an unwelcome thought among most Anglo-Saxonists—whether the Old English were not translated from Bede's Latin.[65]

There is, then, much "eventfulness" to be considered in the manuscripts at this point. Already in 1937 Dobbie noted that the Old English was entered as marginal text in the Latin versions of Bede's text and that it was entered in the text only in a few late manuscripts.[66] The Old English text of the hymn in the oldest manuscript of Bede's Latin text (known as the "Moore" manuscript because it was owned by John Moore, bishop of Ely, and dated *c.* 737)[67] is entered on the last folio, not in Book Four, where Bede gives the Latin, but is apparently written in the same hand as the Latin. Dobbie firmly asserts the then-standard view that the Old English was not "back translated" from the Latin, and conducts a thoroughly Lachmannian analysis of manuscripts of the hymn to reach a conclusion concerning "the words written by Cædmon himself."[68] For Dobbie—and for many Anglo-Saxonists before and after him—Cædmon, simply by virtue of having a text attributed to him by Bede, became a *writer,* which Bede never says, rather than a composer of oral texts.

Other demonstrations of textual eventfulness are apparent. They include the occasional mistranslation from Latin into Old English. For example, Bede says that the harp was passed "for the sake of providing entertainment" ("cum esset laetitiae causa decretum"), which the translator interprets to mean that the harp was passed "þonne þær wæs blisse intinga gedemed," or "when [it] was considered a cause of mirth." Thus the passage says that the instrument was passed as a cause of amusement—which, for Cædmon, it certainly was not—rather than being passed for the sake of amusement.[69] We also find in the Old English that Hild received Cædmon into the monastery "mid his godum," "with his goods," a most unmonastic observation based on a misreading of "cum omnibus suis," meaning that Hild received him "with all her [people]."[70]

Editorial introductions to Cædmon manifest significant attitudes towards the treatment of Old English texts. For example, the Mitchell and Robinson version prints the text of one manuscript, but the editors note that they have "occasionally adopted a reading from one of the other manuscripts when these seem preferable to" the manuscript they use. They do not explain what these changes are, however, or why they make them, nor do they list the manuscripts from which such readings are drawn or explain why the goal of their collection of texts is to present the language in "normalized" form as a way of making certain texts more accessible.[71] Here too is an "event" of the kind teachers of Anglo-Saxon classes often overlook: the version of Cædmon's story in this very good introductory textbook does not reproduce exactly that of any Anglo-Saxon version. Bright's *Reader* is better on this score, giving alternate readings in the textual notes, and *Sweet's Reader* does likewise. It is precisely through discrepancies in manuscript readings that students can be introduced to the manuscript evidence and historical contexts. The normalization of texts through conflation of manuscript readings, a purely theoretical demand of philology for a "standard" or norm, works against history, against language situated in specific social, cultural, and geographical contexts.

Cædmon in Modern Editions ■

When we move from the introductory Old English class to the next level, the manuscript evidence comes into full play and the text's editorial tradition opens a vast field of historical and philological connections. The Old English version of Bede's text has been edited only four times, and each edition reflects a distinctive set of editorial and textual practices, behind which we find equally distinctive understandings of what Bede's text meant and why it was being edited.

The edition published from 1890–1898 by Thomas Miller, a Cambridge scholar then a lecturer in Göttingen, who produced his text for the Early English Text Society, forms a revealing contrast to the edition published soon thereafter by Jakob M. Schipper. Miller was a scholar as close to the manuscript evidence as Sisam or Robinson could hope; his is an edition in which language and manuscript evidence were thoroughly reviewed, an edition in which philological goals were primary. This much is immediately apparent from his short preface, which notes that he began to study the text as he was preparing a work on the syntax of Anglo-Saxon texts attributed to King Alfred. He selected the oldest of the four extant manuscripts, an Oxford version from the first half of the tenth century,[72] and, since it is incomplete at both the beginning and the end, he planned to supplement it with the version in Corpus Christi College, 41, the manuscript containing the three-part "envoi" Robinson edited.[73]

As his work progressed, however, he realized that the scribe of the Cambridge manuscript had "dealt very freely with his author" and had recast parts of the text so that it was "for dialectical [i.e., dialectal] purposes comparatively useless."[74] Since he was primarily interested in the linguistic features of the text, he set this manuscript aside and adopted a "'contamination' of texts," as he called it, using readings from four manuscripts, arranged in order of preference, to construct the archetype or earliest version of the text. Miller's editorial philosophy caused him to set aside the Cambridge manuscript, which we might well consider the most "original" of the versions of Bede in Old English. For Miller's purposes, this version deviated too far from the "original" version of archetype, which, Miller believed, had been written in northern England in the Anglian rather than in the later standard dialect, West Saxon.

Miller's approach illustrates the consequences of his editorial philosophy. Initially, his approach was that of Joseph Bedier. Miller planned to present the "best text" of the surviving manuscripts, and to this end had selected two closely related manuscripts from the same rescension of the text. Later, however, he specifically wished to recreate the archetype or first version of the text rather than a single rescension, and so shifted to the approach of Karl Lachmann. In order to recover the archetype, he had to conflate the evidence of surviving versions. To do this, he relied on the two oldest manuscripts that, linguistically, stood closest to the Anglian archetypes; since these manuscripts descended from different branches of the archetype, they offered independent evidence of its readings.[75]

Miller's edition emphasizes philological detail. The first volume of his two-volume edition contains an extended analysis of the language of the manuscripts; in the second volume he printed the variations of the manuscripts from the printed text (nearly 500 pages of them), so that he made virtually *all* of the textual evidence available to the reader. The textual analysis is impressive. For example, Miller offers nearly 11 pages evaluating the significance of the use of the prepositions "in" and "on," using the predominance of the "in" in Bede to support the case for northern or Anglian provenance of the original and the closeness of his chief manuscripts to this original.[76]

If philology is Miller's strong point and primary objective, then history, it must be said, receives little emphasis. The sole entrance of Anglo-Saxon history into his introduction—and nearly its sole point of connection to the earlier editions I am about to describe—is his reference to the attitude Bede's text takes towards the early Irish church. "The translator shows some familiarity with Scotch localities and circumstances," Miller wrote, "and a tender regard for national susceptibilities." Miller referred here to the controversies regarding clerical tonsure, the date of Easter, and other matters in which Irish practice differed from that of Rome. Bede disapproved of the departure of some Irish monasteries from Roman tradition (the Irish did not observe only one system), but the Old English translator "suppressed" some references to the controversy; Miller took this as a sign of northern origins. Reviewing Miller's discussions on this point, Whitelock conceded that he made "a few minor points" but that "none is convincing."[77] Miller's edition does not engage the scholarship of other Anglo-Saxonists in any unusual way. He comments briefly on the work of previous editors and moves directly to the manuscripts and their language.

Schipper was as concerned with philological apparatus as Miller. The advantage of his edition is that it contains parallel texts from two manuscripts, the Cambridge manuscript (Corpus Christi College, 41) that Miller rejected and Corpus Christi College, 279 (ranked third in importance for Miller). Schipper's textual and linguistic commentary is less extensive than Miller's, although Schipper revises Miller's impressions of the conditions of some of the manuscripts.[78] Miller's edition became standard for several reasons, but no doubt chiefly because of its place in the Early English Text Society. Unlike Schipper, who included the Latin version, Miller translated the Old English version into modern English. His text, however Germanic in its editorial philosophy, was an English version of the Old English version of Bede's *History.*

Cædmon and Bede in Smith's Edition ■

When we move from Miller's or Schipper's edition to that which preceded them, George Smith's text of 1722, we are in very different territory. Smith printed both the Latin and Old English texts but separated them by hundreds of pages. He corrected some of the transcription errors made by Wheelock in his editions of 1643–1644. Smith's chief contribution to the editorial tradition of Bede's *History* is that he was the first to have access to the earliest Latin manuscript of the text (the "Moore" manuscript). Smith is credited with establishing an authoritative version of the Latin text, and his work held the field until Charles Plummer's edition of 1896, whose text "can fairly be described as final."[79] Both Schipper and Miller speak highly of Smith's edition, and Miller keyed the pages of his edition to it.[80]

Smith printed several of Bede's texts, not only the *History;* included are Bede's *Life* of Cuthbert, *De locis sanctis,* and Bede's *Martyrology.* He offers no discussion of the linguistic features of the Anglo-Saxon, but he prints variant readings ("variorum lectionum"). Smith emphasized the Latin rather than the vernacular version, which appears at the end of the volume rather than immediately after the Latin text, and which has no notes, only variant readings. In contrast to both Miller and Schipper, he planned his text as a compendium of Bede's texts. His edition contains several appendices referring to ecclesiastical controversies, keyed to the Latin text. His explicitly political references are confined to the appendices, which are encyclopedic in communicating the entire history of a controversy rather than Smith's own views. Smith was no stranger to controversy, however; the *Dictionary of National Biography* attributes several pamphlets concerning ecclesiastical issues to him, including one entitled, "British and Saxons not converted to Popery."[81]

Smith's edition takes particular interest in regional geography. For example, when Bede describes the reluctance of monks at Bangor Abbey (near Chester) to accept Augustine of Canterbury as their bishop (*EH* 2:2), Smith appends a note about the location of the monastery. Wheelock, we shall see, had pages of commentary about the question of submission to ecclesiastical authority raised by this incident. Smith's treatment of "Cædmon's Hymn" is symptomatic of his scholarly approach. His knowledge of Bede and Cædmon is derived from John Bale (a Protestant) and John Pits (a Catholic), although Smith ignores the extreme hostility between them.[82] Pits (1560–1616) was a Catholic in exile on the Continent during the English Reformation who refuted Bede's theology bitterly (yet trusted him as a source of information).[83] Smith notes that both Bale and Pits believed that Cædmon spoke poems in his sleep that others, overhearing, wrote down, and adds, "Id enim vero Beda non scribit" ("Bede did not in fact write this"). Smith prints two texts of the hymn itself, recognizing some basic linguistic differences between them. Otherwise he passes over the episode in silence.

For all its elaborate editorial apparatus, Smith's edition was aimed at the traveller with a tastes for "antiquities" or historical sites. It includes illustrations, among them an engraving of the east window of Durham Cathedral and another of Bede's tomb.[84] The illustrations illuminate Smith's concept of the past as formally fixed and external, not a focus of excited controversy but rather an object for detached observation. One wants to call his version of Bede's *History* "classic."

Abraham Wheelock's Edition of Bede ■

Compared to Abraham Wheelock's edition of Bede, Smith's is a model of restraint. Wheelock was a librarian at Cambridge who held the first professorship in Anglo-Saxon at Cambridge University. The chair, beginning in 1638, was sponsored by the jurist and historian Henry Spelman, himself a scholar long aware of the importance of the Old English language for the study of early English law and for whom Wheelock worked as a reader in the Cambridge "public" or university library.[85] Wheelock simultaneously held the professorship in Arabic, which was sponsored by a London draper named Sir Thomas Adams, for whom he translated the Gospels into Persian (a work published in 1557, four years after Wheelock's death). Wheelock was, therefore, by profession both Anglo-Saxonist and Orientalist, a connection of genuine interest that has been overlooked but that he recognized. He plays on the connection in the preface to his edition of Bede, where he identifies the "Saxon muses" and the "Arabic sisters" with his patrons (Sig. A4r). He was not the first scholar of early English history to fashion a double identity of East and West in his scholarship, but he was in this—and in other significant ventures—the first to do so as a professional scholar in both cultures.

Bede urged the use of the vernacular to teach the laity; the translation of his *History* at the end of the ninth century was part of a strong movement in this direction in the Anglo-Saxon period. But Bede and Cædmon entered into the recovery of Anglo-Saxon texts and history indirectly at first, and in Latin. There are ironies in examining the textual communities that gathered around Bede and Cædmon in the context of sixteenth-century ecclesiastical history. As monasteries were destroyed and their texts were dispersed, the textual communities known to Bede and seen in his account of Cædmon ceased to exist.

Colgrave and Mynors say that Wheelock's edition ended a long period of English neglect of Bede; they write that only after Wheelock was English historical scholarship, "which had done so little for the *History* in the days of Matthew Parker," ready to make its contribution.[86] The Latin text of Bede's *History*, regularly cited by ecclesiastical historians in their battle against Rome, was first edited in Strasbourg, in 1475–1480 (reprinted in 1500). Catholic scholars who left England because of the Reformation were among the first to draw Bede into the controversy. In 1550, John de Grave expressed hope that the proof of the antiquity of Christianity in England would "discomfit those who think they can reform it."[87] In Basel, Johann Herwagen published the first complete edition of Bede's work in 1563, basing his knowledge of Bede's writing on an illustrious but notoriously unreliable source, Bale's literary history of England, *Illustrium Maioris Britanniae Scriptorum*.[88]

Wheelock printed Bede's *History* but no other texts by Bede. He arranged Latin and vernacular in parallel columns, making it evident where the Old English translator omitted chapters from the Latin. In this and many related details of his treatment of the text, Wheelock manifests a keen sense of history. Miller and Schipper rarely referred to history or to contemporary politics. Smith briefly acknowledged Wheelock and other early scholars, including John Bale, John Pitts, John Leland and William Camden (pp. 116–117). Wheelock, in contrast, was conscious that he shared a horizon with many earlier scholars of Bede's work. His edition is a compendium of Anglo-Saxonists and Anglo-Saxon studies up to the middle of the seventeenth century. To describe the "textual community" around him is to describe the history of Anglo-Saxon studies up to his time. If editions of Bede's text are viewed as "moments" of reception, Wheelock's edition can safely be described as the most complex moment in the history of the text. It is an edition that cannot be understood outside the network of readers and writers gathered around it.

"Gathering" is a mode of operating for Wheelock. It is a historical method that French Fogle has called "history by accretion," an approach that we can contrast to that of a reader who depended extensively on Wheelock's historical vision, John Milton. Milton's *History of England* borrows long stretches from Wheelock's edition of the *History.* Wheelock compiled in the manner of a medieval chronicler; Milton, seeing the need for narrative, synthesized.[89] It is easier to describe Milton's historical method than Wheelock's, for Wheelock's "accretion" calls for simplification but simultaneously resists reduction to straightforward narrative. Milton's style, however prolix, is nonetheless directed; Wheelock writes a history of the Anglo-Saxon church around and even inside the text of Bede.

Wheelock's edition must be approached synchronically, since it brings together and attempts to reconcile various historical accounts and doctrinal disputes, and diachronically, since its collection of texts and authors cannot be sorted out unless they are organized into chronological sequence. A synchronic analysis of his fourth book, which contains the account of Cædmon, will illustrate his method and also demonstrate how Wheelock serves as a focus for a survey of Anglo-Saxon studies from approximately 1460 to Wheelock's time two centuries later. As I said in Chapter 2, I do not intend to repeat the "story" of early Anglo-Saxon studies; it is, as Joseph M. Levine has said, a story that has often been told.[90] Rather, I see this history as many stories, and my recapitulation seeks to demonstrate the complexity of horizons connecting many scholars led by many different desires to work with early English history and its written records. All early Anglo-Saxonists were gatekeepers, in the model I use here, but none stood over as many Anglo-Saxon texts, and as many Anglo-Saxon scholars, as Wheelock. I propose this model not only for Anglo-Saxonists in the Renaissance, but also for Anglo-Saxonists who teach and publish today.

Wheelock has been praised for his accuracy and thoroughness, although corrections to Wheelock's edition began with Smith (who even corrected Wheelock's Latin). Wheelock attended closely to matters we would consider scholarly rather than polemical, "academic" rather than "antiquary." For example, his title page indicates that he worked with three manuscripts of Bede's Latin text, and three manuscripts of the Anglo-Saxon translation; he stresses that some of these manuscripts are the property of the "public library" in Cambridge, now University Library. His textual methods would have pleased nineteenth-century editors; he always indicates his sources with relative precision, and he records variant readings in the margins. His explanatory notes, sometimes nearly as long as the chapters they are appended to, are systematic and elaborately cross-referenced to other places in the edition.

Wheelock's first edition of Bede's *History* appeared in 1643. It incorporated a few Anglo-Saxon texts, chiefly homilies, into notes attached to the text. Some of these documents had already been printed, but others Wheelock printed for the first time, or newly collated. The use of Anglo-Saxon texts, including entire homilies, to explain other Anglo-Saxon texts is a striking feature of the work, and I will return to it shortly. The work was reissued in 1644. In addition to the 1643 texts, it included the first edition of the *Anglo-Saxon Chronicle,* an edition of the laws of Anglo-Saxon kings, and homilies and pastoral letters.

Wheelock's 1644 edition resembles a medieval manuscript compilation, an "accretion" of texts grouped around a governing theme. Wheelock's topic was the documentation of early English history. One manuscript of the Old English Bede known to Wheelock also contains the *Chronicle,* the laws, a genealogy of West Saxon kings to Alfred, "The Seasons of Fasting," and various other texts. This manuscript is London, British Library, Cotton Otho B.xi + Otho B.x; one wonders if it served as a model for Wheelock's own compilation. It was one of the few Anglo-Saxon codices that we know had been read before the Renaissance; Thomas Rudborne, a monk at Winchester, saw this manuscript at Southwick (south of Winchester) in the mid-fifteenth century.[91] Parts of this codex were copied by Laurence Nowell (1520–1598) in 1562 and later recopied, from Nowell's transcript, by William Lambarde (1536–1601). In the seventeenth century, William L'Isle (1569?–1637), whose work was a major source for Wheelock, made notes in the manuscript.

This manuscript illustrates what it means to call Wheelock, in Michel Foucault's language, a "node within a network,"[92] a scholar who leads to the early history of Anglo-Saxon studies in several directions, and on several levels, at once: to texts, to manuscripts, to readers, to other editors. In this preface "ad lectorem," Wheelock refers to nearly the entire range of early Anglo-Saxon scholars, from John Bale, John Foxe, and John Pits (sig. B1r–v), to Matthew Parker, William Camden, John Caius, William L'Isle, William Lambarde, and Henry Spelman. Most of these figures are also cited repeatedly in Wheelock's extensive notes to

Bede's text, where there is even a reference to John Calvin (p. 340). To unravel these references to texts and scholars is to pursue the history of Anglo-Saxon studies in an archaeological manner. Indeed, all these scholars are nodes within networks; each was related to others by specific connections, and the work of each constitutes a moment of reception—a textual event—that requires microscopic analysis. The history of Bede's *History*, seen in terms of these connections, does not emerge as a march of progress from antiquarian amateurishness to philological perfection. Rather, it appears as a dense, thick, and interconnected layer of interpretation, controversy, and experience that resists reduction to linear analysis.

As we trace Bede's *History* amid these networks, we will be struck by the varying importance assigned to Cædmon and his hymn. Cædmon mattered less to Wheelock than he did to Bale, who alloted to Cædmon an authorial status nearly equal to Bede's. Bale's *Illustrium* divides history into units known as "centuries" (although a "century" not corresponding to one hundred years). Both Bede and Cædmon appear in the first "century," which spans the early Christian era to the tenth century. Cædmon's career is described in terms close to those supplied by Bede. Cædmon, known as "Cedmonus Simplex," is credited with a list of works that matches the list of topics about which, according to Bede, Cædmon composed poems. Bale thus helped to establish the opinion that virtually all Anglo-Saxon poetry about biblical history, including the Book of Genesis, the Book of Exodus, and accounts of the Ascension and the Day of Judgment, was Cædmon's (in Bale's *Illustrium,* see p. 40r for the list, and in Wheelock's edition, pp. 327–331). Bede himself was described only as one of the "faithful," but the list of his works appended to the *History* is included and his importance is apparent (pp. 50r–52r; in Wheelock, pp. 492–494).

My approach to Anglo-Saxon studies through Wheelock begins with the multiple discourses that enclose the editor in his immediate, material circumstances, and the ways in which those conditions form a horizon for both the writer and the various audiences he addresses. The edition has not one but two prefaces, one to the sponsor of Wheelock's Arabic post, Thomas Adam (Spelman had already died), and another to the general reader ("ad lectoram"). Both prefaces, as one would expect, are in Latin (a precedent Smith followed), with a smattering of Greek. The dominance of Latin, very important for what it implies about Wheelock's readership, is ironic. Bede's text was translated in an effort to bolster learning in the vernacular; and under Wheelock's direction, the text was making its first appearance in a bilingual edition. But Wheelock used Latin rather than his own English to address his learned audience. Indeed, in the editorial tradition, the language of scholarship was not to move in the direction of a wider reading public for many years. The 1807 inaugural lecture of James Ingram to a professorship in Anglo-Saxon at Oxford lamented the dominance of Latin in terms timely for today, noting that his age was "too indolent and luxurious to submit to the drudgery of learning every thing through the medium of a dead language." The habit of translating Old English into Latin, he said, appeared "to be the principal cause of the neglect of Anglo-Saxon literature."[93] The tradition that forced Smith, Wheelock, and many others to write about Old English in Latin continues to inhibit scholarship, for this tradition is surely a continuing cause of the neglect of early editions of Anglo-Saxon texts.

Wheelock had another, more important reason for writing in Latin: the utter domination of learned discourse in his time by the study of the classics. In the passion for "antiquities" that characterized Anglo-Saxon scholarship throughout the early period, there was little doubt that the proper subject of the antiquaries was the world of Greece and Rome rather than the world of Anglo-Saxon England. But simple comprehensibility explains why Wheelock's edition of Bede's preface is in three parts: Bede's Latin, the Old English, and Wheelock's translation of the Old English into seventeenth-century Latin, a gesture designed to accommodate those who would find the vernacular text difficult to read (Sig. C1r). A concern for the reader is also why Old English material incorporated into his remarkable "annotationes," notes to Bede's text, is also translated into Latin.

The preface to the patron asserts the communion of the Church of England with "the ancient mother church," the ancient "Saxon" tongue being "the instructress of Catholic truth and peace" (Sig. A4rv). The preface "ad lectorum" is considerably blunter in its ideological assertions, cautioning against the "pious deceit of the teachers" ("ad piam docentis fraudem," B2r). The Anglo-Saxon references are meant to exhibit the antiquity of those church practices that some sectarians (that is, Roman Catholics) wish to call novel (Sig A3r). In order to assist the reader in correlating Bede's *History* with ecclesiastical controversies, Wheelock included an index of relevant topics—including the Mass, the wearing of vestments, and preaching—so that the reader could locate evidence that supported the customs of the Church of England against those of Rome (Sig. B1–4; the index is printed after p. 570, the conclusion of Bede's *History* and miscellaneous prayers).

Wheelock's "annotationes" (Sig. A3r) exemplify the principle of "history by accretion," but in a form we might call "argument by accretion." Significantly, Wheelock keyed his notes to the Latin text, not the Old English, since he expected his readers to follow that version rather than the Old English. Among the notes "woven into" the work at different places ("passim intexuimus"), are excerpts from the pastoral letters and homilies of Ælfric (d. *c.* 1012), including Ælfric's homily for Easter Sunday, and from the *Rule of Chrodegang;* all address ecclesiastical practice.

Wheelock's treatment of Ælfric's "Easter homily," "Sermo de sacrificio in die pascae,"[94] sums up the differences between Anglo-Saxon in his age and the age of Parker's Anglo-Saxonism. Parker claimed Ælfric as a witness to the authenticity of Anglican views; Wheelock extended the claim to Bede and to Alfred. To the rather slender evidence available to earlier scholars, a mere handful of excerpts from Old English texts, Wheelock added Bede's *History,* one of the most important texts in English history, and with it the authority of King Alfred, who (so he thought) was the text's first English translator. What others had seen in fragments Wheelock shaped into a complete, and completely argued, synthesis of ecclesiastical tradition and dogma. Wheelock used several of Ælfric's homilies—written at the end of the tenth century—rather than just the one (the only one, apparently) known to Parker, to verify both ninth-century and eighth-century ecclesiastical customs. Theodore H. Leinbaugh says that Wheelock printed the homily "simply as an appendix to Bede's description of Easter observances in Britain."[95] But Wheelock was doing more than insisting once again that the Eucharist was Christ's body in only a figurative sense. The Easter controversy addressed more than this oft-repeated item of doctrine; it was just one of many issues behind the demand for uniform ecclesiastical practice that was as important to Parker in one century, and to Wheelock in the next, as it had been to Bede a thousand years before.

Wheelock's treatment of Ælfric is, indeed, symptomatic of Wheelock's scholarly outlook. At the center for Parker, and for so many later scholars, Ælfric was on the margins for Wheelock, while Bede, not a major figure for Parker, was the center of Wheelock's work. The contrast reveals the sharply expanded world of Anglo-Saxon scholarship available to Wheelock, in which the theological microcosm present in Parker's excerpts was engulfed by the historical macrocosm of Wheelock's compilation. That macrocosm is, above all, a densely textual structure in which entire Anglo-Saxon texts are glosses on others or appendices to them. His edition is a web of interconnected textual evidence, dotted with small letters keyed to notes, filled with asterisks indicating notes to the notes. As Wheelock restructured the Anglo-Saxon literary history written by previous generations of scholars, he drew lines to connect pastoral letters, clerical rules, and homilies in a network centered on Bede's *History,* a text that was written before all the other texts Wheelock used. Bede had always been invoked to establish the precedent for later customs: he was a source for Anglo-Saxon scholars in the age of King Alfred (d. 899), for Ælfric a century later, and for Bale, Stapleton, and many others in the sixteenth century. Wheelock inverted this tradition. He used later customs—that is, the practices of the Anglo-Saxon church in the tenth and eleventh centuries—to establish the authenticity of Bede.

The story of Cædmon serves better than any other to illustrate both Wheelock's method and his meaning. Conditioned by the *Norton Anthology* and a long history of critical commentary to see "Cædmon's Hymn" as an originary moment, we are unprepared for Wheelock's treatment of Cædmon in the context of Bede's fourth book.[96] Of the thirty-two chapters of the fourth book, Wheelock appends notes to seventeen; notes to ten chapters contain Anglo-Saxon texts or references to them. These notes, as we would expect, discuss ecclesiastical and liturgical issues as well as history; among the issues are prayer to God alone rather than to objects (statues) or persons (saints) (ch. 9; Miller, p. 289); the efficacy of the Mass (ch. 22; Miller, p. 327); private confession (ch. 25; Miller, p. 351); and tithing (ch. 29; Miller, p. 375).

The story of Cædmon is followed by four notes, lettered "a" through "d," at the end of the chapter (Wheelock, p. 327). The first refers to the statement that Cædmon's poems caused his hearers to despise the things of the world ("ad contemptum seculi"); the next that "his teachers in turn became his audience" ("doctores suos uicissim auditores suos faciebat"); the third that his songs turned his hearers away from delight in sin ("ab amore scelerum abstrahere"). Wheelock then supplies a chapter from the Anglo-Saxon translation of the *Rule of Chrodegang,* "Concerning Singers" ("Be þam sangerum"), which states that the singer should use music to excite the people to think on and love the joys of heaven, not to sing too fast or too loudly, and use their talent well (pp. 331–332). Wheelock's own note explains that song can lead the ignorant and uncultivated ("inculta rusticitas et barbaries omnes," p. 331) to belief. Accepting a note by one of Parker's assistants in the manuscript (Cambridge, Corpus Christi College, 191), Wheelock believed that this passage was written by Archbishop Theodore and translated into Anglo-Saxon by Ælfric.[97] As the notes make clear, Wheelock found testimony in what he thought was Ælfric's work for the use of music; since the point of Cædmon's story in Bede is the use of music to inspire conversion, the notes here do not strain the Anglo-Saxon text, as Wheelock's notes sometimes do. Singing in church, like other forms of prayer, was closely regulated by the various acts aimed at achieving uniformity in ecclesiastical observance; extreme reformers (later Puritans) were utterly opposed to it as a form of papistry.[98]

Wheelock even manages a note to this note, referring to a later chapter in which Bede says that Cuthbert did not "raise his voice" when he said Mass (4:28; p. 353; Miller, p. 370).

The subject of Wheelock's fourth note to the story of Cædmon is—at least on the surface—Transubstantiation; but Wheelock's link between this controversy and the narrative is, to say the least, tendentious. Shortly before he died, Cædmon asked the brothers attending him, who thought he seemed in good health, if the Eucharist were in the house. It was, and Cædmon asked to receive it. Wheelock takes this opportunity to print not one but two versions of Ælfric's second pastoral letter in Old English to Wulfstan.[99] The letter corrects the view of priests who believe that the Eucharist consecrated at Easter had special powers for healing the sick, warns those who allow animals to eat the Host, and specifies that the Host is not to be kept longer than 14 days (when it should be eaten and new bread consecrated). This is not the focus of Wheelock's attention, however; the prohibition against keeping the Eucharist for long periods was enforced because it would decay, since it was only bread. Thus the prohibition underscores the physical and material nature of the Eucharist, and Wheelock several times stresses the point that the Eucharist was Christ's body only in a figurative sense. Translating the Old English into Latin, Wheelock added capital letters to emphasize the point. "Illa Eucharistia non est Corpus Christi CORPORALITER sed SPIRITUALITER, non corpus illud quo passus est, sed corpus illud de quo locutus est; quando panem et vinum in Eucharistiam . . . consecraverat" (pp. 332–333: "The Eucharist is Christ's body not physically but spiritually, it is not the body in which he suffered but the body concerning which he spoke when he consecrated bread and wine"). He has a similar note to the pastoral letter that follows comments on St. Paul: "non dixit ille, corporaliter, sed spiritualiter" (p. 335: "he did not say physically, but spiritually"). The point is made many times in a few short pages, and Wheelock, not wishing to belabor the point, adds a short note to connect the passage to yet further commentary on the controversy concerning Transubstantiation, leading the reader to the fifth chapter of Bede's *History* (5:22). And there, as a note to the passage in which Bede denounces various customs of the Irish Church (including observing Easter at a time different from that appointed by Rome and method of tonsure), Wheelock prints the text that so many have seen as the origin of Anglo-Saxon studies, the "Easter homily" by Ælfric (pp. 462–479).[100]

Uniform ecclesiastical observance is not what comes to mind, of course, when modern readers think of Cædmon's hymn. That Cædmon was a vernacular poet, whose work would, one expects, appeal to

Wheelock's interest in vernacular preaching, is utterly ignored. Wheelock overlooks the linguistic potential of the episode and does not realize that the hymn, which Bede refers to as "versus" (and the Old English translator as "fers" and "leoþe"), is a poem. Wheelock did not recognize the form of Anglo-Saxon verse either here or in his edition of the *Anglo-Saxon Chronicle,* which contains several poems.[101] For him the episode has none of the philological significance that it has for modern scholars, quite apart from extravagant notions of "schools of Christian poetry" founded by Cædmon; but it is rich in history. And at every point to which he attaches commentary, we see that Wheelock understood the direct relationship of his Church to the history of Bede's English Church and people. The result of his synchronic effort, since it is multi-layered, is sometimes confusing. Wheelock amplifies Bede's voice with Ælfric's, sometimes misunderstanding both (none of Wheelock's predecessors had done any better, however). Later medieval chronicles by Thomas of Walsingham, Walter Hidgen, and others, many of them consulted in the sixteenth century (Walsingham's was printed by Parker), formed a layer over the Anglo-Saxon texts; and then followed commentaries by John Bale, John Foxe, and others.

Just as Anglo-Saxon studies up to the middle of the sixteenth century are summed up in the achievements of Parker's tenure, developments up to the middle of the seventeenth century can be seen through Wheelock's reception of them. Wheelock worked largely by himself with private patrons, of whose support he seems never to have been too sure, while Parker commanded scholars and scribes and enjoyed the incomparable prestige of the Crown. What Wheelock presented in synchronic form cannot actually be described without being reduced. The visual organization of the pages of his edition—rather like the pages of the "envoi" described at the beginning of this chapter—defies verbal description. One needs a camera to communicate its effect; it is a visual artifact for a visually oriented age.

In 1644, Wheelock responded to the controversies that Parker and other Renaissance writers had been engaged in, but Wheelock took a different tone. He built on their historical vision, but he had a fuller knowledge of Anglo-Saxon texts and exercised a more cautious sense of history. This we see in Wheelock's handling of an episode in which Bede describes the resistance to Augustine's episcopate mounted by the monks of Bangor (Chester). In 605, King Æthelfrid slew twelve hundred of these monks, who had assembled to watch a battle. The massacre was interpreted by Parker and his assistants as punishment for the monks' refusal to submit to Augustine's authority (*EH* 2:2). If Augustine were responsible for the slaughter, the Roman mission to

Canterbury would, of course, stand in disgrace. Evidence in the *Peterborough Chronicle* was used to confirm Augustine's guilt.[102] The attempt of Parker's scholars to correlate the dates of Bede's *History* with the *Chronicle* was not undertaken in the spirit of free scholarly inquiry, but it was an early sign of historical method we recognize as modern and reliable. Wheelock, however, had a more acute historical sense and hence saw the controversy differently.

The Latin text of the *History* makes it clear that the carnage happened after Augustine's death, making it difficult to blame the catastrophe on him. The Old English version, however, omitted the passage about Augustine's death. In order to explain this discrepancy, it was decided not that the Old English version was defective, but that the Latin text contained a passage attempting to exonerate Augustine for the crime that was, according to Bishop John Jewel "manifestly forged."[103] The vernacular version of Bede's account was, for Jewel, Foxe and others, above question; the "English" version, thought to have come from Alfred's hand, could be trusted; the trickery had come in the intervening years, when so many Anglo-Saxon records had been "falsified." The matter of falsified records is crucial to understanding the textual practices of the early Anglo-Saxonists, for what they accused the corrupt, Rome-dominated scribes of doing, they did themselves.

The views of Jewel and others concerning these controversies were durable; they survive in John L'Isle's *A Saxon Treatise Concerning the Old and New Testament,* published in 1623.[104] Like Wheelock, L'Isle was a gatekeeper or synthesizer who created a retrospective on earlier textual communities. He printed Ælfric's preface to a translation of the first six books of the Bible, making notes and altering the text in both of the manuscripts he worked with.[105] He then printed the entire text of Parker's *Testimonie,* and followed it with the two versions of Ælfric's letter to Wulfstan concerning the Eucharist. L'Isle also made notes in the manuscript of the *Peterborough Chronicle,* a version of the *Anglo-Saxon Chronicle,* and collated it with one of the manuscripts also containing Bede's *History.*

L'Isle repeats the claim that Augustine of Canterbury was responsible for the killing of the monks who had refused to accept his authority. Wheelock, writing to Sir Symonds D'Ewes in 1638, commented, "What Augustine did concerninge the slaughter of Bangor Monkes, with the blessed Mr. Foxe I say, I cannot tel." All three Latin manuscripts that he consulted agreed that Augustine was dead at the time of the slaughter, Wheelock reported. And although the Old English copies all omitted the passage, he concluded that Augustine "fore-tould and threatned" the monks' death and thus was guilty, in that "he prophesied, that is, threatned the destructions of the fountaines and seminaries of the auncient Britaine Church" so that the Church of Rome could "the better domineire."[106] In his edition of the *History*, Wheelock exercised caution in discussing this controversy. He put the passage concerning the time of Augustine's death in brackets, marking it as corrupt (p. 114), and then included notes referring to Parker's *De Antiquitate Britannicae* and Jewel's *A Defense of the Apologie of the Churche of Englande* (1571), as well as to Joscelyn and Foxe, compiling two pages of notes in Latin and Old English to four pages of Bede's text (text, pp. 110–114; notes, pp. 114–115). Although he retained the position taken by earlier reformers, Wheelock advanced his view with caution, assembled the evidence, and weighed it more carefully than any of the scholars he quotes. Wheelock's work has been identified with the polemic of Anglo-Saxon scholars of the previous century. In Michael Murphy's words, Wheelock's motives were "almost identical" to those of Parker and his associates. Leinbaugh credits Wheelock's "remarkable scholarly achievement," but adds that "[f]ollowing the example of Parker and Foxe, Wheelock is guilty of printing misleading or inaccurate annotations."[107] But these assessments, I believe, sell Wheelock short.

Wheelock's achievement is more readily understandable—and no less impressive—when the contribution of L'Isle is reassessed. By L'Isle's time, the historical and polemical tradition of Anglo-Saxon scholarship had moved closer to the philological and linguistic; L'Isle can be said to have belonged to both. He adhered to some old attitudes. His *Saxon Treatise* borrowed the passage from Jeremiah 6:16 that introduced *A Testimonie of Antiquity:* "Goe into the streets and enquire for the old way, and if it be the good and rigyht way, then goe therein, that you may finde rest for your soules: but they say we will not walke therein." L'Isle subscribed to the full range of views of earlier scholars. He laments the lack of either textual or physical monuments from the British period, the era when England's true faith was born. L'Isle thought that the "Saxon" Bible in the vernacular had been translated by King Alfred (Sig. C1v), that the British, like the Saxons, had had sacred texts in their own tongue, and that all traces of British history had been destroyed. They disappeared not during the Saxon conquest of Britain; rather, these books were "made out of the way since the conquest by some which could not well brooke [their] doctrine" (Sig. M3r), this being but another version of the "conspiracy" theory popularized by Bale and Foxe. For L'Isle, the history of the British Church was only a part of a larger lost history of early Britain (Sig. C1v–2v).

Juxtaposed to his homage to the tradition of Parker and Foxe is a homage to another very different tradition. L'Isle wrote his preface in the style of Virgil's Fourth Eclogue (he published a translation of the

Eclogues in 1628). This act marks him as an antiquary in the sense that the term applied to William Camden and was to be accepted in the next century—that is, as a scholar with a passion for classical antiquity, rather than the antiquity of the English past. L'Isle's interest in Anglo-Saxon had a linguistic focus unlike that of the earlier polemicists' and also different from Wheelock's. He provided a description of how he learned Old English, beginning with a text of Virgil "Scottished by the Reverent Gawin Dowglas," and learned Scottish by comparing the Latin with the translation. He applied this technique to Foxe's edition of the Gospels in Anglo-Saxon and soon found that he could read the language.[108]

That Wheelock has been grouped with the earlier writers is inevitable but unfortunate. His work, like theirs, was part of "a broader stream of patriotic and antiquarian interest in the nation's archives," but the controversies of the sixteenth century had been transformed by Wheelock's time.[109] Although he approached them as a scholar, as no one had before him, he paid the price of conserving a scholarly tradition. He became identified with this scholarly tradition, and his innovations in it, as a result, go unappreciated, overshadowed on the one hand by his illustrious predecessors (Parker in particular) and on the other by a group of scholars to whom theology and the Rome of the pope mattered less than the Roman Empire.

Joseph M. Levine, author of the most recent—and, I think, one of the best—retrospectives on scholarship in the sixteenth and early seventeenth centuries, comments that "almost all antiquarian study was ancillary to some other purpose: either to classical imitation or to religion and politics."[110] Classical imitation was the business of the linguistic and legal tradition of early Anglo-Saxon scholarship, which was to become, after Wheelock, not only more important than the theological application of Anglo-Saxon studies but quite independent of it. Already in L'Isle's time it was possible to view early Anglo-Saxon history without passionate interest in church politics. Camden seems to have set the precedent in this and in many subsequent matters, for although he relied heavily on Bede's *History*, he cared little for controversies that surrounded it. He included the story about Gregory and the "angels" in Rome, for example, without a hint of controversy. He portrayed the English before the Norman Conquest as weak and corrupt and hence as making their overthrow almost inevitable.[111]

I have sought to emphasize the difference between Wheelock and the earlier Anglo-Saxon scholars on whose work he built. However, it is impossible to ignore the fundamental assumptions concerning ecclesiastical history that connect Anglo-Saxon studies from Parker's work in the mid-1550s to Wheelock's nearly a century later. It was only in the early nineteenth century that the historical vision of the polemicists, which contained and guided much if not all of the work with both language and texts in the Renaissance, was dealt a devastating blow. This blow to the pretentions of Reformation scholarship came, as justice would demand, from John Lingard, a Catholic priest. In the most important Anglo-Saxon ecclesiastical history of the early nineteenth century, *The History and Antiquities of the Anglo-Saxon Church,* Lingard called the Saxon invaders of Britain "hordes of ferocious pirates" who were "reclaimed from savage life" when they were converted. They were "unanimously classed with the most barbarious of the nations that invaded and dismembered the Roman empire."[112]

Lingard characterized the Anglo-Saxon conquerors of Britain harshly, but hardly more severely than he portrayed the scholars whose work I have discussed here. He exploded the accounts of the Anglo-Saxon church supplied by Parker and virtually all the ecclesiastical authorities who, before and after him, attacked or denied the Roman Catholic heritage of the English Church. Lingard wrote that these scholars' views on the sacraments, especially the Eucharist and confession, were refuted by "the very homilies which [they] published," and he abolished arguments by Parker, L'Isle, and others about Transubstantiation in the Anglo-Saxon period. "To this formidable phalanx of controvertists, philologists, and historians," he wrote, "may be opposed a still more formidable array of contemporary and unquestionable vouchers."[113] Lingard based his contempt for Parker and other Renaissance scholars on a superior knowledge of texts from the Anglo-Saxon period. He claimed to know more about medieval church history because he knew more about its sources. Indeed, he did; for example, he compared Ælfric's "Easter homily" to its Latin source to disprove the claims made by Parker and his assistants regarding Ælfric's views on the Eucharist.[114] Lingard thus can be said to have believed that he had reached the origin by understanding the true nature of the early English church while his opponents had not. His opponents, of course, had advanced precisely the same argument in their own time, so it is not possible to claim that Lingard himself is a point of origin for the scholarly confidence that became ever more apparent in the nineteenth century and that continues, I have argued, up to the present.

Lingard was contemptuous not only of historians but of "philologists." His use of the term at the beginning of the great age of the "new philology" indicates that, in the early nineteenth century, scholarship concerning Anglo-Saxon history and language was neither highly specialized nor highly regarded. By the end of the century it had become both. Lingard dismissed the Renaissance understanding of Anglo-

Saxon ecclesiastical culture as unscholarly and unhistorical. He did so without Germanic philology or Teutonic myth, neither of which had yet risen to prominence. Lingard's revisionism, which, as we have seen, extended to a new thesis about the authenticity of "Cædmon's Hymn," was possible not only because he read comparatively and more critically than Parker and others, but because he had a vested interest in putting forward a thesis to counter theirs. He had no interest in objectivity or neutrality; rather, his aim was to even the score and to re-establish the Roman Catholic orthodoxy of Anglo-Saxon theology. I hasten to add that I do not wish to suggest that Lingard's motives are equal to the task of scholarship. But I do regard his scholarly rigor as unusual for an age in which scholarship was not yet the contest of methods that was to mark the entry of Germanic philology into the English tradition.

The intellectual climate in which Anglo-Saxon studies were being conducted in Lingard's time, and in which John Mitchell Kemble would introduce some startling ideas about *Beowulf,* is better measured by the work of such figures as Horne Tooke and his protegé, Samuel Henshall, whose contributions I discussed in Chapter 2, than by Lingard's own. Henshall claimed that Latin translations that had been used by Wheelock and so many others to interpret Anglo-Saxon texts were completely inadequate for communicating the character and ideas of "'British-saxon,' 'Anglo-saxon,' or 'Norman-saxon' documents." He believed that Anglo-Saxon texts were virtually transparent and that Latin scholarship had destroyed their "simplicity."

To illustrate the fruits of this learning for Bede's *Ecclesiastical History,* I offer Henshall's translation of "Cædmon's Hymn" and Old English (taken from the *Norton Anthology*); my translation follows.

> Now we shall hearen heaven's Reach word, mighty's might;
> *Nu sculon herigean heofonrices Weard Meotodes meahte*
> and his mode of thought; worked worlds father; so he worlds
> *and his modeþanc weorc Wuldor-Fæder, swa he wundra gehwæs,*
> give was; eke Do-right earth instilled; he erst shaped elder
> *ece Drihten or onstealde. He ærest sceop eorðan*
> Barns Heavens to roof holy Shaping; then middle earth
> *bearnum heofon to hrofe halig Scyppend; þa middangeard*
> men's kind world eke Do-right after tied, free folds from (the) Almighty.
> *moncynnes Weard ece Drihten, æfter teode, firum foldan, Frea ælmihtig.*[115]

Now let us praise of heavenly kingdom the keeper, the might of the creator, and his mind-thought, the work of the gloryfather,

> when he of wonders every one, eternal lord, established the beginning. He first shaped for the children of men heaven as a roof, holy shaper, then middle earth, the keeper of mankind, the eternal lord, afterwards made, as a place for mankind, the eternal Lord.

Henshall's transcription (from Smith's edition of Bede) shows that he did not understand that the hymn was poetry, much less what its grammatical structure was. He was mislead both by errors in word division ("gehwæs," which means "each" in l. 3, was transcribed as "geh wæs" and translated as "give was") and by Tooke's etymological method (e.g., he translated "drihten" [lord] as "do right" in accordance with Tooke's idea that words were "messages," in this case of verb and noun, that communicated meaning in "abbreviated" form).[116] His overwhelming confidence in his method produced some unintended ironies, the chief of which appears on the title page of his book, which bears the motto "Rædende ic tæce" ("reading I teach"). Henshall thought these to be the words of Bede and took them as his motto for reading and teaching of his own. (The words, which gloss "legendo doceo," come from Ælfric's *Grammar.*)[117] "The present investigator relies little on his own knowledge, but is confident of the errors of his opponents," he wrote. He printed transcripts and Latin translations of parts of several Anglo-Saxon texts on one page, and on the facing page his own "simplified" and improved version. His concept of "simplicity" is alarming. In a passage from the Old English *Gospel of Nicodemus,* for example, he miscopied the text (from Hickes) and then attempted to translate it anyway, producing grammatical nonsense to compound the many false etymologies with which he had already confounded the sense of the passage.[118] One readily understands the vehemence with which Lingard railed against "philologists." Lingard operated on *a priori* assumptions of his own, and his work was attacked because of its Catholic sympathies.[119] But his conservative historical methodology would eventually triumph. The work of Henshall, Tooke, and other early philologists has been forgotten, and the ideological apparatus that accompanied the "new philology," characterized by powerful sympathy for the pre-Christian world and an equally strong and anti-Roman bias, has likewise vanished from modern scholarly memory. I attribute the success of Lingard's method not to its inherent superiority but to its transparency. Lingard claimed to have gone directly to the sources of the past in order to study it, and his approach seems more like common sense than scholarship. Lingard was an excellent documentary historian, and documentary history is what medievalists of our time value most highly. The speculations of the mythologists, on the other hand, constructed on elaborate genealogies of pagan gods, did not seek to recover documents but to describe a vanished culture. Their theoretical operations are conspicuous and can be identified as external to the subject and imposed on it, an act that modern scholarship, admiring of claims to neutrality, does not condone.

The "new" philology was already taking shape in Germany when Lingard wrote; in the nineteenth century it would overtake and largely replace both the linguistic research of the Renaissance and eighteenth-century scholars and the worldviews on which that research rested. The transformation of Anglo-Saxon studies into an academic discipline, which depended entirely on the place of philology, classical, and biblical studies in German universities, would result in ridicule of earlier work as amateur speculation. At the same time, Anglo-Saxon culture would be rehabilitated and would become worthy of its place as an origin for Germanic and English peoples. Philologists discovered in *Beowulf* the origin of a culture older even than Rome's, with monuments carved in myth rather than in marble. But their lasting contribution to the scholarly tradition would not be the myths whose origins they sought, but the methods used in the search. In the twentieth century, the methods would become the subject of inquiry, a structure much clearer than a pagan genealogy and as resistant to transformation as a rock.

6

Writing the Unreadable *Beowulf*

Homer and *Beowulf* ■

In an early scene in *The Caxtons: A Family Picture,* the novel published by Edward Bulwer-Lytton in 1850, Augustine Caxton is mulling over the effects of textual criticism on Homer. The precise nature of Homer's achievement, in particular the probability that the poem had been written in a form different from that in which it had been composed, had been a subject of scholarly controversy for nearly three centuries. But "the marriage between textual and literary criticism" that was needed to reveal the historical Homer as an origin, as a center from which one could chart the history of the epics in antiquity, was first realized it the work of the German scholar F. A. Wolf, who published the *Prolegomena ad Homerium* in 1795. Wolf attempted to discover the original form of the *Iliad* by defining detailed criteria that helped reconstruct the state of the text as it had been transmitted century after century; he explained how revisers had altered the poem as it passed from oral to written culture, and in so doing he successfully attacked the unity of the text and the status of its author.[1] As Caxton reads, his wife interrupts to ask what they shall name their new-born son; she assumes "Augustine," after the father, but he objects and suggests "Samuel" instead, a name his young wife abhors. Caxton continues to read; his wife continues to ask about the baby's name. Suddenly he bursts out, "'Pisistratus!'," the name of the Athenian tyrant (600–528 B.C.) credited by some scholars with having fixed the oral text of Homer that the rhapsodists recited at the Panathenaic festival held every four years at Athens.[2] "'Pisistratus Caxton,'" says his wife. "'Thank you, my love: Pisistratus it shall be.'" "'Do you contradict me?'" he replies to her unexpected response. "'Do you side with Wolfe and Heyne, and that pragmatical fellow, Vico? Do you mean to say that the Rhapsodists—'." His wife hastens to assure him that she does not contradict him (nor, indeed, does she know what he is talking about). Caxton, a shy man who hates ceremonies, contrives to miss the baby's christening; he learns to his horror that his son, at his own suggestion, has been named after a sixth-century Greek "enslaver of Athens and disputed arranger of Homer."[3]

Bulwer (1803–1873) was a member of Parliament and a prolific novelist. Although he is not taken seriously by critics of the novel, his historical fiction was as influential in interpreting the Middle Ages for nineteenth-century readers as were the novels of Sir Walter Scott. Bulwer historicized aspects of medieval culture that modern criticism has only begun to notice. One of his historical novels, *Rienzi: Last of the Roman Tribunes,* published in 1835, recounts the life of the fourteenth-century revolutionary Cola di Rienzo. Revolution does not seem to be an obvious subject for an M.P. raised to peerage in 1866, but Lord Bulwer was radical in his politics, and the interest in revolution, heavily sentimentalized, is not so out of place as one might expect. *Rienzi* was translated into German in 1839 and made its way into the hands of a writer with a considerably keener interest in revolutions, Richard Wagner, who fashioned it into his first successful opera, *Rienzi, der Letzte der Tribunen,* staged in Dresden in 1842.[4]

Just as he historicized the Middle Ages, Bulwer helps us historicize his contemporaries. *England and the English,* published in 1833, surveys the national character, educational apparatus, and social structure with the shrewd observations that are also engaged in his fiction.[5] *The Caxtons* is not in Bulwer's historical vein, although the great fifteenth-century printer, William Caxton, supposedly stands at the foot of this family tree. The novel's mild satire on pedantry historicizes textual criticism of the professional, "Germanic" type, as well as publishing and printing, in the context of armchair scholarship still traditional in the middle of the century. Bulwer's joke requires little more than that his audience recognize the importance of Homer and the affront to common sense created by German criticism's attempt to dismantle his identity.

Wolf's work appeared when the foundations of textual criticism and modern scholarship were taking form in German universities. Philology and classical and biblical scholarship were all part of his achievement, and were in turn all deeply influenced by it.[6] Wolf's thesis about Homer influenced Karl Lachmann and, through Lachmann, generations of scholars who contemplated the origins of *Beowulf*. Karl Müllenhoff, one of Lachmann's students, proposed multiple authorship for *Beowulf* in 1869. Müllenhoff's *Liedertheorie* posited the origin of *Beowulf* in folk lays, where Lachmann had placed the origin of the *Niebelungenlied.* Just as the songs of wandering minstrels were the supposed origins of the *Iliad,* folk songs were the supposed origins of *Beowulf*. One of Müllenhoff's inspirations was John Mitchell Kemble, who published the first English edition of *Beowulf* in 1833 (corrected and reissued in 1835), with translation and commentary following in 1837.[7] But when Augustine Caxton contemplated Homer, *Beowulf* was still too obscure to have been a subject for public humor.

That much has changed. Woody Allen advises students not to take "courses where they make you read *Beowulf*,"[8] and *Beowulf* and the *Canterbury Tales* are the only English texts before Shakespeare to merit a place in Maurice Sagoff's *ShrinkLits: Seventy of the World's Towering Classics Cut Down to Size,* which boils the epic down to 26 lines: "Monster Grendel's tastes are plainish. / Breakfast? Just a couple Danish."[9] *Beowulf* survives in the *Norton Anthology of English Literature,* a partner to Bede's *Ecclesiastical History* and the episode of Cædmon in shaping impressions of Anglo-Saxon culture for the undergraduate audience. *Beowulf* is the only Old English text to exist in a *Norton Critical Edition* (although in translation),[10] and it is the only Old English text to merit one of the MLA's "approaches" volumes.[11]

No other Old English text has attained such status, nor is another likely to challenge the position of *Beowulf*. Its reputation among general readers is, of course, dreadful, but this is less the fault of the text than of those who teach it and those who interpret its editorial and textual tradition. Yet, at the levels of reading and instruction discussed in relation to "Cædmon's Hymn," *Beowulf* can be understood as a complex and important cultural event rather than an obscurity people of sense will seek to avoid.

The *Approaches to* Beowulf collection offers an instructive review of attitudes towards the poem. Useful though individual essays are, the collection has three major weaknesses that characterize *Beowulf* scholarship more generally. First, there is, apart from a single essay on women's perspectives, no attempt to address contemporary critical theory, although the importance of philology (never seen as theoretical) is frequently asserted, as if it were in danger of being left out. Second, none of these essays makes integral use of the history of the poem's reception, a matter of great importance, since much was added to and some taken away from *Beowulf* as it emerged in the nineteenth century; nothing at all is made of the poem's reception history before the late nineteenth century. Third, a remarkable degree of consensus prevails, which may also be seen as a lack of dissent over issues that have always animated *Beowulf* criticism and that today are especially controversial. These issues include the date of the poem, which has been confidently placed in the seventh and eleventh centuries, and in all centuries between, and the reliability of the manuscript as an indication of the poem's age, authorship, and historical value.

Controversial issues are usually argued with fierce finality in *Beowulf* criticism, as if they could be settled once and for all. To argue either that the manuscript can plainly support an eleventh-century date for the poem—the position of Kevin S. Kiernan—is no more helpful than maintaining that it "has nothing to tell us about the date of the poem," the position of one of his more hostile reviewers.[12] The meaning of such disagreement is frequently lost. *Beowulf* is an incomplete text, incompletely attested, and it will always be controversial. Its incompleteness is not only a conceptual problem: it is also an event.

Beowulf in Survey Classes ■

The first step in making a classicized text eventful is to break the anthology's hold on the text, to explain how its assertions about Anglo-Saxon culture are selective and even stereotypical, and to show that the text itself offers characterizations of early English culture that the criticism ignores. I see the *Norton Anthology* as a register of received opinions about early English culture; as such, it is worth taking seriously. By challenging what the *Norton* claims about Anglo-Saxon literary culture, we reopen issues that the anthology presents as settled. We see these issues as sites of controversy rather than as given truths, and thereby open *Beowulf* to a discussion of fresh ideas about the historical reception of Anglo-Saxon culture, and the connection of that culture to our own.

Familiar issues provide the framework for expanding our idea of *Beowulf:* translation, which includes translating Old English poetry into modern prose, and transmitting an ancient Germanic text through a Christian culture; historical perspective, and how it is affected by using a poem whose dating is highly controversial to characterize any and all phases of Anglo-Saxon culture; and incompleteness in the text, gaps or defects in the manuscript and silences in the narrative. These issues help us concentrate on the "not Old English" element of the Anglo-Saxon tradition, on "culture" rather than "documents," and on meaning as well as method. A review of the editorial history of *Beowulf* reveals how method developed to produce in the poem a cultural meaning that already existed outside it, a horizon consisting in part of Homeric epic and textual practices that, to Caxton's distress, were being applied to it.

Whether teaching *Beowulf* in a survey course or a course in Old English, one is invariably frustrated by the problem of translation. Translation is interpretation; the translation of *Beowulf* by E. Talbot Donaldson in the *Norton* is an interpretation of the text. Since editors must interpret, editors of *Beowulf* who confront its numerous ambiguities are doing what editors are supposed to do. They are making informed choices for their readers. That they make different choices at different points in history—that editions are "timely" in the sense of "bound by time"—is a positive rather than a negative feature of the tradition, and it is easily addressed in an introductory class in which the poem is read in translation. One need only produce a few pages of other translations—early translations in both Latin and English, for example—to demonstrate that translations differ and to explain why they do. When one compares a translation to a glossary, one sees that the glossary sometimes becomes the translator's gospel.

Examples in *Beowulf* are numerous. The best demonstration I have seen comes from a high-school English literature survey, *England in Literature,*[13] in which four translations of a single short passage—ranging from J. Duncan Spaeth's 1921 version to Michael Alexander's translation published in 1973—are arranged on the page so that students can see how diverse in tone and effect the poem can become in the hands of different translators. Students can be encouraged to explore the source of these differences, the editors' glossaries, which show them that a single word can hold quite different meanings and that the editor's choice is his or her own. For example, in the standard edition of *Beowulf* by Frederick Klaeber, *ellen*—the word so important to Elizabeth Elstob—can mean "courage, valor, strength, zeal," and "deeds of valor" (p. 322); *nið* can mean "(ill-will, envy), violence, hostility, persecution, trouble, affliction," and "battle, contest" (p. 380); *dollic* can mean "foolhardy, audacious, daring" (p. 316). Again, a few photocopied pages—even paragraphs—are sufficient to make the point that editors unavoidably rewrite and interpret the poems they publish.

Teaching translations "against" each other does not cause students to despair at the arbitrariness of editors and translators; instead, it arouses interest in the flexibility of the Old English vocabulary and helps them to see that a translation, and even an edition, is the result of a hermeneutic process. This approach also alerts students to the power of editions they use or will use in other courses. Placing the "definitive" translation in historical context—one can use early as well as recent translations—prepares students to assess the "definitive edition," that institution whose powerful implication of objective editorial standards they will encounter often.

But editors respond to texts, and to manuscripts, as if they were univocal, speaking in one voice only, rather than in several voices at once, some mute, some muddled. The implications of the multiple layers of the manuscript for approaches to narrative in *Beowulf* are too frequently missed because the choices of editors and translators are allowed to stand in place of manuscript and cultural contexts. An obvious, and probably the most important example in *Beowulf,* as in "Cædmon's Hymn," is the mixture of pagan and Christian perspectives. It is usually approached as a compromise between a Christian world view, with its promise of redemption, and the fated universe of Germanic paganism. But this cultural theme is an event; it becomes a conclusion, the solution to a conceptual problem, only through the lexical process of determining how words, including references to fortune, fate, and divinity, will be translated. As Fred C. Robinson has shown, editors and translators juggle the balance of these elements according to the version of Anglo-Saxon culture they have chosen. Pagan or Germanic definitions predominate in some views, while references to the Christian God prevail in others. Often what conveys the decision is an arbitrary use of capitalization: Old English "ælmihtig" becomes "Ælmihtig" and a term with an important ambiguity is reduced to simple statement.[14] Students using translations have no way of knowing, if their teachers are not alert, what is afoot.

This cultural controversy is settled in the *Norton Anthology,* where *Beowulf* is seen as a repository of some of the most important institutions of Germanic culture. The introduction to the Old English period in the *Norton* is a veritable digest of myths about Anglo-Saxon England. There we learn that the "heroic ideal had a very practical bearing on the life of the people whom the king ruled," although there is very little evidence about the lives of those who were ruled, as opposed to those who ruled; and that the Germanic people "never tired of hearing the deeds of their folk heroes," so that "the immortality that the old heroes had sought was achieved through poetry, and poetry in turn gave inspiration to later men in leading their own lives." Men in the meadhall seldom relaxed and wore armor all the time in case Fate should call, and so forth.[15] Thus stereotypes about Anglo-Saxon culture are passed on uncritically, with no thought to the cultural origins of these stereotypes in nineteenth-century criticism. Anglo-Saxonists probably brush aside such characterizations of *Beowulf* and Anglo-Saxon culture as amateur or unspecialized, but students and other readers should be encouraged to question these views on grounds of their exclusivity. The two-part valorization in the *Norton* is doubly deadly: it not only characterizes aesthetic reponse ("never tired of hearing") but asserts a direct relation between hearing poetry and leading an inspired life. Bulwer would have approved, but how are readers who are aware of postmodern possibilities to regard such assessments? We should regard them with skepticism, I believe, and with the awareness that they are the product of desire.

One of the strongest desires evident in *Beowulf* criticism is the wish to invoke the historical perspective of ancient Germanic institutions as background to the poem. The view of Anglo-Saxon culture taken in the *Norton* is not Anglo-Saxon at all; it is drawn from Tacitus's *Germania*, written in the first century. Tacitus was a Roman historian, but his influence over Anglo-Saxon literary history is great. Klaeber observes that the poem is "a veritable treasure-house of information on 'Germanic antiquities,' in which we seem at times to hear echoes of Tacitus' famous *Germania*."[16] Thus Tacitus looms large in the *Norton* introduction, and has been cited in a long list of Anglo-Saxon literary histories: C. L. Wrenn's portrait of the heroic in Anglo-Saxon literature;[17] the assessment of Stanley B. Greenfield and Daniel G. Calder;[18] and Margaret Goldsmith's view.[19] Tacitus too has to be interpreted before he can be used to interpret, and scholars needing a pure Germanic past for *Beowulf* have invented it in *Germania*, treating Tacitus as an objective reporter of Germanic customs and applying his fragmentary analysis of a first-century culture wholesale to Anglo-Saxon culture six centuries later. Rare is the caution of Milton McC. Gatch, who, unlike so many who write about the Germanic roots of Anglo-Saxon culture, hesitates to take Tacitus at face value and instead portrays him as a cynical observer of urban Roman culture who found in the provincial north a rustic culture to romanticize.[20] Tacitus has become a beginning for *Beowulf* earlier than English culture; not unexpectedly, he is a classical and Roman point of reference, an anchor to antiquity, a link between the wilds of the North and the civilized pursuits of Anglo-Saxon culture. Once such views of Tacitus have been repeated and asserted enough times, they become institutionalized; readers of *Beowulf*—especially students pondering this long and confusing text as the first masterpiece of English literature—automatically integrate institutionalized ideas into their view of the text. Those received ideas are little more than conventional wisdom; they are readily dislodged by discussion of the text's reception, which, instead of dishing up fixed assessments, asks readers to use their own experience as a point of entry into the text: in other words, to identify a shared horizon, and work from it.

One can offset these traditional, institutional assertions about *Beowulf* by historicizing the function of the poem as a version of English history. Early scholars saw *Beowulf* as a record of English Germanic origins and mined it for evidence of the heroic civilization that distinguished the Anglo-Saxon past. This view has been out of fashion ever since J.R.R. Tolkien challenged the historical approach in an essay widely accepted as the starting point (i.e., the beginning) of literary criticism of *Beowulf*.[21] Thereafter, almost any historical approach to the text, as opposed to a literary critical approach, seemed antiquated. But the poem's historical function, as I see it, is not only its account of the Anglo-Saxon era, but its reception in the nineteenth century, when it mirrored world views of its editors and translators and thus helped to shape the course of Anglo-Saxon studies.

Tolkien asserted powerfully, for the first time, that *Beowulf* was a text no less worthy of "literary criticism" than any other. Part of Tolkien's task was celebratory. He lamented the prominence given to the poem as history, as witnessed, for example, in the view of Archibald Strong, published in 1921, that *Beowulf* is "the picture of a whole civilization, of the Germania" of Tacitus, when Tolkien himself wished its poetry to overshadow its historical function. Tolkien asserted that more than one modern poem was inspired by *Beowulf* since "*Beowulf* escaped from the dominion of students of origins to the students of poetry."[22] Here is a dichotomy worth analysis: poetry, or literary merit, as defined by aesthetics, set in opposition to history as expressed in a search for origins. Tolkien functioned as a gatekeeper in the history of *Beowulf* criticism, not only because he made a case for the poem as literature but because he felt it necessary to rescue *Beowulf* from historians to whom it was "a quarry of fact and fancy" rather than "a work of art."[23]

Tolkien dismissed the idea that *Beowulf* is a "quarry of fact and fancy," but as a work of art it is, of course, just that. Rather than see the *poem* as a "quarry," however, we can apply that concept to the *manuscript* and subject it to Foucauldian archaeology, a study of all that has grown up around the manuscript and that filters the text and conditions its reception. We can undertake this pursuit with the *Beowulf* manuscript rather than the poem because the poem was discovered long after the manuscript (London, British Library, Cotton Vitellius A.xv). The first readers of *Beowulf* did not know what an Anglo-Saxon poem was. They had no horizon of Old English verse into which to insert it. Tolkien put an end to the "old historicism" of those who wanted to use the poem in positivist historical ways; but without realizing it, he handed *Beowulf* over to New Criticism, which developed as the "literary" channel for "higher criticism," while philology continued to direct the flow of "lower criticism." Together the two came to constitute the "traditional" approach to medieval studies, Anglo-Saxon studies included.

The alternative to this neat pair of New Criticism and old history is not "New Historicism,"[24] but a historicism that attempts to understand earlier editors and readers and to establish a sympathetic perspective in which their work is valued rather than dismissed. Like any damaged ruin—like the monuments mourned by Camden and the manuscripts reconstructed by Parker—*Beowulf* must be restored before it can be understood. But what one era "appreciates" and so reconstitutes in the poem is, in a later era, a layer through which one must seek the monument. One makes this point by showing students that between the *Beowulf* manuscript and us are many layers of emendations, solutions to cruces, proposed by these scholars. The editorial and critical history of *Beowulf*—its reception—is not a process of removing error or late accretions in order to disclose a pristine Ur-text; rather, it is a process of adding to such accretions, layer upon layer. The manuscript history is an archive of the development of Anglo-Saxon studies. The oldest layer of that archive, the manuscript, already comprises several layers of data: corrections, erasures, a palimpsest, damaged and rebound pages. Surrounding this text is a long and contentious history of transcripts, translation, editions, and critical analysis or literary interpretation. This accumulated body of evidence attests to the cultural significance of *Beowulf* and to its power to command scholarly attention and readership. Placed at the center of our understanding of the poem, the manuscript shows us not how *Beowulf* was created, but how we have created it, making and remaking not just its literary meaning but its language.

Anyone who sees a facsimile of a few of the manuscript's badly damaged pages knows why editing *Beowulf* amounts to writing it. Dealing with defects has always been a necessary part of its reception, as we see in the facsimile edited by Julius Zupitza for the Early English Text Society,[25] Joseph Tuso's well-presented facsimile page in the *Norton* critical edition, which contains a transcription and an edited version of the text,[26] or Kiernan's several pages reproducing the manuscript. Incompleteness of this sort is, as I have said earlier, a feature of many Anglo-Saxon texts. Teaching that engages this aspect of the text can illustrate how scholars, as a necessary condition of their work, help to shape their subject by restructuring textual evidence.

Beowulf in Introductory Old English Classes ■

We can raise the questions of translation, historical reception, and incompleteness when teaching *Beowulf* in translation in a survey course. All these issues raise themselves in introductory Old English courses, when students learn about the condition of manuscripts and the nature of textual emendations, although rarely from *Beowulf,* which modern introductory Anglo-Saxon textbooks seldom include. The omission is due to the traditional format for presenting Anglo-Saxon in the curriculum in a two-course sequence; the first course consists of grammar, taught chiefly through prose, and the second course consists of *Beowulf.* But older texts include excerpts from *Beowulf* as a matter of routine. *The Elements of Old English,* by Samuel Moore and Thomas A. Knott, includes several early episodes: Grendel's raids, Beowulf's arrival at Heorot, and his fight with the monster.[27] Henry Sweet chose several parts of the poem in *First Steps in Anglo-Saxon,* inserting his own subheads (in Old English, no less), to introduce each excerpt.[28] In *The Threshhold of Anglo-Saxon* (an interesting response to Sweet's title), A. J. Wyatt managed to incorporate the whole poem, interspersing excerpts with the summary of William Morris.[29] R. C. Alton's *An Introduction to Old English* includes a few sections only.[30] The two most popular introductory texts, *A Guide to Old English,* by Bruce Mitchell and Fred C. Robinson, and *Bright's' Reader,* edited by F. G. Cassidy and Richard N. Ringler, omit *Beowulf* entirely.[31] My survey is not systematic (such a survey would be useful), but it is apparent even from a brief accounting that *Beowulf* has left the middle ground of Anglo-Saxon studies and can be found chiefly in introductory surveys and in seminars for those who have already studied some Old English.

The values formerly attached to *Beowulf* in introductory courses can be seen in *Sweet's Anglo-Saxon Reader,* first published in 1876 and revised many times. It includes the episode in which Beowulf fights with Grendel's mother (lines 1251–1651), which he calls "one of the most vivid parts of the poem." Sweet believed that the "poet's Christian intention is shown by the unequivocal claim that Beowulf owed his victory over Grendel to his faith in God."[32] Sweet's choice of episodes reveals his view of the poem as a Christian epic and his expectation that vivid action, on the level of an adventure tale, is an important aesthetic consideration. His capitalization illustrates the Christian perspective he claims for the poem; "anwalda," meaning ruler, appears as "Anwalda," indicating the Christian God (l. 1272), and "alwalda," meaning "omnipotent one," appears as "Alwalda," meaning God (l. 1314).[33] That the capitalization is an interpretation of the manuscript readings—a Christianizing of them—is left for the student to determine; in his prefatory note apparently explaining all, Sweet is silent on this count.

The relationship of translation to interpretation is the very subject of an introductory course in Old English. Equally important is the linking of interpretation to incompleteness. Students learn about incompleteness by another name, the "crux," a term designating not only "a difficult problem, a puzzling thing," but also "a critical moment, a crucial point," even "the essential or most important point."[34] This word, *crux,* and this concept in Anglo-Saxon scholarship, like so many other fundamental notions of textual criticism, come to us from the Latinate vocabulary of early textual critics and classicists. It is a fascinating term, meaning "cross," coming from "crucio," "to crucify," to torture or to torment. Alexander Pope was one of the eighteenth-century writers for whom the link between antiquarian study and pointless pain was already clear; *The Dunciad* scoffs at those who "Old puns restore, lost blunders nicely seek, / And crucify poor Shakespear once a week."[35]

For Anglo-Saxonists, a "crux" is traditionally seen as a riddle or a puzzle that can be solved by the proper application of critical and scholarly ingenuity to the linguistic facts at hand. The crux usually involves a manuscript reading that does not fit its context. Cruces are sometimes generated by the expectation that *Beowulf* must set a standard for grammatical usage and meter. Since *Beowulf* is not only the earliest English literature, but also the only medieval epic in English, the poem is expected to preserve the earliest forms of Anglo-Saxon language and art—the primary data for the analysis of meter, vocabulary, and even style. Metrical restorations seek to present the poem in strict conformity with the rules of Old English meter as they were formulated in the nineteenth century; *Beowulf* is used to test other Old English poetry for metrical regularity, thereby setting the standard for all Old English verse. Just one of many possible examples is the comment by T. P. Dunning and A. J. Bliss, in their edition of *The Wanderer*, that "The metre of *The Wanderer* conforms in general with the strict standards of the *Beowulf* poet."[36] Ashley Amos characterized the "proper rules for the meter of *Beowulf* " as the "classical" meter of Old English poetry, but notes disagreement on the application of these rules to other poems.[37]

But some cruces are related to a different kind of unreadability. They may involve not only missing letters and difficult readings, but also style and subject matter—not "cruces," in the narrow sense, but aesthetic defects that can be seen wherever the epic does not meet the expectations of editors and critics. For *Beowulf* is a repository of literary and linguistic institutions, including poetic style, type scenes, and lexicography. Expectations appropriate to *Beowulf* as the earliest example of these features create the unreadability they seek to remedy; they are only academic notions, critical conventions of what an Anglo-Saxon epic poem ought to be. It ought to be highly serious, universal, unified, correct, and *complete.* To demand completeness of a poem essentially incomplete is, of course, unwise, since the manuscript makes the physical fact of incompleteness apparent, and since the poem periodically fails strict metrical or grammatical criteria. The poem's incompleteness, manifest in fragmentary episodes and occasional defects in meter, has something important to tell us about the text and about how its gaps guide our teaching and scholarship, our reading and writing of *Beowulf.*

The Poem and Scholarly Editing ■

Desire for a complete *Beowulf*—for *Beowulf* as a pure point of origin—has inspired editors to create its wholeness by writing supplements to fill the gaps in the text. These gaps, or cruces, are of two kinds: literal gaps, where the text cannot be read and where important information is suppressed, leaving the plot incomplete; and figurative gaps, where the text can be read, but not to the satisfaction of metrical standards or other criteria that scholarship imposes on the manuscript. The first kind of gap requires editors to emend the manuscript and publish their emendations simply as *Beowulf;* they indicate their changes with brackets or italics, as tradition dictates, but their corrected text, not the manuscript of *Beowulf,* is the one put before the reading public. The second kind of gap requires that we "write," meaning "interpret," whenever we undertake to make a text conform to our image of it, our concept of its possibilities. The narrative gaps must be addressed when *Beowulf* is taught in translation, so I begin with them.

The most notorious of the textual episodes, usually referred to as "digressions," are the obscure fight at Finnsburgh (1068–1159b), the Sigemund digression (874b–897b), the complex sequence about Onela at the end of the poem (2345–2509b, 2910–2998b), and the account of Beowulf's later years as king, including the conditions that surround the appearance of the dragon (2210b–2231a, 2669–2820b) who ends the hero's life. These episodes prevent us from knowing what we need to know to make the poem complete. The incompleteness of the poem is evident in what it does not discuss; what *Beowulf* leaves unsaid, including the thoughts of most of its women characters, must be spoken for when the poem is spoken about. Attention called to this function of the poem's incompleteness—its stimulus to speaking—complicates and enriches a student's introduction to it. Gillian R. Overing's link between women and death in *Beowulf* describes the feminist and semiotic possibilities of the poem's silences and omissions powerfully.[38] The gaps are untold parts of the story; they unsettle its telling.

These gaps remind us that *Beowulf* exists in the form of a copy, not an original. Kiernan's recent arguments that the poem was partially rewritten in the eleventh century is only the latest version of a position that the poem is a copy.[39] Indeed, the widely accepted view that *Beowulf* is an ancient poem reworked in later cultures, which has been the standard paradigm of its reception, altered only by Kiernan's argument that the poem was revised in the eleventh century, poses a model for narrative study based on the existence of gaps (their presence), rather than on the usual scholarly response of filling them in (their absence).

The narrative and textual gaps in *Beowulf* are intertexts, distinct but interactive "sign systems" or narrative units. My argument about these intertexts and the poem's intertextuality is a return to the premise of the *Liedertheorie,* but it is not the *Liedertheorie* made new. The thesis that *Beowulf* is composed of separate *Lieder* is only a claim for the existence of texts within the text and for the creation of *Beowulf* through the interplay of these individual textual voices. The merits of this claim, as the *Liedertheorie* advances it, have not been welcome, even though the "unity" of *Beowulf* has always been controversial. Kiernan sees the poem as a conflation of two texts brought together for the first time by an author, who created neither poem, in the eleventh century. He argues for two authors for *Beowulf* but rejects the *Liedertheorie* because it is an "impotent assault on the artistic integrity of the poem"; he maintains that the poem has descended to us in "unquestionably unified" form, but not everyone agrees.[40] Tolkien argued that *Beowulf* is composed of separate texts not entirely happily joined. Explicitly theological parts of the poem—an early passage condemning the monsters and the later passage absurdly known as "Hrothgar's sermon"—were, he thought, liable to have been expanded or revised; they had a "ring" unlike the rest of the poem.[41] C. L. Wrenn proposed moving some lines to eliminate inconsistencies in tone (i.e., unwarranted Christian references).[42]

Anglo-Saxonists become understandably impatient when the issue of multiple authorship is raised in *Beowulf,* not wanting the problems of a poem with more than one author (or one reader?) written in more than one century. But a contemporary critical model, such as M. M. Bakhtin's "dialogized imagination," and a contemporary concept of authorship, such as Michel Foucault's idea of "the disappearance of the author," offer complex and divergent models that actually demand, rather than merely allow for, historical perspective.[43] These more complex narrative models do not disregard the "hard" evidence of manuscript tradition and editorial practice. Foucault wrote about narrative in the novel, not in the epic; and though Bakhtin discusses the epic, he positions its narrative qualities in contradistinction to the "dialogic" qualities of novelistic narrative. Nevertheless, their concepts are more fluid and precise ways to discuss "inner history" than Anglo-Saxonists have yet explored. Bakhtin's concept of a "dialogized" text—a text with several voices—or Said's concept of a repressive text whose hidden melodies can still be heard, is a far more promising model than the tradition of "the poet" and "the *Beowulf* poet," the Anglo-Saxon counterpart to Homer, whose nonexistence, should anyone dare to proclaim it, would, at the end of the twentieth century, provoke a reaction not too different from Augustine Caxton's a century and a half earlier.

It is not surprising that today few dare to advocate origins for *Beowulf* in several poems composed by different authors; nor, as a result, is it surprising that another plausible idea—that *Beowulf* generates meaning through the interplay of individual textual voices generated by its external and internal readers—has likewise gone unobserved. We are too busy admiring the poet and correcting his language in our search for a unified literary experience. Our obsession with the need for a pure, complete origin in *Beowulf* has inspired criticism to focus on the unities and achievements of the text rather than its gaps and fissures. "Gaps" and "fissures" are, to some medievalists, irritatingly contemporary terms, synonymous with that urge in contemporary criticism to look at what is not in the text and claim for it as much significance as what traditional criticism has put there. Let us recall that it is a function of history to invent origins. When we see how origins of various kinds have been invented for *Beowulf,* by which I mean the set of traditions surrounding the poem, we can, in a sense probably more literal than he meant it, second Edward Irving's statement that "Beowulf is the product of centuries"[44]—not centuries preceding the poem, however, but the centuries that have come after it.

Gaps of two kinds, both textual and narrative, can serve (and have served) as sites for reading and writing; these activities align the horizons of characters in the poem, the scribes who copied it, and the early nineteenth-century scholars who recovered the poem.[45] My focus on reading and writing *Beowulf* has two sides: the manuscript itself and what must be written to make it readable; and the interpretive act, what must be written about *Beowulf* in order to interpret it. I shall take issue with the extent to which "writing" in the form of reconstruction of physical evidence has been permitted, and will encourage the conception of criticism as another kind of writing. The ways in which the poem's incompleteness can contribute to its effectiveness are to be found in the history of its reception.

An act of reception in the poem that all critics recognize is Hrothgar's welcome to Beowulf and his entourage when they arrive in Heorot. At lines 389–390 (fol. 138v8–11), Hrothgar tells his messenger, Wulfgar, to make haste in admitting the visitors to the king's presence.[46]

> "Gesaga him eac wordum   þæt hie sint wilcuman
> Deniga leodum."   Word inne abead:
> "Eow het secgan   sigedrihten min. . . ." (389–391)
> "Say to them in words that they are welcome to the
> people of the Danes." He spoke the words within: "I am
> commanded to tell you that my glorious leader. . . ."

The half-lines of line 390 do not alliterate. They should do so, and in 1857 Christian W. M. Grein wrote two more half-lines, as follows, to supply alliteration for the a-verse of line 390, making the existing half-line into the b-verse of the next line:[47]

> "Gesaga him eac wordum   þæt hie sint wilcuman
> Deniga leodum."   (Ða wið duru healle
> Wulfgar eode,)   word inne abead.
> "Eow het secgan   sigedrihten min. . . ."
> "Say to them in words that they are welcome to the people of the
> Danes." (Then Wulfgar went to the door of the hall.) He spoke
> the words within: "I am commanded to tell you that my glorious
> leader. . . ."

All editors follow suit, but most change the text, as did Klaeber, from "Wulfgar eode" to "widcuð hæleð"("widely known warrior").[48] Thus *Beowulf* acquired an entire line to remedy a metrical defect.

A restoration on the most badly damaged folio (fol. 179r) solves a crux that is not even recognized as an emendation but that instead has been regarded as a manuscript reading. At *Beowulf* 2221, two manuscript readings, one obscure, one plain, are involved. The second word in the line cannot be read; Zupitza suggested "mid":

> Nealles mid gewe(a)ldum wyrmhord a(b)ræ(c)
> sylfes willum. . . .
> Not deliberately, for his own desires, did he [break into
> the dragon's hoard]

The consequence of Zupitza's reading is that the sentence lacks a verb, and this in turn necessitated the rewriting of *cræft,* which is perfectly plain in the manuscript, to *abræc.* Neither Klaeber nor Wrenn-Bolton marks "mid" as a restoration, and Birte Kelly, in a long, two-part discussion of editorial emendations, does not list it either.[49] The rewriting of "cræft" at least merits a note in Klaeber and Wrenn-Bolton. Seeking to keep the manuscript reading, Kiernan suggests "næs" for Zupitza's "mid":

> Nealles næs geweoldum wyrmhorda(n) cræft
> sylfes willum. . . .

But that this line *is* a crux only Kiernan seems aware.[50] "Cræft" became "abræc" in the hands of Max Kaluza, a metricist who suggested the emendations to Holthausen, through whom it passed into the poem. Here we have, then, three cruces; two of them are pseudo-cruces, and one is a crux that is not even recognized as such. There are other examples.

Editorial emendation is sometimes a necessary rewriting. I wish to look at another kind of rewriting that *Beowulf* forces on its readers. Sometimes when we write *Beowulf,* we add something to the poem, not to restore or emend its meter and grammar but to voice its silences. I want us to consider as a "crux" what is said about writing and reading in the poem. "Intertextuality" has a wide semantic range; it revives and redefines the concept of an "inner history" of *Beowulf* and likewise alters our concept of the poem's readability. Eugene Vance describes it as the relationship "between a single text and the network of *other* texts that constitutes its cultural horizon."[51] Julia Kristeva introduced the term to French criticism in *La Révolution du langage poétique* to describe "transposition of one or more *systems* of signs into another, accompanied by a new articulation of the enunciative and denotative position."[52] The "other texts" or systems I shall discuss in intertextual relation to *Beowulf* are the incomplete episodes of *Beowulf,* its "digressions." They appear in narratives of the *scop* in Hrothgar's court, in recollections by the poet of *Beowulf,* and on the hilt of a sword. Taking a cue from a pun on "writing" and "cutting through," I shall also identify a story "written" by Beowulf when he pierces the dragon.

The intertextual relationship between the writing instruments and their carving action is clarified in Michael Riffaterre's definition of intertextuality through *syllepsis,* "the trope that consists in understanding the same word in two different ways at the same time, one meaning being literal or primary, the other figurative, with the second meaning "tied to the first as its polar opposite," as the two sides of a coin are joined. The relationship of the suppressed subtext to the text of the poem is intertextual because "the intertext is partly encoded within the text and conflicts with it because of stylistic or semantic incompatibilities." In "intratextual" intertextuality, Riffaterre says, "the syllepsis symbolizes the compatibility, at the significance level, between a text and an intertext incompatible at the level of meaning."[53]

I propose that we see "writan" and the element "writan" in "forwritan" as a *syllepsis,* as a structure joining writing and death in a pun on opposite meanings. Jonathan Culler discusses such words as "points of condensation," when "a single term brings together different lines of argument or sets of values."[54] Intertexts, I propose, can be identified in references to writing and reading as acts that surround texts, recognizing and receiving them. Some intertexts are created by critics and by editors whose technical practices govern our knowledge of *Beowulf,* intercepting the manuscript and writing the poem for us. Reading and writing also occur *within Beowulf,* and this I will demonstrate by examining these key words, "writan" and "forwritan," words which pun on "to write" and "to carve" and represent analogues for "to interpret."

"Writan," "to write," occurs only once in *Beowulf* (1688b), where the word is, with a nice irony, now only partially written; it survived as "writen" in the early nineteenth century, however, as recent work shows.[55] We may be surprised to find it in a poem said to reflect an oral rather than a written culture, a poem transmitted in oral form and about stories transmitted orally rather than in writing. I will juxtapose this word with another that occurs only once in *Beowulf* and that, in addition, appears only here in all of Old English, "forwritan" (2705a), meaning "to cut through" or "to cut in two." Given the choices possible for describing this very common action of hewing or cutting, this word too seems unexpected. Both words are linked to weapons. In Fitt 24, "writen" (past participle) refers to a story about monsters engraved on the hilt of a magic sword taken from the cave of Grendel's dam; I quote the passage at some length.

Hroðgar maðelode— hylt sceawode,
ealde lafe, on ðæm wæs or writen
fyrngewinnes, syðþan flod ofsloh,
gifen geotende giganta cyn,
frecne geferdon; þæt wæs fremde þeod
ecean Dryhtne; him þæs endelean
þurh wæteres wylm Waldend sealde.
Swa wæs on þæm scennum sciran goldes
þurh runstafas rihte gemearcod,
geseted and gesæd, hwam þæt sweord geworht
irena cyst ærest wære
wreoþenhilt ond wyrmfah. (1687–1698)

Hrothgar spoke—he examined the hilt, the ancient heirloom, on which was written the origins of ancient strife when the flood, the rushing ocean, slayed the race of giants. They suffered terribly, those people alien to [their] god; their ruler sent them their final reward through the surging waters. On the shining metal handle [of the sword] it was marked, set down, and said through secret letters, clearly, by [or for] whom the best of irons first was made, with a twisted hilt and with curved ornaments.

Hrothgar reads a story about the race from which Grendel and his mother descended. He examines the remnant ("lafe"), on which is written the origin of ancient strife; this bright gold sword hilt declares "through secret letters" for whom the sword was made. The engraved hilt constitutes a text, not simply a set of pictures, as the usual interpretation of "runes" implies.

In Fitt 37, "forwritan" (preterite, "forwrat") is used to describe how Beowulf cuts through the middle of the dragon once the monster has been wounded by Wiglaf:

Ða gen sylf cyning
geweold his gewitte, wæll-seaxe gebræd
biter ond beaduscearp, þæt he on byrnan wæg;
forwrat Wedra helm wyrm on middan. (2702b–2705)

The king still controlled his own senses; he drew the belt-knife, pointed and battle-sharp, that he wore on his shirt of mail; he, the protector of the Weders, carved the worm in the middle.

These two weapons accomplish Beowulf's revenge on three monsters. The magic sword of Fitt 23 is the "bil" that penetrated the dam (1567b) and cut off Grendel's head (1590b); he retrieves only the hilt from the cave, for the sword itself has mysteriously melted (1615b–1617b). The later sword "cuts through" (forwrat, 2705) the fire dragon in the last of the hero's three encounters with monsters.

Hewing and carving align these weapons with instruments for engraving and writing, in the sense of inscribing. "Writan" and "forwritan" derive from the same root, meaning "to cut" or "to carve." But "forwritan" may also translate "proscribere," meaning "to outlaw" or "to banish"; "forscrifen" (106) means "to proscribe," and "scrifan" means "to assign penalty," a secular as well as an ecclesiastical term.[56] Although the second sword's act of carving evokes writing—"forwriting" as it creates death, so to speak—this is not the direction in which the wordplay leads us. "Forwritan" is a *hapax-legomenon* (a sole occurrence of a word), but its etymological roots are those of "writan," and we have no other examples in Old English to contradict or to offset our response to the second element of the compound: "forwritan" means "to cut through" just as "writan" means "to write (by means of carving)." These words suggest that *Beowulf* contains subtextual references to reading and writing as yet uninterrogated; runes may be secret or magic writing, but they are writing nonetheless.[57]

I wish to use "writan" and "forwritan" in their immediate lexical context in *Beowulf* to discuss what I call the suppressed textuality of the poem. By juxtaposing these two words, we connect writing to death. "Runstafas" (1695) is a compound for "secret letters." A three-part apposition locates the letters: they were "gemearcod, geseted, and gesæd": "gemearcod" from "mearcian," "to mark;" "geseted" from "settan," "to set down;" and "gesæd" from "secgan," "to say." The textuality of the passage is developed by appositional verbs referring to one act of inscribing in three different but closely similar ways. These three appositives sharpen the link between "marking" and "telling." We are told this not once, then, but three times—to mark, to set down, to say; only the former pertains exclusively to carving, only the latter exclusively to telling.[58] The "-staf" element appears shortly after this passage at l. 1753, in "endestæf," which occurs only in *Beowulf*. It is usually translated "end," but it means "final letter" in Hrothgar's famous speech in which he says, "in the end," the body will decay. This is a striking reference, coming as it does after the "runstafas" on the sword hilt. What these "secret letters" convey is not conveyed to the reader, nor is it interpreted for us by those who read the runes in the poem.

My immediate concern is with the first sword (Fitt 24), on which is written a story about the race from which Grendel and his mother descended; this is the only story in *Beowulf* transmitted in written rather than oral form. The magic sword, as a text, has therefore already been "cut through": a "pen" (an engraving instrument) has written on the sword, cutting through the metal to create the text and, in the context of *Beowulf*, cutting through time to record the history of the race of Cain. We remember, of course, as we think about the relationship between swords and monsters, that part of Grendel's power is that such weapons cannot harm him, since he is protected from them (by a magic spell?) ("he sigewæpnum forsworen hæfde," 804). In any case, Grendel cannot be cut through by a sword, although his mother is not protected in this way.[59]

By juxtaposing "writan" and "forwritan," I juxtapose the sword as a text, an object that preserves the past and hence serves as a beginning, with the sword as a weapon, an object of destruction and ending. We can thereby juxtapose and relate writing and reading and, by implication, origins and ends. The juxtaposition as framed by writing ("writan," "forwritan") is, for us, admittedly coincidental. But coincidence here and elsewhere has the merit of helping us to see the familiar anew. *Beowulf* is about writing as well as about "cutting through," and therefore about the pen as well as the sword, because it is about both story-telling and stories. Frequent references to the *scop* remind us that texts lie within *Beowulf* and that we must view the work intertextually. The so-called digressions prevent us from knowing what they contain, what they narrate. As such, they are stories whose meaning, contained in their details, we will never know. Each episode is a text, a history partially written in *Beowulf* and partially lost. The Sigemund episode is an example.

Certain parallels between the Sigemund episode and Beowulf's own career as a swordsman are arresting. Surrounded with references to story-telling and mystery, the Sigemund episode is the most enigmatic of these tales and the most obvious account of story-telling. Sigemund, like Beowulf, uses his sword to cut through ("þurhwod," 890) a dragon. Sigemund is the *scop*'s subject; the *scop* tells everything ("welhwylc") he has heard about Sigemund, but also mentions many strange things—feuds and crimes—unknown to men because Sigemund told no one except his nephew, Fitela, about them. What should the reader of *Beowulf* make of this discussion? After all, these exploits are unknown to men, yet they alone preserve Sigemund's great fame. The episode of the sword and Sigemund serves as an example of bravery in battle, and more generally good kingship, of the type Beowulf himself will later demonstrate. This mysterious passage is followed by a perfectly clear one, and one that contrasts sharply with the Sigemund episode: the severely critical summary of Heremod's career as an unworthy king and Sigemund's predecessor. The contrast needs no further comment.

Like the Sigemund digressions, the episode involving Hrothgar and the sword hilt relates an event no one has witnessed. Beowulf uses the sword ("bil") to kill the dam and sever Grendel's head (the latter at last succumbing to the weapon powerless against him in life). As we have seen, Beowulf retrieves only the hilt from the cave, since the sword itself has mysteriously melted (1615b–1617b). The writing on the hilt, not noticed until the feast following Beowulf's victory, is another fragmentary story, told not by the *scop* who tells us about Sigemund, or the poet who tells us so little about Finnsburg. Instead it is read—and not told—by Hrothgar alone. And the reference to the text on the hilt comes at a crucial juncture in *Beowulf:* it is Hrothgar's act immediately before he begins the long narrative known as his "sermon." Criticism of the poem, to the extent that it notices the sword hilt, imagines that Hrothgar's harangue somehow expounds on or constructs an exegesis of the story on the hilt. We have been invited to suppose that the sword hilt and Hrothgar's speech contain the same lesson; I now invite us to suppose that these two texts diverge and that Hrothgar's speech counteracts the text on the hilt. The sword hilt contains only one—a single story not about the heroes, Beowulf, Hrothgar, Hygelac, Sigemund and others, but about their enemies.

Not all readers agree. James W. Earl, like Margaret Goldsmith, did not consider this passage a crux; both demystified the text on the hilt, saying that it records a story about the race of Giants punished by the flood (Genesis 6:4). The sword, according to Earl, reveals a divine judgment on the race of Cain after that judgment has been executed. Earl's link between Grendel, his mother, and the race of Cain is a traditional strategy that implies more than it needs to. This strategy invites us to assume that when Beowulf kills the monsters, the doom of their race, forecast on the sword, has been fulfilled. The hilt, the work of giants, may tell of the origin of the conflict, the "beginning of the ancient warfare;" this may be the flood that supposedly destroyed the race of giants, the fallen angels incestuously joined to daughters descended from Cain.

The sword hilt, therefore, may not depict the end of the race of Cain, but rather the flood that tried unsuccessfully to end that race. There is a large apocryphal literature about the creatures who escaped destruction, creatures who, if not like Grendel and his mother, are at least distantly related to them. The sword hilt is not necessarily a story of endings; it may quite possibly be a story of beginnings. It may tell of the beginning of an evil line, rather than its end, and in *Beowulf* it may serve to establish continuity between the curse of Cain, the descendants of creatures who escaped the flood, and the evil that has escaped Beowulf's own retribution and that will destroy him.

Beowulf's death is exchanged for cultural immortality. His people, the Geats, want to compose poetry at his funeral pyre ("wordgyd wrecan ond ymb w(er) sprecan," or so line 3172 is reconstructed), fittingly praising their leader "when he must (go forth) from his home" (3176–3177). The juxtaposition of writing and death—of the writing Beowulf performs, and the writing of *Beowulf,* with the deaths he is responsible for, and with his own death—prompts one to connect the poem to Foucault's essay, "What is an Author?," which deploys the notion of a multifaceted "author-function." Foucault maintains that in the modern world writing is linked to death. He contrasts this link to the conception of classical epic (and thus, for Anglo-Saxonists, the epic world of *Beowulf*), which "was designed to guarantee the immortality of a hero," and to the related phenomenon, as witnessed in *The Arabian Nights,* of stories that had "as their motivation, their theme and pretext, this strategy for defeating death"—that is, telling stories to postpone the moment of silence, to avert the unnameable.

Foucault's concern with how we conceptualize the creative consciousness at work in a text poses a challenge to criticism of anonymous texts. What sort of "author-function" do we prescribe for works by unknown hands? An "author-function" is responsible for many procedures that authenticate texts: a uniform level of quality, conceptual or thematic coherence, stylistic consistency, and even historical credibility. Unevenness in the text is "ascribed to changes caused by evolution, maturation, or outside influences."[60] Readers of *Beowulf* have much to think about after reading Foucault. *Beowulf* is an epic whose hero is "most eager for fame." The price of fame—lasting signification and heroic reputation—is death; a meaning that outlives time is purchasable only by death. To be present for eternity, Beowulf must become absent in the world in which he seeks to be remembered.

But this is not where the reader would expect a desire for origins to lead. When we turn back to "writan" and "forwritan," and ask again what difference it makes that we consider these verbs as puns, we can contemplate a horizon between readers and writers in the poem, and those outside it reading—and writing—their vision of history into *Beowulf.* As readers of *Beowulf,* we may wish to take these references to writing as warnings against rigorous interpretation. No one knows or will ever know what is written on the sword hilt, what Sigemund told Fitela, or what took place in the Finn episode. We shall never decipher the hermeneutic role of Hrothgar, whose "sermon," a commentary on a text we cannot read, creates our only textual link to the sword hilt. Swords supposedly put an end to the monsters, but in fact they did not; and pens continuously try to put an end to the stories of *Beowulf* by writing the deeds of the swords. But writing is a subject in the text and of the text, and so long as we read and write with it in view, the traditional valorization of the epic as a fixed monument to English culture is an indulgence.

I have tried to demonstrate that the illusive and allusive nature of writing and reading in *Beowulf* discourages us from acts of closure, and indeed prevents those acts of interpretation, of "cutting through," sought by conventional criticism. In order to interpret, one has to "cut through," a violent act that results in "death" in the text—calling a halt to the interplay of signs and sign systems—so that the critical act can be completed (art must die in order that criticism, so to speak, may live). There is a difference in *Beowulf* between what cannot be understood (i.e., known for certain) and what cannot be interpreted. Editorial conjecture and critical analysis are both attempts to understand that produce interpretations, even though the attempts remain incomplete. Indeed, they produce meaning *because* they remain incomplete.

Beowulf in History ■

Linking the study of Anglo-Saxon texts to the history of their reception requires an initial gesture of defamiliarization. Deconstruction and "Cædmon's Hymn," intertextuality, writing, and death in *Beowulf*, are means by which I hope to wrest these texts from comfortable interpretive paradigms of which those in the *Norton Anthology* are only the most obvious.[61] One reason that we have learned to ignore the history of texts is that philology has become a given of literary interpretation: philology seeks to account for *all* past knowledge of the manuscript, the text, and its language, and hence to constitute the culmination of the past. At this point, we need to recall Hans Robert Jauss's discussion of literary history at the end of the nineteenth century. Just as literary history saw the present as culminating in the past, so philology sees the past of the history of *Beowulf*'s reception culminating in its own mode of analysis. The literary critic uses philological data, which is regarded as factual assessment and which, therefore, stands for history, to mediate the text aesthetically.[62]

This is a profoundly unsatisfactory mode of operation. It reduces the cultural testimony—the reading and writing, the textual experience—of generations of previous readers to documentary evidence. Because their understanding of the text, its date and language, is seen as inferior to our understanding, their experience can be set aside; this demand, generated by the paradigm of progress, has narrowed the interpretive tradition to a process, which, at its worst, amounts to little more than a competition among readings of the texts as various cruces are variously solved in the interest of producing different literary interpretations. Examples in *Beowulf* criticism are numerous: Is Beowulf a Christian hero? Is he guilty of avaricious misjudgment at the end of the poem?

A study of the poem's reception is a vigorous alternative to this speculation. If we ask how the text incorporates reading and writing, themselves acts of reception and textual production, we establish a point of common interest between ourselves and characters in the poem, as well as its author and transcribers. Everyone who reads *Beowulf* today does so through a consciously perceived method; a related part of my strategy in this book is to stress hermeneutic self-consciousness, especially on the part of those who have taken to making final pronouncements about *Beowulf* and other texts. *Beowulf* may be a cliché and a joke inside as well as outside the profession, but it is a very young text all the same: it has had readers for barely two hundred years, while Bede's readership is of nearly thirteen hundred years' standing. The emergence of *Beowulf* into literary-historical time reveals the remarkable fact that its first readers, including Sharon Turner, John Conybeare, and Benjamin Thorpe, were both the poem's editors and its translators. That is, the lack of interpretive tradition for the vernacular epic, and the utter unfamiliarity of the text, forced them to translate—to interpret in the language of the day—what they transcribed and edited.[63]

Their hermeneutic mission was obvious, and the experimental nature of their work allowed them to change their minds, to correct their mistakes, and to alter their conclusions with impressive frequency. About the meaning of the poem they had little doubt. They seem to have decided what it meant chiefly by situating it in a horizon of texts constituted by the *Iliad* and the *Aeneid,* two texts often mentioned by early scholars of *Beowulf*. But *Beowulf* did not emerge as epic; it was first seen as romance and first admired by scholars reacting to the classicizing bias of the eighteenth century. In 1826, John Josias Conybeare, who had been the Rawlinson professor of Anglo-Saxon at Oxford from 1809–1812, noted, "it may even excite a smile to hear a production so little resembling the purer models of classical antiquity dignified by the name of poetry, or considered an object of criticism." Like Turner and others who, to Tolkien's dismay, admired *Beowulf* as history, Conybeare understood the poem chiefly as "a picture of manners and opinions, and in some measure even as a historical document," although it was in style more like to "the father of the Grecian epic, than to the romancers of the middle ages." The Finnsburg fragment he understood, with *Beowulf,* as "having constituted a portion of a similar historical romance."[64] Romance was an important attribute to document in Anglo-

Saxon literature for the simple reason that romance could then no longer be considered a French tradition introduced into Anglo-Saxon culture by the Normans.

Turner's discussion of *Beowulf* indicates some of the prejudice against which Anglo-Saxonists of his generation labored. Referring to the notorious "philologer" Joseph Ritson, Turner remarked, "It was asserted by Mr. Ritson, in conformity with the prevailing opinion of antiquaries, that the Anglo-Saxons had no poetical romance in their native tongue." Ritson's charge was of a piece with the view, common in the eighteenth century, that Anglo-Saxon England was a barbarous place with a barbarous civilization only lifted to respectability by the Norman Conquest. By demonstrating that *Beowulf* was a "poetic romance," Turner was able to claim that the merits of English literature after the Conquest were also evident before the Conquest; it was perhaps the first time that the "literary merit" of Anglo-Saxon texts was asserted in defending the Anglo-Saxon period against charges of barbarism.[65] No doubt the prejudice of Ritson and others against Anglo-Saxon literature had helped to delay the study of *Beowulf*. Turner introduced his summary of *Beowulf* in the 1823 edition of his *History* by observing, "The origin of the metrical romance has been lately an interesting subject of literary research; and as it has not been yet completely elucidated, it seems proper to enquire whether any light can be thrown upon it from the ancient Saxon poetry."[66]

As we would expect of scholars working in the vernacular, Anglo-Saxonists took their methods from the established routines of classical scholars. They knew what *Beowulf* meant, but they had to discover how to explain the certitude of that knowledge, and eventually how to defend it. They reversed the expected relationship between method and meaning. For us, the former creates the latter, but for them, I believe, the latter created the former. They knew what *Beowulf* was: a historical romance, akin to a national epic, and an account of national origins at once historical and mythical. Their pressing need was to explain why they were right. Like "Cædmon's Hymn," *Beowulf* was only rudimentary as poetry; but it contained the seeds of later greatness, and therein lay its value.

There is no record of anyone having read or understood *Beowulf* in the sixteenth or seventeenth century, although the manuscript came to the attention of seventeenth-century readers. These included Richard James (between 1628 and 1638) and Francis Junius (the Dutch scholar and publisher of the "works" of Cædmon, who lived in England from 1620–1650).[67] *Beowulf* was, for practical purposes, the discovery of Humphrey Wanley, who was the first Anglo-Saxonist to describe the manuscript, which he did in his catalogue of 1705. An earlier catalogue by Thomas Smith (1696) made no reference to *Beowulf*. Laurence Nowell wrote his name in the manuscript in 1563; Kiernan suggests that he acquired it through William Cecil and that John Bale might have owned it earlier, but there is no clear evidence of ownership before Nowell. Someone in Nowell's time underlined passages in the manuscript, but the markings are not those of Parker's assistants.[68] We have already seen that nearly a hundred years later neither Abraham Wheelock nor John Milton recognized an Anglo-Saxon poem when they saw it; "Cædmon's Hymn" had no status as a poem apart from sanctioning the use of music to instruct the faithful. Given the importance of ecclesiastical prose texts in sixteenth-century Anglo-Saxonism, one cannot be sure what those who could have read *Beowulf* at that time would have thought of it.

But at the end of the century Richard Verstegan and William Camden had begun writing about the continental origins of the English language. The study of "northern antiquities" became a preoccupation of Anglo-Saxonists in the eighteenth century, but even then *Beowulf* went nearly unnoticed and obviously unread. Its syntax made it much more difficult to read than the relatively straightforward prose—for example, the laws, the *Anglo-Saxon Chronicle*, even Bede's *History*—that was the scholars' chief concern. Even in the nineteenth century, Anglo-Saxonists were not sure of the nature or form of Old English poetry. The printed verse form of *Beowulf* fluctuated throughout the nineteenth century, sometimes appearing as individual half-lines (as in Benjamin Thorpe's edition of 1855) rather than the two-part lines modern readers are accustomed to, and sometimes in "long lines," or two full lines printed as one.

Wanley described the poem as an account of "Beowulf the Dane" against the Swedes; his description caught the attention of another reader. An eighteenth-century Danish archivist, Jakob Langebek (1710–1775), noticed *Beowulf* in Wanley's catalogue and wondered why no English scholar had studied this "Poema Anglosaxonicum vestustum & egregium" (Wanley's description). Langebek's notice in turn came to the attention of Grimur Jonsson Thorkelin (1752–1829), an Icelander in the service of the Danish government who went to England to look for manuscripts about Danish history and who became the first editor of *Beowulf*. Thorkelin transcribed the poem and hired a copiest to make another transcript some years later; he published his edition in 1815 with a Latin translation—a gesture reminiscent of many earlier Anglo-Saxonists' work, and a sign that he did not expect a scholarly audience to read Anglo-Saxon.[69]

Thorkelin's edition was ready for the press much earlier, but it was destroyed, in a staggering irony, when his house burned during the British bombardment of Copenhagen in 1807. Two years earlier, Sharon Turner had become the first English scholar to make prominent mention of *Beowulf*. Turner checked Thorkelin's transcriptions. "I have commonly found an inaccuracy of copying in every page," he noted, "but for a first publisher he has been, on the whole, unusually correct." Turner formed his own impressions of the poem; since he knew little Anglo-Saxon, he made numerous errors in describing the poem's events, but his views of 1805 were significantly different when the fourth edition of his *History* appeared in 1823. What Turner said about *Beowulf* would be repeated many times. "It is the most interesting relic of the Anglo-Saxon poetry which time has spared to us," he wrote; "and, as a picture of the manners, and as an exhibition of the feelings and notions of those days, it is as valuable as it is ancient."[70] His views were durable; they find an echo in the *Norton Anthology*.

Turner was asserting the value of Anglo-Saxon literature and history against a prejudice deeper than that concerning literary taste. As we saw in Chapter 2, the eighteenth century was hostile to Anglo-Saxon antiquities, and Turner and other scholars had much prejudice to combat as they sought to make way for the poem. Turner's view of the history recounted in the text reflects some of this bias; the view that Beowulf was a pirate, which I have traced to John Lingard's *The History and Antiquities of the Anglo-Saxon Church*, is a good example. Chauncey B. Tinker attributes some of Turner's misunderstandings to a misplaced page in the manuscript, which led him to an amusing mistake. The misplaced sheet (fol. 137) had been inserted to follow line 90 of the poem, with the result that the end of fol. 130v, which describes a *scop* singing a "creation hymn," the "swutol sang scopes" (90–98) that has been compared to Cædmon's, was immediately followed by the account of Grendel's first assault on Heorot after Beowulf has arrived, so that line 91b and line 740a were continuous: "feorran reccan" (91b) "feng hraðe forman siðe (740).[71] The result was a jarring juxtaposition of the scop's graceful narrative with a description of a warrior being slain by the monster:

> He who knew
> The beginning of mankind
> From afar to narrate.
> "He took wilfully
> By the nearest side
> The sleeping warrior.

He slew the unheeding one
With a club on the bones of his hair."[72]

After he published this translation in 1805, Turner realized that a leaf was misplaced early in the codex and corrected his translation. His view of the piratical nature of Beowulf's voyage was not related to this mistake, however, and it appears in both the first and the fourth editions of his work. Turner's view that Beowulf appeared in the poem as "preparing for a warlike or predatory venture," and later, in the court, can be traced to Unferth's challenge to the hero: "Art thou Beowulf, he that with such profit labours on the wide sea, amid the contests of the ocean? There you for riches and for deceitful glory, explore its bays. . . ."[73] Turner directs Lingard's view of the piratical nature of the Saxons at his hero.

The rehabilitation of Anglo-Saxon studies brought about by the study of *Beowulf* was greatly assisted by the next English scholar of the poem, Conybeare. Conybeare's work was not published until 1826, after his death, and it included studies that he carried out as a pastor after leaving Oxford. Conybeare's achievements were many. In addition to publishing texts from the *Exeter Book* for the first time, he began the study of Old English meter, and greatly assisted the effort to win recognition for poetry in Old English, correctly perceiving that its value as literature depended on this link. Conybeare asserted that Old English poetry was undervalued and that the fault lay with "our still imperfect knowledge" of the construction of Anglo-Saxon poetry rather than with the poetry itself. Conybeare was conscious of the work of contemporary philologists, and wrote that certain elements in *Beowulf* "do assuredly bear, if it may be so termed, an oriental rather than a northern aspect," noting that certain scholars were claiming Gothic and Sanskrit "as cognate dialects."[74] He was the first to connect *Beowulf* not only to northern antiquities, but to the Orient. His views of Anglo-Saxon poetry, along with those of Benjamin Thorpe, another translator of *Beowulf* who was working in Denmark, were incorporated by Henry Wadsworth Longfellow, who turned some of Conybeare's text into modern English.[75]

Conybeare's work with meter and his comparative studies (between Old English and Scandanavian poetry) indicated his awareness of the need for method. Method came to nineteenth-century Anglo-Saxon studies in the person of John Mitchell Kemble, who was, as we saw in Chapter 2, influenced by Jakob Grimm, and who was nineteenth-century England's most important Anglo-Saxonist. Kemble edited *Beowulf* twice, in a limited edition in 1833 that he improved and corrected and published again in 1837. In 1837 he published his translation and notes, dedicating it to Jakob Grimm. Kemble describes Grimm as the "founder of that school of philology, which has converted etymological researches, once a chaos of accidents, into a logical and scientific system."[76] But it was more than scholarly method that Kemble brought to England; he brought with it historical meaning in the form of a pure, pagan, Germanic origin that would serve as the foundation of scholarly ideas about Anglo-Saxon England for more than a century.

Kemble first believed that *Beowulf* was historical, as did Turner and Conybeare, and dated it to the mid-fifth century, close to "the coming of Hengest and Hors into Britain." He believed that the poem was brought by these settlers and that the manuscript was only a "careless copy" of "an older and far completer poem." The implications of his view for editorial method are considerable. Kemble believed that manuscript readings should be kept rather than emended, since they "serve sometimes as guides and clues to the inner being and spiritual tendencies of the language itself." He lamented the continuing decline of the manuscript, the "progressing evil" of letters falling away.[77] Kiernan estimated that some two thousand letters were lost between the time of Thorkelin's transcripts and the rediscovery of *Beowulf* in the mid-nineteenth century.[78] Kemble rather apologetically made corrections to Thorkelin's transcripts (again, one can compare Kemble to Turner in this regard).

Kemble's 1837 preface contained a great deal of backtracking; it declared the 1833 preface "null and void." His view of the historical significance of *Beowulf*, which he attributed to the Danish historian Suhm, Kemble now renounced. *Beowulf* became instead "a confused remembering of heathen myth," and its main character but a "shadow" of the "earlier Beowulf," who was a divinity. Kemble traced extremely elaborate genealogies for Germanic and Scandanavian deities he saw hovering in the text of *Beowulf*. Beowulf's name itself had taken many forms—Beow, Beowine—that connected him to "the Olympus of the North," as John Earle later put it.[79] Kemble showed the capacity of philology to produce extravagant speculation, richly supported by arcane learning, much of it mythological and most of it thoroughly romantic. His preface to his edition and translation of the text bristle with learning forced into abstractly perfect patterns, finding, through some very fine differentiation of proper names, twenty-four mythic heroes, "the ancient mythic genealogy of our kings nearly as it was known to our forefathers in the heathen times."[80] Thus the genealogy of the pagan gods did not, in the end, remove *Beowulf* from the scene of national literary history. The poem asserted a direct relation of the past ("our forefathers") to the present ("our kings").

Kemble's two prefaces illustrate the important consequences of method for meaning. His growing grasp of philological criticism and its relation to mythology caused him, in just two years, to repudiate a whole set of assumptions about the poem and its history. The more "scientific" his method, the more remote and exotic the meaning. Kemble ascended these rather dizzying heights in order to proclaim the greatness of Grimm and the philological method; his speculations are a potent reminder of the fundamental romanticism of Grimm's own thinking about language, myth, and history.

Kemble's most important influence on *Beowulf* came through a scholar inspired by him and by Lachmann, Lachmann's pupil Karl Müllenhoff, who applied the *Liedertheorie* to *Beowulf* and so put scholarship of the English epic on the level of that of Homer's. Müllenhoff sent *Beowulf* flying in several directions. Tracing the "inner" history of the poem required some remodeling and house cleaning. In particular, its Christian content had to be identified as added and interpolated, an excrescence to be rejected so that the poem could be newly restored to its original purity. The theory was better received in the next century, when, in 1905, L. L. Schücking endorsed it in *Beowulfs Rückkehr,* and later scholars, including Berendsohn in 1935, and, most prominently in 1950s, Francis P. Magoun, Jr., explored the idea.[81] However, this attempt to recover origins conflicted with emerging claims for the achievement of Anglo-Saxon culture in unifying Christian and pagan world views.

But Müllenhoff's was not the most radical scholarship of the poem in the nineteenth century. That distinction, I believe, belongs to one of its Danish scholars, Thorkelin's successor as custodian of the poem, Nikolai F. S. Grundtvig. Although a part of the poem had been translated earlier by Ebenezer Henderson, who used Thorkelin's transcript to translate the *scop*'s songs into English,[82] Grundtvig produced the first full-length paraphrase of *Beowulf.* Discussions of the poem, after Müllenhoff, become notorious for designating certain parts of the poem as interpolations and arguing that they be excised; Grundtvig was the first to make *Beowulf* longer. This he did twice, first in 1820. As his title—*Bjowulfs Drape* ("Beowulf's Burial")—indicates, Grundtvig wrote a conclusion for the poem. In his edition of *Beowulf,* published in 1861, he incorporated the whole of the "Finnsburg Fragment" into the text after line 1160. Thorkelin protested the first addition, as one might expect; Grundtvig's achievement remains underappreciated. What he wrote is no mere continuation of the poem, however, but an account of Beowulf's last words by a Danish *skald*. The poet implores that the "clan of the Angles, now alienated from the North, might remember old Denmark."[83]

Grundtvig's edition of *Beowulf* of 1861 is important for several reasons. Earle considers it the most extreme edition in its incorporation of emendations. In fact, Grundtvig began correcting Thorkelin's transcripts without having seen the manuscript itself. "Almost all his corrections proved to be identical with the reading of the manuscript," Earle reports, and Grundtvig was subsequently accorded "a demonstrated right to correct the manuscript itself."[84] This view corresponds to Kemble's 1837 preface, which claims that a modern edition by a scholar well-versed in Anglo-Saxon "will in all probability be much more like the original than the [manuscript] copy."[85]

But Grundtvig mastered details of *Beowulf* that no one before him had understood. His most famous discovery was the identification of Hygelac in *Beowulf* with Chochilaicus, a king mentioned by Gregory of Tours, an important historical connection that Grimm borrowed in his *Geschichte der Deutschen Sprache*.[86] Grundtvig's text—but not his compendious editorial apparatus—was adopted by Grein, whose edition of the poem in 1867 was notable for its conservatism. Grein relied on Grundtvig for the simple reason that Grundtvig had collated Thorkelin's transcripts against the manuscript in England (between 1829–1831) and was assumed to have an unparalleled knowledge of it.

Early scholars of *Beowulf* both edited and translated the text, and could not do one without the other. Kelly's recent study notes that over half the emendations of *Beowulf* accepted by editors from 1950 onward had already been proposed by Grein in 1857. Kelly adds—and this is usually forgotten—that numerous errors and inconsistencies were introduced into the text during this same period because, until 1888 and Zupitza's facsimile and edition, no one had yet edited the poem from the manuscript itself: all editors before Grundtvig worked with transcripts only.[87] In other words, over half the emendations of *Beowulf* accepted in modern scholarship are based on the work of editors who never saw the manuscript.

Beowulf as History ■

What emerges in the early history of *Beowulf* scholarship is not a march of progress, or a transition from one view to another, but a picture of ongoing disputes about method and the poem's meaning. In Denmark, we can compare Thorkelin to Grundtvig; in Germany, we can compare

Müllenhoff to Grein; in England, Kemble to Thorpe. The lines dividing scholars were not national, although their scholarship was often intensely nationalistic. Rather, the major arguments were about methods of textual criticism. We can see that the early history of *Beowulf* scholarship is, therefore, relevant to teaching the poem as a record of how the methods of studying Anglo-Saxon poetry were developed, so to speak, in the laboratory of the text—a figure of speech some of the scholars would have approved of. The first phase of reception was historical, as we see in Thorkelin and Grundtvig, both of whom continued a Danish antiquarian tradition for several decades; and in Turner and the Kemble of 1833. The second phase emphasized poetry and mythology, as we see in Conybeare, the Kemble of 1837, and Müllenhoff's application of the *Liedertheorie,* an extension of Kemble.

The history of this scholarship is rich in summary views. That which I have found most useful is Earle's of 1892, sympathetic in regard to early scholars, jaundiced in regard to those who came later, especially to scholars who advocated the *Liedertheorie,* which he called "that passion for discovering the sutures of poetic workmanship which they have excited among themselves through generations of competitive theorizing about Homer."[88] One phrase in particular here leads me to my conclusion: "competitive theorizing." Let me set Earle's disdain for competitive theorizing against a similar sentiment from a highly regarded source, R. W. Chambers, whose great study, Beowulf: *An Introduction to the Study of the Poem,* is a retrospective on scholarship that in some ways stands in relation to *Beowulf* as Wheelock's edition stands in relation to Bede's *History.* After nearly four hundred pages that examine a century's worth of historical evidence, including the consequences of claims for the "inner history" of the poem, Chambers pointed to the synthesis of views in Klaeber's edition, and remarked, "It [the edition] *has* shown that, *if we can agree upon the method to be used,* a good many problems can be settled" (his emphasis). A few paragraphs later he acknowledged differences dividing his views, Klaeber's, and those of several other scholars, and wrote, "The essential thing is the agreement."[89]

I have said several times in this study that conflict is a meaningful rather than distasteful part of scholarship. Earle's dismay at German competitiveness (which reminds us of Sweet's fear of "Germanizing himself," seen in Chapter 2), and Chambers's insistence that shared method would bring agreement, are statements from two very different scholars about issues fundamental to my study of Anglo-Saxon scholarship and my views of the profession as it enters its postmodern age. For I believe in teaching conflict rather than endorsing methodological uniformity to obliterate it; and I believe in encouraging a diversity of methods that renews conflict productively and meaningfully. The history of *Beowulf* scholarship demonstrates the effect of reading and writing in *Beowulf* on *Beowulf*. Textual reception and textual production express a desire for origins. Activities exterior to the origin they desire, they themselves constitute the origin, and *Beowulf* scholars, as if unaware of the paradox, pursue each other rather than the epic they claim to study.

7

Nationalism, Internationalism, and Teaching Anglo-Saxon Studies in the United States

Pedagogy and Politics ■

My goal in this book has been to explore some of the political links between scholars and their subjects that make Anglo-Saxon studies "worldly" and that therefore require worldly criticism. Worldly Anglo-Saxon scholarship challenges the orthodoxies of Anglo-Saxon studies and treats the pillars of orthodoxy with purposeful irreverence, demythologizing, deconstructing, and dismantling them. To assert the meaning of "method" is to return method to the worldly circumstances in which it developed; to examine the cultural and social constructions excluded by narrow documentary analysis is to situate texts in a timely rather than a timeless sense; to connect "not old English" to Old English is to demonstrate the power of Anglo-Saxon language and culture as events that are still taking place, reaching readers and writers, and serving human interests.

Worldly criticism, as defined by Edward W. Said, is culturally specific, committed, and skeptical of authority. In "Religious Criticism," Said compares culture to religion. He writes that "grand ideas," such as Orientalism, "have something in common with religious discourse" in that each can become "an agent of closure, shutting off human investigation, criticism, and effort in deference to the authority of the more-than-human, the supernatural, the other-worldly." The communal sense that religion and culture sometimes create can work against worldly or "secular" criticism, which Said defines as "a sense of history and of human production, along with a healthy skepticism about the various official idols venerated by culture and by system." These scholarly instincts are disadvantaged by "appeals to what cannot be thought through and explained, except by consensus and appeals to authority."[1]

Appeals to consensus and authority are routine in Anglo-Saxon studies. How badly they have served the subject we can see in textbooks used to teach the language. Almost without exception, they confront introductory-level students—those who, by registering for a course in Old English, have already expressed willingness to learn it—with a formidable array of phonological rules and paradigms that presume on that willingness and ignore the need to build interest in the subject. Introductory chapters of older textbooks revised only a few years ago look almost exactly as they did in the last century; rather than address large, cultural aspects of the subject or examine the history of the discipline, they dive immediately into the wonders of sound changes. R. C. Alston speaks to the point when he protests that there is too much phonology in philology. Wary of the rise of belletristic criticism, he rightly anticipated that Old English and language study generally were being presented to students far too narrowly.[2]

Examples of the emphasis on phonology in philology—at the expense, I might add, of the history of philology—are abundant. *Bright's Grammar and Reader,* revised in 1971, one of the best all-around texts since it supplies detailed textual notes and facsimile manuscript pages, is nevertheless one of the worst offenders in this regard; its chapters on phonological changes, written with a professional audience in mind, raise immediate, intimidating barriers.[3] *A Guide to Old English,* by Bruce Mitchell and Fred C. Robinson, handles linguistic material much better, and remembers to define parts of speech, which even graduate students sometimes do not know. But it homogenizes texts into a nonexistent standard or "normalized" dialect and thereby defeats the point of learning about phonology. Henry Sweet's *Primer,* first published in 1882, revised by Norman Davis in 1970, remains by comparison a clear and concise gem. But Sweet himself explained that his "primer" was intended "for students who have already had some linguistic training—especially those who know German," and he produced a simpler version, *First Steps in Anglo-Saxon,* for those "whose memories will not bear the strain of having to master a grammar of some length before proceeding to the texts."[4] There are students whose memories will bear the strain of mastering grammar, but they rightly expect to be given good reasons for doing so. Introductory texts that treat grammatical paradigms *as* texts—as constructions open to analysis, discovery, and discussion—would effectively break down the paralyzing procedure of "first the grammar, only then the literature" that has made Old English so tedious for so long. Grammar is historically constructed; it is a shifting discourse of power, and learning about its regularities is not a priestly rite of initiation which only the most devoted should expect to survive.

Old English textbooks treat linguistic methods but conceal the process, and the meaning, of their historical development. Neither *Bright's Grammar* nor the Mitchell-Robinson introduction explains "Grimm's Law" or "Verner's Law" as historically produced, or recognizes that to describe sound changes as "laws" is to perpetuate the misleading idea that language change is both as regular and as independent of human agency as the laws of gravity. H.C.G. von Jagemann saw the dangers of this assumption long ago. "Thus it is now well recognized that the term *law,* as applied to linguistic processes, cannot be used in the same sense as in speaking of purely physical phenomena. Every linguistic process is immensely more complicated than any purely physical one, or, to speak more accurately, in the latter we get down much sooner to certain universal truths . . . ."[5] The difference between a "law" and the phenomenon it describes should be explained, not assumed, and made a point of interrogation rather than an article of faith. The presentation of orthodoxy in Anglo-Saxon textbooks may not rival the "theology" surrounding studies of the Orient, but Anglo-Saxon scholars have venerated the practices of the past with something like religious fervor. There is much evidence of this veneration to be found in the dedications of monumental Anglo-Saxon texts and in historical (and therefore theoretical) reflections of medievalists on their occupation. Among the most revealing of all "not Old English" texts, these prefaces and forewords manifest the social world of Anglo-Saxonists themselves and stand, quite literally, between each respective "culture" and the "system" of Anglo-Saxon editions and critical studies; I return to them in my conclusion.[6] I want first to define some distinctively American developments in Anglo-Saxon studies in the last century and view them as a prelude to developments in the next.

Jefferson's Plans for Anglo-Saxon ■

My first chapter cited the importance of Jefferson's design for the Great Seal of the United States: On one side he wanted to picture the mythical Anglo-Saxon warriors, Hengst and Horsa; on the other, he wanted to portray the Chosen People following a pillar of fire. Jefferson saw Hengst and Horsa as ideal leaders of a free and democratic people who were, at least in Jefferson's imagination, "chosen" to live in a free world of individual rights and communal blessings. The English Constitution and Common Law were Saxon "legacies" for Jefferson, reflections of "primitive democracy." He saw pre-Conquest England as a time of wide-spread liberties for freedom-loving Anglo-Saxons, a pre-Christian Paradise destroyed by Norman-led feudalism and restored by the Magna Carta. In his *Summary View of the Rights of British America* in 1774, he compared the arrival of the settlers in America to the arrival of the Saxons in England from the woods of northern Europe. Their leaders were Hengst and Horsa.[7]

Jefferson was among those who believed that the Norman Conquest did not destroy the Anglo-Saxon political foundations of Europe. "The battle of Hastings, indeed, was lost," Jefferson wrote, "but the natural rights of the nation were not staked on the event of a single battle. Their will to recover the Saxon constitution continued unabated, and was at the bottom of all the unsuccessful insurrections which succeeded in subsequent times." He noted that the "Whig historians of England . . . have always gone back to the Saxon period for the true principles of their constitution, while the Tories and Hume, their Coryphaeus, date it from the Norman conquest, and hence conclude that the continual claim by the nation of the good old Saxon laws, and the struggles to recover them, were 'encroachments of the people on the crown, and not usurpations of the crown on the people.'"[8]

Because he believed that Saxon laws were the foundation of American democracy, Jefferson, with a literalness we may find startling, applied technical terms from Anglo-Saxon law in his writing about how law should be taught in the United States. He even copied out parts of the Virginia Constitution in Old English characters. Referring to an Anglo-Saxon unit of land measure called the "hundred," frequently mentioned in the laws of King Alfred, Jefferson proposed in the Land Ordinance of 1784 that the American West be measured out in units of "hundreds," ten-mile square sections. In a letter to Major John Cartwright, Jefferson proposed dividing the counties of Virginia into six-mile squares that "would answer to the hundreds of your Saxon Alfred."[9] His practical interest in education is symbolized in his plan to divide every county into hundreds "of such size that all the children of each will be within a central school in it," calling these units "little republics" which "would be the main strength of the great one."[10] It is clear that Jefferson's interest was in the practical application of the

Anglo-Saxon language, not in the investigation of its literature. By his own account, Jefferson began to study "the Northern languages" after his law-student days at William and Mary. He pursued these studies as part of his education in political history all his life. In a letter of November 1825, just a year before his death, Jefferson wrote to J. Evelyn Denison (M.P.) that, "Literature is not yet a distinct profession with us. Now and then a strong mind arises, and at its intervals of leisure from business, emits a flash of light. But the first object of young societies is bread and covering; science is but secondary and subsequent."[11] Anglo-Saxon studies were not to be a distinct profession for many years. But if Jefferson's pursuit of Old English was a secondary, it was not insignificant.

Jefferson's Anglo-Saxon scholarship linked law and education through Anglo-Saxon grammar. For Jefferson, the study of language was preparatory to the study of law; hence he wished everyone who attended the University of Virginia to learn it. In a letter to John S. Vater in 1812, Jefferson revealed his belief in the connection between language and national identity. It precisely parallels the thesis of many Oriental scholars of the nineteenth century that language is the basis of nationality and that a nation is a cultural rather than a political unit. Jefferson wrote to Vater, "I have long considered the filiation of languages as the best proof we can ever obtain of the filiation of nations."[12] He knew that nothing could be done to propagate Anglo-Saxon institutions without improving methods for learning the "dialect," a term which shows that he did not see Anglo-Saxon roots as remote from his own and that he understood the Anglo-Saxon language to be the immediate source of his own. Jefferson's accomplishments in Anglo-Saxon, the extent of his interest in the grammar and the means to teach it, are remarkable. Old English orthography, which reflects dialectal and historical changes, seemed to Jefferson the consequence of the ill training of scribes. Thus Jefferson developed a system for simplifying the orthography to lessen "the terrors and difficulties presented by its rude alphabet," finding the forms of the "black-letter" type "rugged, uncouth, and appalling," and advocating clean, simple Roman type in its place.[13] In other words, for a pure language, Jefferson wanted a clean type.

Jefferson knew the laws of the Anglo-Saxons, at least the laws attributed to Alfred, in detail, and undertook a textual study of them. No advocate of organized religion, he insisted that "the common law existed while the Anglo-Saxons were yet pagan, at a time when they had never heard the name of Christ pronounced, or ever knew that such a character had ever existed." The laws of Alfred are highly unusual in their frequent quotations from the Book of Exodus and the Acts of the Apostles; but then Alfred was an unusually learned king. Jefferson regarded references to Scripture as interpolations and attributed them to "Anglo-Saxon priests" who corrupted the "common law" and attempted to appropriate it in a "conspiracy" between Church and State.[14] His view resembles that of John Foxe, John Bale, and other passionate reformers of the sixteenth century. Jefferson was naive about the development of law codes; his desire to remove the contaminating influence of Christianity in order to recover the "pure" or "native" origins of the Saxon laws recalls the efforts of Matthew Parker, John Foxe, and others to emend and thus rewrite Anglo-Saxon texts to make them conform to early Anglican visions of English history.

Thanks to Jefferson, courses in Anglo-Saxon language and law appeared in the United States first in the curriculum of the University of Virginia, where they were for years the only English courses taught. In his letter of June 1824 to Cartwright, Jefferson set forth his whole philosophy on the English constitution and his plans for teaching Anglo-Saxon. He directed that the curriculum of the University of Virginia, then taking shape, should include agriculture, a "professorship of the principles of government," and Anglo-Saxon. Anglo-Saxon was actually to be used to teach government, as he wrote: "As the histories and laws left us in that type and dialect, must be the text-books of the reading of the learners, they will imbibe with the language their free principles of government." Commenting on the curriculum at William and Mary, then the only public college in Virginia, Jefferson noted that there was a professor for Modern Languages but none for Anglo-Saxon. He suggested that one should be added "for the ancient languages and literature of the North, on account of their connection with our own language, laws, customs, and history."[15]

Jefferson's grammar of Old English proposed sweeping revisions of methods for the presentation and teaching of the Anglo-Saxon language. Eager to divest the subject of its antiquarian, obscurantist aspect and brighten it for a new American audience, he complained that those who had written the grammars had given it "too much of a learned form" and had endeavored

> to mount it on all the scaffolding of the Greek and Latin, to load it with their genders, numbers, cases, declensions, conjugations, etc. Strip it of these embarrassments, vest it in the Roman type which we have adopted instead of our English black letter, reform its uncouth orthography, and assimilate its pronunciation, as much as may be, to the present English, just as we do in reading

> Piers Plowman or Chaucer, and with the cotemporary [sic] vocabulary for the few lost words, we understand it as we do them.[16]

His aim was to make Old English look as much like modern English as possible; he sought to recover obsolete words and so to restore some of the Anglo-Saxon vocabulary to popular speech.

Jefferson won the wars of westward expansion but lost the battle of philology. The pedagogical rigidity he deplored had barely emerged when he wrote, for the full apparatus of Germanic philology was just being invented. Jefferson would have been pleased to know that Francis B. Gummere proposed, before the MLA in 1885, that English philology be taught in the elementary school—an essay quoted in my preface—but I doubt if he would have been delighted at the state of Anglo-Saxon studies a century after his death.[17]

Post-Jefferson, Pre-Modern ■

Jefferson was an Anglo-Saxonist, not a philologist. But not long after his death the distinctive American uses of philology and Anglo-Saxon studies were apparent. Among those who taught Old English at the University of Virginia, George Blätterman and Schele de Vere published significant scholarship, and a group of Anglo-Saxonists were trained by them, including J. L. Johnson and others who taught at universities in the South. One of the most remarkable of these early scholars, an acquaintance of Blätterman at Virginia, was Louis Frederick Klipstein (1813–1878), a graduate of Hampden-Sydney College who seems to have been the first American to publish on Anglo-Saxon. Klipstein published *The Study of Modern Languages* in 1845, *A Grammar of Anglo-Saxon* in 1848 and a collection of texts, *Analecta,* in 1849. All appear to have been commercial failures, although the author had hopes that they would make him rich.

Klipstein's Orientalism emerges in his "ethnographical essay," the introduction to the *Analecta,* in which, "on philological principle," he traces the origins of the Anglo-Saxons to the East and demonstrates the closeness of Persian and Teutonic dialects. "If this opinion is correct," he wrote, "an opinion which is supported by historical facts, though dim, but especially by philology, the occupation of the East by the British arms, and by British enterprise, will eventually be like the return of a stream to its source in fertilizing showers."[18] Klipstein, unlike Jefferson, was abreast of continental and English scholarship. In London, in 1850, Edward Bulwer-Lytton did not link *Beowulf* to Wolf's Homeric scholarship, but in the United States in 1848, Klipstein did. "Even if the poem of Beowulf was composed in the days of Hengist, as some think," he wrote, "we need not conclude that it was at once committed to writing, as it may have been preserved in the memory of minstrels, and thus handed down to later times, like the Homeric Rhapsodies, and all literary productions in the early unlettered stages of a people" (p. 80).

Klipstein was writing in the pre-Civil War America; his expansionist politics portray a bright and indeed unlimited national future. "There is something morally sublime in the advance of the American people westward," he wrote (thinking chiefly of the conquest of Mexican territory). In order to conquer a nation, it was only necessary for American enterprise to enter it, for in the face of commercial success there could be no military failure. He saw the United States as "a giant in youth—in infancy, shall we say?" and asked, "What will not the American branch be in vigor of manhood, unfettered as it is, in the career which its inherent destiny has assigned to it, and being unfettered, capable of developing powers to overawe the world?" (pp. 96–97).

Although he saw himself as a scholar as well as a Presbyterian minister, Klipstein represents a counterpart to the polemical and popular rather than the academic and scholarly tradition of Anglo-Saxon scholarship. He is closer in kind to John Bale and John Foxe than to John Leland or William Camden, closer to Sharon Turner than to John Mitchell Kemble. Klipstein ended his life a drunk "living among the Negroes" of Charleston, says the *Dictionary of American Biography.*[19] The pre-eminent figure of the other, strictly scholarly line of American Anglo-Saxonism, Francis A. March (1825–1911), met a better fate.

March can be considered the most important of the American Anglo-Saxonists of the nineteenth century. Long on the faculty of Lafayette College (Easton, Pennsylvania), March was the first professor of English and comparative philology in the United States and author of several books on teaching Anglo-Saxon and philology. Three of his works demonstrate the similarity of his thinking to Jefferson's and also identify a key difference. In *Methods of Philological Study of the English Language,* March compared classical philology to the philology then taught in American schools. The inquiry ranged wide, connecting grammar to "etymology, rhetoric, poetry, and criticism," and also to questions of psychology. Because "the general laws of language are on one side also laws of mind," he wrote, language "includes the study of the history and character of a race and their language, and of the nature in which they have lived, since from these result the peculiar laws and idioms of a language, and the power of special words and phrases over the national heart." All this sounds promising and expansive, but the preface includes a sober note. "Similar questions are iterated and reiterated; the teacher should reiterate without end, that the dullest may be made to run in the right rut."[20]

Analyzing the "General Prologue" to *The Canterbury Tales,* March supplied two pages of questions (in tiny type) related to each word (and even individual letters) of the first two lines (pp. 90–93). Questions included, "What kind of letter is *d*—labial, palatal, or lingual? Why so called? Name the labials!" Grimm's law is frequently mentioned; opportunities for humor are few, and none is taken, not even for "Marche" (as in "the droght of Marche"), which prompts the question, "From what language is *Marche?*" March offered to relieve the pain of compositions for students by urging that writing out scraps of lecture notes and investigating them make composition "97% less horrible." He does not discuss the pains of reading such compositions, which he believed was all that the professor of rhetoric could do "toward the study of the English language and of English literature."[21]

Gerald Graff portrays some of the horrors of March's method, the practice of which is, he says, "grotesquely illustrated" by March's textbook.[22] It is not a pedagogical style one would want to emulate, but Graff's charges against him are rather superficial. In fact, March constantly mixed questions about language with questions about culture. Both subjects were no doubt conceptualized in a very narrow way, but March expected his students to know a great deal of historical information about the texts they took apart. My own students, reading his book, have been able to see past the mechanical nature of the presentation to a familiarity with tradition they envy. March also seems to have selected his passages with particular care, holding up Chaucer's Squire as a model young man, for example, and choosing selections from John Bunyan's *Pilgrim's Progress* with obvious edifying content.

In 1875, March reported on a survey of the teaching of Anglo-Saxon in the United States. "It is strange that there should have been no more study of Anglo-Saxon, the mother of our mother tongue," he wrote. "There is talk enough about it. From the way our orators and critics dilate upon the glories of the Anglo-Saxon tongue, and the beauty and power of an Anglo-Saxon style, one would suppose that everybody studies it."[23] March gave some very good Jeffersonian reasons why Anglo-Saxon should be studied. "Languages are studied for discipline, as a key to their books, as tools for further investigation, and as models or other aids in our own talking and writing." Inflected languages—Latin, Greek, and Anglo-Saxon are his examples—require mental discipline to learn; they are records of "mind and law." Anglo-Saxon he considered especially important for knowledge of modern English.

This emphasis on mechanical learning has a venerable place in the humanistic tradition. Anyone reading the descriptions of how knowledge was transmitted in the Renaissance classroom, vividly described by Anthony Grafton and Lisa Jardine, will understand that rote memorization—transcription of what the teacher dictated—was not an innovation in Germanic philology, but a continuation of standard pedagogical practice.[24]

In his *Introduction to Anglo-Saxon: Primer and Reader* March wrote that because every scholar should have a scholarly knowledge of the English language "every scholar ought to study Anglo-Saxon."[25] March, ever methodical, outlined three ways to learn languages. The first method was "offhand," guessing at meaning by picking up a word here and there and supposing the rest to be clear. French, he said, was commonly read this way, and it was also how March supposed Jefferson to have studied Anglo-Saxon. Latin and Greek required a different approach, which March called "historical and esthetical study." This method focused on connections of thought and attention to modes and tenses, "so as fully to get the thought" and "recreate the environment." Since this approach was more systematic, March approved of it. The third was "philological study," used "in a few of the best colleges," and also the best method. As March had shown in his earlier publication, this method required "careful scrutiny of every word in view of the modern science of language." "The best students," he said, prepared etymologies of every word, as well as comparative syntax, and had to "scrutinize word after word and phrase after phrase with minute attention" (pp. 5–6). March admitted that Anglo-Saxon was "hard to prepare, and needs the stimulus of interesting applications," but he regrettably gave no indication of what these were to be, and his own philological handbook, as we have seen, is no help. We can, however, see the obvious association of methods with cultures studied: lax method for French, historical and aesthetic for Latin and Greek, scientific and disciplined for the Germanic tongues.

March thought that there was something particularly appropriate about the pursuit of Anglo-Saxon studies in the United States, where he thought that, in 1875, the subject was making "great progress" in a time "when the natural sciences are crowding everywhere." He tracked the professorship of Anglo-Saxon established by Jefferson at the University of Virginia, where he estimated that some several hundred students had studied English language in the fifty years since the University was founded; many of them had gone on to be professors at southern universities, where they "have exerted a considerable influence in favor of this study" (p. 8). But there were many difficulties.

At Harvard, up to twenty students might enroll in the first-year Old English class, but only five or six would take the second year, when *Beowulf* was studied, and small enrollment could cause the class to "fail altogether."

Yet March concluded that nowhere in the world was more being done to further the study of Old English than in the United States. He reported the response to his survey given by Francis James Child, who said that "Anglo-Saxon is *utterly* neglected in England—at present there is but one man in England that is known to know anything of it—and not *extensively* pursued anywhere in America" (a rather fantastic assessment singling out, presumably, Henry Sweet).

At the MLA meeting in 1892, March repeated Child's extraordinary misperceptions but identified them as accurate for the time they were given. Since then, the Germans had been put right by the Early English Text Society, "and the press has teemed with critical studies as well as text-books." March did not think this was necessarily an improvement. "The early professors had no recondite learning applicable to English, and did not know what to do with classes in it. They can now make English as hard as Greek."[26]

March's 1875 paper began with a complaint about "the way our orators and critics dilate upon the glories of the Anglo-Saxon tongue." A curious example of this dilation links language to politics in a way, one fears, that was distinctively American. *A Handbook of Anglo-Saxon Derivatives* was published "By a Literary Association" as part of a series known as "The American System of Education."[27] The book's preface sums up some statistics for the benefit of the skeptical teacher. There are, it says, approximately eighty thousand words in English, of which twenty-three thousand derive from the Anglo-Saxon. Some seven thousand are the "choicest" of these twenty-three thousand words, and of them one thousand are root words to which sixteen prefixes and suffixes can be joined to make up all the others. Thus, by learning just one thousand words, the student could build a tremendous vocabulary. Joseph Bosworth, in *A Compendious Anglo-Saxon and English Dictionary*, published in 1881, put the number of words in English at only thirty-eight thousand, however, but also believed that twenty-three thousand of them, "or more than five-eighths, [were] of Anglo-Saxon origin."[28] Modern assessments offer illuminating comparisons. *Bright's Grammar* reports that eighty-three percent of the one thousand most common English words are of Old English origin, that the rate remains at about thirty percent for less common words, and that fifty-five percent of the one thousand most frequently used words in Anglo-Saxon poetry have survived "in recognizable form" into Modern English.[29]

The "Literary Association" organized its system for teaching vocabulary according to the "law of the mind," which stated than humans acquired languages first with nouns, then adjectives, and finally verbs. There was no doubt that the system was aimed squarely at the practical matter of vocabulary. There was evidently no other reason to study the Anglo-Saxon language. At the end of its short list of facts to guide the teacher (a very compressed teacher's manual), the Association noted that English literature dated back only six centuries (to about 1250), but that "all that is really valuable has been produced during the last three hundred years," or since about 1550, saving Spenser and Shakespeare but dismissing even Chaucer.

The Association had drawn its inspiration from an address by "Dr. Wisdom" extolling "the Saxon part of our language." Dr. Wisdom identified the basic stock of the English vocabulary as its "Saxon part," and declared that "the other elements, which enter into its composition, are puny exotics." The Saxon vocabulary included "words of home, heart, and life," sensible things, words of practical life, he said, words of domestic virtue, words of law and order. The French part of the English vocabulary, Dr. Wisdom warned, was "associated with wrong and oppression." He thus reinforced the view taken in the book's preface that "the English language was ascertained to be a composit[e] one, and, like the Great American Nation, *Unum e Pluribus*." The Anglo-Saxon part was the "stock" of the vocabulary, and all others—"the Celtic, Gothic, (embracing the German, Swedish, Danish, and Norwegian), French, Latin, and Greek elements"—were "only *engraftures* " (p. iv). Here, if it needs pointing out, one sees the isolationist drift of the *Handbook* and no doubt of the "Association" that produced it; the list of "engraftures" reads like a list of populations immigrating to the New World. This is inspired nonsense of the sort, perhaps, that March recognized as "oratory" and critics' dilation. It is also something besides linguistic hucksterism, although Dr. Wisdom's call to arms strikes one as clownish:

> The time is at hand when the professor of the English language shall sit side by side with the doctors of Latin and Greek; but he shall do so on the condition of placing the old Anglo-Saxon above the classics, and making Alfred and Bede more honorable than Virgil and Homer. Gentlemen, our old mother-tongue has endured two captivities: one under the Norman-French, the other under Latin and Greek. From the former, it was delivered under the reign of a king; from the latter, it is about to return under a president. (p. x)

The political aspects of Anglo-Saxon language study in this bizarre paean are obvious, and they can be connected to the stress on "opportunities" awaiting industrious young men who wished to pursue careers as Anglo-Saxonists. March ended his 1875 report on his survey by stressing that Anglo-Saxon studies had "prizes to offer as tempting as any," including professorships, and "then the eminence which waits on successful original work in a prominent field." (The prominence of Anglo-Saxon studies could, evidently, be assumed.) "Two or three American scholars, devoted to Anglo-Saxon," March concluded, "would have a great field to distinguish themselves in, undisputed by Englishmen" (p. 10). The study of the past became, in these exhortations, a chance to get ahead. Study of the past had been an opportunity for "advancement" for Matthew Parker, and for many who used Anglo-Saxon for political ends; others, like Elizabeth Elstob and her brother, William, were all but ruined by their pursuit of scholarship. Study of the Anglo-Saxon language and history had been overtly racialist for over a century when March and the "Association" published. But when, if ever, had it been so plainly commercial?

Teaching the Tradition ■

My sketch of Anglo-Saxon studies in the last century demonstrates some important aspects of the subject, including its linguistic basis, its political investment, its basis in the study of law, its competition with classical studies for status in the academy. Both Old English and classical studies were considered essential to good college and university programs well into the twentieth century. In 1922, Lane Cooper repeated a venerable defense for both the classics and Germanic philology with an emphasis on Anglo-Saxon that March himself would have endorsed. Cooper was especially concerned with justifying the place of Old English and the classics in doctoral degree programs.[30] March was only one of many who rationalized the place of Old English in terms of the modern languages and argued that one could not teach English at any level, from any period, without being a philologist—that is, without being a scholar of Old English. This rationale was precisely the rationale Cooper used when he claimed that one could not do either Anglo-Saxon or the rest of English literature without understanding the classics. The point was that one needed Anglo-Saxon in order to know so much else—in fact, in terms of the English Department, in order to know everything else. Today, those who know everything else—theory, criticism, and modern literature, at least—are in a very good position to understand the importance of Old English and to learn it. We can reverse the traditional paradigm in which Anglo-Saxon was a requirement for higher kinds of learning. Today, in order to know Old English, one needs to know a great deal that is "not Old English," both literary history and literature after the Anglo-Saxon period, and the history of textual, linguistic, and cultural study for large stretches of the Western tradition.

With the historical and cultural contexts of language study in mind, I would like to address six hypotheses to all those who teach the tradition, in departments of English and history with and without Anglo-Saxonists, and to all those students, undergraduate, graduate, or graduated, who are interested in the culture of the Middle Ages. I have compiled this list in the course of reading and thinking about the problem of Anglo-Saxon studies in the postmodern era; reasons why Anglo-Saxon was studied in previous ages have shaped my list of reasons why it should be studied now. I address these statements to revisionists as well as to traditionalists; both will, I hope, experiment with Anglo-Saxon studies in their educational programs.

First, Anglo-Saxon studies confront and help redress the diminishing linguistic training of undergraduates and graduate students. Anglo-Saxon survives in modern speech, and, however foreign it appears, is not foreign. Students who learn about Anglo-Saxon language and literature are learning about early forms of the language they speak—its grammar and syntax as well as its vocabulary—and about the cultural beginnings of the literature they read; such knowledge will contribute to the improvement of their language skills and help them understand how linguistic heritage explains cultural privilege.

Second, language is political. The Anglo-Saxon language and its literature and history have for centuries been used to debate fundamental moral and political issues. To study these issues, teachers and students must cross disciplinary lines and range widely over topics as politically-charged as racism and language skills. For this reason, Anglo-Saxon studies belong to cultural studies, which are unavoidably historical. Our legal tradition, our language, and even our label for a certain part of the population as "White Anglo-Saxon Protestant," are just a few of the ways in which daily parlance recalls, however superficially, the power of our Anglo-Saxon past.

Third, Anglo-Saxon studies challenge us to situate our own scholarship politically. It is ironic that Anglo-Saxon studies have become culturally weak in part because they are politically volatile, while language study has become weak because it no longer seems relevant, much less explosive. Many Anglo-Saxonists are unwilling to acknowledge their relationship to ideological and cultural traditions they rightly distrust, but such defensiveness is unnecessary. The study of racism does more to discourage racism than to promote it; the study of political controversies surrounding Anglo-Saxon texts invites students and teachers to see the relationship between the past and present forms of such disputes.

Fourth, Anglo-Saxon studies also balance the overwhelming bias in favor of student specialization in modernism and the neglect of premodern periods; that bias is created in part by the daunting linguistic and cultural expertise needed to study "dead" languages and ancient cultures. By drawing attention to political and critical contexts for the study of Anglo-Saxon culture, teachers cannot make learning Old English easy, but they can help their students discover compelling connections and in them reasons to know the past as Anglo-Saxon records, and as the study of those records, preserve it.

Fifth, the history of Anglo-Saxon studies connects Anglo-Saxon texts and history to more recent texts and histories and rejoins the segments into which the academy has divided and subdivided the material it studies, such as the periods into which history and literature are organized, without limiting the expertise necessary to any of those subdivisions. The large and integrated views that the study of Anglo-Saxon culture can create are not the only terms in which the academy can conduct its business, obviously, but such views are indispensable to the integration of graduate research with undergraduate teaching and the integration of academic work with the wider interests of culture. Surveys of the teaching of Anglo-Saxon in America show that introductory Anglo-Saxon courses frequently enroll both graduate and undergraduate students.[31] This pattern allows these supposedly disparate student groups to become acquainted in a way beneficial to all parties concerned, especially graduate students who aspire to teach undergraduates.

Sixth, Anglo-Saxon texts and artifacts were among the first to be edited and analyzed by textual critics, historians, art historians, and archaeologists; learning Anglo-Saxon is not only a good way to learn about language and history, but a good way to study the formation and conduct of scholarly disciplines themselves. Anglo-Saxon studies offer scholars a chance to contemplate the roots of their institutions and to renew their sense of place in the scholarly tradition. In England and Germany, Anglo-Saxon scholars have fairly easy access to manuscripts; in America manuscripts are very rare, but early editions of Anglo-Saxon texts are not. Many of the early editions I have discussed here are available in college and university libraries, large and small, across the United States; Anglo-Saxonists who take an interest in the history of their discipline can incorporate these texts into both introductory classes and advanced seminars, and in the process help their students learn about rare books and specialized library collections.

The sweeping effects of contemporary criticism on this tradition in the humanities disciplines have left some readers in the dark and many dismayed. I sympathize with those who see some of this change as innovation for its own sake. I too am dismayed at the left-leaning political orthodoxy demanded by many of the leaders in theoretical innovation, such as Said's embarrassing willingness to oblige any aspect of the Palestinian cause, a prominent feature of his cultural criticism,[32] or Terry Eagleton's Marxist-feminist mockery of New Criticism in a book that never subjects Marxism or feminism to even cursory scrutiny.[33] Nevertheless, I think many who consider themselves traditionalists have reason to take heart. These movements have broken the hold of belletristic criticism on the study of English language and literature. In doing so they have opened the way for the "cultural studies" in the curriculum. These studies usually focus on popular culture—film, rock music, and other media—but "cultural studies" also include the "prose of ideas," as it is sometimes called, including writing about language, and historical and political tracts. Having for decades used history as a "background" to literature, scholars are learning what it means to recognize that texts can make history as well as illustrate it. And if custodians of the New Critical, art-appreciation approach must now deal with more than lyric poetry and the language's only Anglo-Saxon epic, scholars who wish to explore the politics of gender, race, and class (the holy litany of those who "call into question" the tradition they have conveniently totalized so that it can be dismissed and denounced) must deal with history, of which there is more than they might have thought, and with languages, which take longer to learn than any of us could wish. That is the work of the "new philology" of our own age.

Otherness and Culture ■

To raise the topic of cultural criticism is to polarize one's subject, and one's reading audience, so I choose my terms carefully. I am using "revisionist" and "traditionalist" to describe participants in this discussion about the place of theory and specialization in higher education and in Anglo-Saxon studies in particular. Revisionists—"Professors of Otherness"—believe that education should critique society and lead to change; traditionalists—"Professors of Culture"—believe that education celebrates and teaches reverence for cultural achievements.[34] There are many differences between the new theories and the old, but those most relevant to the future of Anglo-Saxon studies concern broad disagreements about the purpose of educating students in history and literature.

Many traditional scholars, whose views I generally share, are uneasy with the role of politics in scholarship and teaching because they believe that political analysis, if it does not dishonor the subject, encourages disrespect that in turn excuses or encourages ignorance of tradition (i.e., the assumption that since tradition is prejudiced, it can be ignored). They see the function of scholarship as celebrating, upholding, and continuing culture, rather than criticizing it. A prominent proponent of this view is Lynne W. Cheney, currently the head of the National Endowment for the Humanities. Cheney believes that too many scholars "reduce the study of the humanities to the study of politics, arguing that truth—and beauty and excellence—are not timeless matters, but transitory notions, devices used by some groups to perpetuate 'hegemony' over others."[35] A study of how Anglo-Saxon language, literature, and history have influenced later intellectual and academic developments would, presumably, fall into the trap of reducing a humanistic subject "to the study of politics."

Cheney's comments echo the trenchant analysis of Allan Bloom's *The Closing of the American Mind.* Bloom argues that modern education has substituted "relativism"—the view that beliefs are only "preferences" or "accidents of their time and place"—for the moral conviction that one's own country, and one's own culture, are in a real and basic sense *better* than the countries and cultures of others. Bloom describes relativism as a movement away from ethnocentrism—from a concept of what makes "us" uniquely "us"—and emphasizes the irony that relativism in American education has resulted in "openness" to non-Western culture. Most students, Bloom thinks, acquire only a superficial acquaintance with such cultures. He argues that "if students were really to learn something of the mind of these non-Western cultures—which they do not—they would find that each and every one of these cultures is ethnocentric. All of them think that their way is the best way, and all others are inferior."[36]

Bloom seems to be convinced that information about tradition matters for the sake of tradition. Such a view fails to consider that the history of previous ages, including the history of Anglo-Saxon studies, is nothing more than a study of "relativism"; the traditional canon of great writers appears to transcend relativism only when it is isolated from context and enshrined as timeless, unchanging, and classic—that is, only when it is taken out of that moment in history in which its greatness was declared. Any concept of history, any reconstruction of the past, is supported by certain theoretical principles—some preconceptions governing the reconstruction—no matter how deeply these principles may be submerged. The separation of "literary history"—the timeless level of permanent and unchanging value—from "literary theory"—the realm of relativism—is plainly superficial.[37] Cheney's view that politics has no place in scholarship is itself a political statement informed with theoretical assumptions about politics, scholarship, and the social value of the academy.[38]

The approach of traditionalists to Anglo-Saxon studies is a proven failure. Old English was never, I believe, taught "for its own sake," and anyone who attempts to project it onto a plane of timeless and unchanging excellence and beauty is in for a shock—not because there is no excellence or beauty in Old English language or literature, but because both the language and the literature are timely. They are a means of measuring the time of language, which is measured against the earliest forms of English, "old" to "middle" and "modern." A subject that measures time is therefore *rooted* in time, and its antiquity is one reason for its difficulty. If tradition is timeless, there can be no place for Anglo-Saxon studies in it. It is precisely the timeliness of Anglo-Saxon culture that explains its presence in our tradition.

From the moment of their inception in the sixteenth century, Anglo-Saxon studies were used to explore, define, and propagate fundamental ideas about what made the English "English," and also—and somewhat ironically—what made the Americans "American." Anglo-Saxon studies formed the heart of English and American ethnocentrism, and this is an obvious reason why Anglo-Saxon studies should be important to traditionalists. However, such a perspective on Anglo-Saxon studies directly contravenes Cheney's distinction between "history" and "theory." Great figures in the medieval tradition—Bede, Chaucer, and King Alfred, for example—are never seen as political unless their politics are to be praised as humanistic. In short, I do not expect traditionalists to welcome my proposals for teaching Anglo-Saxon studies in terms of their historical and political contexts.

It might seem odd that historically oriented Anglo-Saxon courses could find a place in universities influenced by revisionists, famous for their attacks on ethnocentrism, but I think this may be true. It is evident that, in the academic and theoretical climate clearly dominated by the relativism that Bloom and others deplore (reasonably, in my view), Anglo-Saxon studies are at the moment an anathema. Revisionists are, I submit, particularly offended by Anglo-Saxon culture and its historical identity as the *origin* of white, male, violent, heroic, and, in addition, piously Christian values. The culture stands for what many revisionists regard as the worst not only in American but in Western culture, a legacy to be escaped, and indeed combated, not reclaimed. There are, in any case, oppressors much easier to target than philologists, including Nazi Germany, the ultimate result of Germanic nationalism in the nineteenth century, a spirit that suffused Anglo-Saxon scholars at the time. Moreover, in order to study Anglo-Saxon forms of oppression, one has to learn Old English, which is encumbered with tedious scholarly (philological) apparatus that may itself be seen as a sign of oppression. One does not need to study Jefferson's views on Anglo-Saxon spelling, or learn paradigms of nouns and pronouns or the seven classes of strong verbs, in order to form strong views on racialism and imperialism.

The place of Anglo-Saxon studies on the revisionist agenda sinks even lower in the face of a new development, the institutionalization of minority or alternative and oppositional perspectives on traditional history—as, for example, in *required* courses in ethnicity and racism. This is a nice irony, since courses in Western culture or American history are rarely required, which is why eighty percent of college students graduate without taking them; and students' failure to study foreign languages compounds the new left provincialism. Left-leaning college students from the 1960s have risen to administrative and professorial power; having been freed of required courses that perpetuated an Old World view, their first achievement seems be to require courses in a world view of their own.

Their views of the Western tradition are not encouraging for Anglo-Saxonists. At Stanford University, we can contemplate the fate of John Locke, whose writings form an essential strand in the social theory of language. A Stanford dean has written that Locke's views on social justice "seemed indispensable" half a century ago. but that the "interdependent world order" of our own decade suggests that "someone like Frantz Fanon, a black Algerian psychoanalyst, will get us closer to the answer we need." In this formulation, Fanon, a radical extremist as well as a psychoanalyst (although this is not mentioned by the dean), *replaces* Locke. The psychoanalyst rather than the philosopher "will get us closer to the answer we need." The singular "answer," the plural "we." This is language as presumptuous as any the most retrograde traditionalist could spout. Bloom can be forgiven for dismissing Fanon as "the ideologue of currently popular movements," and for concluding that the dean's remarks, "the very definition of the closing of the American mind," are a "stunning confirmation" of his thesis.[39]

Yet, despite their excesses and self-congratulatory sense of superiority, revisionists hold out more hope than traditionalists for a new age of Anglo-Saxon studies. A study of ethnocentrism in American culture, how it has developed, and—as we see in our culture at present—is changing, would necessarily include attitudes towards language. The place of the Old English language in American culture, and of attitudes toward Anglo-Saxon culture more generally, would, for such a study, be of great importance. Or so one would like to think, if those mandating curricular revision could offer such a course. Under present conditions, many professors cannot teach a course in the politics of Anglo-Saxon linguistic and historical study because they have never taken a course in Old English.

Contemporary criticism has been politicized, but those who have seized the moral high ground, claiming to speak for the oppressed, may find the second stages of their revolution more difficult than the first. Those who would speak for the past, whether they imagine it as voices and "hidden melodies" (Said's characteristically poetic and ambivalent term) waiting to be liberated and heard, or as Foucault's "dehumanized" monument of discourse waiting to be dismantled, must first learn its languages—its icongraphies, its systems of signs and objects, its vocabulary and its syntax. I mean none of these languages in one sense only; the grammar of noun declensions and verb conjugations is linguistic, but belongs to the regularities of larger, interrelated social grammars and social systems. One cannot translate the past unless one speaks its languages and listens to one's predecessors through it. But a scholar who speaks only academic languages and rarified discourse, whether the subject is word order or world order, will find ever fewer listeners. The proliferation of "theory" as an academic obsession has produced "fieldspeak," in Gerald Graff's term, for a small, inbred audience who, as they refine, define, and delimit, write more and more about less and less.[40]

At the start of this chapter I said that prefaces and forewords to Anglo-Saxon texts and studies contain important parts of the "not Old English" tradition I wish to revitalize. I cite the example of R. W. Chambers' great work, Beowulf: *An Introduction to the Study of the Poem with a Discussion of the Stories of Offa and Finn.* Chambers first published this work in England in 1921; he dedicated it to W. W. Lawrence, an important American Anglo-Saxonist, because Lawrence had assisted Chambers' research, and also because, Chambers wrote, "the debt" was "no longer purely personal." He continued, "We in this country can never forget what we owe to your people," including food sent from the U. S. to Europe after World War I, which Chambers called "the miracle of those loaves," and the founding of a new college at Oxford under American sponsorship. He ended his dedication with a quotation from Hrothgar's farewell to Beowulf: "I know that our people will stand united towards friend and foe, in the old way, blameless in all."[41]

Chambers' remarks play lightly across the irony of America's support for the nation's one-time colonial master. My concluding example of a personal, culturally situated voice in medieval studies is that of the great German medievalist, Ernst Robert Curtius, speaking after World War II. Curtius is one of Said's "extraterritorial" critics: that is, cosmopolitan rather than nationalist, and concerned with general applications of knowledge rather than specialization.[42] Curtius's "Foreword," a stirring account of a career in its worldly situation, notes that he opposed the "barbarization of education and the nationalistic frenzy which were the forerunners of the Nazi regime" and did so under the influence of the American medievalist, Edward Kennedy Rand. During the war, he wrote *European Literature and the Latin Middle Ages,* published in Germany in 1948. In 1949, Curtius came to Denver to address the Goethe Bicentennial Convocation. He reflected on the tradition of medievalism in the United States. The "phenomenon" of "American medievalism is highly interesting," he wrote, "and one I should like to study some time. I believe that it has a deep spiritual meaning." He went on:

> When America became conscious of herself she strove to acquire the cultural inheritance of Europe. American literature and scholarship can boast of a number of pioneers who, as it were, conquered the European past. Some went to Spain, like Washington Irving or Ticknor, some to Italy, others to France and Germany. But what strikes me most is this: The American mind might go back to Puritanism or to William Penn, but it lacked that which preceded them; it lacked the Middle Ages. It was in the position of a man who has never known his mother. The American conquest of the Middle Ages has something of that romantic glamour and of that deep sentimental urge which we might expect in a man who should set out to find his lost mother.[43]

Curtius paid no attention to Anglo-Saxon studies in the United States—to Thomas Jefferson, for example—noting that "medieval thought and expression became creative only around 1050," a date convenient to the anniversary his paper commemorated (1750) but disheartening to Anglo-Saxonists. Already in the twelfth-century "renaissance" the union of poetry and philosophy began to be undone. Amid waning respect for the ancients, John of Salisbury saluted law and medicine as "new domains of learning." For Curtius this was a turning away from letters to science, natural history, and metaphysics. Curtius thus found in the twelfth century the first of the unceasing humanist laments that new sciences threatened ancient arts. He looked to America, even without a medieval past, for a new humanistic synthesis.

March also complained that his was a time "when the natural sciences are crowding everywhere"; ours is a time when the sciences are crowding still, and humanists are still bewailing the trend. March's response was to put Anglo-Saxon studies on the same footing as "modern science," but his approach failed, and even he criticized those who followed it and helped to make English (Old English, that is) "as hard as Greek."[44] Curtius referred to the methods of "the natural sciences," and wrote, "Geometry demonstrates with figures, philology with texts. Philology too ought to give results which are verifiable." Nonetheless, he said, "philology is not an end in itself"; he had not written his book for "purely scholarly interests." Instead, it "grew out of vital urges and under the pressure of a concrete historical situation" (Foreword, p. x). Curtius was afraid for the survival of Western culture; his brilliantly rich, deeply "philological" book sought to preserve that culture by mediating it, not celebrating it, for a wide audience. Anglo-Saxonists fearful of the nuclear destruction that ended World War II mediated Anglo-Saxon textual culture by founding, with the support of Sir Winston Churchill, a project to ensure that manuscripts would survive another war, if only in facsimile.[45] This is a series for "purely scholarly interests," but the Anglo-Saxonists who study these and other texts ought to heed Curtius's example as a reminder that their work ought to have a purpose beyond philology.

Traditional Anglo-Saxon studies have opted for philology and excluded all else—culture, social meaning, and "not Old English." Revisionists wish to see and study Anglo-Saxon language, literature, and history in terms of their connections to other periods and cultures, and include the "other." Those excluded elements are to be found nowhere but in the language, manuscripts, and artifacts that have been read and misread in the eight hundred years (more or less) since Old English became "not Old English" and the present began its attempts to force closure on the past. My desire is not to direct Anglo-Saxon studies away from closure, for without closure the past cannot be studied. Work with Anglo-Saxon culture, textual and material, should look for more connections to the worldly aspects of cultural production than our discipline now makes and should spend less time in rarified battles whose only basis is a positivistic belief in the conclusiveness of human science. I am reminded again of Raymond Williams' boyhood home, the site of roadways from many centuries crossing each other in layer upon layer. These connections can be defined simply as points of contact that have been forgotten. In the end, we cannot care for what we do not know about. If as readers and writers we educate readers and writers to remain ignorant of the past, its grammars, and its people, we ensure only our own oblivion.

Old English, New Language ■

I began this book with a discussion of the isolation of Anglo-Saxonists from general readers and even from other specialists in the academy. I wish to conclude it with a discussion of the division of Anglo-Saxonists from each other. The impact of contemporary critical theory for a subject whose governing disciplinary theories are a century old or more has been particularly sweeping. The division separates those who "do theory," meaning, for example, intertextuality, semiotics, deconstruction, and feminist criticism, and other applications of theory, and those who do not, meaning those who practice traditional methods of linguistic analysis, textual criticism, source study, and historical as well as belletristic criticism. But this division between the theoretical and the non-theoretical will be less and less apparent as more and more Anglo-Saxonists catch up to colleagues in other disciplines and other periods of English studies. Another division exists, and it, I believe runs deeper. It is the separation between those who consider the history of their discipline part of the discipline, and those who consider this history a specialized topic that does not have significant consequences for disciplinary practices. Concerning classical studies, which is the subject of several works in which he analyzes key episodes in the history of the subject, Anthony Grafton writes,

> In Germany or Italy, there would be no need to defend this method. The history of scholarship is there accepted as a normal field of historical inquiry and practised by eminent intellectual historians. But in England and the United States, both historians and classicists tend to regard such studies as exercises in antiquarianism. Old scholarship is for them dead scholarship; to rake up the embers of dead philological controversies seems to them tedious and unprofitable. After all, the technicalities of classical

> studies are not now of much concern to many people, or even to many intellectuals. The history of classical studies is *a fortiori* even less interesting.[46]

The history of Anglo-Saxon studies likewise seems to be a limited topic which not even Anglo-Saxonists want to pursue. Yet I believe that it is this very history that offers Anglo-Saxon scholars a sure way to revive their subject and renew its place in intellectual life.

This book has been based not only on the premise that the place of Anglo-Saxon studies in modern intellectual life is marginal, but also on the larger and equally obvious premise that, with the exception of a small number of hallowed names and titles, the literature and history of earlier ages are themselves routinely dismissed. The academy seems to be valued only as a place where the young can be trained for jobs, and the mature who have jobs taught to enjoy life. Within the Department of English, academic activity revolves around literary criticism and the study of modern literatures, emphasizing aesthetic enjoyment more than professional preparation. Historians themselves wonder what scholars in the Department of English do; even within the academy, English professors who teach and write about cultures that predate the modern era seem to be conveyors of the most irrelevant and archaic disciplines of all. Yet few scholars of medieval culture wonder about the larger goals of the expertise and training they have acquired and offer to others. To train more experts and to contribute to the growing stockpile of expertise in esoteric subjects are dubious accomplishments as long as the broad-based concerns of society remain neglected. Bruce Wilshire is one teacher who has analyzed this problem recently, in terms that everyone concerned with the place of education in the working world will appreciate. In his masterful critique of the university and its construction of knowledge, *The Moral Collapse of the University: Professionalism, Purity, and Alienation*, Wilshire, like Grafton, sees the future in the past.[47] Wilshire believes that academic departments have become weak and ineffective because they have become specialized, and that they have become specialized not only because specialization is necessary to education, but also because it is essential to professionalism. Wilshire is correct, I think, in his assessment of the negative consequences of professionalism for higher education, in his view that fundamental rethinking is needed if the university is to fulfill its aim of educating the whole person, and in his claim that the construction of academic departments is one of the chief causes of the compartmentalization and rarification of higher education. Indeed, if Anglo-Saxon studies in particular and medieval studies more generally are to have a vigorous future, they will have to seek it outside the Department of English and outside the rigid limits of language study, literary criticism, and history that contain them.

Institutions persist, and the Department of English will persist in spite of the numerous charges lodged against its elitest and self-serving ways, including its dismissal of the history of language, its dismissal of the ancient past, and its fondness for critical trends that supply new paradigms within which dominant universities can exercise power and shape the future of the profession. Critical self-consciousness will not, by itself, be enough to integrate the Department of English into the social framework, and contemporary critical theory, no matter how aggressively it is applied to the work of rereading the canon, will not serve to return Anglo-Saxon studies to an engagement with political realities.[48]

But there is hope for change. One recent and encouraging sign that a better future for Anglo-Saxon studies is not merely a fantasy is the emergence of "cultural studies," a concept dependent on Marxist thought and richly historical in its areas of investigation.[49] Cultural studies require that we break the "taboo" of mixing disciplines and crossing from one's own field into another. ("Taboo" is Wilshire's term for this phenomenon.) At present, academics do not tend to stray outside the narrow confines of their respective disciplines, or even outside the immediate concerns of their specialized parts of it, whether that be the dating of *Beowulf* or the meter of "Cædmon's Hymn." Each academic's specialty provides all the subject matter needed for a successful, even an illustrious career. Cultural studies also require that we break the taboo of so-called disinterestedness in scholarship and consider the political place of our work; cultural studies require that we confront the history of our disciplines.

For medieval studies to take the form of cultural studies, medievalists will have to reconsider the history of the discipline and the function of that history, not merely as a backdrop to their work but in fact as its basis. It is clear that such reconsideration is now underway. The Medieval Academy of America has recently devoted an issue of its journal, *Speculum,* to "The New Philology," a volume of essays seeking to explain how the scholarly past relates to the present.[50] Most of the contributions emphasize the culture of the "high" or later Middle Ages, however, and the emphasis is on France; Anglo-Saxon language and literature are barely mentioned, much less discussed, and other medieval languages, literatures, and indeed whole disciplines are completely ignored.

Likewise, another recent essay collection specifically addresses cultural study and "rewriting" the Middle Ages, but also contains no work on Old English or other subjects that constitute medieval studies.[51] Anglo-Saxon studies must be part of this revisionary process, however, not because they concern the oldest part of the language and literature the Department of English studies, but because they contain the oldest part of the Department of English itself.

It is the connectedness of Anglo-Saxon studies that matters, not their age. I have tried to show here that the history of Anglo-Saxon studies is intimately connected to all phases of English literature and history subsequent to the Anglo-Saxon age. Such issues as expansionism, linguistic imperialism, and cultural colonization link our own age, the previous ages in which Anglo-Saxon culture has been studied, and the Anglo-Saxon texts themselves: Hengst and Horsa, the place of Rome in the Renaissance and in Anglo-Saxon texts, the partnership of writing and death in *Beowulf*. Yet these links go unexplored because the history of the discipline written into the history of Anglo-Saxon studies is a past that Anglo-Saxonists have chosen to ignore. As a result, the human experience that shaped the discipline has been excluded from the practices of the discipline. This history is a tradition of lived lives that can be purposefully integrated into Anglo-Saxon studies, now that the legitimacy of the practices of the discipline has been challenged by critical self-consciousness. Indeed, it is a tradition that will have to be taught. Anglo-Saxonists, medievalists more generally, and everyone who teaches literature and history—who teaches what *has been* written and done—are always teaching the tradition, whether in Old English or in the new languages of deconstruction, feminist theories, or New Historicism. We represent and continue the tradition even as we critique it. Our own place in the tradition requires not only that we understand our predecessors but also that we see ourselves in them. We have a great deal in common with those whose experience and ideas shaped our discipline, more than we might expect, more than we might wish, and from them we have much to learn.

Notes

Preface ■

1. Francis B. Gummere, "What Place Has Old English Philology in Our Elementary Schools?" *PMLA* 1 (1884–1885):170–178; see p. 170.

2. Reginald Horsman, *Race and Manifest Destiny: The Origins of American Racial Anglo-Saxonism* (Cambridge, MA: 1981; reprinted 1986). I am not sure where the term "Anglo-Saxonism" originated, but Horsman's use is the first that I consider significant.

3. George Campbell, *The Philosophy of Rhetoric,* ed. Lloyd F. Bitzer, forward by David Potter (Carbondale, IL, 1963; originally published London, 1776), p. 56; all references taken from entries on "philology" and "philologer" in the *Oxford English Dictionary*, 2nd ed., 20 vols. (Oxford, 1989).

4. Fritz Stern, *The Varieties of History* (New York, 1956), p. 11.

5. R. G. Collingwood, *The Idea of History* (Oxford, 1946), p. 282.

6. The definition of textual criticism is taken from the *Princeton Encyclopedia of Poetry and Poetics,* ed. Alex Preminger, Frank J. Warnke, and O. B. Hardison, Jr. (Princeton, 1974), p. 849. A good general introduction is James Thorpe, *Principles of Textual Criticism* (San Marino, CA, 1972); a more technical introduction is Martin L. West, *Textual Criticism and Editorial Technique* (Stuttgart, 1973).

7. Johann Gottfried von Herder, *Ideas on the Philosophy of the History of Mankind* (1784–1791); quoted in Raymond Williams, *Keywords: A Vocabulary of Culture and Society*, rev. ed. (New York, 1983), p. 89.

8. John P. Hermann, *Allegories of War: Language and Violence in Old English Poetry* (Ann Arbor, 1989); see pp. 199–208.

9. Hayden White, *Tropics of Discourse: Essays in Cultural Criticism* (Baltimore, 1978), p. 81.

Chapter 1. Desire for Origins: Postmodern Contexts for Anglo-Saxon Studies ■

1. Antiquaries were active in more areas than literature, including archaeology, numismatics, music history, and textual editing; see the discussion in Philippa Levine, *The Amateur and the Professional: Antiquarians, Historians and Archaeologists in Victorian England, 1838–1886* (Cambridge, 1986), pp. 7–23.

2. My references are to M. H. Abrams *et al.*, eds., *The Norton Anthology of English Literature,* 2 vols., fifth edition (New York, 1986), vol. 1.

3. Both Pope and Sheridan are quoted from A. C. Baugh and Thomas Cable, *A History of the English Language* (Englewood Cliffs, NJ, 1978), p. 260.

4. The first quote is from Richard Ohmann, *English in America: A Radical View of the Profession* (New York, 1976), p. 303, the second from Ohmann's *Politics of Letters* (Middletown, MA, 1987), p. 8.

5. William E. Cain, "English in America Reconsidered: Theory, Criticism, Marxism, and Social Change," *Criticism in the University*, ed. Gerald Graff and Reginald Gibbons (Evanston, 1985), pp. 85–104.

6. Terry Eagleton, *Literary Theory: An Introduction* (Minneapolis, 1983).

7. Raymond Williams, *Politics and Letters* (London, 1979); *Problems in Culture and Materialism* (London, 1980); *The Country and the City* (New York, 1973).

8. Gerald Graff, *Professing Literature: An Institutional History* (Chicago, 1987); Gerald Graff and Reginald Gibbons, eds., *Criticism in the University* (Evanston, IL, 1985); Gerald Graff and Michael Warner, eds., *The Origins of Literary Studies in America: A Documentary Anthology* (New York, 1989).

9. Robert Scholes, *Textual Power: Literary Theory and the Teaching of English* (New Haven, 1985), p. 25.

10. William Bennett, *To Reclaim a Legacy,* Report of the NEH Study Group on the State of Learning in the Humanities in Higher Education (Washington, D.C., 1984).

11. E. D. Hirsch, Jr., *Cultural Literacy: What Every American Needs to Know* (Boston, 1987); *A Dictionary of Cultural Literacy* (New York, 1988); Allan Bloom, *The Closing of the American Mind* (New York, 1987).

12. Hirsch's view differs from the others here, especially from Bloom's. Hirsch believes that knowledge of the tradition, like command of standard English, is important not simply for cultural literacy, but for access to power. See the exceptionally balanced essay by Jeff Smith, "Cultural Literacy and the Academic 'Left,'" *Profession 88* (1988): 25–28, for a defense of Hirsch and a clear distinction between his views and Bloom's.

13. Bloom has translated Plato's *Republic;* his book draws heavily on the classical, philosophical tradition; Hirsch's book, as I show below, stresses the importance of knowledge of classical subjects.

14. E. G. Stanley, *A Collection of Papers with Emphasis on Old English Literature,* Publications of the Dictionary of Old English 3 (Toronto, 1987), pp. 3–114; and *The Search for Anglo-Saxon Paganism* (Cambridge, 1975), pp. 12–82.

15. Eleanor N. Adams, *Old English Scholarship in England from 1566 to 1800* (New Haven, 1917), p. 5.

16. Carl T. Berkhout and Milton McC. Gatch, eds., *Anglo-Saxon Scholarship: The First Three Centuries* (Boston, 1982); for a bibliography of secondary studies on the history of Anglo-Saxon scholarship up to 1980, see Berkhout and Gatch, pp. 183–192.

17. Michael Murphy, "From Antiquary to Academic: The Progress of Anglo-Saxon Scholarship," in Berkhout and Gatch, *Anglo-Saxon Scholarship,* pp. 1–17.

18. Lee Patterson, *Negotiating the Past: The Historical Understanding of Medieval Literature* (Madison, WI, 1987), pp. 9–10.

19. Patterson, *Negotiating,* p. 71.

20. See Anthony Grafton and Lisa Jardine, *From Humanism to the Humanities: Education and the Liberal Arts in Fifteenth- and Sixteenth-Century Europe* (Cambridge, MA, 1986).

21. Hirsch, *Cultural Literacy*, pp. 146–215.
22. Hirsch, *Cultural Literacy*, pp. 84–85.
23. Abraham Mills, ed., *Lectures on Rhetoric and Belles Lettres* (Philadelphia, 1850), p. 4.
24. Robert F. Yeager, "Some Turning Points in the History of Teaching Old English in America," *Old English Newsletter* 13 (1980):9–20; see p. 18 for data: three schools dropped the requirement before 1964, sixteen between 1964 and 1971, and three more between 1975 and 1979. Joseph Tuso discusses the teaching of Old English in "The State of the Art: A Survey," in *Approaches to Teaching* Beowulf, ed. Jess B. Bessinger, Jr. and Robert F. Yeager (New York, 1984), pp. 33–39.
25. Results of my Spring 1989 South Atlantic Modern Language Association (SAMLA) Survey were discussed at the November 1989 SAMLA meeting in Atlanta.
26. Yeager, "Some Turning Points," p. 12.
27. I report these statistics from *Speaking for the Humanities* (New York, 1989), reviewed by Tzvetan Todorov, "Crimes Against Humanities," *The New Republic* (3 July 1989):23–30.
28. Bessinger and Yeager, *Approaches*, pp. xiii-xiv.
29. See the notice in the *Old English Newsletter* 16.2 (1983): 7.
30. Bessinger and Yeager, *Approaches*, p. xiv, and, for commentary, John P. Hermann, *Allegories of War: Language and Violence in Old English Poetry* (Ann Arbor, 1989), p. 207.
31. Bruce Mitchell, *On Old English* (Oxford, 1988).
32. For other such assessments, see Fred C. Robinson, "Anglo-Saxon Studies: Present State and Future Prospects," *Mediaevalia* 1 (1975):63–77; Antonette di Paolo Healey, "Old English Language Studies: Present State and Future Prospects," *Old English Newsletter* 20 (1987):34–45.
33. Roberta Frank and Angus Cameron, eds., *A Plan for the Dictionary of Old English* (Toronto, 1983); Antonette di Paolo Healey and Richard L. Venezky, *A Microfiche Concordance to Old English* (Toronto, 1985), and *A Microfiche Concordance to Old English: The High Frequency Words* (Toronto, 1986).
34. See Jane Roberts, "Towards an Old English Thesaurus," *Poetica* 9 (1978):56–72.
35. J.D.A. Ogilvy, *Books Known to the English, 597–1066* (Cambridge, MA, 1967); Ogilvy printed corrections in "Books Known to the English, 597–1066: Addenda et Corrigenda," *Mediaevalia* 7 (1981):281–325.
36. Both projects are described in the *Old English Newsletter* 19 (Fall 1985): 22–23.
37. William Schipper, "Old English Studies in Japan," *Old English Newsletter* 19 (1988):24–31; and Tadao Kubouchi, William Schipper, and Hiroshi Ogawa, "Old English Studies from Japan," *Old English Newsletter*, Subsidia 14 (1988).
38. The *Mediaeval English Studies Newsletter* 18 (1988): 1–3 contains a discussion of Anglo-Saxon teaching in France that suggests France is far behind Australia, New Zealand, Japan, and Scandinavian countries.
39. Charles L. Sykes, *ProfScam: Professors and the Demise of Higher Education* (Washington, D.C., 1988). In reference to *Beowulf* criticism, Sykes cites an essay written when the idea for this book was taking shape, Allen J. Frantzen and Charles L. Venegoni, "The Desire for Origins: An Archaeological Analysis of Anglo-Saxon Studies" *Style* 20 (1986):142–56; see Sykes, p. 208.
40. Dominick LaCapra, *History and Criticism* (Ithaca, 1985), p. 29.
41. This topic has been splendidly analyzed by Reginald Horsman, *Race and Manifest Destiny: The Origins of American Racial Anglo-Saxonism* (Cambridge, MA, 1981; reprinted 1986), pp. 18–23. See also Stanley R. Hauer, "Thomas Jefferson and the Anglo-Saxon Language," *PMLA* 98 (1983): 879–898.
42. Winston Churchill, *History of the English-Speaking Peoples* 4 vols. (London, 1956–1958), 1:51; on Hengst and Horsa, see Bertram Colgrave and R. A. B. Mynors, eds., *Bede's Ecclesiastical History of the English People* (Oxford, 1969), Book I, ch. 15, and F. M. Stenton, *Anglo-Saxon England*, 3rd. ed. (Oxford, 1971), pp. 16–17.
43. Quoted by Horsman, *Race and Manifest Destiny*, p. 22.

44. See Hauer, "Thomas Jefferson and the Anglo-Saxon Language," pp. 894–895, for the contents of Jefferson's library.

45. *Beowulf* appears in the *Norton Anthology of English Literature,* 5th ed.; see 1:47–48 on Hengst.

46. This was the argument of Sharon Turner, an Anglo-Saxon literary historian I discuss in Chapter 2; see Chauncey B. Tinker, *The Translations of* Beowulf: *A Critical Bibliography*, with updated bibliography by Marijane Osborn (Hamden, CN, 1974), p. 12.

47. Hauer, "Thomas Jefferson," p. 893. My differences with Hauer's view of Jefferson's politics do not diminish my appreciation for his important and informative essay and in particular for its careful analysis of the stages of Jefferson's progress on his grammar.

48. Quotation from Hauer, "Thomas Jefferson," p. 883.

49. See Horsman, *Race and Manifest Destiny*, pp. 18–19.

50. John Frow, *Marxism and Literary History* (Oxford, 1986), p. 3.

51. I discuss these concerns in my concluding chapter; see Jefferson's 1825 letter to J. Evelyn Denison, *The Writings of Thomas Jefferson,* ed. Andrew A. Libscomb and Albert Ellery Bergh, 20 vols. (Washington, D.C., 1903), 16:129–135.

52. Raymond Williams, *Keywords: A Vocabulary of Culture and Society,* rev. ed. (New York, 1983), pp. 87–93.

53. For example, by Martin Mueller, "Yellow Stripes and Dead Armadillos: Some Thoughts on the Current State of English Studies," *ADE Bulletin* (1989): 5–12.

54. Wlad Godzich, "Foreword" to Michael Nerlich, *Ideology of Adventure: Studies in Modern Consciousness 1100–1750,* 2 vols. (Minneapolis, 1987), 1: viii-ix.

55. Hans Aarsleff, *The Study of Language in England 1780–1860* (Princeton, 1967; Minneapolis, 1983), pp. 9–10.

56. The distinction is adapted from M. H. Abrams, *A Glossary of Literary Terms* (New York, 1957), pp. 137–138; a good short summary is found in the *Princeton Encyclopedia of Poetry and Poetics,* ed. Alex Preminger, Frank J. Warnke, and O. B. Hardison, Jr. (Princeton, 1974), p. 663; a standard discussion of the topic is Lois Whitney, *Primitivism and the Idea of Progress in English Popular Literature of the Eighteenth Century* (Baltimore, 1934).

57. Edward W. Said, *Beginnings: Intention and Method* (New York, 1975), pp. xii-xiii, 5–6. See also Said, *The World, the Text, and the Critic* (Cambridge, MA, 1983), pp. 133–135 for related arguments about originality.

58. John Frow, *Marxism and Literary History*, pp. 1–2.

59. This description of the hermeneutic circle is from Eagleton, *Literary Theory*, p. 74.

60. For a recent discussion, see Peter Novick, *That Noble Dream: The "Objectivity Question" and the American Historical Profession* (Chicago, 1988).

61. I cite just two of many examples: Arthur Bryant, *The Story of England: Makers of the Realm* (Boston, 1954); and David Baldwin Leland, *God's Englishmen* (Boston, 1954). Baldwin is especially specific in his discussions of stereotypes of Northern as opposed to Mediterranean races.

Chapter 2. Origins, Orientalism, and Anglo-Saxonism in the Sixteenth and Nineteenth Centuries ■

1. Quoted from G. M. Young, ed., *Macaulay: Prose and Poetry* (Cambridge, MA, 1967), p. 722; quoted (with errors) by Edward W. Said, *The World, the Text, and the Critic* (Cambridge, MA, 1983), p. 12.

2. On Macaulay and India, see Eric Stokes, *The English Utilitarians and India* (Oxford, 1959).

3. See Said, *The World,* pp. 222–224, and *Orientalism* (New York, 1978). For historical and critical responses to this book, see essays edited by Robert A. Kapp, *Journal of Asian*

Studies 39 (1980):481–517, especially David Kopf, "Hermeneutics versus History," pp. 495–506.

4. Raymond Schwab, *La Renaissance orientale* (Paris, 1950); English ed. *The Oriental Renaissance,* trans. Gene Patterson-Black and Victor Reinking, foreword by Edward W. Said (New York, 1984).

5. Wilhelm Halbfass, *India and Europe: An Essay in Understanding* (Albany, 1988); German ed. *Indian und Europa,* 1981.

6. Donald S. Lach, *Asia in the Making of Europe,* 3 vols. (Chicago, 1981), 2:520–540; see Hans Aarsleff, *The Study of Language in England 1780–1860,* 2nd ed. (Minneapolis, 1983), pp. 115–161, for the introduction of Orientalism into England.

7. Said, *The World,* p. 47.

8. Said, *The World,* p. 223.

9. These figures are taken from *The Dictionary of National Biography*, 22 vols. (Oxford, 1917; reprinted 1959), 12:415. The article on Macaulay was written by Sir Leslie Stephen.

10. The first two volumes were published in 1848; volumes 3 and 4 in 1855; volume 5 appeared in 1861, after his death. See the six-volume text, *The History of England,* ed. Charles Harding Firth (London, 1913); I quote the Everyman Library edition, *Macaulay's History of England,* with an introduction by Douglas Jerrold, 4 vols. (London, 1906; reprinted 1957), 1:3.

11. For discussions of Macaulay's place in the tradition of Whig historiography, see Joseph Hamburger, *Macaulay and the Whig Tradition* (Chicago, 1976); and J.G.A. Pocock, *Virtue, Commerce, and History* (Cambridge, 1985), pp. 300–306.

12. Reginald Horsman, *Race and Manifest Destiny* (Cambridge, MA, 1981; reprinted 1986), p. 11.

13. H.C.G. von Jagemann, "Philology and Purism," *PMLA* 15 (1900):74–96; quote from p. 74.

14. Sharon Turner, *The History of the Anglo-Saxons,* 3 vols. (London, 1823), quote from 3:257.

15. Turner, *History* 3:264–265.

16. On Kemble's Whig politics, which nearly drew him into a Spanish revolution, see Gretchen P. Ackerman, "J. M. Kemble and Sir Frederic Madden: 'Conceit and Too Much Germanism'?" in *Anglo-Saxon Scholarship: The First Three Centuries,* ed. Carl T. Berkhout and Milton McC. Gatch (Boston, 1982), pp. 167–181.

17. Quoted from the preface to J. M. Kemble, *Beowulf* (London, 1883), p. xxxii.

18. This is Kemble's "Letter to M. Francisque Michel," published in *Bibliothèque Anglo-Saxonne,* part 2 of M. Thomas Wright, *Anglo-Saxonica,* trans. M. de Larenaudiere (Paris, 1836), pp. 1–45; see p. 25 for quote.

19. I quote this remark from the introduction by Douglas Jerrold to the Everyman's Library edition of the *History*, 1:vii.

20. John Mitchell Kemble, *The Saxons in England,* rev. Walter de Gray Birch (London, 1876), pp. v (Kemble), x (Birch).

21. Rudborne's *Historia* was edited by Henry Wharton, *Anglia sacra sive Collectio Historiarum,* 2 vols. (London, 1691), 1:183 (the passage quoted from Bede concerns St. Alban; Bede's *Ecclesiastical History*, Book 1, ch. 7). Wharton's text was reprinted by Anna Gurney, *Ancient History, English and French* (London, 1830).

22. On Rudborne (c. 1460), see N. R. Ker, *Catalogue of Manuscripts containing Anglo-Saxon* (Oxford, 1957), pp. xliv, xlix.

23. Ker, *Catalogue,* pp. xlviii-xlix.

24. Ker, *Catalogue,* pp. xlviii-xlix; I do not want to exaggerate the significance of these counts; the broad outlines are clear.

25. Ker, *Catalogue,* pp. liii-liv.

26. Patrick Conner's work on Exeter manuscripts offers evidence that Old English was read and used before the sixteenth century. Conner has demonstrated that a list of books in the Exeter Cathedral Library was translated into Modern English by someone

with a knowledge of Old English in the early fifteenth century, when a new library was built and the extant collection rebound. Patrick Conner, "An Exeter Anglo-Saxonist of the Early Fifteenth Century," presented at the 1988 meeting of the MLA. I thank Professor Conner for allowing me to consult this work, part of his forthcoming study, *Anglo-Saxon Exeter: A Tenth-Century Cultural History.*

27. See C. E. Wright, "The Dispersal of Monastic Libraries and the Beginnings of Anglo-Saxon Studies," *Transactions of the Cambridge Bibliographical Society* 1 (1949–1953): 208–237. For documents, see G. R. Elton, *The Tudor Constitutions: Documents and Commentary* (Cambridge, 1965), pp. 392–396 (for the Act of 1549), and J. R. Tanner, *Tudor Constitutional Documents A. D. 1485–1603* (Cambridge, 1948), pp. 113–115 (for the Act of 1550).

28. For documents from Mary's and Elizabeth's reigns, see Tanner, *Tudor Constitutional Documents,* pp. 121–139, and Elton, *Tudor Constitutions,* pp. 399–404.

29. Wright, "The Dispersal," 227.

30. My discussion of Bale makes use of the excellent discussion by Leslie P. Fairfield, *John Bale: Mythmaker for the English Reformation* (West Lafayette, IN, 1976), and May McKisak's compact, detailed analysis in *Medieval History in the Tudor Age* (Oxford, 1971), pp. 11–20.

31. See Anne Hudson, *The Premature Reformation: Wycliffite Texts and Lollard History* (Oxford, 1988). For an older but very good study of this movement, see May McKisak, *The Fourteenth Century, 1307–1399* (Oxford, 1959), pp. 289–291, 510–515.

32. The book was published in Germany, but some copies were given a title page indicating that the book had been published at Ipswich, a ruse designed to circumvent the ban on foreign books put into effect in 1534. J. Bale, *Illustrium Maiorus Brittaniae Scriptorum* (Wesel, 1548); the copy at the Newberry Library, Chicago, carries a title page saying it was printed at Ipswich.

33. Fairfield, *John Bale,* pp. 75–77.

34. For Bede's text, see Bertram Colgrave and R.A.B. Mynors, *Bede's Ecclesiastical History of the English People* (Oxford, 1969), pp. 133–135; Book 2, ch. 1.

35. John Bale, *The Actes of Englysh Votaryes* (London, 1548), pp. 22–23a.

36. Thomas Stapleton, *The History of the Church of England Compiled by Venerable Bede, Englishman* (Antwerp, 1565), "Preface to the Reader," p. 3b.

37. John Foxe, *Acts and Monuments of Matters Most Speciall and Memorable,* 4th ed. (London, 1583); see the dedication to Queen Elizabeth I, p. ir.

38. See Foxe, *Acts and Monuments,* p. iiiia on the "stampe of antiquitie," pp. 1135–1137 for the Acts, and pp. 1141–1146 for his reference to "newcome doctrine," and his edition and translation of Old English texts. For the text of the Acts, see Elton, *Tudor Constitution,* pp. 389–392; there is a good discussion by Tanner, *Tudor Constitutional Documents,* p. 95.

39. McKisak, *Medieval History*, pp. 75–76.

40. James McConica, *English Humanists and Reformation Politics under Henry VIII and Edward VI* (Oxford, 1968); see pp. 48–49 and p. 239; see also John King, *English Reformation Literature: The Tudor Origins of the Protestant Tradition* (Princeton, 1982), pp. 211–12. The best recent study of continental humanism is Anthony Grafton and Lisa Jardine, *From Humanism to the Humanities* (Cambridge, MA, 1986), especially pp. 122–160 on the northern European traditions.

41. Joseph M. Levine, *Humanism and History: Origins of Modern English Historiography* (Ithaca, 1987), p. 79.

42. McKisak, *Medieval History,* pp. 1–3 and 6–7.

43. Excellent discussions of Leland are to be found in Levine, *Humanism and History*, and McKisak, *Medieval History,* pp. 1–7.

44. Ker, *Catalogue,* p. l-li, for a list of these manuscripts.

45. Ker, *Catalogue,* p. l.

46. The manuscript is London, British Library, Cotton Otho B.xi + B.x; see Ker, *Catalogue,* no. 180, pp. 230–234; see Robin Flower, "Laurence Nowell and the Discovery of England in Tudor Times," *PBA* 21 (1935):46–73.

47. This is British Library, Stowe 944 (Ker no. 274, pp. 338–340).

48. See the account of Nowell's work by Kenneth Sisam, *Studies in the History of Old English Literature* (Oxford, 1953), pp. 232–258.

49. See Wilbur Dunkel, *William Lambarde: Elizabethan Jurist* (New Brunswick, 1956).

50. Ker, *Catalogue,* pp. l-li.

51. McKisak, *Medieval History,* pp. 26–27.

52. Berkhout and Gatch, eds., *Anglo-Saxon Scholarship,* p. ix.

53. See John Strype, *The Life and Acts of Matthew Parker,* 4 vols. (Oxford, 1821), and McKisak, *Medieval History,* pp. 26–49, for a thorough discussion.

54. See Stanley B. Greenfield and Fred C. Robinson, *A Bibliography of Publications on Old English Literature to the End of 1972* (Toronto, 1980), p. 302 (no. 5276), for a full description of the contents of the anthology and information about its history of reprinting. For the contents of Ælfric's pastoral letters, see Milton McC. Gatch, *Preaching and Theology in Anglo-Saxon England* (Toronto, 1977), pp. 41–44, and Bernhard Fehr, *Die Hiertenbriefe Ælfrics in altenglischer und lateinischer Fassung* (Hamburg, 1914; reprinted Darmstadt, 1966), pp. xxix-xxxi.

55. Thorpe, *Homilies,* 2:262–282.

56. Dorothy Whitelock, *The Peterborough Chronicle,* Early English Manuscripts in Facsimile, 4 (Copenhagen, 1954), pp. 22–23.

57. The edition is based on Oxford, Bodleian Library, Bodley 441 (Ker, *Catalogue,* no. 312, p. 375).

58. John Jewel, *A Defense of the Apologie of the Churche of Englande* (London, 1571).

59. Galbraith is quoted in McKisak, *Medieval History*, p. 36.

60. Strype, *The Life and Acts,* 1:500–501.

61. Strype, *The Life and Acts,* 1:513.

62. Noted by Elizabeth L. Eisenstein, *The Printing Press as an Agent of Change* (Cambridge, 1979), p. 415.

63. See Ker, *Catalogue,* no. 53, p. 94, and Foxe, *Acts and Monuments,* p. 1141. For the "Cannons of Worcester Librarye" referred to by Parker, also with Parkerian markings, see Oxford, Bodleian Library, Junius 121, f. 111; Ker no. 338, but see p. 73.

64. Foxe's treatment of the homily is analyzed closely by Theodore H. Leinbaugh, "Ælfric's *Sermo de Sacrificio in Die Pascae:* Anglican Polemic in the Sixteenth and Seventeenth Centuries," in *Anglo-Saxon Scholarship,* ed. Berkhout and Gatch, pp. 56–58.

65. Wright, "The Dispersal," p. 211; see also McKisak, *Medieval History,* pp. 3–4.

66. See R. B. Wernham, "The Public Records in the Sixteenth and Seventeenth Centuries," *English Historical Scholarship in the Sixteenth and Seventeenth Centuries,* ed. Levi Fox (Oxford, 1956), pp. 11–30.

67. See Richard Clement, "Thomas James's *Ecloga Oxonio-Cantabrigiensis,*" *Journal of Library History* 21 (1987): 1–22.

68. Levine, *Humanism and History*, p. 73.

69. See A. C. Baugh and Thomas Cable, *A History of the English Language* (Englewood Cliffs, NJ, 1978), pp. 193–198, and David Wallace, "Chaucer's Continental Inheritance: The Early Poems and *Troilus and Criseyde,*" *The Cambridge Chaucer Companion,* ed. Piero Boitani and Jill Mann (Cambridge, 1986), pp. 19–37.

70. See McKisak, *Medieval History*, pp. 155–169, for a discussion of the Society and its activities.

71. William Camden, *Remaines of a Greater Worke, Concerning Britaine, the Inhabitants Thereof, Their Languages, Names, Surnames, Empreses* (London, 1605). The book went through many editions, and each was augmented by the addition of more material concerning Roman Britain; see Levine, *Humanism and History*, pp. 93–95, and references.

72. Camden, *Remaines,* pp. 16–23.

73. Richard Verstegan, *A Restitution of Decayed Intelligence: In Antiquities. Concerning the most noble and renowned English Nation* (Antwerp, 1605).

74. Philip H. Goepp, II, "Verstegan's 'Most Ancient Saxon Words'," in Thomas A.

Kirby and Henry Bosley Woolf, eds., *Philologica: The Malone Anniversary Studies* (Baltimore, 1949), pp. 249–255.

75. William Somner, *Dictionarium Saxonico-Latino-Anglicum* (London, 1659; reprinted Menston, England, 1970).

76. George Hickes, *Institutiones grammaticae Anglo-Saxonicae et Moeso-Gothicae,* 3 vols. (Oxford, 1689).

77. Humphrey Wanley, *Librorum Veterum Septentrionalium, qui in Angliae Bibliothecis extant* (Oxford, 1705); Thomas Smith, *Catalogus Librorum Manuscriptorum Bibliothecae Cottonianae* (Oxford, 1696).

78. Kenneth Sisam, "Humphrey Wanley," *Studies in the History of Old English Literature,* pp. 259–277; quotation from p. 277.

79. Eleanor N. Adams, *Old English Scholarship in England from 1566 to 1800* (New Haven, 1917), p. 91, and, for the best survey, David C. Douglas, *English Scholars 1660–1730* (London, 1951).

80. Edward Lye, *Dictionarium Saxonico et Gothico-Latinum* (London, 1772).

81. The poem, one of several commending Somner in this volume, is anonymous; it follows p. 2b in the 1659 edition; in the 1970 reprint, see pp. 1–3.

82. On Hickes' career, see Douglas, *English Scholars,* pp. 96–100, and Sisam, *Studies,* p. 263–264.

83. See R. J. Smith, *The Gothic Bequest: Medieval Institutions in British Thought, 1688–1863* (Cambridge, England, 1987), pp. 11–42, for an overview of the constitutional debates and the Revolution of 1688.

84. Levine, *Humanism and History*, p. 94.

85. I quote Baugh and Cable, *A History*, p. 254. See pp. 253–294 for a good survey of eighteenth-century attitudes towards language.

86. Sisam, *Studies,* p. 276; compare Levine's view in *Humanism and History*, pp. 95–97, and Adams, *Old English Scholarship,* pp. 108–110.

87. Douglas, *English Scholars,* pp. 272–284. For other studies, see Emma Vorlat, *The Development of English Grammatical Theory*, *1586–1737* (Leuven, 1975).

88. Janice Lee, "Political Antiquarianism Unmasked: The Conservative Attack on the Myth of the Ancient Constitution," *Bulletin of the Institute of Historical Research* 55 (1962):166–179.

89. John Fortescue-Aland, *The Difference between an Absolute and a Limited Monarchy*, *by Sir John Fortescue-Aland* (London, 1714); I quote from the preface, pp. xlii-xlvii.

90. Elizabeth Elstob, *The Rudiments of Grammar for the English-Saxon Tongue, First Given in English, with An Apology for the Study of Northern Antiquities* (London, 1715); a facsimile was published by R. C. Alston in 1968. So long neglected, and so often patronized and dismissed, Elstob is now the subject of much feminist research; her time has come at last.

91. See Baugh and Cable, *A History,* pp. 261–264.

92. Douglas, *English Scholars,* p. 183; both quotations from p. 193.

93. Guy Miège, *The English Grammar* (London, 1688; reprinted Menston, England, 1969), sig. A4.

94. Thomas Stackhouse, *Reflections on the Nature and Property of Language in General* (1731; rep. 1970); see pp. 3, 9, 58; for Johnson's view on "fixing" the language, see Baugh and Cable, *A History*, pp. 267–268.

95. L. D. Nelme, *An Essay Towards an Investigation of the Origin and Elements of Language and Letters* (1772; reprinted Menston, England, 1972). On the dictionary, see A. W. Read, "Projected English Dictionaries, 1755–1828," *Journal of English and Germanic Philology* 36 (1937):188–205, 347–366.

96. Rowland Jones, *Origin of Languages and Nations* (1764; rep. Menston, England, 1972); Camden is referred to on Sig. B3.

97. John Williams, *Thoughts on The Origins and Method of Teaching the Language* (1783; rep. Menston, England, 1972), pp. 7–8, 14–15.

98. Aarsleff, *The Study of Language,* p. 3.

99. Reginald Horsman, *Race and Manifest Destiny*, p. 33 (the quotation from Hegel), and pp. 4, 5, 44.

100. John Horne Tooke, *The Diversions of Purley,* 2 vols., rev. Richard Taylor (London, 1829). Aarsleff's chapters on Tooke are excellent: *The Study of Language,* pp. 44–114. See also David Simpson, *The Politics of American English, 1776–1850* (New York, 1986), pp. 81–90.

101. These examples are from *Diversions,* 1:334–338 (through), 378 (by and with), 382 (beyond). Modern scholarship holds that "beyond" derives from the Old English "geon," meaning "person or thing over there," and is related to the Old English "geond," meaning both "over there" and "through." See Eric Partridge, *Origins: A Short Etymological Dictionary of Modern English* (New York, 1959), p. 816.

102. These examples are taken from Tooke, *Diversions,* 2:182–183 and 402–405; on "treow," see Patridge, *Origins,* pp. 740–741.

103. Aarsleff, *The Study of Language,* pp. 77–78.

104. Samuel Henshall, *The Saxon and English Languages Reciprocally Illustrative of Each Other* (London, 1798), p. 49.

105. On the composition of Anglo-Saxon verse in the seventeenth century, see Francis L. Utley, "Two Seventeenth-Century Anglo-Saxon Poems," *Modern Language Quarterly* 3 (1942):243–261.

106. Aarsleff, *The Study of Language,* p. 73.

107. Kemble, *History,* 2:412–413.

108. Adams, *Old English Scholarship,* p. 5.

109. The last three comments come from contributors to *Anglo-Saxon Scholarship,* ed. Berkhout and Gatch; see p. 10 for the first, pp. 13–14 for the second, and p. 149 for the third. For a bibliography on Anglo-Saxon studies in this period, see F. Smith Fussner, *The Historical Revolution: English Historical Writing and Thought 1580–1640* (New York, 1962).

110. Daniel G. Calder, "Histories and Surveys of Old English Literature: A Chronological Review," *Anglo-Saxon England* 10 (1982):201–244; quote from p. 244. At a meeting of the Old English Division of the 1988 MLA, Calder identified these remarks as insertions by Professor Peter Clemoes, editor of the journal in which this article appears.

111. Hans Robert Jauss, *Toward an Aesthetic of Reception,* trans. Timothy Bahti (Minneapolis, 1982), pp. 3, 7.

112. Hayden White, *Metahistory: The Historical Imagination in Nineteenth-Century Europe* (Baltimore, 1973), p. 79.

113. Aarsleff, *The Study of Language,* p. 151.

114. Jauss, *Toward an Aesthetic,* p. 7.

115. Robert F. Yeager's essay appeared in the *Old English Newsletter* 13 (1980): 9–20.

116. Elizabeth Elstob, *An Anglo-Saxon Homily on the Birth-Day of St. Gregory: Anciently Used in the English-Saxon Church* (London, 1709), pp. 15–17.

117. Halbfass, *India and Europe,* p. 53; emphasis in original.

Chapter 3. Sources and the Search for Origins in the Academy ■

1. Philip Styles, "Politics and Historical Research in the Early Seventeenth Century," in *Historical Scholarship in the Sixteenth and Seventeenth Centuries,* ed. Levi Fox (London, 1956), p. 64.

2. T. A. Birrell, "The Society of Antiquaries and the Taste for Old English, 1705–1840," *Neophilologus* 50 (1966):107–117, quote from p. 115.

3. Hans Aarsleff, *From Locke to Saussure: Essays on the Study of Language and Intellectual History* (Minneapolis, 1982), and *The Study of Language in England 1780–1860* (Minneapolis, 1983); James H. Stam, *Inquiries into the Origin of Language* (New York, 1976).

4. Aarsleff, *The Study of Language,* p. 36.; for the quotation from G.W.F. Hegel, "On Classical Studies," see Gerald Graff, *Professing Literature: An Institutional History* (Chicago, 1987), p. 29.

5. Eugene Vance, *From Topic to Tale* (Minneapolis, 1987), p. 42.

6. J. M. Kemble, *The Poems of* Beowulf (London, 1833), p. xxiv.

7. Hans Aarsleff, "Scholarship and Ideology: Joseph Bedier's Critique of Romantic Medievalism," in *Historical Studies and Literary Criticism*, ed. Jerome J. McGann (Madison, 1985), pp. 93–113.

8. Aarsleff, "Scholarship and Ideology," p. 93.

9. Martin Bernal, *Black Athena: The Afroasiatic Roots of Classical Civilization* (New Brunswick, 1987), 1:205. See also E. G. Stanley, "The English Branch of the German Tree," in *The Search for Anglo-Saxon Paganism*, ed. E. G. Stanley (Cambridge, 1975), pp. 5–7.

10. Aarsleff, *From Locke to Saussure*, p. 294; Aarsleff's chapter, "Breal vs. Schleicher: Reorientation in Linguistics during the Latter Half of the Nineteenth Century," pp. 293–334, is an excellent discussion of language theory during this period. The subject is explored from a somewhat different angle by Colin Renfrew, *Archaeology and Language: The Puzzle of Indo-European Origins* (New York, 1988).

11. Jeffrey H. Tigay, *Empirical Modes for Biblical Criticism* (Philadelphia, 1985), p. 3; his introduction is very good, pp. 1–20. See also comments by Anthony Grafton in F. A. Wolf, *Prolegomena to Homer*, trans. with an introduction and notes by Anthony Grafton, Glenn W. Most, and James E. G. Zetzel (Princeton, 1985), pp. 19–20.

12. Bernal, *Black Athena*, p. 215; see comments by Aarsleff, *The Study*, pp. 179–182.

13. On the history of classical scholarship that forms the background to these developments, see E. J. Kennedy, *The Classical Text* (Berkeley, 1974); Herbert Butterfield, *Man on His Past* (Boston, 1960); P. H. Reill, *The German Enlightenment and the Rise of Historicism* (Berkeley, 1974).

14. The best summary of Lachmann's assumptions, and their cultural environment, has been written by Aarsleff in his discussion of Bedier; standard expositions of Lachmann's theories can be found in F. W. Hall, *A Companion to Classical Texts*, and J. P. Postage, "Textual Criticism," in *A Companion to Latin Studies*, ed. J. E. Sandys (Cambridge, 1921).

15. Aarsleff, "Scholarship," p. 94; see Bernal, *Black Athena*, pp. 214–215, for a similar view.

16. Sebastiano Timpanaro, *La Genesi del Metodo del Lachmann* (Florence, 1963). See also articles cited in the *Princeton Encyclopedia of Poetry and Poetics*, ed. Alex Preminger, Frank J. Warnke, and O. B. Hardison, Jr. (Princeton, 1974), "Textual Criticism," pp. 849–853; Lee Patterson's summary is very good; see "The Logic of Textual Criticism and the Way of Genius: The Kane-Donaldson *Piers Plowman*," *Textual Criticism and Literary Interpretation*, ed. Jerome J. McGann (Chicago, 1985), pp. 55–91; see pp. 81–85. Reprinted in Patterson, *Negotiating the Past: The Historical Understanding of Medieval Literature* (Madison, 1987).

17. James Thorpe, *Principles of Textual Criticism* (San Marino, CA, 1972), p. 114. In addition to Tigay, see Said, *Beginnings: Intention and Method* (New York, 1975), pp. 214–215.

18. Patterson, "Logic," p. 83.

19. Karl Lachmann, *Betrachtungen über Homers Ilias* (1837–1841; reprinted Berlin, 1847).

20. Karl Lachmann, *Zwanzig alte Lieder von der Nibelungen* (Berlin, 1840).

21. Aarsleff, "Scholarship," p. 102.

22. Patterson, "Logic," p. 83.

23. Aarsleff, "Scholarship," p. 106.

24. Raymond A. Wiley, ed., *John Mitchell Kemble and Jakob Grimm: A Correspondence* (Leiden, 1971).

25. Rasmus K. Rask, *Angelsaksisk Sproglære, tilligemed en kort Læsebog* (Stockholm, 1817), translated as *A Grammar of the Anglo-Saxon Tongue, with a Praxis* (London, 1830); the translation includes some new material by Rask.

26. Jakob Grimm, *Deutsche Grammatik*, I (Göttingen, 1819), pp. xviii-xix. For discussion of Grundtvig, see Aarsleff, *The Study of Language*, pp. 185–189.

27. Louis L. Synder, *Roots of German Nationalism* (Bloomington, 1978), pp. 35–54

28. John M. Ellis, *One Fairy Story Too Many* (Chicago, 1983), pp. 35–36.

29. Synder, *German Nationalism,* p. 50; see his reference to V. Petrova and A. Vibakh, "Nazi Literature for Children," *The Living Age* 347 (1934):365–366. For an explicitly Marxist critique of fairy-tale literature, see Jack Zipes, *Breaking the Magic Spell: Radical Theories of Folk and Fairy Tales* (New York, 1979), and *Fairy Tales and the Art of Subversion: The Classical Genre for Children and the Process of Civilization* (New York, 1983). The 1979 work contains a discussion of how the tales have been "reutilized" by the German left to critique conservative political positions; see pp. 45–70. Ellis's devastating commentary does not extend to Zipes' 1979 work, unfortunately; one would like to know how the left-wing revival of this literature contributes to the process Ellis traces.

30. Quotations from Stanley, *Search,* pp. 14, 26.

31. Stam, "Reconstruction of the *Ursprache,*" in *Inquiries,* pp. 216–241; the quotation is from p. 224.

32. E. Prokosch, *A Comparative German Grammar* (Philadelphia, 1939), p. 55.

33. Stanley, *Search,* p. 8 and p. 17.

34. Ashley Crandell Amos, *Linguistic Means of Determining the Dates of Old English Literary Texts* (Cambridge, MA, 1980), pp. 4, 6–7.

35. Kemble, "Letter to M. Francisque Michel," *Bibliothèque Anglo-Saxonne,* part 2, ed. M. Thomas Wright, *Anglo-Saxonica,* trans. M. de Larenaudiere (Paris, 1836), pp. 27–28.

36. See K. M. Elisabeth Murray, *Caught in the Web of Words* (New Haven, 1977), p. 77.

37. Henry Sweet, ed., *King Alfred's West-Saxon Version of Gregory's Pastoral Care,* EETS, O. S. 45, 50 (London, 1871; reprinted New York, 1973), pp. vi, ix.

38. Henry Sweet, *The Oldest English Texts.* EETS, O. S. 83 (London, 1885; reprinted 1966), p. v.; quoted by Stanley, *The Search,* p. 37; see further comments by Allen J. Frantzen and Charles L. Venegoni, "The Desire for Origins: An Archaeology of Anglo-Saxon Studies," *Style* 20 (1986):142–56; see p. 146.

39. Aarsleff, *The Study of Language,* pp. 181–182, citing the *Encyklopaedia und Methodologie der Englischen Philologie* of Gustav Körting (Heilbronn, 1888).

40. John Churton Collins, *The Study of English Literature* (Cambridge, 1891); see Gerald Graff and Michael Warner, eds., *The Origins of Literary Studies in America: A Documentary Anthology* (New York, 1989), pp. 77–81.

41. Daniel G. Calder, "Histories and Surveys of Old English Literature: A Chronological Review," *Anglo-Saxon England* 10 (1982):201–44.

42. Quoted by R. W. Chambers, *On the Continuity of Old English Prose from Alfred to More and his School,* EETS, O.S. 191a (London, 1932), pp. lvi-lvii, lxiv-lxv.

43. Chambers, *On the Continuity,* pp. lxiv-lxxxi.

44. Brooke's remark, Calder says, is the "epitome" of cultural narcissism; Calder, "Histories and Surveys," p. 220.

45. See C. Diehl, *Americans and German Scholarship, 1770–1870* (New Haven, 1978).

46. Philology was also important in France, of course. For a discussion of the history of philology and Old French language and literature, see R. Howard Bloch, "New Philology and Old French," *Speculum* 65 (1990):38–58.

47. Gerald Graff, *Professing Literature,* p. 114; James Wilson Bright, "Concerning the Unwritten History of the Modern Language Association of America," *PMLA* 18 (1903):xli–lxii. The text is *Bright's Old English Grammar and Reader,* ed. F. G. Cassidy and Richard N. Ringler (New York, 1971).

48. Quoted from Gerald Graff and Michael Warner, *The Origins,* pp. 44, 49.

49. James Morgan Hart, "The College Course in English Literature, How it May Be Improved," in *The Origins,* ed. Graff and Warner, pp. 34–37.

50. On the vast literature admiring King Alfred, see Allen J. Frantzen, *King Alfred* (Boston, 1986), pp. 1–3, and references there.

51. Woodrow Wilson, "Mere Literature," *The Atlantic Monthly* 1893; reprinted in Graff and Warner, *The Origins,* pp. 82–89.

52. Hiram Corson, *The Aims of Literary Study* (New York, 1895), pp. 42–44; quoted from Graff and Warner, *The Origins,* p. 91; see Graff, *Professing Literature,* p. 47.

53. Graff and Warner note Wilson's opposition to any systematic approach; *The Origins,* p. 82.

54. R. C. Alston, "The Study of English," in *The English Language,* ed. W. F. Bolton (London, 1975), p. 347.

55. Graff describes the use of texts to discipline students in *Professing Literature,* pp. 28–35 and 72–74; of course, any learned material—not just literature and language—could be abused this way.

56. Graff, *Professing Literature,* p. 28; see also 36.

57. Robert F. Yeager, "Some Turning Points in the History of Teaching Old English in America," *Old English Newsletter* 13 (1980):10–11; see also Frantzen and Venegoni, "The Desire for Origins," p. 148.

58. See Graff, *Professing Literature,* pp. 38–40, 55–64.

59. For a spirited account of New Criticism, see Terry Eagleton, *Literary Theory: An Introduction* (Minneapolis, 1983), pp. 46–51; and, more soberly, Graff, *Professing Literature,* pp. 145–148.

60. Rene Wellek, "American Literary Scholarship," in *Concepts of Criticism* (New Haven, 1963), p. 311.

61. Graff, *Professing Literature,* p. 149; Eagleton, *Literary Theory,* pp. 44–46.

62. Graff, *Professing Literature,* p. 152.

63. Edward B. Irving, Jr., *A Reading of* Beowulf (New Haven, 1968); Stanley B. Greenfield, *A Critical History of Old English Literature* (New York, 1965). The stress on patterns in Irving's reading is particularly strong; see, for example, his comments, pp. 1–2.

64. J. M. Campbell, "Patristic Studies and the Literature of Mediaeval England," *Speculum* 7 (1933):465–478.

65. D. W. Robertson, Jr., "Historical Criticism," *English Institute Essays, 1950,* ed. A. S. Downer (New York, 1951); and "The Doctrine of Charity in Medieval Literary Gardens: A Topical Approach Through Symbolism and Allegory," *Speculum* 26 (1951), reprinted Lewis E. Nicholson, ed., *An Anthology of* Beowulf *Criticism* (Notre Dame, 1963; reprinted 1980), pp. 165–188. Augustine first articulates this idea at *De Doctrina Christiana* 2. 62.

66. E. Talbot Donaldson, "Patristic Exegesis in the Criticism of Medieval Literature: The Opposition," in *Critical Approaches to Medieval Literature: Selected English Institute Papers, 1958–59,* ed. Dorothy Bethurum (New York, 1960; reprinted 1967), pp. 1–26.

67. R. E. Kaske, "Patristic Exegesis in the Criticism of Medieval Literature: The Defense," Bethurum, *Critical Approaches,* pp. 27–60.

68. R. S. Crane, *The Idea of the Humanities,* 2 vols. (Chicago, 1967), 2:246–258.

69. Hans Robert Jauss, *Alterität und Modernität in der Mittelalterlichen Literatur* (Munich, 1967).

70. D. W. Robertson, Jr., *A Preface to Chaucer* (Princeton, 1962); quotations cited in text. See Kaske's review in *English Literary History* 30 (1963): 175–192.

71. C. L. Wrenn, *A Study of Old English Literature* (New York, 1967), p. 57. George K. Anderson, *The Literature of the Anglo-Saxons,* rev. ed. (Princeton, 1966).

72. Greenfield, *A Critical History,* p. 4; Stanley B. Greenfield and Daniel G. Calder, *A New Critical History of Old English Literature* (New York, 1986), p. 5; Fred C. Robinson has pointed out that "the unintended amphibole resident in 'New Critical' is appropriate"; see the *Mediaeval English Studies Newsletter* 17 (1987):4–5.

73. Paul E. Szarmach, ed., *Studies in Earlier Old English Prose* (Albany, 1986), "Introduction," p. 13.

74. Stanley B. Greenfield and Fred C. Robinson, *A Bibliography of Publications on Old English Literature to the End of 1972* (Toronto, 1980); see numbers 52–82, and, in addition, E. G. Stanley, "The Scholarly Recovery of the Significance of Anglo-Saxon Records in Prose and Verse: A New Bibliography," *Anglo-Saxon England* 9 (1981): 223–262; see pp. 235, 247–248. On the EETS, see Aarsleff, *The Study of Language,* pp. 212–213, 262–263.

75. Roberta Frank and Angus Cameron, eds., *A Plan for the Dictionary of Old English* (Toronto, 1983), p. vi.

76. Helmut Gneuss, "Guide to the Editing and Preparation of Texts for the Dictionary of Old English," in Frank and Cameron, *A Plan,* pp. 11–24; see p. 15; see also Frantzen and Venegoni, "The Desire for Origins," p. 151.

77. Aarsleff, "Scholarship and Ideology," pp. 93–113; quote from p. 103.

78. *Fontes Anglo-Saxonici: A Register of Written Sources Used by Authors in Anglo-Saxon England*, forthcoming.

79. Paul E. Szarmach, ed., "Sources of Anglo-Saxon Literary Culture," 1987 brochure.

80. One can compare the published lists.

81. My observations on this matter appear in "Value, Evaluation, and Twenty Years' Worth of Old English Studies," *Old English Newsletter*, Subsidia 18 (1989):43–57.

82. See John Miles Foley, *The Tradition of Oral Composition* (Bloomington, IN, 1988.)

83. Paul E. Szarmach, ed., *Sources of Anglo-Saxon Culture* (Kalamazoo, MI, 1986), p. ix. The meeting was held in May 1983.

84. Thomas D. Hill, "Literary History and Old English Poetry: The Case of *Christ I, II, III*," Szarmach, *Sources*, pp. 3–22; see p. 4.

85. Hill, "Literary History," pp. 7, 10.

86. Colin Chase, "Source Study as a Trick with Mirrors: Annihilation of Meaning in the Old English 'Mary of Egypt'," Szarmach, *Sources*, pp. 23–33.

87. John Lingard, *The History and Antiquities of the Anglo-Saxon Church*, 2 vols., 2nd ed. (Newcastle, 1810), p. iv.

88. Chase, "Trick with Mirrors," pp. 23–24.

89. McGann, "The Monks and the Giants: Textual and Bibliographical Studies and the Interpretation of Literary Works," in *Textual Criticism and Literary Interpretation*, pp. 184–185.

90. McGann, "The Monks and the Giants," pp. 186–189, cites several scholars who narrow textual criticism to editing, and gives special credit to M. L. West, in *Textual Criticism and Editorial Technique* (Stuttgart, 1973) for recognizing the hermeneutic function of textual criticism (West, pp. 8–9); but West's perspective is much more confined than McGann's own, in "The Monks and the Giants" and in *Critique of Modern Textual Criticism* (Chicago, 1983).

91. James Thorpe, *Principles*, pp. 50–51.

92. Carl T. Berkhout, "The Future," in *The Bibliography of Old English*, edited with a forward by Stanley B. Greenfield, Old English Newsletter, *Subsidia* 8 (1982):16–17.

93. A definition taken from Raymond Williams, *Keywords: A Vocabulary of Culture and Society*, rev. ed. (New York, 1983), p. 156.

94. This is Friedrich Engels, "Feuerbach," pp. 65–66, quoted in Williams, *Keywords*, p. 155. See the observations by Lee Patterson, "'No man his reson herde': Peasant Consciousness, Chaucer's Miller, and the Structure of the *Canterbury Tales*," *South Atlantic Quarterly* 86 (1987): 457–495, especially p. 458.

95. See, for example, A. Campbell, *Old English Grammar* (Oxford, 1959), pp. 1–3; Randolph Quirk and C. L. Wrenn, *An Old English Grammar* (London, 1976), pp. 1–7.

96. See Aarsleff, *The Study of Lanuage*, p. 184.

97. H. Munro Chadwick, *The Nationalities of Europe* (Cambridge, 1945; reprinted New York, 1973), pp. 1–11.

98. Translated by James Steven Stallybrass (London, 1882).

99. Quoted by Aarsleff, *The Study of Language*, p. 162; Aarsleff discusses the Danish contribution on pp. 162–166.

100. See Aarsleff, *The Study of Language*, pp. 299–300.

101. Chadwick, *The Nationalities*, p. 143.

102. See Chadwick, *The Nationalities*, p. 123, 138–139.

Chapter 4. Deconstruction and Reconstruction of the Origin ■

1. Eugene Vance, *From Topic to Tale* (Minneapolis, 1987), pp. xxiv-xxv; Vance quotes Wilhelm Dilthey, "The Rise of Hermeneutics," trans. Frederick Jameson, *New Literary History* 3 (1972):233. On Dilthey, see Collingwood, *The Idea of History* (Oxford, 1946), pp. 171–176.

2. Vance, *From Topic,* p. xxv.

3. J.G.A. Pocock, "Texts as Events: Reflections on the History of Political Thought," in *The Politics of Discourse: The Literature and History of Seventeenth-Century England,* ed. Kevin Sharpe and Steven N. Zwicker (Berkeley, 1987), pp. 21–34; I quote from a slightly earlier version of Pocock's work, *Virtue, Commerce, and History* (Cambridge, 1985), pp. 18–21. For recent comments, see Gabrielle M. Spiegel, "History, Historicism, and the Social Logic of the Text in the Middle Ages," *Speculum* 65 (1990):59–86.

4. P. Carpenter, *History Teaching: The Era Approach* (Cambridge, England, 1964), pp. 38–39. This is a brief, direct, and persuasive book about secondary-school teaching in England.

5. For a summary of the deconstructionist critique of "philosophical humanism," see David Hoy, "Jacques Derrida," in *The Return of Grand Theory to the Human Sciences,* ed. Quentin Skinner (Cambridge, 1985), pp. 41–64; see pp. 47–50.

6. Michael Ryan, *Marxism and Deconstruction: A Critical Articulation* (Baltimore, 1982), p. 49; further references are given in the text.

7. See Ryan, *Marxism,* pp. 51–52 for the parallel to Marxist thought concerning positivism and the relations of production. Since my aim here is to develop deconstructive rather than Marxist constructs, I give more space to Derridian than to Marxist ideas throughout this summary.

8. Hayden White, *Metahistory: The Historical Imagination in Nineteenth-Century Europe* (Baltimore, 1973), p. 47; see also pp. 74–80.

9. See Margaret Schlauch, *English Literature and its Social Foundations* (1956; reprinted New York, 1971); Vida Dutton Scudder, *Social Ideals in English Letters* (New York, 1898), and *On Journey* (New York, 1937); excerpts from the second work are printed by Gerald Graff and Michael Warner, *The Origins of Literary Studies in America: A Documentary Anthology* (New York, 1989), pp. 171–178.

10. Raymond Williams, *The Country and the City* (New York, 1973), pp. 3–4.

11. Robert Scholes, "Some Problems in Current Graduate Programs in English," *Profession* 87 (1987):40–42; quote from p. 40.

12. Frank Lentricchia, *After the New Criticism* (Chicago, 1980), p. 209.

13. Rodolphe Gasché, *The Tain of the Mirror: Derrida and the Philosophy of Reflection* (Cambridge, MA, 1986), pp. 180–182.

14. Jacques Derrida, "Structure, Sign, and Play in the Discourse of the Human Sciences," *The Languages of Criticism and the Sciences of Man,* ed. Richard Macksey and Eugenio Donato (Baltimore, 1970), pp. 247–265.

15. The concept of supplementarity is, of course, a much more complex concept than I am able to go into here. See Gasché, *The Tain,* pp. 207–210 for the discussion I draw from.

16. Jonathan Culler, *On Deconstruction: Theory and Criticism after Structuralism* (Ithaca, 1982), p. 86, quoting Nietzsche, *The Will to Power,* ed. Karl Schlechta, *Werke,* 3 vols. (Munich, 1966), 3:804.

17. Culler, *On Deconstruction,* p. 129.

18. Culler, *On Deconstruction,* p. 129.

19. Culler, *On Deconstruction,* p. 248.

20. See Ryan, *Marxism,* p. 3.

21. J.R.R. Tolkien, "*Beowulf:* The Monsters and the Critics," in Lewis E. Nicholson, ed., *An Anthology of* Beowulf *Criticism* (Notre Dame, 1965), pp. 51–103.

22. Among Michel Foucault's works I shall discuss "Nietzsche, Genealogy, History," in *Language, Counter-Memory, Practice: Selected Essays and Interviews by Michel Foucault,* ed. Donald F. Bouchard, trans. Donald F. Bouchard and Sherry Simon (Ithaca, 1977), pp. 139–164; *The Archaeology of Knowledge* and *The Discourse on Language,* trans. A. M. Sheridan Smith (New York, 1972); and *The Order of Things: An Archaeology of the Human Sciences* (New York, 1973). Further references to *The Archaeology of Knowledge* will be given in the text.

23. Among these commentators are Frank Lentricchia, Edward W. Said, and Hayden White; in addition, essays by Mark Poster and E. M. Henning examine Foucault's histor-

ical methods, rephrase and clarify them, and critique their limitations: see below nn. 24, 25, 32.

24. My caution here reflects Hayden White, "Foucault Decoded: Notes from Underground," *Tropics of Discourse: Essays in Cultural Criticism* (Baltimore, 1978), p. 237.

25. Mark Poster seems closer to Foucault than is White, who describes Foucault as "an antihistorical historian," who "writes 'history' in order to destroy it." See White, "Foucault Decoded," p. 234. Poster argues that Foucault attempts to reconstitute history, not to destroy it; Poster, "The Future According to Foucault: *The Archaeology of Knowledge* and Intellectual History," in *Modern European Intellectual History: Reappraisals and New Perspectives,* ed. Dominick LaCapra and Steven L. Kaplan (Ithaca, 1982), pp. 137–52; see p. 143. Poster reasserts this view in *Foucault, Marxism, and History* (Cambridge, 1984), pp. 70–94.

26. See Stewart Clark, "The *Annales* Historians," in Skinner, *The Return of Grand Theory*, pp. 177–198.

27. For commentary, see Poster, "The Future," pp. 144–145

28. White, "Foucault Decoded," p. 239.

29. Here I follow Poster, *Foucault, Marxism, and History*, pp. 78–83.

30. Hayden White, "Foucault Decoded," p. 239.

31. Paolo Valesio, *Novantiqua: Rhetorics as a Contemporary Theory* (Bloomington, IN, 1980), pp. 62–63.

32. Foucault, *The Order of Things,* p. 31. For syntheses of archaeological analysis and deconstruction, see Edward W. Said, "Criticism Between Culture and System," *The World, the Text, and the Critic* (Cambridge, MA, 1983), pp. 178–225; for Said's important criticism of Foucault and some scholars inspired by him, see pp. 242–247. For additional commentary, see E. M. Henning, "Archaeology, Deconstruction, and Intellectual History," in LaCapra and Kaplan, *Modern European Intellectual History*, pp. 153–196.

33. Said, *The World,* p. 47.

34. Said, *The World,* pp. 244, 246.

35. Foucault, "Nietzsche," pp. 142, 146.

36. Hans Robert Jauss, *Toward an Aesthetic of Reception,* trans. Timothy Bahti (Minneapolis, 1982), pp. 108–9; further references will be given in the text. Jauss further clarifies his theoretical concepts and illustrates practical results of his approach in *Question and Answer: Forms of Dialogic Understanding,* translated by Michael Hays (Minneapolis, 1989). (These essays are selected from *Ästhetische Erfahrung und literarische Hermeneutik* [Frankfurt, 1982], Jauss's second collection of essays by the title; the first, *Äesthetische Erfahrung und literarische Hermeneutik I,* was published in Munich in 1977, translated by Michael Shaw as *Aesthetic Experience and Literary Hermeneutics* [Minneapolis, 1982].) The genesis of reception criticism is outlined by Robert C. Holub, *Reception Theory: A Critical Introduction* (London, 1984).

37. Brian Stock, *The Implications of Literacy* (Princeton, 1983), p. 90.

38. Levine L. Schücking, *Die Soziologie der literarischen Geschmacksbildung,* 3rd ed. (Bern, 1961); English translation of 3rd ed., *The Sociology of Literary Taste,* trans. Brian Battershaw (Chicago, 1966), pp 50–52; see Holub, *Reception Theory*, pp. 49–51, for a summary of Schücking's work.

39. Said, *The World,* p. 4.

40. Dominick LaCapra, *History and Criticism* (Ithaca, 1985), p. 11; LaCapra's proposals for "interactive" models of understanding history apply to the sources projects and parallel applications of reception theory. See pp. 35–38.

41. I summarize ideas expressed by Pocock, *Virtue,* pp. 19–23 and "Texts as Events," pp. 21–23.

42. Jerome J. McGann, "The Monks and the Giants: Textual and Bibliographical Studies and the Interpretation of Literary Works," in *Textual Criticism and Literary Interpretation,* ed. Jerome J. McGann (Chicago, 1985), pp. 180–199. See also McGann's introduction to *Historical Studies and Literary Criticism,* ed. Jerome J. McGann (Madison, 1985), pp. 3–21.

43. Valesio, *Novantiqua,* p. 66.

44. Pocock, *Virtue,* p. 26.
45. Pocock, *Virtue,* p. 24.
46. Paul Zumthor, *Speaking of the Middle Ages,* trans. Sarah White (Lincoln, NE and London, 1986), pp. 22–26.

Chapter 5. Polemic, Philology, and Anglo-Saxon Studies in the Renaissance ■

1. Brian Stock, *The Implications of Literacy* (Princeton, 1983), p. 90.
2. Stanley Fish, "Interpreting the *Variorum,*" *Critical Inquiry* 3 (1976):183–190; reprinted in Jane Tompkins, *Reader Response Criticism* (Baltimore, 1980), pp. 164–184, and quoted from p. 182 there. The concept of "eventfulness" I use here, and describe in the last chapter, is not related to Fish's idea of reading as an "event" as elaborated in "Literature in the Reader," *New Literary History* 2 (1970):123–162. Robert Scholes points out some of the weaknesses of Fish's concept in *Textual Power: Literary Theory and the Teaching of English* (New Haven, 1985), pp. 149–165.
3. Humphrey Wanley, *Librorum Veterum Septentrionalium* (Oxford, 1705).
4. Sisam's 1935 lecture, "Humphrey Wanley," is printed in *Studies in the History of Old English Literature* (Oxford, 1953), pp. 259–277; quotation from p. 277.
5. Fred C. Robinson, "Consider the Source: Medieval Texts and Medieval Manuscripts," *Medieval Perspectives* 2 (1987):7–16.
6. Fred C. Robinson, "'Bede's' Envoi to the Old English *History:* An Experiment in Editing," *Studies in Philology* 78 (1981):4–19; see p. 5 and pp. 12–19 for the text and commentary. Robinson developed his argument concerning this text more fully in "Old English Literature in Its Most Immediate Context," *Old English Literature in Context,* ed. John Niles (Bury St. Edmunds, 1980), pp. 11–29.
7. Text from Robinson, "'Bede's'" Envoi," pp. 12–14; Robinson also translates the text; the translation here is my own.
8. Robinson, "'Bede's' Envoi," p. 7.
9. Robinson, "Old English Literature," p. 20.
10. Identified by Raymond J. S. Grant, *Cambridge, CCC 41* (Amsterdam, 1979), pp. 106–107.
11. These texts are identified by N. R. Ker, *Catalogue of Manuscripts Containing Anglo-Saxon* (Oxford, 1953), p. 45.
12. Quoted by Eugene Vance, *From Topic to Tale* (Minneapolis, 1987), p. xxiv; see the introduction to chapter 4 for further discussion.
13. See the dialogue about the relation of Old to Modern English in *Bright's Old English Grammar and Reader,* rev. F. G. Cassidy and Richard N. Ringler, 3rd ed. (New York, 1971), pp. 33–34 and 37–38.
14. Excerpts from Ælfric's *Colloquy* are printed in Bruce Mitchell and Fred C. Robinson, *A Guide to Old English* (Toronto, 1982), pp. 183–191. Unfortunately, they "normalize" spellings and follow the syntax of the text as it was rewritten by Henry Sweet in "idiomatic Old English" as an aid to beginners. The practice is understandable as an aid to beginners; but it distorts the point of "unidiomatic" syntax in a text used to teach Latin through Old English. See Sweet, *First Steps in Anglo-Saxon* (Oxford, 1897), p. viii-ix.
15. G. N. Garmonsway, *Ælfric's Colloquy* (London, 1947); the Mitchell and Robinson *Guide* omits the Latin entirely.
16. Quoted from Mitchell and Robinson, *A Guide,* p. 174.
17. Text quoted from M. H. Abrams, et al., eds., *The Norton Anthology of English Literature,* 5th ed., 2 vols. (New York, 1986), 1:19–22; the translation is mine.
18. Bruce Mitchell, *On Old English* (Oxford, 1989), prints a note on line one, and another on line three, pp. 91–95 and pp. 69–72 respectively.
19. *Norton Anthology,* 1: 19–22.

20. The Latin text is edited and translated by Bertram Colgrave and R.A.B. Mynors, *Bede's Ecclesiastical History of the English People* (Oxford, 1969); all quotations are taken from this edition and translation (the text is hereafter referred to as *EH*). On the date of the Roman expedition, p. 20.

21. A very good survey of Bede's works and his achievement can be found in recently collected essays by James Campbell, *Essays in Anglo-Saxon History* (London, 1986), pp. 1–48.

22. Colgrave and Mynors, *EH*, p. xliii.

23. On the manuscript tradition, see Dorothy Whitelock, "The Old English Bede," *Proceedings of the British Academy* 48 (1962):57–90; reprinted in *From Bede to Alfred* (London, 1980). See pp. 85–89.

24. Thomas Stapleton, *The History of the Church of England Compiled by Venerable Bede, Englishman* (Antwerp, 1565).

25. Abraham Wheelock, *Historiae Ecclesiasticae Gentis Anglorum* (Cambridge, 1644); his name is also spelled "Wheloc" and "Wheelocke," but, after Michael Murphy, I will use "Wheelock." For a good discussion of Wheelock's edition, see Murphy, "Abraham Wheelock's Edition of Bede's *History* in Old English," *Studia Neophilologica* 39 (1967):46–59.

26. Johannis Smith, *Baedae Historia Ecclesiastica Latine et Saxonice* (Cambridge, 1722); John Stevens, *The Ecclesiastical History of the English Nation* (London, 1723).

27. J. A. Giles, ed., *Venerabilis Bedae opera quae supersunt* (London, 1843–1844).

28. Charles Plummer, *Baedae Historia Ecclesiastica gentis Anglorum: Venerabilis Baedae opera historica,* 2 vols. (Oxford, 1896).

29. Thomas Miller, *The Old English Version of Bede's Ecclesiastical History of the English People,* EETS O.S. 94–95, 110–111 (Oxford, 1890–1898; reprinted 1959).

30. Jakob M. Schipper, *König Alfreds Übersetzung von Bedas Kirchengeschichte* (Leipzig, 1899).

31. J.G.A. Pocock, "Texts as Events: Reflections on the History of Political Thought," in *Politics of Discourse,* ed. Kevin Sharpe and Steven N. Zwicker (Los Angeles, 1987), pp. 22–24.

32. Robert Scholes, *Textual Power,* pp. 18–21.

33. See Ker's *Catalogue,* no. 334.

34. Edited by George Philip Krapp, *The Anglo-Saxon Poetic Records* 1 (New York, 1931).

35. My quotations are from Colgrave and Minors, *EH,* pp. 415–418.

36. *Norton Anthology,* 1:19; Stanley B. Greenfield and Daniel G. Calder, *A New Critical History of Old English Literature* (New York, 1986), p. 227.

37. F. M. Stenton, *Anglo-Saxon England,* 3rd ed. (Oxford, 1971), p. 196.

38. J. M. Wallace-Hadrill, *Bede's Ecclesiastical History of the English People: A Historical Commentary* (Oxford, 1988), pp. xxiv, 166.

39. C. L. Wrenn, "The Poetry of Cædmon," *Proceedings of the British Academy* 32 (1946):277–295; see p. 286; André Crépin, "Bede and the Vernacular," *Famulus Christi,* ed. Gerald Bonner (London, 1976), pp. 170–192; see p. 179.

40. Plummer, *Baedae Opera,* 2:256–257.

41. See Donald K. Fry, "Cædmon as a Formulaic Poet," in *Oral Literature,* ed. Joseph Duggan (New York, 1975), pp. 41–61; Jess B. Bessinger, Jr., "Homage to Cædmon and Others: A Beowulfian Praise Song," *Old English Studies in Honor of John C. Pope,* ed. Robert B. Burlin and Edward B. Irving, Jr. (Toronto, 1974), pp. 91–106; and Virginia Day, "The Influence of Catechetical 'Narratio' on Old English and Some Other Medieval Literature," *Anglo-Saxon England* 3 (1974):51–61. The creation theme in the hymn is the subject of a forthcoming essay, "Cædmon and the Germanic Tradition," by Laura Morland, who kindly allowed me to consult a typescript of the work.

42. Fred C. Robinson, Beowulf *and the Appositive Style* (Knoxville, 1985), pp. 30–31, 90.

43. Jonathan Culler, *On Deconstruction: Theory and Criticism after Structuralism* (Ithaca, 1982), pp. 214–215.

44. Pocock, "Texts as Events," p. 22.

45. Quoted from the *Old English Version,* ed. Miller, p. 344.

46. On the monastic practice of "rumination," André Crépin, "Bede and the Vernacular," p. 187.

47. Rodolphe Gasché, *The Tain of the Mirror* (Cambridge, MA, 1986), p. 180; see also Derrida's comments on Rousseau and origins in *Of Grammatology*, trans. Gayatri Chakravorty Spivak (Baltimore, 1976), pp. 165–268; see pp. 243–245.

48. I quote from Gasché, *Tain,* p. 180; see Colgrave and Mynors, *EH,* pp. 418–419, for the quotation from Bede.

49. G. Shepherd, "The Prophetic Cædmon," *Review of English Studies,* n.s. 5 (1954):113–122.

50. Richard A. Lanham, *A Handlist of Rhetorical Terms* (Berkeley, 1968), the source for this understanding of prolepsis (and the related feature of procatalepsis), pp. 79, 81.

51. George Hardin Brown, *The Venerable Bede* (Boston, 1987), p. 99.

52. For example, David Knowles claims that scholars feel for Bede "quite spontaneously a reverence and affection unmixed with any reserve." Fry explains that we trust Bede "because [he] convinces us that we should." See Donald Fry, "The Art of Bede II: The Reliable Narrator as Persona," *The Early Middle Ages, Acta* 6 (1979):63–82; quotation from pp. 63–64.

53. Edward W. Said, *The World, the Text, and the Critic* (Cambridge, MA, 1983), p. 40.

54. *Bright's Old English Grammar and Reader,* pp. 105–134; Mitchell and Robinson, *Guide,* pp. 208–217.

55. *Sweet's Anglo-Saxon Reader in Prose and Verse,* rev. Dorothy Whitelock (Oxford, 1970), pp. 42–50.

56. Otto Funke and Karl Jost, *An Old English Reader,* Bibliotheca Anglicana, 1, 6th ed. (Bern, 1974), pp. 32–38.

57. *Sweet's Anglo-Saxon Primer,* rev. Norman Davis (Oxford, 1971).

58. Colgrave and Mynors is the best Latin edition; it has a facing translation; a widely available translation is that by Leo Shirley-Price, *A History of the English Church and People,* revised by R. E. Latham (Baltimore, 1968).

59. *English Historical Documents* I, *c. 500–1042,* ed. Dorothy Whitelock (London, 1979), pp. 799–810.

60. Greenfield and Calder, *A New Critical History*, p. 231.

61. Brown, *The Venerable Bede,* p. 94.

62. John Lingard, *The History and Antiquities of the Anglo-Saxon Church* (2nd ed. Newcastle, 1810), pp. 521–522. John Josias Conybeare, *Illustrations of Anglo-Saxon Poetry*, ed. William Daniel Conybeare (London, 1826; reprinted New York, 1964), p. 7.

63. My comments on this matter have benefitted from discussions with Kevin Kiernan, whose help I wish to acknoweldge.

64. The Latin is quoted from Colgrave and Mynors, *EH,* p. 416.

65. For a recent discussion, see D. N. Dumville, "Beowulf Come Lately," *Archiv* 225 (1988):49–63.

66. Elliot van Kirk Dobbie, *The Manuscripts of Cædmon's Hymn and Bede's Death Song* (New York, 1937), p. 11. See Katherine O'Brien O'Keeffe, "Orality and the Developing Text of Cædmon's *Hymn,*" *Speculum* 62 (1987):1–20.

67. Now Cambridge, University Library Kk.5.16, written in Northumbria "in or soon after the year 737"; see Colgrave and Mynors, *EH,* pp. xliii-xliv.

68. Dobbie, *The Manuscripts,* pp. 47–48.

69. I quote the translation from Colgrave and Minors, *EH,* pp. 415–417, and the Old English from Miller 1:342; see the note in *Sweet's Anglo-Saxon Reader,* p. 243; *Bright's Old English Grammar,* p. 127, l. 15; and Mitchell and Robinson, *A Guide,* p. 217.

70. See *Bright's,* p. 131, l. 54.

71. On the text, Mitchell and Robinson, *A Guide,* p. 213, where they cite changes in five lines; the first four entries are "normalized," but thereafter, although texts tend to be taken from individual manuscripts, conflation continues. Mitchell and Robinson do the same with King Alfred's Preface to his translation of Gregory's *Cura Pastoralis;* see p. 197.

72. Oxford, Bodleian Library, Tanner 10; no. 351 in Ker's *Catalogue*. Miller thought it was "somewhat earlier" than the end of the tenth century, the date then accepted (see p. xv). Three short fragments published, by Zupitza in 1886, are earlier, but obviously cannot be considered as a version of the text; see Ker no. 151 and Miller, pp. xx-xxi.

73. A manuscript once owned by Matthew Parker; no. 32 in Ker's *Catalogue,* dated by Ker s. xi 1.

74. Miller, *Old English Version,* p. iv.

75. Miller, *Old English Version,* p. xxviii.

76. Miller, *Old English Version,* pp. xxxiii-xliv.

77. See Miller, *Old English Version,* p. lviii, and Whitelock, "The Old English Bede," p. 64. See her comments on the translator's nationalism, pp. 62–65.

78. Schipper, *König Alfreds Übersetzung,* p. xxvi.

79. Colgrave and Mynors, *EH,* pp. lxxii-lxxiii.

80. See Schipper, *König Alfreds Übersetzung,* p. xxxi, on Smith's success in reproducing the "original Latin."

81. The *Dictionary of National Biography* reports that the pamphlet appears among Smith's papers at Oxford.

82. Smith, *Baedae Historia Ecclesiastica Latine et Saxonice,* pp. 168, 170–171.

83. John Pits, *Relationum Historicarum de Rebus Anglicis,* 2 vols. (Paris, 1619), vol. 1.

84. The first engraving is opposite the first page, the second opposite p. 805; Smith also prints Bede's epitaph (Sig. B1) and the inscription over the tomb (Sig. B2v-B4r). Here and elsewhere, "signature" ("sig.") refers to signatures, enumerated units of four pages lettered and gathered in alphabetical order; "A4v" indicates the verso side of the fourth sheet of the first signature.

85. Wheelock reports that he was Spelman's "anagnosta"; *Historiae,* Sig. B1v. For Spelman's career and his role in the "discovery of feudalism" see J.G.A. Pocock, *The Ancient Constitution and the Feudal Law: A Study of English Historical Thought in the Seventeenth Century* (Cambridge, 1957; reprinted 1987), pp. 91–123.

86. Colgrave and Minors, *EH,* p. lxxii.

87. Colgrave and Mynors, *EH,* p. lxxi.

88. Herwagen mistakenly attributed a commentary on two of Bede's works, *De Natura Rerum* and *De Temporum Ratione,* to the Anglo-Saxon monk Byrhtferth of Ramsey. See Peter S. Baker, "Byrhtferth of Ramsey and the Renaissance Scholars," in *Anglo-Saxon Scholarship: The First Three Centuries,* ed. Carl T. Berkhout and Milton McC. Gatch, (Boston, 1982), pp. 69–77; an enlarged version was published in Basel in 1557.

89. John Milton, *The History of Britain,* ed. French Fogel, *Complete Prose Works of John Milton,* ed. Don M. Wolfe, 8 vols. (New Haven, 1953–1982), 5:xxxii–xxxvi.

90. Joseph M. Levine, *Humanism and History: Origins of Modern English Historiography* (Ithaca, 1987), pp. 89, 247.

91. The manuscript was badly damaged in the Cotton Library fire of 1731. See Ker, *Catalogue,* no. 180, pp. 230–234, and Dorothy Whitelock, "The Old English Bede." On Rudborne (*c.* 1460), see Ker, *Catalogue,* pp. xliv and xlix.

92. Michel Foucault, *The Archaeology of Knowledge,* trans. A. M. Sheridan Smith (New York, 1972), p. 23.

93. James Ingram, *An Inaugural Lecture on the Utility of Anglo-Saxon Literature* (Oxford, 1807), pp. 11–12.

94. In Wheelock, see pp. 462–479. For the text, see Benjamin Thorpe, *Homilies of the Anglo-Saxon Church,* 2 vols. (London, 1844), 2:252–281.

95. Theodore H. Leinbaugh, "Ælfric's *Sermo de Sacrificio in Die Pascae:* Anglican Polemic in the Sixteenth and Seventeenth Centuries," in Berkhout and Gatch, *Anglo-Saxon Scholarship,* pp. 51–68; see p. 61.

96. Wheelock inserted and numbered chapters from the Latin that his Anglo-Saxon manuscripts omitted; in Book Four these are chs. 14, 19, and 20. I follow the chapter and page numbers in Wheelock with the page number in Miller's edition.

97. Neither authority can be connected with the text; see Arthur S. Napier, *The Old English Version of the Enlarged Rule of Chrodegang,* EETS O.S. 150 (London, 1916;

reprinted New York, 1971), chapter 48, pp. 56–57 for the passage and vii on the manuscript.

98. For example, the Act against Superstitious Books and Images of 1550 (Edward VI), printed by J. R. Tanner, *Tudor Constitutional Documents, A.D. 1485–1603* (Cambridge, 1948), pp. 113–114. Tanner's documents have been revised by G. R. Elton, *The Tudor Constitution: Documents and Commentary* (Cambridge, 1965).

99. Bernhard Fehr, *Die Hirtenbriefe Ælfrics in altenglisher und lateinischer Fassung* (Hamburg, 1914; reprinted Darmstadt, 1966), "Brief III," pp. 178–181, sections 86–93.

100. The Easter controversy was among the signs of "nationalism" for Miller, *The Old English Version,* p. 62–65.

101. Fogle notes that neither Wheelock nor Milton identified the "Coronation of Egdar" or the "Battle of Brunanburgh"; see Fogel, *Milton's History,* p. 323, n.24.

102. Dorothy Whitelock, *The Peterborough Chronicle,* Early English Manuscripts in Facsimile, 4 (Copenhagen, 1954), pp. 22–23.

103. John Jewel, *A Defense of the Apologie of the Church of England* (London, 1571), p. 520.

104. John L'Isle, *A Saxon Treatise Concerning the Old and New Testament* (London, 1623).

105. London, British Library, Cotton Claudius B.iv (Ker no. 142) and Oxford, Bodleian Laud Misc. 509 (Ker no. 344).

106. Sir Henry Ellis, *Original Letters of Eminent Literary Men of the Sixteenth, Seventeenth, and Eighteenth Centuries* (London, 1843; New York, 1968), pp. 158–159.

107. Murphy, "Wheelock," p. 50; Leinbaugh, "Anglican Polemic," p. 62.

108. L'Isle, *A Saxon Treatise,* Sig. B3r–B4v.

109. Eleanor N. Adams, *Old English Scholarship in England from 1566 to 1800* (New Haven, 1917), p. 30. See also David C. Douglas's account in *English Scholars 1660–1730* (London, 1951), pp. 1–29; and Fehr's little-noticed discussion of the Renaissance reputation of Ælfric and the Anglo-Saxon texts associated with him, *Hirtenbriefe,* pp. xxiii-xxxiv.

110. Levine, *Humanism and History,* p. 99.

111. William Camden, *Britain, or a Chorographicall Description of the Most Flourishing Kingdomes,* trans. Philomon Holland and revised by Camden (London, 1610), pp. 136–137, 143.

112. Lingard, *The History and Antiquities of the Anglo-Saxon Church,* p. iv; see also pp. 45–50. The book was revised in 1845 and was translated into both French and German. See Stanley B. Greenfield and Fred C. Robinson, *A Bibliography of Publications on Old English Literature to the End of 1972* (Toronto, 1980), p. 42, no. 461.

113. Lingard, *The History,* pp. 202, 491–506; quote from p. 492.

114. Lingard, *The History,* pp. 499–500.

115. Samuel Henshall, *The Saxon and English Language Reciprocally Illustrative of Each Other* (London, 1798), pp. 1, 49–53. Hans Aarsleff comments on Henshall's work with the hymn in *The Study of Language in England 1780–1860* (Minneapolis, 1983), pp. 76–77.

116. John Horne Tooke, *The Diversions of Purley,* 2 vols., revised by Richard Taylor (London, 1829). See Aarsleff, *The Study of Language,* pp. 44–114.

117. J. Zupitza, ed. *Ælfrics Grammatik und Glossar* (Berlin, 1880; reprinted, 1966), p. 135. See Henshall, *The Saxon and English Languages,* pp. 46–47.

118. Henshall, *The Saxon and English Languages,* pp. 16–17. The Old English reads in part: "and aa ðu ord-fruma ealra yfela and la ðu fæder ealra flymena. and la *ðu þe* ealdor wære ealles deaðes, and la ordfruma ealra modignysse. for hwig gedyrst læhtest *þuþe* þæt ðu geþanc." When he copied the passage from Hickes (whose transcription and Latin translation are both accurate), Henshall elided the passage between the italicized words, producing "ðu ðe þæt ðu þæt geþanc on þaet," which he then translated as "and la thu the the that, thou that gethanc." I quote the Old English from the edition by William H. Hulme, "The Old English Version of the Gospel of Nicodemus," *PMLA* 13(1898):457–542, p. 506.

119. See Lingard, "A Reply to the Observations of the *Edinburgh Review* on the Anglo-Saxon Antiquities," *The Pamphleteer: Respectfully Dedicated to Both Houses of Parliament,* vol. 14 (London, 1816), pp. 531–544.

Chapter 6. Writing the Unreadable *Beowulf* ■

1. F. A. Wolf, *Prolegomena to Homer, or Concerning the Original and Genuine Form of the Homeric Works and their Various Alterations and the Proper Method of Emendation* (1795), trans. with an introduction and notes by Anthony Grafton, Glenn W. Most, and James E. G. Zetzel (Princeton, 1985); quotations from p. 12; see the Introduction, pp. 1–35, on Wolf's education and his influence.

2. The tradition that Pisistratus did fix the text of Homer is "late and untrustworthy," according to Moses Hadas, *A History of Greek Literature* (New York, 1950), p. 27.

3. Edward Lytton Bulwer, *The Caxtons: A Family Picture* (London, 1850; reprinted New York, 1902), pp. 12–13.

4. See Raymond Mander and Joe Mitchenson, *The Wagner Companion* (New York, 1977), pp. 47–55.

5. Edward Lytton Bulwer, *England and the English,* edited with an introduction by Standish Meacham (Chicago, 1970).

6. For an analysis of Germanic scholarship in this period, see P. H. Reill, *The German Enlightenment and the Rise of Historicism* (Berkeley, 1975); additional bibliography can be found in Grafton et al., *Prolegomena,* pp. 249–254.

7. Fr. Klaeber, ed., Beowulf *and* The Fight at Finnsburg, 3rd ed. with supplements (Lexington, MA, 1953). All quotations will be taken from this edition, and further references will be given in the text; see pp. cxxxix-cxlii for studies of individual legends related to the poem. John Mitchell Kemble, ed. *The Poems of* Beowulf, The Traveller's Song, *and* the Battle of Finnes-burh (London, 1833); the second edition appeared in two volumes, vol. 1 in 1835, with same title as the first edition, vol. 2, *A Translation of the Anglo-Saxon Poem of* Beowulf in 1837 (both London).

8. Quoted by James W. Earl, "*Beowulf* and the Origins of Civilization," *Speaking Two Languages: Traditional Disciplines and Contemporary Theory in Medieval Studies,* ed. Allen J. Frantzen (Albany, forthcoming).

9. Maurice Sagoff, *ShrinkLits: Seventy of the World's Towering Classics Cut Down to Size* (New York, 1980).

10. Beowulf: *The Donaldson Translation, Backgrounds and Sources, Criticism,* ed. Joseph F. Tuso (New York, 1975).

11. Jess B. Bessinger, Jr., and Robert F. Yeager, *Approaches to Teaching* Beowulf (New York, 1984).

12. Kevin S. Kiernan, Beowulf *and the* Beowulf *Manuscript* (New Brunswick, 1981). I quote the review by R. D. Fulk, *Philological Quarterly* (1982):341–359, quote from p. 357.

13. *England in Literature* (Glenview, IL, 1985), pp. 22–23.

14. Fred C. Robinson, Beowulf *and the Appositive Style* (Knoxville, 1985), pp. 34–35.

15. M. H. Abrams et al., eds., *The Norton Anthology of English Literature,* 2 vols. (New York, 1986), 1:3–5.

16. Klaeber, *Beowulf,* p. lxiii.

17. C. L. Wrenn, *A Study of Old English Literature* (New York, 1967), pp. 74–76.

18. Stanley B. Greenfield and Daniel G. Calder, *A New Critical History of Old English Literature* (New York, 1986), pp. 134–136.

19. Margaret Goldsmith, *The Mode and Meaning of* Beowulf (London, 1970), pp. 60–61.

20. Milton McC. Gatch, *Loyalties and Traditions* (New York, 1971), pp. 54–55.

21. J. R. R. Tolkien, "*Beowulf:* The Monsters and the Critics," *An Anthology of* Beowulf *Criticism,* ed. Lewis E. Nicholson (Notre Dame, 1963; reprinted 1980), pp. 51–103.

22. Tolkien, "*Beowulf:* The Monsters," pp. 53, 65.

23. Tolkien, "*Beowulf:* The Monsters," p. 52.

24. On the assumptions and assertions of "New Historicism," I recommend Edward Pechter, "The New Historicism and Its Discontents," *PMLA* 102 (1987):292–303.

25. Julius Zupitza, ed., Beowulf: *Reproduced in Facsimile from the Unique Manuscript,*

British Museum MS. Cotton Vitellius A.xv, with a Transliteration and Notes, 2nd ed. EETS O.S. 245 (London, 1967).

26. Tuso, *Beowulf,* pp. 194–196.

27. Samuel Moore and Thomas A. Knott, eds., *The Elements of Old English* (Ann Arbor, 1940), pp. 280–284.

28. Henry Sweet, ed., *First Steps in Anglo-Saxon* (Oxford, 1897; reprinted 1925), pp. 39–67.

29. A. J. Wyatt, *The Threshold of Anglo-Saxon* (Cambridge, 1926; reprinted 1950), pp. 35–59.

30. R. C. Alton, ed., *An Introduction to Old English* (Evanston, IL, 1961), pp. 109–113.

31. Bruce Mitchell and Fred C. Robinson, *A Guide to Old English* (Toronto, 1982); F. G. Cassidy and Richard N. Ringler, *Bright's Old English Grammar and Reader,* 3rd ed. (New York, 1971). (The recent revision of the *Guide* includes *Beowulf* excerpts.)

32. Dorothy Whitelock, ed., *Sweet's Anglo-Saxon Reader in Prose and Verse* (Oxford, 1967), pp. 102–115; quotation from p. 102.

33. Klaeber capitalizes both words as well; in Sweet, see p. 103, l. 22, and p. 104, l. 64, where Sweet notes that the manuscript reads "alfwalda."

34. These definitions are from the *Oxford English Dictionary,* 2nd ed., 20 vols. (Oxford, 1989), 4:91.

35. Alexander Pope, *The Dunciad* (1728 text), Book I:163–164, quoted from *The Poems of Alexander Pope,* ed. John Butt (New Haven, 1963), p. 363.

36. T. P. Dunning and A. J. Bliss, eds., *The Wanderer* (London, 1969), p. 74.

37. Ashley Crandell Amos, *Linguistic Means of Determining the Dates of Old English Literary Texts* (Cambridge, MA, 1980), p. 15, pp. 6–7.

38. Gillian R. Overing, "Swords and Signs: A Semiotic Perspective on *Beowulf,*" *American Journal of Semiotics* 5 (1987):35–57; Overing, *Language, Sign, and Gender in* Beowulf (Carbondale, IL, 1990).

39. See Klaeber, *Beowulf,* pp. lxxxviii-lxxxix.

40. Kiernan, *Beowulf,* p. 250.

41. Tolkien, "Monsters," pp. 93–95 (concerning Hrothgar) and pp. 101–102 (concerning the monsters).

42. C. L. Wrenn, ed., Beowulf, rev. W. F. Bolton (London, 1973), pp. 62–67. Stanley discusses several of these views, *The Search for Anglo-Saxon Paganism* (Cambridge, 1975), pp. 40–53.

43. M. M. Bakhtin, *The Dialogic Imagination,* ed. Michael Holquist, trans. Caryl Emerson and Michael Holquist (Austin, TX, 1981); Michel Foucault, "What Is an Author?," in *Language, Counter-Memory, Practice: Selected Essays and Interviews by Michel Foucault,* ed. Donald F. Bouchard, trans. Donald F. Bouchard and Sherry Simon (Ithaca, 1977).

44. Edward Irving, *A Reading of* Beowulf (New Haven, 1968), p. 1.

45. The following discussion is abridged from my essay, "Writing the Unreadable *Beowulf:* Writan and Forwritan, the Pen and the Sword," forthcoming.

46. All quotations are taken from Klaeber's edition of the poem.

47. Christian W. M. Grein, ed., Beowulf *nebst den Fragmenten Finnsburg und Valdere* (Kassel, 1867).

48. Klaeber's second supplement has the same second half-line—"Wulfgar eode"—as Grein.

49. Birte Kelly, "The Formative Stages of *Beowulf* Textual Scholarship: Part I," *Anglo-Saxon England* 11 (1983): 247–274; "The Formative Stages of *Beowulf* Textual Scholarship: Part II," *Anglo-Saxon England* 12 (1984): 239–275.

50. Kiernan, *Beowulf,* p. 237.

51. Eugene Vance, *From Topic to Tale* (Minneapolis, 1967), p. xxvii.

52. Julia Kristeva, *Desire in Language: A Semiotic Approach to Literature and Art,* ed. Leon S. Roudiez, trans. Thomas Gora, Alice Jardine, and Leon S. Roudiez (New York, 1980), p. 15 (quoted from the editor's introduction). Her definition is used by Martin Irvine, who defines intertextuality as "the principle that a text presupposes prior texts, forms of expression, modes of signifying and representing, and codes of intelligibility." Martin Ir-

vine, "Anglo-Saxon Literary Theory in Old English Poems," *Style* 20 (1986):157–181, quote from p. 158.

53. Michael Riffaterre, "Syllepsis," *Critical Inquiry* 6 (1980):625–638; quotes from p. 629 and p. 627. In addition, see Riffaterre's discussions in "The Intertextual Unconscious," *Critical Inquiry* 13 (1987):371–385.

54. Jonathan Culler, *On Deconstruction: Theory and Criticism after Structuralism* (Ithaca, 1982), pp. 213–214.

55. Kevin S. Kiernan, *The Thorkelin Transcripts of* Beowulf, Anglistica 25 (Copenhagen, 1986), p. 71.

56. I thank James W. Earl for these observations.

57. But see Paul Beekman Taylor, "Grendel's Monstrous Arts," *In Geardagum* 6 (1984):1–12, for comments which, although brief, do raise the issue of reading and writing in the poem. John Earle related "writing on the sword" to the transition from "heathen magic" to Christianity in *The Deeds of Beowulf* (Oxford, 1892), p. 165.

58. Little has been made of these references to writing in *Beowulf.* The Wrenn-Bolton edition notes at line 1696 simply that "the name of the first owner of the sword is carved in runes on the thin gold plating" of the hilt (p. 160). Readers traditionally translate "runstafas" simply as "runes" and the sequence of verbs that I take to designate writing and narrating instead as "set down, said, marked."

59. The spell is disputed, but see Klaeber's notes to l. 804 (p. 157) and l. 1523 (p. 187).

60. Michel Foucault, "What is an Author?," pp. 117, 128.

61. See Ian Duncan, "Epitaphs for Æglæcan: Narrative Strife in *Beowulf,*" for some stimulating remarks on defamiliarization and this poem. In Beowulf: *Modern Critical Interpretations,* ed. Harold Bloom (New York, 1987), pp. 111–130.

62. For a selective survey of *Beowulf* criticism, see Douglas Short, Beowulf *Scholarship: An Annotated Bibliography* (New York, 1980).

63. The history of the work's reception is compact but extensive. See Chauncey B. Tinker, *The Translations of* Beowulf: *A Critical Bibliography,* with a revised bibliography by Marijane Osborn and a forward by Fred C. Robinson (Hamden, CN, 1974), and E. G. Stanley, *The Search for Anglo-Saxon Paganism* (Cambridge, 1975).

64. John Josias Conybeare, *Illustrations of Anglo-Saxon Poetry*, ed. William Daniel Conybeare (London, 1826; reprinted New York, 1964), pp. 79–81. There is a good assessment of his achievements by Daniel G. Calder, "The Study of Style in Old English Poetry: A Historical introduction," in *Old English Poetry: Essays on Style,* ed. Daniel G. Calder (Los Angeles, 1979), pp. 9–13.

65. See Earle, *The Deeds,* pp. xvi-xvii concerning Ritson and Turner; Earle incorrectly dates Turner's first reference to the poem to 1807.

66. Sharon Turner, *The History of the Anglo-Saxons: Comprising the History of England from the Earliest Period to the Norman Conquest,* 4th ed., 3 vols. (London, 1823), 3:280.

67. On the history of the manuscript, see Kiernan, *Beowulf,* pp. 65–85.

68. Kiernan, *Beowulf,* p. 162, n. 69.

69. Thorkelin's acquaintance with the manuscript is the subject of Kiernan's, *Thorkelin Transcripts,* pp. 1–34. See also R. W. Chambers, Beowulf: *An Introduction to the Study of the Poem with a Discussion of the Stories of Offa and Finn* (Cambridge, 1959), pp. 419–450. For an early, and lively, account of Danish scholarship concerning Anglo-Saxon England, see Earle, *The Deeds,* pp. x-xvii.

70. Turner, *The History*, 3:280–281, 283, n. 9.

71. See the facsimile by Zupitza, pp. 5, 36.

72. Tinker, *The Translations,* p. 12; Kiernan prints Turner's translation, *Beowulf,* p. 137.

73. Turner, *The History*, p. 285, n. 17 concerning the transposed leaf; p. 283 concerning Beowulf's motives and p. 291 for Unferth's speech.

74. Conybeare, *Illustrations,* p. 80.

75. See Henry Bosley Woolf, "Longfellow's Interest in Old English," in *Philologica: The Malone Anniversary Studies,* ed. Thomas A. Kirby and Henry Bosley Woolf (Baltimore, 1949), pp. 281–289.

76. Kemble, Preface to 1833 edition, p. xxxii.

77. Kemble discusses *Beowulf* and pagan beliefs in *The Saxons in England: A History of the English Commonwealth till the Period of the Norman Conquest*, 2 vols. (London, 1876), 1:413–432. The comments on language and the manuscript are taken from the 1833 Preface, pp. xix–xxiv.

78. Kiernan, "The Legacy of Wiglaf," *The Kentucky Review* 6 (1986):27–44; see p. 28.

79. Kemble, 1837 edition, p. xliv. Earle, *Deeds*, p. xxiv.

80. This material was published by Kemble as "Über die Stammtafel der Westsachsen" in Munich in 1836; Kemble reported that Grimm reviewed the article favorably.

81. There is a good summary of the issue in Kiernan, *Beowulf*, pp. 250–257; see also Wrenn, *Beowulf*, pp. 65–67. For the quotations from Kemble, see the 1837 Preface, pp. xliv, xxviii–xxix.

82. Ebenezer Henderson, *Iceland, or the Journal of a Residence in that Island* (Edinburgh, 1818), 2:329–330.

83. I quote the English translation of the Danish by Fred C. Robinson, distributed at the 1987 meeting of the International Society of Anglo-Saxonists at the University of Toronto. See N.F.S. Grundtvig, *Beowulfes Beorh eller Bjovulfs-Drapen* (Copenhagen, 1861).

84. Earle, *Deeds*, p. xxxvii.

85. Kemble, 1837 ed., p. xxiv.

86. See Franklin D. Cooley, "Contemporary Reaction to the Identification of Hygelac," pp. 269–274, and David J. Savage, "Grundtvig: A Stimulus to Old English Scholarship," pp. 275–280. Both essays are found in Kirby and Woolf, *Philologica: The Malone Anniversary Studies*.

87. Kelly, "The Formative Stages," Part 2, pp. 246–248.

88. Earl, *Deeds*, p. lii.

89. Chambers, *Beowulf*, p. 396, 398.

Chapter 7. Nationalism, Internationalism, and Teaching Anglo-Saxon Studies in the United States ■

1. Edward W. Said, *The World, the Text, and the Critic* (Cambridge, MA,1983), p. 290.

2. R. C. Alston, "The Study of English," in *The English Language*, ed. W. F. Bolton (London, 1975), pp. 350–351.

3. See chapters 6 and 8, for example; ed. F. G. Cassidy and Richard N. Ringler, 3rd ed. (New York, 1971), pp. 21–22, 30–31.

4. Henry Sweet, *First Steps in Anglo-Saxon* (Oxford, 1897; reprinted 1925), p. iii.

5. H.C.G. von Jagemann, "Philology and Purism," *PMLA* 15 (1900):74–96; pp. 80–81.

6. "Criticism Between Culture and System" is the title of an important chapter in *The World*, pp. 178–225.

7. See Charles Francis Adams, ed., *Familiar Letters of John Adams and his Wife Abigail Adams* (Boston, 1875), p. 211, where Jefferson's plan is reported; quoted by Reginald Horsman, *Race and Manifest Destiny: The Origins of American Racial Anglo-Saxonism* (Cambridge, MA, 1981; reprinted 1986), p. 22; see also Stanley R. Hauer, "Thomas Jefferson and the Anglo-Saxon Language," *PMLA* 98 (1983): 879–898; p. 880.

8. Thomas Jefferson, *The Writings of Thomas Jefferson*, ed. Andrew A. Libscomb and Albert Ellery Bergh, 20 vols. (Washington, D.C., 1903), 16:127–128. There are two very good studies of language in Jefferson's period. I refer the reader to David Simpson, *The Politics of American English, 1776–1850* (New York, 1986), and Robert A. Ferguson, *Law and Literature in American Culture* (Cambridge, MA, 1984).

9. Jefferson, *Writings*, 16:46; quoted by Hauer, "Thomas Jefferson," p. 880, notes 6–7.

10. Jefferson's letter to Governor Tyler, May 26, 1810; see *Writings*, 12:391–394.

11. Jefferson, *Writings*, 16:135–135.

12. Hauer, "Thomas Jefferson," p. 880; *Writings*, 13:61.

13. For the quotation concerning the "terrors," see Jefferson's letter to John Adams of August 15, 1820, *Writings*, 15:270. For the discussion of typeface, see Jefferson, "An Essay towards Facilitating Instruction in the Anglo-Saxon Language for the Use of the University of Virginia," *Writings*, 18:367 (quoted by Hauer "Thomas Jefferson," p. 886). The text has yet to be edited in complete form, as Hauer notes; for the currently available edition, see Jefferson, *Writings*, 18:365–411.

14. Jefferson, *Writings*, 16:48, 51.

15. Jefferson, *Writings*, 16:51; for Jefferson's "Notes on the State of Virginia," see *Writings*, 2:210.

16. Jefferson, *Writings*, 16:131.

17. Francis B. Gummere, "What Place has Old English Philology in our Elementary Schools?" *PMLA* 1 (1884–1885):170–178; see Wallace Douglas, "Accidental Institution: On the Origin of Modern Language Study," *Criticism in the University*, ed. Gerald Graff and Reginald Gibbons (Evanston, IL, 1985), pp. 35–61.

18. Louis F. Klipstein, *Analecta* (New York, 1849), pp. 14–15; further references in the text. Klipstein provided further thoughts on the inherent superiority of Western races in *A Grammar of the Anglo-Saxon Tongue* (New York, 1848), the introduction to which contrasts the drugged and indolent races of the East with their industrious counterparts in Europe, and in England in particular.

19. See the article by George Harvey Genzmer in the *Dictionary of American Biography*, ed. Dumas Malone, 20 vols. (New York, 1943), 10:446–447. See also J. B. Henneman, "Two Pioneers in the Historical Study of English—Thomas Jefferson and Louis F. Klipstein: A Contribution to the History of the Study of English in America," *PMLA* 8 (1893): lxiii-xlix.

20. Francis A. March, *Methods of Philological Study* (New York, 1865), p. iii.

21. March, *Method*, p. iv.

22. Gerald Graff, *Professing Literature: An Institutional History* (Chicago, 1987), pp. 38–39.

23. *The Study of Anglo-Saxon;* no publisher or date is given in the Newberry Library copy, Bonnapart Collection, no. 11640, p. 3.

24. Anthony Grafton and Lisa Jardine, *From Humanism to the Humanities: Education and the Liberal Arts in Fifteenth- and Sixteenth-Century Europe* (Cambridge, MA, 1986), pp. 161–182.

25. Francis A. March, *Introduction to Anglo-Saxon: Primer and Reader* (New York, 1890 [1870]), p. 81 and Preface.

26. March's MLA address is excerpted in *The Origins of Literary Study in America*, ed. Gerald Graff and Michael Warner (New York, 1989), pp. 25–27.

27. *A Handbook of Anglo-Saxon Derivatives*, The American System of Education (New York, 1854).

28. Joseph Bosworth, *A Compendious Anglo-Saxon and English Dictionary* (London, 1881), p. iv.

29. Cassidy and Ringler, *Bright's Old English Grammar and Reader*, pp. 3–4.

30. Lane Cooper, *Two Views of Education* (New Haven, 1922), pp. 264–266, and passim.

31. See Robert F. Yeager, "Some Turning Points in the History of Teaching Old English in America," *Old English Newsletter* 13 (1980):9–20, confirmed in a survey of institutions in the South Atlantic MLA in 1989.

32. Edward W. Said, "Representing the Colonized," *Critical Inquiry* 15 (1989): 205–225 for claims demolished in "West Bank Fratricide," an editorial in *The New Republic*, 11 September 1989, pp. 10–11.

33. Terry Eagleton, *Literary Theory: An Introduction* (Minneapolis, 1983). Eagleton does not consider either Marxist or feminist criticism to be "literary criticism' as opposed to rhetorical or possibly cultural criticism. See pp. 204–205.

34. I am drawing on David Bromwich's review of Michael Oakshott, *The Voice of Liberal Learning: Michael Oakshott on Education*, ed. Timothy Fuller (New Haven, 1989); Bromwich's review appeared in *The New Republic*, 10 July 1989:33–36.

35. Quoted by Maria Margaronis from Lynne W. Cheney, *Humanities in America: A Report to the President, the Congress, and the American People,* in "Waiting for the Barbarians," *Voice Literary Supplement* (January–February 1989):17.

36. Allan Bloom, *The Closing of the American Mind* (New York, 1987), pp. 30–36.

37. See her exchange with Barbara Herrnstein-Smith in the *MLA Newsletter* 20.3 (1988):12. Herrnstein-Smith made this discussion the subject of 1988 MLA presidential address, "Limelight: Reflections on a Public Year," *PMLA* 104 (1989):285–293.

38. See Barbara Herrnstein Smith, "Contingencies of Value," in *Canons,* ed. Robert von Hallberg (Chicago, 1984), pp. 5–39, and, more recently, *Contingencies of Value: Alternative Perspectives for Critical Theory* (Cambridge, MA, 1988).

39. I quote Allan Bloom's letter "Educational Trendiness," from *The Wall Street Journal* (21 January 1989) p. A15, written in reply to a January 6 letter by Charles Junkerman of Standford University.

40. Graff, *Professing Literature,* p. 208.

41. R. W. Chambers, Beowulf: *An Introduction to the Study of the Poem with a Discussion of the Stories of Offa and Finn* (Cambridge, 1959); preface; the lines from *Beowulf* (1861–1865) are given in my translation.

42. Said, *The World,* p. 166.

43. Ernst Robert Curtius, "The Medieval Bases of Western Thought," *European Literature and the Latin Middle Ages* (New York, 1953), pp. 585–596; quote p. 585.

44. March, "The Study," p. 8.

45. Fred C. Robinson, "Anglo-Saxon Studies: Present State and Future Prospects," *Mediaevalia* 1 (1975):63–77.

46. Anthony Grafton, *Joseph Scaliger: A Study in the History of Classical Scholarship* (Oxford, 1983), p. 5.

47. Bruce Wilshire, *The Moral Collapse of the University: Professionalism, Purity, and Alienation* (Albany, 1990).

48. John P. Hermann concludes his provocative study, *Allegories of War: Language and Violence in Old English Poetry* (Ann Arbor, 1989), with a call for Anglo-Saxonists to "do theory," as if "theory" will somehow cause those whose criticism has ignored the world to become worldly, in Said's sense, in a beneficial and constructive way. I disagree; indeed, "doing theory" seems to be only the latest way that the academy has found to do itself in by not dealing with the world.

49. See Richard Johnson, "What is Cultural Studies Anyway?" *Social Text* 16 (1986):38–80, and Giles Gunn, *The Culture of Criticism and the Criticism of Culture* (New York, 1987). I discuss medieval studies as cultural studies in "Documents and Monuments: Difference and Interdisciplinarity in the Study of Medieval Culture," in *Speaking Two Languages: Traditional Disciplines and Contemporary Theory in Medieval Studies,* ed. Allen J. Frantzen (Albany, forthcoming).

50. See *Speculum* 65, January 1990, edited by Stephen G. Nichols.

51. See the *Journal of Medieval and Renaissance Studies* 18 (1988), edited by Lee Patterson; see also his introduction, pp. 133–135.

Index